SINGING LIKE GERMANS

SINGING LIKE GERMANS

BLACK MUSICIANS IN THE LAND OF BACH, BEETHOVEN, AND BRAHMS

KIRA THURMAN

CORNELL UNIVERSITY PRESS

Ithaca and London

First published 2021 by Cornell University Press

Library of Congress Cataloging-in-Publication Data

Names: Thurman, Kira, author.
Title: Singing like Germans : Black musicians in the land of
    Bach, Beethoven, and Brahms / Kira Thurman.
Description: Ithaca [New York] : Cornell University Press,
    2021. | Includes bibliographical references and index.
Identifiers: LCCN 2021012388 (print) | LCCN 2021012389
    (ebook) | ISBN 9781501759840 (hardcover) |
    ISBN 9781501759857 (epub) | ISBN 9781501759864 (pdf)
Subjects: LCSH: Musicians, Black—Germany—History—
    20th century. | Musicians, Black—Austria—History—
    20th century. | Musicians, Black—Germany—
    History—19th century. | Musicians, Black—
    Austria—History—19th century. | African American
    musicians—Germany—History—20th century. | African
    American musicians—Austria—History—20th century. |
    African American musicians—Germany—History—19th
    century. | African American musicians—Austria—
    History—19th century. | Music—Social aspects—
    Germany—History. | Music—Social aspects—Austria—
    History. | Music—Political aspects—Germany—History. |
    Music—Political aspects—Austria—History. | Music
    and race.
Classification: LCC ML3917.G3 T58 2021 (print) | LCC
    ML3917.G3 (ebook) | DDC 306.4/8428—dc23
LC record available at https://lccn.loc.gov/2021012388
LC ebook record available at https://lccn.loc.
    gov/2021012389

To my parents, Don and Carol Thurman

Contents

ACKNOWLEDGMENTS

Choosing to write a hundred-year-long transatlantic interdisciplinary history between three countries was perhaps not the wisest decision I ever made. But encouraging feedback from teachers, colleagues, and friends convinced me that it was the right one. The reason why this book exists today has everything to do with the people and institutions who have supported this endeavor.

The book first began as a conversation with Beverly Weber, who told me that I could, in fact, research and write about the history of Black people in German-speaking Europe. Celia Applegate was kind, enthusiastic, and generous in her support for my research. Because she never doubted me, I never doubted myself. I benefitted greatly from the guidance and insights of Jean Pedersen and Ralph Locke.

The Fulbright Program, the Botstiber Foundation, and a faculty research grant from the University of Akron gave me the funding to visit archives in Germany, Austria, and the United States. Residential fellowships through the Peters Fellowship at the University of Notre Dame, the American Academy in Berlin, the Institute for Cultural Studies in Vienna (IFK), and the Institute for Advanced Study in Princeton provided me with precious time and space to sit down, flail about, and try to put words on a page. The AMS 75 PAYS Fund of the American Musicological Society, supported in part by the National Endowment for the Humanities and the Andrew W. Mellon Foundation, provided me with a publication subvention to pay for the images that appear in this book.

My project would have been impossible to execute if not for the digitization of Black historical newspapers, which occurred right when I began to look more earnestly for the musicians who lived and worked in Germany and Austria. Instead of trying to find needles in haystacks upon my arrival to German-speaking Europe in 2009, I was able to visit archives with exact names and dates and confirm my hunch that more Black classical musicians had performed in Germany and Austria than secondary scholarship suggested.

This project is based on documents I was able to find in those archives. In Germany, I received support from the Akademie der Künste Archives (especially Peter Konopatsch and Petra Uhlmann), the Bayerische Staatsbibliothek, the Berliner Philharmoniker archive at the Staatliche Institut für Musikforschung, the Bundesarchiv Berlin-Lichterfelde, the University of Music and Theater "Felix Mendelssohn Bartholdy" (HMT) Leipzig Archives (many thanks to Ingrid Jach), the Monacensia Library of the Münchner Stadtbibliothek, the Richard Wagner Museum, the Music and Newspaper Departments of the Staatsbibliothek zu Berlin–Preußischer Kulturbesitz, and the Berlin University of the Arts (UdK) Archive (Antje Kalcher). Yolande Korb at the American Academy in Berlin also aided me with my research in the fall of 2017. In Austria, Peter Poltun at the Vienna State Opera Archives, Dr. Silvia Kargl at the Historical Archives of the Vienna Philharmonic, and the archivists at the Vienna City Library also helped me find documents for the book.

Archivists in the United States have also been generous with their knowledge and support. I am especially indebted to Romie Minor and Carla Raczek at the Detroit Public Library; the late and great Beth Howse, as well as Chantel Clark, DeLisa Harris, and Brynna Farris at Fisk University's Special Collections; Sierra Dixon at the Connecticut Historical Society; and Holly Smith and Kassandra Ware at Spelman College, who pointed me in the direction of Josephine Harreld Love's letters home to her parents from Salzburg in 1935. April James, Eric Dillalogue, and John Pollack at the Kislak Center for Special Collections, Rare Books, and Manuscripts at the University of Pennsylvania and Brittany Newberry and Tiffany Atwater Lee at the Robert W. Woodruff Library went above the call of duty.

As an assistant professor at the University of Akron, I benefitted from the leadership and guidance of my colleagues Stephen Harp, Constance Bouchard, Janet Klein, and Toja Okoh. At the University of Michigan, I was fortunate to find community in both the German and History departments. My German colleagues—Kerstin Barndt, Julia Hell, Johannes von Moltke, Andreas Gailus, Kristin Dickinson, Tyler Whitney, Scott Spector, Helmut Puff, and Peter McIsaac—were kind and thoughtful in their criticisms. In History, my colleagues Kathleen Canning, Geoff Eley, Joshua Cole, Pamela Ballinger, Rita Chin, Stephen Berrey, Dario Gaggio, Paulina Alberto, Kisha Simmons, and Jesse Hoffnung-Garskof were generous with their feedback and support.

Three workshops have also shaped the outcome of this book. In addition to a workshop at Michigan organized by LSA and led by Scotti Parish, I benefitted from a second that generated new directions in my work while also better anchoring it. Joy Calico and Andrew Zimmerman were pivotal interlocutors who made sense of what I had produced at a time when I still couldn't quite see the forest through the trees. A third workshop, funded by the Thyssen Foundation that I co-organized with Stefan Hübner in the summer of 2017, brought wonderful colleagues together from around the world to read my work and show me how to make it better.

Friends and colleagues in different disciplines have contributed to this project in intangible ways. In musicology, I thank Alex Stefaniak, Douglas Shadle, Kristen Turner, Kim Hannon Teal, Emily Richmond Pollock, Naomi André, Lauron Kehrer, Laurie McManus, and Lucy Caplan for enriching my work. In German history and German studies, Eve Rosenhaft, Jeff Bowersox, Priscilla Layne, Jonathan Wipplinger, Tiffany Florvil, Maureen Gallagher, and the Rosa Luxemburg Group (Willeke Sandler, Jen Lynn, Deb Barton, Lauren Stokes, and Julie Ault) made my book stronger and my arguments more focused.

Over the years, writing buddies Aimee Slaughter, William Calvo-Quirós, Julian Lim, Aglaya Glebova, Sugi Ganeshananthan, and Anne-Marie Angelo have been there to make sure that I got out of bed, grabbed a cup of coffee, and got to work. I am forever grateful to the Black communities in Berlin and Vienna (especially ADEFRA, Soul Sisters Berlin, and the "Black People in Vienna" Facebook group) for being my anchors of support while I was conducting and writing my research in Germany and Austria.

Anna Rose Nelson transcribed the musical scores that appear in this book; as a graphic designer Laura Koroncey was a terrific pinch-hitter in the last inning. Emily Andrew has been a dream editor at Cornell University Press, and I am so thankful for her kindness, intellect, and musical curiosity. Jennifer Savran Kelly, Julia Cook, and Allegra Martschenko made the publication process smooth and efficient. I am indebted to Hilary Bown, my editor, warrior, and friend who has read every single word I've put to the page since 2013.

Lastly, I thank my family for their care, love, and support on this long journey to publication. I know that in my darkest hour, I can always turn to my brother Jonathan Thurman to provide me with a funny meme, usually mined from the deep archives of Black Twitter. His insouciance reminds me to lighten up a little; it's just a book. Erica Haldi is the most obnoxious cheerleader and best big sister a scholar could ask for. My nieces Ellie and Lia are two of my greatest inspirations. Joel Bentley demonstrates every day the true meaning of partnership. My parents, Don and Carol Thurman, have made countless sacrifices for the sake of their children. This book is not only a manifestation of their hard work but an expression of my profound gratitude.

Note on Translation

Unless stated otherwise, all translations from German into English are my own.

SINGING LIKE GERMANS

Introduction

Grace Bumbry glittered in gold. The African American soprano glided around the set of the Bayreuth Festival Theatre, shimmering under a dim glow of light filtered through laced netting that flooded the stage in gentle waves. Playing the role of Venus in the nineteenth-century German composer Richard Wagner's 1845 opera, *Tannhäuser*, Bumbry sparkled with each turn, embodying the tempting seductress she had been cast to perform, singing of love and lust to an enraptured audience of nearly two thousand listeners, including international dignitaries, high-ranking classical musicians, music critics, and socialites.

Built between 1872 and 1876, the Bayreuth Festival Theatre where Bumbry sang was a national monument of sorts, a shrine to the works of Wagner, and every summer pilgrims flocked to the small Bavarian town to hear Wagner's operas performed in the house he had built. But in the summer of 1961, news that Wagner's grandson Wieland Wagner had hired a young Black soprano to sing inside Bayreuth's hallowed halls sent shockwaves across West Germany. Prior to her performance that warm July evening, hundreds of letters of protest had bombarded the opera house, declaring that Bumbry's presence in Bayreuth would have that most "German" of composers rolling over in his grave.

Bumbry ignored them all. And on the first night of her appearance, the aspiring diva received a thirty-minute standing ovation. Her performance earned her international accolades and vaulted her to stardom.

Bumbry's Bayreuth debut brings to light many different themes in German history that were hiding in plain sight. First, it illustrates how German audiences' understandings of classical music—long heralded as the "most German of the arts"—could shift depending on the political era.[1] No composer better symbolized how swiftly listeners could change their positions on music than Richard Wagner himself, an ardent anti-Semite and German nationalist, whose music Adolf Hitler later publicly avowed and generously supported. After WWII, however, Wagner's operas came under close scrutiny by Allied forces because of the composer's perceived proximity to Nazism, and many performances of his operas were either banned outright during the early occupation years or strongly discouraged. To bring Wagner back from the dead, the Bayreuth Festival Theatre embarked on a rescue mission. The music of Wagner could survive, the administrators believed, if given a new set of tools with which to perform and listen to it. One such tool was Grace Bumbry, a soprano with absolutely no experience singing Wagner.

The administration's insistence on hiring her anyway—and the public's vociferous response to her debut—illuminates another important theme in German history: namely, how cultural institutions wrestled with questions of race and racism. Bayreuth's reclamation of Wagner through a Black singer was not only a bold act of rehabilitation but also an intentional insistence on rejecting the kinds of racist audiences who extolled the noxious ideologies Wagner espoused. Out of the ashes of Nazism, they proclaimed, West Germany had risen like a Phoenix to become a democratic society, and Bumbry's performance on Bayreuth's recently denazified stage was evidence of a new political era of racial acceptance. Her debut was meant to usher in a vibrant new moment in German history.

The initiative was deeply flawed. In order to disengage from a previous racial order, Wagner and the opera production team ultimately turned to historical myths of deviant Black female sexuality to transform Bumbry into an erotic goddess on stage. Called the "Black Venus" in newspapers and in casual conversation, Bumbry quickly came to symbolize earlier representations of sexualized Black women in European history, from Sara Baartman to Josephine Baker. Bayreuth's 1961 production illustrates the problems and paradoxes of dislodging a cultural institution from its racist past by relying on historical stereotypes of Black people to do it. But even while Bumbry sang in scandalous dress and smeared in glitter, her symbolic significance as the vanguard of a new era could not be shaken.

To see Bumbry as representing a new era in German history, however, misses a greater story. Her premiere takes on new meaning when we treat it not as the beginning of something new but rather the product of almost one hundred years of Black networking and transatlantic activity. Since at least the 1870s, African American classical musicians were involved in the production and dissemination of classical music on German soil.[2] Other Black musicians such as Sissieretta Jones, an opera singer who performed in 1890s Berlin, and the contralto Marian Anderson, who lived and performed in 1930s Germany and Austria, made Bumbry's path to stardom a little more feasible.

The fact that audiences persistently viewed Bumbry's debut as a novelty also occludes the most telling fact: Bumbry was not the first Black singer to grace the Bayreuth stage. In fact, the Afro-European contralto Luranah Aldridge had been invited by the Wagner family to reside with them in Bayreuth in the 1890s. Welcomed into the arms of Cosima Wagner and her daughters, Aldridge was supposed to perform as a Valkyrie in Wagner's Ring Cycle before falling ill in 1896.[3]

Bumbry's Bayreuth debut takes on greater meaning, then, if we understand it as one of many Black performances that caused a listening public to work out the ties between music, race, and nation. Performances like Bumbry's were especially powerful because they challenged the deeply entrenched notion in German history that Blackness and Germanness were discrete categories. Angry protestors against Bumbry's debut argued that a Black musician performing Wagner was paradoxical in nature, thus reinforcing the notion that Germanness was synonymous with whiteness and that Black people existed outside of it. Bumbry's insistence on singing Wagner rejected the sonic and racial boundaries that white German audiences had constructed.

Bumbry's debut is important because it placed a Black musician at the center of a national debate. But her premiere wasn't the only time a Black musician had been called upon to perform this important cultural labor. Using documents collected from over thirty archives in Germany, Austria, and the United States, this book traces the long history of Black classical musicians—both singers and instrumentalists—from the Americas, the Caribbean, and Europe who studied and performed in Germany and Austria, the musical heartland of Europe. It narrates this story across the nineteenth and twentieth centuries, beginning in the 1870s after the abolition of slavery in the United States and German unification and ending in the early 1960s and the construction of the Berlin Wall in August 1961, one month after Bumbry's debut. It follows Black musicians through every political era in modern Germany and Austria, starting with imperial Germany and Austria (part 1), the vibrant and volatile 1920s and 1930s (part 2), and the creation of three separate political states after 1945 (part 3): Austria, the Federal Republic of Germany (FRG), and the German Democratic Republic (GDR).

What my book demonstrates is that by virtue of what they performed, where they performed, and how they performed it, Black classical musicians consistently challenged their audience's ideas of Blackness, whiteness, and German national identity. White German and Austrian listeners frequently assumed that the categories of Blackness and Germanness were mutually exclusive. Yet Black performances of German music suggested that these typologies were not as fixed as listeners had been conditioned to expect. Audiences, I demonstrate, oscillated between seeing Black classical musicians as rightful heirs and dangerous usurpers of Austro-German musical culture.

It might seem strange to associate Blackness with German national identity in performances of classical music, but it is precisely this strangeness I wish to confront. Although we now recognize the long history of German antisemitism, scholars and others have been more reluctant to pay heed to Germany and Austria's Black populations (past and present) and identify anti-Black racism in Central European history. Since the 1980s, a growing Afro-German movement, spearheaded by figures such as the Black lesbian feminist poet Audre Lorde and the Afro-German poet May Ayim, has called for the recognition of Afro-Germans in society as both Black and German.[4] When people of African descent in Central Europe appear in public discourse, they are usually described as a post-WWII phenomenon, thus ignoring the long history of Black diasporic migration to Europe over centuries. In general, transatlantic discourses of Black people in Europe explain them as a current manifestation of globalization, as immigrants and outsiders, reinforcing the assumption that Black people lack the historical connection to claim European identities or truly be European citizens.[5] Afro-Germans, however, have been declaring themselves German since at least 1919.[6] Many white, German-speaking institutions have refused to recognize them for just as long.

Yet musical performances, I argue, had the power to render racial categories malleable or fluid. Repeatedly, Black classical musicians' interpretations of "the great masters" suggested to audiences that identities were not stable categories passed down genetically but instead were transmutable through the very act of performance. Their performances suggested that cultural identities had the power to supplant racial ones and that German national identity was something that could be mastered through performance and study rather than being inherited biologically through whiteness. In the concert hall or opera house, Black people musically performed both Blackness and Europeanness, collapsing the categories of Blackness and whiteness, "foreignness" and Germanness, race and culture.

This book, however, is also a study of how white audiences then responded to those epistemological collapses by shoring up hegemonic boundaries anew on European soil. Musical reception reveals that listeners constantly policed the boundaries of Blackness and whiteness in performance arenas. Across political eras and amid competing and even opposing political ideologies, white German and Austrian audiences consistently participated in the practice of racial listening, one that frequently rendered Blackness alien and foreign, as far removed from German culture as possible, even while their own ears contradicted that fact. Occasionally, however, music critics recognized the daring possibilities that Black interpretations of classical music performed: German music could be recreated and represented by "outsiders." In other words, the music of Bach, Beethoven, and Brahms might be discoverable, translatable, and reproducible after all.

Beethoven Goes Global: Musical Universalism and Black Migration

When asked by an American journalist in 1897 if there was a difference in her reception between American and European audiences, Sissieretta Jones responded, "Yes, a marked difference. In Europe there is no prejudice against my race. It matters not to them in what garb an artist come, so he be an artist . . . It is the artist['s] soul they look at there, not the color of his skin."[7] About a decade later, the African American violinist and recent transplant to Europe Clarence Cameron White made the same argument in an interview with the African American newspaper the *New York Age*: "On every side you find [that] the European musician and music-lover [sic] as well, realizes that music is too broad and too universal to be circumscribed by the complexion of the skin or texture of the hair."[8] Both performers turned to powerful notions of classical music's universality and to myths of European color blindness to explain why they believed Black classical musicians were better received in Europe than in the United States.

Their reasons for doing so were not rooted entirely in praise of European culture. Throughout the nineteenth and twentieth centuries, Black classical musicians expressed their righteous anger and frustration with the American classical music market, which used extreme measures to exclude them.[9] While many had trained at conservatories of music such as Oberlin College or the New England Conservatory of Music (NEC) since the late nineteenth century, once they stepped off the podium at graduation they encountered constant institutional barriers to their success. Although Americans now laud Marian Anderson for breaking the racial barrier at the Metropolitan Opera House in 1954, countless Black musicians had been available to sing prior to her debut. And where were they to perform?

Take, for instance, an incident in 1925, when the Italian opera singer Edo-ardo Ferrari-Fontana staged a competition at the Metropolitan Opera House in New York City to find a Black woman to sing Verdi's *Aida*, an opera about an Ethiopian princess who must choose between the Egyptian general Rad-amès (her father's enemy) and her loyalty to Ethiopia. Ferrari-Fontana con-fessed, "It has always been a mystery to me why impresarios have not sought a Negro voice for an opera like *Aida*."[10] Much to the shock and later horror of the Metropolitan Opera House, over two hundred and fifty women re-sponded to Ferrari-Fontana's request for Black singers, all stating that they were ready to sing the part. And many of them were: classically-trained sing-ers such as Muriel Rahn, who in 1959 became the first Black musical director of what is now the Frankfurt Opera, and Florence Cole Talbert, the first Black woman to perform Verdi's *Aida* in Europe, were both shortlisted. Yet despite the overwhelming proliferation of letters and telegrams seeking an audition, the Metropolitan Opera House shut down this vocal experiment.

Spurned by classical music institutions in the United States, by the late nineteenth century African American musicians began to argue that Europe was a place of racial acceptance for their musical gifts. Black praise of Eu-rope, however, frequently had less to do with European racial attitudes than with African Americans' dissatisfaction with life in the United States.[11] None-theless, Black musicians claimed that while classical music in the United States operated along rigid racial fault lines, in Europe classical music was simply too universal to be debased by racism; European support for their per-formances, they said, was proof that musical universalism was transcendent.

Yet if music is a universal language, it has a strong German accent. The compositions of Mozart or Beethoven in particular have earned a reputation for universality because of their supposed ability to transcend national bound-aries as they transport listeners to another realm. By the mid-nineteenth cen-tury, musicians and critics such as Robert Schumann had come to argue that only music "speaks the most universal of languages, one by which the soul is freely, yet indefinably moved; only then is it at home."[12] More important, according to these critics, only German art music remained pure enough, spiritual enough, and sufficiently unmarked by the aesthetic and moral de-pravation of Italian or French music to express the universal message of art. By proposing that universal music was serious, pure, and soulful and by posi-tioning German music as the only true expression of these universal values, German aesthetes, nationalists, and even politicians transformed a universal-ist message into a nationalist idea. Simultaneously belonging to all and also authentically German, the Austro-German musical canon paradoxically tied the universal to the nation like no other.

Much to the surprise of German-speaking audiences, it was precisely classical music's paradoxical nature that led Black musicians such as Clarence Cameron White to claim it. The fact that Black classical musicians in the Caribbean, the United States, and Latin America came to espouse the gospel of musical universalism is, if anything, a testament to German music's hegemonic and expansive reach. Indeed, as we will see, many of the Black musicians who traveled to Germany and Austria had been reared on the Austro-German canon by German immigrant teachers. One of the reasons why Black musicians could preach the gospel of German music so effectively was because their German teachers had taught it to them.

It is no accident that the majority of Black classical musicians performing in Germany and Austria were from the United States. Due to the transatlantic slave trade and Afro-Caribbean migration, by the late nineteenth century the United States possessed both a large Black diasporic population and elite conservatories of Western art music such as Oberlin College—modeled after German schools of music—that trained Black students. Moreover, German musicians also taught or collaborated with Black students at historically Black colleges and universities (HBCUs) such as Fisk University. German immigrants were a formidable force in the lives of Black classical musicians and often worked behind the scenes to procure their students concertizing opportunities and teachers abroad. Imbued with the teachings of "the great masters," African American classical musicians, like many white Americans, were eager to book passage across the Atlantic Ocean to pursue their dreams of living, studying, and performing in the musical promised land.

Black longing to visit the musical capitals of Vienna and Berlin demonstrates that German-speaking Europe functioned as its own metropolis for Black travel and migration, and for reasons that differed entirely from those surrounding England, France, and other regions that have dominated historical narratives of Black lives in Europe. British imperialism functioned as a key determinant connecting Anglophone Black intellectuals and artists across the Atlantic Ocean from Kingston, Jamaica, to London, England.[13] In the Francophone world, intellectuals such as René Maran and Léopold Senghor strengthened and complicated Black diasporic politics in the twentieth century.[14] Soviet Moscow became a site of Black intellectual and cultural production in the twentieth century, in part because a global vision of Marxism invited thinkers and artists to the capital city from across the Black diaspora.[15] But in the case of Black classical musicians, their reasons for living and working in Germany and Austria had little to do with empire or popular entertainment, thus providing us with a peculiarly German origin to a form of Black travel and migration. German music itself was the draw.

Moreover, the social worlds of Black classical musicians in Germany and Austria functioned differently from those of Black jazz musicians or African colonial migrants in Europe. They partook in the elite social customs and rituals expected of professional classical musicians more generally, adhering to an apprenticeship system that emphasized highly individualized musical instruction and joining patronage and pedagogy networks whose aims were to promote classical musicians in their endeavors. The concert hall as an active musical and social space also differentiated Black classical musicians from Black entertainers.[16] Performance venues such as the Sing-Akademie in Berlin or the Musikverein in Vienna functioned as sites of legitimation that granted Black performers musical credibility and even authority in a manner that other musical spaces could not. The fact that Black classical musicians had infiltrated these sacred locales was testament to their exceptional qualities in the eyes and ears of many of their listeners.

What also distinguished Black classical musicians from popular entertainers concerns the discourse surrounding Western art music itself. Transatlantic musical discourse upheld the belief that edification and uplift distinguished art music from popular or vernacular music, which classical musicians eschewed for its commercialistic overtones. An intense, all-consuming enterprise, classical music supposedly demanded complete and utter devotion. Hours of solitary practice, individual lessons, and rehearsals in symphony orchestra halls or opera houses cultivated distinct social rules—rules that Black classical musicians also wished to obey. Studying with the right teacher, attending a prestigious conservatory of music in Germany or Austria, and auditioning for a management agency were equally important pursuits. Tapping into established patronage networks, Black classical musicians formed intimate relationships with white Germans and Europeans, many of whom advocated both formally and informally on their behalf. Their worlds were uniquely Germanocentric, for what had brought them to German-speaking Europe and what made it possible for them to form these ties was Austro-German musical culture itself.

Yet at the same time, these musicians' Black diasporic identities obviously informed their experiences. As I discuss throughout the book, they often sought out other Black classical musicians and intellectuals abroad and formed intimate relationships with white Germans and Europeans at a time when most white Americans refused to acknowledge them. The pianist Portia Washington, daughter of Booker T. Washington, benefitted from her fellow pianist Hazel Harrison's connections to find housing and teachers in Berlin in the early twentieth century. Marian Anderson mentored the pianist

Josephine Harreld while Harreld studied abroad in Salzburg in the summer of 1935. African American opera coach Sylvia Olden Lee pulled a young Jessye Norman aside in 1960s West Berlin to discuss with her how to navigate her career in opera as a Black woman.

Their experiences were also gendered. Black women overwhelmingly dominated the world of opera, in part because Black men were rarely cast as romantic heroic leads with white women. Black men trained and performed in German-speaking Europe as conductors, an opportunity denied most women. The gender of Black musicians certainly shaped their encounters with their fellow musicians, their auditions, their concerts, and the audience's reception of them as well. As we will see, Black men and women were sexualized and fetishized by the German and Austrian press and by their fellow musicians. Black performers were also often vocal in rejecting how German and Austrian media portrayed them.

In short, what the experiences of Black classical musicians in Germany and Austria reveal is the global dialectical power of "musical Germanness" and the ways in which it transformed lives and institutions across the Atlantic Ocean.[17] Its endurance and mutability in transatlantic musical discourse suggest the lengths to which musicians and audiences were willing to go to maintain it. The global function of "musical Germanness" ultimately encouraged everyone, including non-Germans, to reinforce its hegemonic power. Indeed, Hoi-eun Kim argues that this is precisely how Germanness has operated in modern global history. Rather than seeing Germanness as an essence, Kim suggests that we consider it as "a collective sum of variable attributes of a nation and its members that both German nationals and non-Germans envisioned, articulated, and even embodied."[18] Germanness, he posits, has long been "subject to global production and articulation by non-Germans who wanted to define it for their own interests and agendas."[19] Black performances of classical music belong to this greater story of how discourses of German musical greatness were produced and reproduced around the world.

Settling down in cities such as Berlin, Leipzig, Vienna, and Salzburg, Black musicians performed the music of German composers and indulged long-held dreams of residing in their musical homeland. Some came for a summer. Some came for the rest of their lives. Their feet planted firmly on German soil, they made it their mission to study "the great masters" and sing like Germans. Audiences frequently responded to Black performers with rounds of applause. But, as Inga Clendinnen asks, how real was the listener's comprehension?[20]

Hearing Race: Blackness as Discourse in German History

While Black classical musicians often sang their praises for Austro-German music in a universalist key, white German and Austrian responses to their performances suggest that they were attuned to a different ideological modality. Austrian and German modes of listening to Black performers of Wagner or Brahms often belied the transnational and supposedly transcendental relationships fostered in the name of German music. Decade after decade, white German and Austrian listeners expressed surprise and even shock when hearing Black musicians perform the music of "the German masters." More important, however, their critical reception of the performances produced and reproduced nationalist and racist discourses of music. Their criticisms are proof that audience reception is never a passive experience but rather an active process where social, cultural, and political categories are constantly arbitrated.[21]

In order to interrogate how audiences listened to Black classical musicians, I draw on theories of listening that have been developed by historians, musicologists, and sound studies scholars over the last decade. Their work fundamentally rejects the assumption that listening is a universal, objective experience—namely, that listeners all hear the same sounds in the same way.[22] Rather, they argue, listening has historically functioned as a method of social boundary drawing. Audiences listen along racial lines, drawing from preexisting racial vocabularies and systems of knowledge to contextualize the sounds that they hear.[23] Over time, audiences learned how to listen for Blackness and used sounds they coded as "Black" and "white" to draw what Jennifer Lynn Stoever calls the "sonic color line," creating a hierarchical division between Blackness and whiteness.[24] This practice of racial listening, beginning in earnest in the nineteenth century, made it possible for white elite audiences to see themselves as arbiters of taste, citizenship, and personhood.

Owing its methodology to new theories of racial listening, this book also investigates when and how audiences began to associate classical music with whiteness. Mark Burford, for example, argues that certain genres became white in the ears and minds of many "because of the barriers, caveats, bargains, and apologias performers of all races and ethnicities have faced when attempting to perform and voice complex selves through it."[25] White German and Austrian audience responses to Black classical musicians, therefore, may tell us just as much about their own constructions of whiteness and German national identity as they do about their perceptions of Blackness.

One of the ways in which classical music became associated with whiteness was through the insidious practice of racial un/marking. Classical music, like whiteness itself, is frequently racially unmarked and presented as universal—until people of color start performing it.[26] Audiences, in turn, then employ practices of racial listening to compose the sonic color line in classical music anew, even as they consider the porousness of its boundaries. As we will see, German-speaking music criticism consistently fell along racial lines, at various times praising or condemning Black classical musicians for sounding either "white" or "Black," German or un-German. Across decades, listeners tuned their ears for inaudible social cues and drew on racial discourses to make aesthetic judgments on performances of Schubert or Brahms. Their sonic observations were never benign or objective. Rather, they produced and maintained racial difference.

For example, in the 1920s listeners praised Black classical musicians such as Marian Anderson and Roland Hayes as "Negroes with white souls," which suggested that through their dedication to classical music they had overcome their Blackness and the limitations it posed. The practice of describing "good" Black people as white has its origins in German colonialism. In 1912, for example, the German ethnographer Leo Frobenius praised an African sergeant named Bida along the same lines during his time in Sudan. "Above all," he writes, "I must praise my hardworking Sergeant Bida, who, although of dark skin, has demonstrated that he has a white heart."[27] During the American occupation of West Germany after 1945, white German commentators used a similar rhetorical device when pleading with Germans to be more accepting of children born to African American soldiers and white German women. Heide Fehrenbach writes, "In efforts to establish the children's 'innocence' and untainted moral state, liberal commentators would remark that while they might be Black on the outside, on the inside—where it counts—the children had a 'white heart.' "[28] Even in the case of Black Germans today, "if their Blackness is recognized, their Germanness is not, and if they are allowed to be German, they are not so Black, after all," argues Fatima El-Tayeb.[29] German national identity, scholars find, has operated in a Black-white binary that has been difficult to dismantle.

In sum, German and Austrian reception of Black classical musicians reveals the limits of German musical universalism despite its global reach. Listeners' evaluations illustrate how universalizing beliefs actually obfuscated music's role in reinforcing racial hierarchies and shaping ideologies of cultural belonging. Confronted by the politics of race and nation, listeners fiddled with the timbre and tone of German musical universalism in response to the different kinds of performers praising it. However much the audience believed in the transcendental powers of the Austro-German canon, and however much Black classical musicians praised European society for being more receptive to their musicianship than the United States, race still informed white audiences' criticisms of Black performers and their renditions of the supposedly universal music of Bach, Beethoven, and Brahms.

Crossing Time and Space: German History over the *Longue Durée*

Searching for Black people in German musical spaces has occasionally felt akin to chasing ghosts. While some musicians reached international stardom and continue to live on in public memory, others such as Hazel Harrison, who performed with the Berlin Philharmonic in 1904, have fallen into obscurity. Many names are simply unknown in African American history because their careers and lives flourished entirely on German soil. The African American conductor George Byrd, for example, was a protégé of Herbert von Karajan and a conductor who worked on both sides of the Berlin Wall from the 1960s until the collapse of the GDR in 1990. Claudio Brindis de Salas, an Afro-Brazilian violinist, spent well over a decade in Germany in the late nineteenth century before retiring to Argentina. J. Elmer Spyglass, a graduate of Ohio's Toledo Conservatory of Music, traveled abroad to Germany in the early 1910s and simply never came back. At the end of WWII, he was among a crowd of German villagers greeting American soldiers who had defeated Nazi rule.

In order to find these individuals, I turned to print media as the primary source base for my histories of transatlantic musical exchange, even though I recognize the difficulties of relying on concert music criticism to inform historical and musicological scholarship. Although many American and Austrian newspapers have been digitized and made text searchable, German newspapers still exist primarily in analog form and are accessible only through archival research.[30] I supplement historical newspapers with memoirs, unpublished speeches, musical scores, concert programs, private letters, and personal diaries located in German, Austrian, and American archives in order to create a panoramic perspective of how music critics, audiences, Black performers, their teachers, and their friends understood Blackness, whiteness, and German musical culture.

While sound recordings are worthy of investigation, I have privileged eyewitness accounts, interviews, diaries, and memoirs over musical albums to focus on audiences' reflections on their encounters with Black performers on Central European stages. It was simply more important to me to counter myths of European historical whiteness by providing irrefutable evidence that Black people traveled to, lived in, and performed in front of German and

Austrian audiences than it was to analyze sonic materials, divorced as they are from the Black men and women that produced them. The advantage to privileging live performances over sound recordings lies precisely in illustrating how Black musicians performatively detangled the relationship between sight and sound, race and culture, in front of their audiences for nearly one hundred years.

Writing a *longue durée* of this kind offers many advantages, the first being that it becomes possible to see how musical performances can change their meaning in a new political context. Anderson's renditions of Handel, Bach, and Schubert made her an international superstar in the 1930s. In 1950, she offered a recital featuring much of the same music she had sung in previous decades. But the context had completely changed. She performed in Berlin in front of German music lovers and American soldiers at the behest of the US military, who hired Black classical musicians to perform in Germany in order to "teach the Germans a racial lesson."[31] Her performances of Schubert were now heard in a different key.

Second, narrating a longer history reveals both how historical agents were shaped by the political and cultural context in which they resided and also how the varying discursive practices in which they were engaged had, in actuality, preceded them. Following Neil Gregor's observation that the "same underlying habits of thought" structured the way Germans listened to the composer Anton Bruckner's music across the twentieth century, this book also provides occasional clues to patterns of reception that undergirded Austro-German musical culture.[32] Rather than seeing German and Austrian audiences, patrons, and social networks as static or unchanging over time, it presents moments of intense political rupture and change while also uncovering underlying logics that continued to generate theories of racial difference or musical sameness.

Third, taking the long view of German musical reception also encourages us to listen carefully to German constructs of Blackness across time, to see how they drew from earlier archives and repositories of knowledge and how they curated an ever-changing body of rhetoric, iconography, and musical vocabulary to make sense of what they perceived as novelty. For this reason, white German audiences' comparisons of Black musicians to their Black predecessors or contemporaries actually matter more than when they were compared to Jewish musicians or others labeled as different. Being attentive to how German audiences compared Black musicians across time reveals how past and present notions of Blackness piled atop one another and incited public interest.[33] In a concert hall, listeners frequently located older Black references, demonstrating a remarkable awareness of Black musicianship in different political eras—even while occasionally still expressing surprise at seeing a Black classical musician in front of them.

Fourth, by addressing moments across time when German and Austrian listeners tapped into racial discourses, this book also challenges conventional forms of periodization. It intentionally pushes through well-established vanishing points such as Hitler's rise to power in 1933 or the end of WWII in 1945, choosing to see them neither as beginnings nor endings of important conversations about race or music. Transgressing the 1945 barrier in German history becomes especially important for writing histories of race and racism because for a long time many postwar historians operated under the assumption that the problem of racism disappeared after the demise of the Nazi state. In doing so, they propagated the postwar notion that constructs of race were no longer necessary to define or understand.[34] Yet German reception of Black classical musicians demonstrates how difficult it was for audiences to dislodge their perceptions of Black talent and musicianship, even in a new era of Allied occupation. Their praise for, or rejection of, a Black performer's voice and appearance often relied on older racial vocabularies, in spite of their new political reality.

Yet as much as this book offers us a history of durable memory, of drawing on older racial practices to make sense of the new, it is also a history of forgetting. Or, perhaps more fitting, it is about how German and Austrian listeners employed what Katrin Sieg calls technologies of forgetting in order to maintain certain kinds of public memories. Forgetting historical knowledge, she argues, is a complex and deliberately dishonest process: "The work of forgetting faces a conceptual dilemma: how to forget something you cannot acknowledge knowing, since that acknowledgment would consign matter to memory rather than oblivion?"[35]

The act of forgetting made it possible for listeners to feel a sense of discovery and novelty each time a Black musician performed on stage, thus presenting Black performances as rare occurrences. This pattern of forgetting or erasure recurs time and again. For example, audiences today still assume that André Watts was the first Black pianist to perform with the Berlin Philharmonic in 1967 when in fact Hazel Harrison broke that barrier in 1904. Likewise, our assumption that Grace Bumbry was the first Black singer in Bayreuth erases Luranah Aldridge's experience. The career of the Juilliard-trained conductor George Byrd is also a striking example of this history of forgetting: when he conducted the Berlin Philharmonic in 1959, newspapers in both the United States and Germany reported that he was the first Black conductor to do so.[36] Yet fourteen years prior, Rudolph Dunbar had conducted the ensemble in one of their first concerts following the end of WWII.

White German denial or erasure of the presence of Black classical musicians within German history was a complex process. Because Black classical musicians were often rendered as exceptions to German understanding of Black musicianship, with its emphasis on jazz or popular music, they were easy to forget—or, to put it more succinctly, they could be made forgettable. Black classical musicians could exist as strange aberrations outside of German history as opposed to being a part of it. German histories of forgetting were simultaneously histories of compressing, of repeatedly associating Black musicianship with jazz, popular music, and degenerate entertainment, thus presenting classical musicians as an extraordinary anomaly. Across time, a curated iconography of Black popular entertainment overlaid performances by Black classical musicians, rendering them potentially inscrutable on their own terms.

In addition to crossing time, this book also travels across borders. In particular, it transgresses the Austro-German boundary that has shaped much of German historiography. The reasons for this are many. First, Black classical musicians themselves rarely stayed within national borders. Their musical migrations between Berlin, Munich, Vienna, and Salzburg suggest instead a fluidity of movement in what they perceived to be a shared cultural space. Especially after the 1933 rise of Hitler, Black classical musicians left Germany and took advantage of musical communities and markets in Austria to continue staging their concerts. Similarly, after 1945, Black classical musicians were also willing to cross the Berlin Wall into East Germany to advance their careers.

Music-making has also always been a transregional and transnational activity, and many musicians and audiences in German-speaking Europe found various ways to lay claim to the Austro-German musical canon.[37] I do not wish to conflate all regions of German-speaking Europe, but rather to recognize the tensions that developed between cultural space and geographic place and to identify if or how these tensions changed in response to the arrival of transnational actors.[38] Indeed, the strength of crossing political and regional borders is that we may bring German-speaking cultural centers into conversation with one another.[39] It makes it possible to see how audiences in Vienna, Salzburg, Munich, Leipzig, and Berlin claimed cultural and musical Germanness throughout the nineteenth and twentieth centuries in different ways, and to see how they held figures such as Beethoven and Brahms central to their cultural identities.

Music was not the only value Germans and Austrians shared. Consideration of how notions of Blackness crossed borders also illuminates a history of anti-Black racism that likewise knew no national boundary. While the historiography of Black migration to Germany has grown considerably, sub-stantially less scholarship exists on Blackness in Austria.[40] Yet Austrians and Germans frequently relied on their presumed whiteness to understand per-formances of German music, even when their political situations differed. Germans and Austrians often assumed a shared culture when it came to dis-cussing Black musicians. Most disconcerting, their comments suggest a racist comprehension of musical Germanness, one that betrayed its universalist spirit. Although critics in Austria and Germany did not always agree on what musical Germanness was, this book demonstrates that they all nonetheless believed Blackness lay outside of it, even when provided sonic evidence to the contrary. In twentieth-century Germany, Priscilla Layne writes, "Black-ness [was] posited as always already outside of German culture and in op-position to German culture, foreclosing the possibility of being both Black and German."[41] One thing was for certain: musical Germanness was defined along racial lines, even during moments of international support and univer-salist aspirations.

Resisting White Expectations

This book is not about jazz. It is not about hip hop, gospel, or other genres of music that we associate with Black identity. It is, however, about the as-sumptions, expectations, and desires that white audiences placed on Black bodies across the Atlantic Ocean and that they ascribed to Black musician-ship of whatever genre. In fact, the strength of this book is its location of Black performances within the realm of classical music, which has escaped many of our historiographical conversations on race and Blackness.[42] Black musicians performed in German-speaking Europe long before the invention of jazz and have performed long since. Yet our historiographies of Black musical migration and travel have given us the most limited sense of their accomplishments. Repeatedly, books on Black musicians in the diaspora have refused to examine anything outside of a narrowly-defined conception of "Black music." There must be space in scholarship for Black cultural activity and agency that both expands and calls into question what we have come to define as Black aesthetics. Discussing these activities does not diminish or jeopardize the work of racial justice.[43] Instead, it bolsters us to consider new definitions of Blackness and music in ever-shifting global contexts.

Black performances of classical music in Germany and Austria take on new meaning when we consider them not only as musical interpretations of canonical works but also as performances of cultural citizenship in Europe. The question of whether different racial minorities can claim a German or

Austrian identity has only become more urgent in the twenty-first century.[44] Black musical renditions of Brahms or Beethoven are especially powerful in this light because these performances struck right at the heart of German culture and how its listeners understood it. Black musicians' rigorous study and successful execution of German music suggest that, contrary to contemporary conservative, essentialist claims to German national identity, Germanness is something that can not only be performed but also learned.

Yet by the time the popular African American choral ensemble known as the Fisk Jubilee Singers arrived in Germany in 1877, German demands for a particular kind of musical Blackness had become a powerful force of their own. For over a century, white German-speakers continually demanded a Black musical authenticity that often countered what the musicians themselves wished to perform. In the 1890s, Kaiser Wilhelm II's son requested African American spirituals when the Hampton Institute Choir came to visit, and in the 1920s, Afro-Germans took up American jazz music to satisfy white German interest—in spite of the fact that they had little training in the music or familiarity with it. Even in Nazi concentration camps in the 1930s and 1940s, Nazi officers demanded that Black prisoners perform jazz. After 1945, Black musicians still found themselves the objects of a particular kind of musical desire. The mezzo-soprano Shirley Verrett, who spent the majority of her career in the 1960s and 1970s in West Germany, recalled giving recitals in Europe in which she had omitted African American spirituals from the text of her concert program, only to be obliged to sing them anyway after hearing repeated calls for "spiri-chu-elles" from the back of the concert hall.[45] At the request of the West German government, Sylvia Lee taught spirituals to German choruses during her seven-year residency in West Germany, where she also worked at the Bavaria State Opera.[46] Trapped by German expectations of Black authenticity, Black musicians were supposed to give German and Austrian audiences the sounds of themselves.

The title of this book, however, encourages us to consider what happened when Black classical musicians defied those expectations, to linger in those moments when they sang music that did not supposedly "look" like them, when they performed brilliantly and under considerable scrutiny. So let us hear what they gave their listeners instead.

PART I

1870–1914

CHAPTER 1

How Beethoven Came to Black America

*German Musical Universalism and Black Education
after the Civil War*

Carl Reinecke's Piano Sonatina in D Major,
op. 47, no. 2 might seem like a strange piece of music to find in Tuskegee,
Alabama in 1890. Published in Germany in 1855, the light-hearted sonatina
appears out of place in the land of sharecropping, the site of the Great Migration and the violent terrain of Jim Crow. A playful exchange between
the right and left hands defines most of the first movement: the right hand
begins a phrase that the left hand then directly copies a beat later, almost
as if lagging behind by a step. The sonatina's second movement whizzes
by quickly, beginning with a chromatic melody lurching forward in a dizzying, hurdy-gurdy motion, followed by a breezy baritone tune. The third
and final movement concludes in a fashion popular in its day: a theme with
variations. Set in the style of a German chorale, the theme is a classic German children's song called "Wer hat die schönsten Schäfchen?" ("Who has
the prettiest lambs?"). Composed by Johann Friedrich Reichardt in 1790 and
then set to text by German Romantic poet August Heinrich Hoffmann von
Fallersleben in 1830, the tune was—and remains—a popular German lullaby.

Reinecke's piano sonatinas were a beloved staple in many a piano teacher's pedagogical repertoire in the nineteenth and early twentieth centuries,
a practical and handy tool in their toolkit. And for good reason. A professor
(and later director) at the Leipzig Conservatory of Music starting in 1860,
Reinecke earned a reputation for being committed to students' musical

Piano Sonatina in D Major

THEMA.   Carl Reinecke, Op. 47 No. 2

FIGURE 1. The third movement of Carl Reinecke's Piano Sonatina in D Major, op. 47, no. 2, mm. 1–16. It is a theme and variations using the children's song, "Wer hat die schönsten Schäfchen?" ("Who has the prettiest lambs?") by August Heinrich Hoffmann von Fallersleben and Johann Friedrich Reichart, first composed in 1830.

development, steeping them in a musical training that he pragmatically saw as a thorough grounding in both the basics and the classics.[1] His piano sonatinas were no exception, offering this unique mixture of German Romantic musical styles and useful technical instruction.

In Tuskegee, Reinecke's sonatinas came to life again in the hands of African American students, who most likely spent hours on the piano in the newly built chapel of the Tuskegee Institute practicing tricky passages, connecting musical dots to bring out the sonatinas' melodies, and developing their piano peddling so the pieces would not sound too muddy.[2] Reinecke's popular German Romantic *Hausmusik*, which emanated from pianos in many homes of the middle-class intellectuals (*Bildungsbürgertum*) throughout German-speaking Europe, found a new home on Black students' recital programs in the United States.

How did a piano sonatina by a German Romantic composer end up in the hands of formerly enslaved peoples in rural Alabama? The idea that the music of Reinecke and other German composers floated freely out of the windows of chapels or concert halls on African American campuses of higher education in the 1890s might strike some readers as strange or jarring since it counters our historical narratives of the rise of Black popular music in that same era.[3] Yet its pervasiveness in African American musical life was no accident. Its prominence in musical education is a testament to the global power of German music in the nineteenth century and to the fierce determination of African Americans invested in performing it.

In the decades following the US Civil War (1861–65), many African Americans embarked on a project to study, perform, and teach the music of Reinecke and others. Part of the mass movement to educate African Americans in general between the 1870s and 1918, music education promised to cultivate new generations of politically minded, culturally sophisticated, and socially aware Black citizens to advance their rights in a nation that still refused to recognize them. Some believed that the respectability afforded to art music offered African Americans a way to fight denigration by white people. Racially mixed institutions of higher learning such as Oberlin College had made it their mission to educate many African American students, and the boom in Black institutions of higher learning (HBCUs) such as Fisk University, Tuskegee Institute, Howard University, Spelman College, and Morehouse College during the era of Reconstruction also played a new and significant role in transforming Black American lives.

What all of these institutions espoused, and what music teachers across the United States also insisted, was that if Black students were to advance in society, they would do so through performing and listening to the "right" kind of music. The right kind of music was classical music—and even more specifically, I argue, German art music. Course offerings at HBCUs did not instruct students on the musical qualities of Black popular music, even if African American students performed it in concerts for outside audiences. Rather, students learned two-part inventions by Johann Sebastian Bach, lieder by Franz Schubert, and choral music by Felix Mendelssohn. If music was going to launch a new generation of African Americans into an era of racial equality, the music best suited to accomplish this difficult feat was that of Bach, Beethoven, and Brahms.

This chapter explores the transatlantic and transformative power that classical music, and German music in particular, brought to African American lives in the Post-Bellum and Pre-Harlem era (1870s–1918). Central European musicians and pedagogues who had emigrated to the United States were instrumental in extolling the virtues and values of classical music across America, including in Black American homes. African Americans, in turn, internalized German Romantic ideals of musical universalism and used them to articulate their politics of racial uplift and social advancement in the nineteenth and twentieth centuries. In so doing, Black musicians recomposed what musical universalism looked like or sounded like, anchoring it in the racial politics of the United States and beyond.

How African American students were able to pick up and study classical music is remarkable when one considers how many impediments stood in their way. Black Americans lived in a racist, white supremacist society that employed violence and the threat of violence, erected oppressive legal systems, and dedicated resources and people to ensure that Black people had a status unequal to white Americans. Rape and lynching, white vigilantism in the South and racialized policing in the North defined many Black experiences.[4] Black classical musicians, emboldened by transatlantic discourses of German music's accessibility, overcame significant barriers to perform it. As this discourse of musical universalism reached new shores, it ultimately convinced Black musicians to set sail for Europe. German musicians, we will see, were integral to this generation of a new Black Atlantic network, in part because they were everywhere.

The German Music Teacher

In 1890s Niagara Falls, New York, Nathaniel Dett, a Black teenager, squirmed at the piano bench. His Austrian teacher was visibly frustrated. Dett eventually became one of the most important early composers of African American art music, but as a gifted young student he couldn't quite seem to figure out the first movement of Beethoven's Piano Sonata in F Minor. "I still have a memory of this excitable Teuton tearing his hair when I persistently played wrong notes," Dett shared decades later in an interview. Believing Beethoven's quick and fiery Piano Sonata in F Minor to be sentimental, Dett played it far too slowly until his teacher stopped him. The teacher demanded that Dett perform the music "as indicated and taught [him] the significance of the printed musical terms."[5]

Although Dett may not have appreciated his teacher's antics very much, the fact that he received instruction from a German-speaking musician is revealing. German musicians were highly sought-after commodities in American music, critical "agents of German *Kultur*" who disseminated German music to American audiences and quickly came to dominate the musical landscape.[6] In fact, the German musical establishment in the United States was so powerful that in places such as New York City, Berndt Ostendorf writes, "it led some people in the music business to change their names from English to German for reasons of marketability (Clapp to Dockstader, from Gumm to Von Tilzer)."[7]

In the nineteenth and twentieth centuries, African Americans also promulgated the notion that German musicians were superior. For example, James Monroe Trotter's seminal 1878 text, *Music and Some Highly Musical*

People—the first book written by and about African American musicians—is full of praise for German music. Espousing the principles of musical universalism, Trotter writes, "I have said that music speaks a language all its own, and one that is universal."[8] Yet how quickly Trotter pivots from a broad universalism to extolling the composers of the Austro-German musical canon. "The German race," he concludes, "is remarkable for the intelligence, steadiness, and industry of its members, and their love for and cultivation of the art of music—these latter characteristics prevailing to a most pleasing degree among all classes of the race. *Indeed, it is rare to find a German not, in some sense at least, a musician.*"[9] For decades, texts by Black writers and intellectuals on music espoused the same belief. On the eve of WWI in 1914, a writer for the prominent African American civil rights newspaper the *Chicago Defender* placed Germany at the center of musical greatness. "Certainly," the author professes, "no other nation can show greater music than that which was composed by Beethoven, Mozart, and other artists from the Fatherland."[10] And no other people possessed such a mastery of it.

Indeed, the preference among African American families for Germans to teach their sons and daughters the music of Beethoven was so prevalent that the *Negro Music Journal* complained about it in 1903. In an editorial for the journal, the first ever Black publication dedicated to Black musicians and Black music, J. Hillary Taylor complained that too many Black families were repeatedly boasting, "'My child is studying under a German teacher.'" He demanded that African Americans hire instructors "on their merits as teachers rather than on account of color or nationality."[11]

Why did German music reign supreme in the United States? For one thing, Western art music supposedly demonstrated the triumph of reason and rational thought over intellectual backwardness and primitive cultures.[12] The sophisticated harmonies, structures, and forms of instrumental music and symphonic music in particular were somehow proof of German music's supremacy in particular, showcasing Central Europe's advanced intellectual development and evolution away from more primitive modes of music-making.[13] Imbued with bourgeois values, the theory of German music's universality meant that those who did not appreciate this edifying music were themselves found lacking. It became a moral imperative to reach the culturally backward, educate the less fortunate, and uplift those in need of social and cultural transformation. However, David Gramit warns, "the status of German musical culture rested on a precariously double-edged claim: serious (and most often German) music was held to be universally valid, even though, at the same time, maintaining its prestige demanded limiting access to it along the lines of existing social divisions."[14] German musical universalism reinforced social hierarchies, in other words, even while its rhetoric of transcendentalism obscured them.[15]

Both white and Black Americans in the late nineteenth century saw classical music as a way to uplift American society because they linked it to moral improvement and to social status.[16] Admiration of German art music was, in these terms, proof of one's good taste. "There can be no doubt," Douglas Shadle writes, "that the sacralization of art, fueled by the desire for German music (of whatever brand), left a lasting imprint on the culture of classical music that is still with us today."[17] By the late nineteenth century, German music dominated symphony orchestra repertoires, piano teachers assigned it in middle class American homes, American opera houses performed it, and religious communities sang it throughout the United States. German music—from Mendelssohn's oratorios and Brahms's *German Requiem* to Beethoven's symphonies and Wagner's overtures—was pervasive, permeating many aspects of American life.

But there was a racial dimension to this aesthetic appreciation as well, for African Americans came to believe that classical music could be a vehicle that they could use to cross the color line. Black American elites especially sought out classical music as a way to challenge white American racist constructions of Blackness that were often tied to minstrelsy. In the midst of violence and oppression, Kevin Gaines writes, Black elites strove to distinguish themselves as "bourgeois agents of civilization" and championed the phrase "uplifting the race"—"so purposeful and earnest, yet so often of ambiguous significance."[18] Unfortunately, racial uplift often meant reinforcing social divisions among Black people and upholding middle-class Victorian values rather than undoing them.

Classical music was imbricated in these social entrenchments defining Black American cultural life in the late nineteenth and early twentieth centuries. But German art music also allowed Black Americans to envision a musical world beyond the United States. The aesthetic and professional choices of Black classical musicians cannot be reduced to a binary pole of assimilation into white America on the one hand or the cultivation of an "authentically" Black identity on the other.[19] As we will see, German music teachers were instrumental in forming an alternative to this binary because they supported Black students' quests for transatlantic careers. German musicians were highly sought-after teachers who instructed African American students individually in cities around the United States, from big East Coast metropolises such as Boston and New York to Midwestern hubs like Cleveland and the western locales of Denver and San Francisco.

Working closely together in weekly lessons and sharing small physical spaces either in someone's home or studio, German musicians and African

American students formed intimate bonds. Music lessons demand close proximity, the sharing of instruments, a teacher's hand on a student's body to illustrate a particular technique or gesture. In musical lessons, a student and a teacher collaborate together to smooth out musical phrases, hammer out a tricky technical passage, and develop a musical idea. Lessons require both the student and the teacher to make themselves intellectually and even physically vulnerable for the sake of musical education.

Musical instruction also required a cross-racial collaboration and intimacy that both parties had to be willing to develop. In agreeing to take on a Black student (which many white teachers would not), a white teacher made a performative statement that he or she desired to share a space with someone to whom white American society was openly hostile. Black students, eagerly seeking knowledge, sometimes put themselves at risk of psychological or even physical abuse. Perhaps because of the intimacy that music lessons require, they frequently fostered lifelong bonds between Central European teachers and African American students, leading to a teacher's advocacy and support for the student as a musician and intellectual in his or her own right. (A successful student also vindicates the teacher's decision to admit him or her and enhances the teacher's reputation.)

We know that these bonds between German teachers and African American pupils were long-lasting and transformative because many African American musicians spoke of them in such terms. Prominent Black classical musicians at the turn of the century such as Daisy Tapley, William Kemper Harreld, Felix Weir, Justin Holland, and Hazel Harrison touted their private training with German teachers in interviews and in press materials.[20] Moreover, many of the early titans of African American popular music had studied at a young age with German teachers, including James Reese Europe and the Hyers Sisters.[21] Speaking favorably of one's former German music teacher was a useful strategy, for it signaled to concert-goers a musician's prestige, rigorous training, and commitment to perfecting the musical art.

Two cases in particular illustrate the transformative power, long-lasting bonds, and professional advantages that Black students gained from working with German music teachers: African American composers Scott Joplin and Harry Lawrence Freeman. Arguably the most famous composer of ragtime music, Joplin studied in the 1880s with Julius Weiss, a Jewish-German immigrant from Saxony who taught his young pupil in Texarkana, Texas, even when Joplin's family could no longer afford a piano tutor. Years later, a financially successful Joplin sent money to an impoverished Weiss for over a decade, an act demonstrating his dedication to and admiration for his first teacher.[22]

Joplin also won the support of a second German music teacher in the twentieth century who became an advocate for Joplin's music. In 1901 Joplin became a student of the pianist and conductor Alfred Ernst, who had come to St. Louis in 1894 to conduct the St. Louis Choral-Symphony. Under Ernst's instruction, Joplin learned music theory and discovered Richard Wagner's opera, *Tannhäuser*.[23] That same year, the *St. Louis Dispatch* reported, "So deeply is Mr. Ernst impressed with the ability of [Joplin] that he intends to take with him to Germany next summer copies of Joplin's work, with a view of educating the dignified disciples of . . . European masters into an appreciation of the real American ragtime melodies."[24] Ernst's public proclamation of Joplin's talent and abilities most likely benefited the young composer's career. By suggesting that Joplin's music could find a German audience, he indicated that Joplin's talents had merits that reached beyond white Americans and their refusal to recognize them. German audiences were the real tastemakers, after all, and if they admired Joplin's music, then it meant his compositions were indeed worthy of listening. But by insisting that Joplin's work could find an audience outside of the United States, Ernst, like other German teachers, planted a seed in Black students' minds: their musicianship was appreciated beyond the shores of the United States. If white Americans would not accept them, perhaps Germans might.

Harry Lawrence Freeman, a composer of dozens of operas during the Harlem Renaissance, used his relationship with the German American composer and conductor Johann Heinrich Beck to advance his career. Born in Cleveland, Ohio, in 1869, Freeman resolved to become a composer at the age of eighteen when he heard a performance of Wagner's *Tannhäuser*. Following this musical epiphany he began writing operas and debuted two of them—*Epthalia* and *The Martyr*—at Denver's Deutsches Theater while he was living in the city in the early 1890s. It was his time studying with Beck, however, that transformed Freeman's career. Returning to Cleveland in 1893, Freeman trained with Beck (the first conductor of what would eventually become the Cleveland Orchestra) and became immersed in the musical language of many opera composers, including Wagner.

Beck, in turn, championed Freeman's career and praised Freeman for his work as an opera composer. Beck helped sponsor the premiere of Freeman's opera, *The Martyr*, at Cleveland's Germania Hall on May 2, 1900, and attended a casual listening session of the opera at Freeman's home.[25] Beck also conducted one of Freeman's works, *Nada*, with the Cleveland Orchestra in March 1900, and he kept a copy of the score with him throughout his life.[26] Beck praised Freeman as having "some of the important qualities of character that made Wagner great. His compositions are wonderfully big in conception, the music faithfully portraying the sentiment of the words."[27] Freeman used Beck's ringing endorsement in his own press materials. Perhaps because of Beck's association with Wagner in print, Freeman was dubbed the "Colored Wagner," a title he proudly maintained throughout his career.[28]

African American students and performers managed to keep in touch with former Central European teachers for years—sometimes even throughout their whole careers. Their memoirs, letters, and interviews with local press testify to the intimacy and adoration of these relationships. Their close bonds tell us that although white Americans were often reluctant or unwilling to teach or foster Black students, many Central European musicians were not, perhaps because they did not feel the same social pressures of American racism or because people's perceptions of them as cosmopolitan Europeans permitted them to break social rules and work with Black students (or both).

It would be naive or foolish to believe that Central European musicians were somehow free from the politics of American racism. Nor should we see them as rescuers of Black musical talent, plucking young African Americans from a path of obscurity to reveal their true musical promise. African Americans, of course, were hungry for training, compelled by a desire to sing, play, and listen to music that consumed their thoughts. They sought out teachers, requested auditions, and set up music lessons for their own musical and intellectual growth, often at great financial and social expense.

But what remains striking is the transnational nature of these collaborations. If a Black musician were to succeed in the world of classical music, the likelihood that a musician from Central Europe—or at least from outside the United States—was behind his or her career was fairly high. They endorsed and promoted students and encouraged them to travel not only around the United States but around Europe.[29] The transnational nature of their relationship might have permitted German teachers to imagine how their students could build careers for themselves that were not limited to the United States. These teachers' backgrounds, in other words, freed them from seeing Black lives and potential careers solely through the lens of American race relations. Operating outside of established institutions, together both student and teacher explored the range and fulfilled the promise of Black musical potential.

Black Students at White Institutions

The reason why African American students worked with teachers outside of conservatories of music is that many established music institutions were hostile to Black students. The number of Black students admitted at the New England Conservatory of Music (NEC), the Curtis Institute of Music, and other schools was never high. Moreover, some institutions such as the Peabody Institute and the University of Cincinnati College-Conservatory of Music refused to accept Black students well into the mid-twentieth century— Peabody did not admit Black students until 1949.[30] As Loren Kajikawa argues, music conservatories were historically "built on a culture of exclusion" that privileged white bodies and musical traditions over all others.[31]

Silence shrouds many histories of Western art music institutions and their participation in maintaining racial segregation in the nineteenth and twentieth centuries. The profound consequences of the myth of Western art music's color blindness and proclaimed meritocracy coupled with the historical realities and legacies of racism in the United States have created a fraught body of literature on the history of racial minorities at music conservatories. The few institutional histories of American music schools that mention race routinely find ways to laud their conservatories for their race relations in the nineteenth and twentieth centuries. Such praise often espouses the kind of color-blind mythology that frees classical music from any social responsibility for racism.[32]

For example, when approached by the Kennedy administration in 1963 to create directives against discrimination in light of the civil rights movement, NEC's board boastfully replied, "There has never been a color bar in either the admissions or the placement policies of the Conservatory."[33] But Black students nonetheless experienced racism at NEC. Take, for example, the experience of the NEC student Maud Cuney Hare in Boston in the 1890s. Hare was a forceful figure of the Harlem Renaissance and a musicologist whose 1936 book, *Negro Music and Musicians*, was a landmark piece of scholarship on Black music history. Attending the conservatory to study with Emil Ludwig and Edwin Klahre, Hare faced protest from her white roommates upon entering her college dormitory. School authorities took her roommates' side.[34] Hare's experience counters the NEC board's boast of racial harmony.

The perceived lack of a color bar did not historically guarantee positive or progressive action to grant Black students access to classical musical education. In fact, the legacies and consequences of color blindness, meritocracy, and musical universalism shaped classical musical education itself. On the one hand, because of their belief in musical universalism, classical musical institutions admitted some Black students for study at times when they were denied access to education elsewhere. Committed to sharing classical music's edifying powers and virtues with all of society, some teachers and musicians took on Black students who demonstrated musical talent and interest, thus practicing the gospel of musical universalism they themselves preached. On the other, the premise of "art for art's sake" and the belief that the politics of race played no role in musical admissions or the aesthetic pleasure of a musical concert glossed over classical music's complicity in racism and ignored the classist, racist, and gendered structures in the United States that operated against Black students.

Nonetheless, one institution played a prominent role in educating Black music students: Oberlin College.[35] It was such an obvious choice for African American musicians that prominent performers such as William Grant Still and Will Marion Cook publicly stated it was the only place for Black students to study.[36] Oberlin was in a unique position to musically educate Black students for two reasons. First, Oberlin's commitment to educating African Americans in the nineteenth and twentieth centuries was unparalleled. The core mission of Oberlin as an institution was one of radical egalitarianism. Accepting and educating Black students was essential to the institution's identity from its founding in 1833. From 1833 until 1916, for example, Oberlin used its pre-college preparatory school as a feeder into its bachelor degree programs, thus successfully pipelining Black students into the college.[37] By 1899, Oberlin—a white-majority school—educated the most Black students outside of the South.[38] Especially prior to the end of the Civil War and the consequent founding of historically Black Southern institutions such as Fisk or Howard Universities, Oberlin shone brightly as a beacon for Black education.

What also distinguished Oberlin was its conservatory of music. In the United States, the German model of the conservatory of music served as the foundation for American conservatories of music, and Germans and German Americans were those institutions' founders and first teachers. Founded in 1865, Oberlin's conservatory of music was no different. Of the twenty-three faculty listed in their 1901 course catalog, only five lacked either a personal or a professional connection to Germany or Austria, and those five were lower-tiered instructors who mostly taught in the preparatory music program.[39] All of the primary faculty, in other words, were either German themselves (such as the music theorist Friedrich Johann Lehmann) or had studied, performed, or attended concerts there.[40] For decades, the directors of the conservatory were all German-trained musicians. Well through the 1950s, it remained a requirement for American faculty at Oberlin to have studied extensively in Central Europe.[41]

With its commitment to educating Black students and its prestigious German-led conservatory of music, Oberlin offered a rigorous musical education to Black classical musicians that was unmatched by any other predominantly white institution.[42] Indeed, many of the musicians who traveled to Germany and Austria in the nineteenth and twentieth centuries trained at Oberlin or later took lessons from Oberlin graduates. Between 1890 and 1945, Oberlin awarded over eighty degrees in music to African American students, including the composers Nathaniel Dett and William Grant Still and the pianists Roy Tibbs and Sylvia Lee, both of whom studied and made careers in German-speaking Europe.

Black students' recital programs also show how steeped Oberlin music students were in the German musical canon.[43] In their senior recitals, pianists performed works by Carl Maria von Weber, Brahms, Schumann, and Mendelssohn, while organists showcased fugues by Bach and Dieterich Buxtehude.[44] German faculty at Oberlin such as Friedrich August Goerner (a product of Weimar's Orchestra School and a student of Leopold Grützmacher) and Maurice Koessler (a graduate of the Royal Academy of Musical Performing Arts in Berlin) often played on Black student recitals as well, offering up pieces such as Josef Rheinberger's Trio no. 3, op. 121. Oberlin faculty also wrote letters of recommendation for Black students, such as that by Arthur Heacox, a string bass player and music theorist trained in Munich, applauding Edith Baker for her discipline, scholarship, and knowledge of harmony, keyboard, counterpoint, musical form, music history, and piano literature.[45]

African American musicians studied at other conservatories of music as well. But only Oberlin produced a substantially large number of musicians with wide-ranging careers. Some became music teachers at elementary schools, private piano instructors, or high school choir teachers, and others became nationally known composers or conductors. Belonging to the first generations of college-educated music students, they were instrumental in establishing music programs for Black students in the United States.

Teaching Music to the Talented Tenth: Classical Music at HBCUs

The music of Bach, Beethoven, and Brahms was also important to Black colleges and universities in the United States, who sought to uphold the values of racial uplift and create a liberally educated Black middle class.[46] Black university students were, in the words of W. E. B. Du Bois, the "talented tenth," an elite group of African Americans who would use their cultivated intellects and cultured selves to lead a new generation of African Americans into a more promising and brighter future. Established in the aftermath of the Civil War, HBCUs such as Fisk, Howard, Spelman, and Morehouse are institutions whose educational goals of intellectual and social advancement have drawn generations of African American students to them.

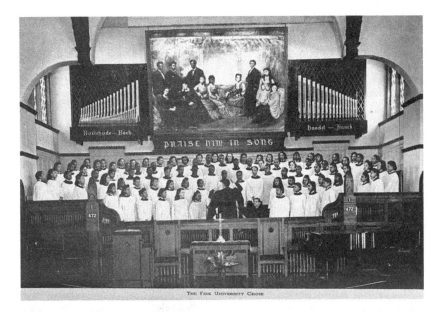

FIGURE 2.   The Fisk University Choir, singing inside the Memorial Chapel, which was completed in 1892. *Fisk Herald*, February 1942, 12. Fisk University, John Hope and Aurelia E. Franklin Library, Special Collections.

One mission for many HBCUs was to create a conservatory of music, and they explicitly imitated schools such as NEC or Oberlin to accomplish this goal. Spelman's 1890 course catalog, for example, states that their curriculum is "modern and progressive, employing New England Conservatory plans of teaching."[47] By 1894, Spelman music students were learning Chopin nocturnes and singing major choral-orchestral works like Bach's *St. John's Passion* or Mendelssohn's *Elijah*.

To launch their brand-new conservatories of music, HBCUs hired Oberlin's first Black music graduates to become the leaders and founders of their conservatories of music. Oberlin's dominance in Black schools of music was so prevalent that Oberlin alumna Edith Baker commented on it to her classmates in 1931 from her position at Fisk. "I am now in my third year teaching Harmony, School Music Methods, and Counterpoint," she writes, "and I am also the conductor of the orchestra in the Music School of Fisk University of Nashville, Tennessee. There is a little Oberlin here for the director of the Music School and *five of the teachers of nine on the faculty are Oberlinites*."[48] The list of Oberlin graduates who taught at various Black institutions was extensive.

Fisk's department of music offers us a strong example of how classical music functioned on an HBCU campus. One of the most prestigious conservatories of music at an HBCU, the department had 132 pupils study-ing voice, piano, or organ by 1896. By the 1915–16 academic year, Fisk had "twenty pianos, including three concert grands, and a pedal piano, and three cabinet organs, one of which has pedals and two manuals after the man-ner of pipe organs, and one pipe organ," and their music library contained over 4,000 copies of musical scores.[49] The library collected original letters by composers such as Franz Liszt, Beethoven, Wagner, and Weber.[50] By 1922, a twenty-five-member student and faculty orchestra had organized to perform symphonies and choral-orchestral works for the local community.[51]

For decades, the Mozart Society, a mixed choral ensemble that had formed in 1881, was a source of pride for Fisk. Throughout its history, the choir, ranging from forty to eighty students at its height, sang oratorios, requiems, and other standard choral-orchestral works by composers such as Mendelssohn, Haydn, Mozart, Brahms, and Beethoven. Although the Fisk Jubilee Singers—the more famous of the university's two choirs—sang Afri-can American spirituals to outsiders around the United States to raise money, the Mozart Society was the choir that serviced the musical needs of the in-stitution. One of society's primary functions was to officiate at ceremonies, and the music they sang gave college rituals their pomp and circumstance: the Benedictus from Mozart's Requiem and "Et resurrexit" from Mozart's Mass in C Minor for commencement week, and George Frideric Handel's "Hallelujah" chorus at holidays.[52]

While the Fisk Jubilee Singers traveled away to perform, the Mozart Soci-ety earned adoration from students such as Du Bois at home.[53] After hearing the ensemble perform Mendelssohn's *Elijah Oratorio*, Du Bois wrote in the *Fisk Herald* that the Mozart Society's concert proved that "our race, but a quarter of a century removed from slavery, can master the greatest musical compositions."[54] If we look at a list of the musical works performed by the ensemble, it becomes clear that the "greatest musical compositions" referred to by Du Bois were from the Austro-German canon. Meeting and perform-ing steadily throughout the early to mid-twentieth century, the group ex-panded their repertoire to include Bach's B Minor Mass, Brahms's *German Requiem*, Mendelssohn's *St. Paulus Oratorio*, Mendelssohn's *Elijah*, and Joseph Haydn's *Creation Oratorio*.[55] "No student ever left Fisk without a deep and abiding appreciation of real music," Du Bois boasted in his autobiography. Real music, of course, meant classical music, and usually the music of Ger-man composers.

Fisk students occasionally snuck off campus to attend concerts in Nash-ville. "In the gay Nineties during my college days at Fisk University," the pianist Raymond Augustus Lawson recalled, "Walter Damrosch came to

THE MOZART SOCIETY

They made a successful appearance in Chicago on March 17 and followed up with a brilliant rendition of Brahm's **Requiem** at the recent Spring Festival.

FIGURE 3. The Mozart Society choir at Fisk University. *Fisk News*, November 1937, 13. Fisk University, John Hope and Aurelia E. Franklin Library, Special Collections.

Nashville with the Metropolitan Opera Company and gave a performance of *Tannhäuser*. It was a thrilling experience, being the first time we had heard an opera in the South with a fine conductor, chorus, and orchestra."[56] Listening to Wagner in segregated Nashville while attending a university often under threat of attack by white supremacists was a bold act. Yet German art music, held up as the model of progress and universalism, was the object of many music students' affection.

In addition to hiring German-trained teachers for their music programs, Black colleges also ensured that all students took music theory and music history classes to cultivate a greater and more intimate knowledge of classical music. Their courses in theory and history also reveal the extent to which the German worldview of musical performance had been inculcated into Americans. The primary textbook assigned to students at Spelman and Fisk in the 1910s, for example, embodied these German ideals of music pedagogy. Written by two Oberlin professors, Friedrich Johann Lehmann and Arthur Heacox, the book, called *A Guide Through Lessons in Harmony*, emphasized a thorough training in tonal music. Students learned how to compose in the style of Martin Luther or Bach through instruction on writing four-part chorales and were also exposed to formal analysis of the music of German composers. The piano instruction offerings from Fisk University's 1896 course catalog, as shown in figure 4, illustrate the overwhelming hegemony of the Austro-German musical canon.

German music also permeated life on HBCU campuses, and schools such as Tuskegee, Howard, and Fisk were instrumental in teaching generations of African American students about German music. In the 1880s and 1890s, many colleges and universities strove to cultivate a rich and robust musical life on their campuses. Students at Clark College and Atlanta University attended "Mozart evenings" or "Wagner evenings" to improve their musical education. On such an occasion, a student usually gave a public presentation on the life of a composer and one of the college's music ensembles provided a live performance of the composer's music.[57] Musical activities on Black campuses, in other words, encouraged students to perform and listen to Western art music.

Most of the repertoire that students learned at Black conservatories of music was aesthetically conservative. Students did not rehearse the music of Arnold Schoenberg, for example, and composers such as Claude Debussy, Gabriel Fauré, and Francis Poulenc did not appear with much frequency on student recital programs or in their classroom instruction. Moreover, many institutions discouraged the study of opera, especially for Black women, on the grounds that it was not respectable enough for an aspiring student of a middle-class background. Rather, they focused on presenting music deemed universally great for students and the public attending their concerts.

An undertone of stoic conservatism also resonated in music pedagogy for Black students more generally. For example, the pianist Raymond Augustus Lawson, an 1896 Fisk graduate and a pupil of Ossip Gabrilowitsch in Germany, preached the values of self-discipline that were necessary to the pursuit of high art in his article for the student newspaper, the *Fisk Herald*, in 1915.[58] In an essay full of platitudes and beatitudes extolling in Weberian tones the virtues of hard work, he ties art music to racial advancement and portrays music as morally purposeful with proclamations. Arguing that through musical practice African Americans could "advance slowly but surely," he preaches that classical music has the power to create moral and upstanding citizens.[59]

The musical styles of Central Europe were especially desirable models for aspiring young Black musicians because of the music's perceived seriousness and sense of purpose. Like the majority of white American classical musicians in these decades, African American classical musicians believed that works such as Mendelssohn's *Elijah Oratorio* or Beethoven's Fifth Symphony

COURSE IN
PIANOFORTE

1ST GRADE	Emery, Foundation Studies; Czerny's One Hundred Progressive Lessons; Spindler, op. 131, Koehler, op. 162; Kunz Canons; Major scales in one and two octaves, Exercises for developing ease in the use of wrist and fingers.
2ND GRADE	Koehler, op. 151; Gurlitt, op. 83; 50 Kunz Canons; Spindler, op. 44; Burgmüller, op. 100; Clementi, op. 36, Reinecke, op. 107; Major scales, three octaves; Minor scales, one octave; Arpeggios. Daily finger and wrist exercises.
3RD GRADE	Czerny, op. 802; Koehler, op. 50; 50 Kunz Canons; Burgmüller, op. 100; Le Couppey, op. 17; Kuhlau, op. 55; Gade, op. 36; Schumann, op. 68; Kullak, op. 62; Major scales, four octaves; Minor scales, three octaves. Wrist exercises in intervals of a fifth, sixth, and octave. Exercises for developing a clear legato touch.
4TH GRADE	Döring, op. 8; Czerny, op. 636; Czerny, op. 718; Heller, op. 47; 75 Kunz Canons; Beethoven, op. 49; Gade, op. 19; Mozart's Sonatas; Schumann, op. 124; Mendelssohn's "Songs Without Words." Scales in groups of 6 and 8. Arpeggios and Octaves.
5TH GRADE	Czerny, 848; Czerny, 718; Duvernoy, op. 120; Heller, op. 46; Bach, Twelve Little Preludes; Haydn's Sonatas; Mozart's Sonatas; Mendelssohn's "Songs Without Words;" Beethoven's Sonatas; Schmitt, op. 114; Krause, op. 2. Scales, Arpeggios, and Octaves.
6TH GRADE	Le Couppey, op. 20; Löschorn, op. 66; Heller, op. 45; Döring, Octave Studies; Bach, Two Part Inventions; Mendelssohn's "Songs Without Words;" Sonatas by Haydn, Mozart, and Beethoven; Selections from Schumann, op. 94, and Schumann, op. 142. Selected technical exercises.
7TH GRADE	Matthews' Graded Studies, Book 6; Czerny, op. 299; Schumann, op. 12; Heller, op. 45; Bach, "Two Voiced Inventions;" Chopin's Nocturnes; Beethoven's Sonatas; Gade, op. 18; Döring, op. 24. Scales in thirds and sixths.
8TH GRADE	Löschorn, op. 67; Bach, Well-Tempered Clavichord; Selections from Schumann and Chopin; Beethoven's Sonatas. Scales in Canon form and contrary motion.

FIGURE 4. Fisk University Course Catalog, 1896–97. Fisk University, John Hope and Aurelia E. Franklin Library, Special Collections.

far surpassed the frivolities of Italian operas or French chansons. Ergo, African American art music would be made more beautiful and listened to more seriously if its composers used German compositional techniques to express Black musical ideas and truths. In 1899, for example, a student writing for Atlanta University's newspaper, the *Scroll*, asked, "Where is the great Negro composer who shall take those sweet old plantation melodies—the only distinctively native music ever produced on American soil—and use them as a basis for fugues, lullabies, nocturnes, and sonatas?"[60] For many, the future of African American art music could only be built upon a German musical foundation.

Black popular music such as ragtime, on the other hand, was the enemy. A genre of popular music that thrived between the 1890s and 1910s, it carried with it the connotations of Black minstrelsy and Black popular culture. Its most predominant musical trait was its rhythmic syncopation, a sonic signifier to many of Black American popular music. It is also precisely because of ragtime's perceived African American musicality that white Americans mocked it. In response, Black elites argued that the music was undignified and called for African Americans to move away from it.[61] For these reasons, HBCUs offered no instruction on Black popular or improvisational music, nor did they encourage students to perform it on campus.

Black institutions' hostilities towards Black popular music cohered with established Black music criticism on the moral purposes of music education. The writers and editors of the *Negro Music Journal*, for example, also held the position that only art music, rather than ragtime and popular music, offered Black Americans a morally and musically sound education. Its editor J. Hillary Taylor denounced ragtime and lauded classical music on moral grounds in 1903, declaring that the "day of low, trivial, popular music should be cast aside forever."[62] African Americans deserved a "better art," and the supposedly pure and noble music of Mozart and Beethoven was best suited to advance their cause of musical progress, if not enlightenment.

On the surface, musical education at HBCUs looked quite similar to the education that students at Oberlin or the NEC received. And, certainly, modeling their course catalogs and concert programming on other conservatories of music was intentional. The faculty's degrees from those institutions also guaranteed that students at HBCUs would learn similar repertoire, musical styles, and techniques for mastering the music of "the great masters." Yet the motivations behind learning classical music differed greatly, dictated as they were by the sharp and violent politics of racism and racial segregation in the United States.

Heading to Europe

In 1890s Niagara Falls, Nathaniel Dett's training with his Austrian music teacher frustrated them both. But an encounter with a German visitor and acquaintance of the composer Antonín Dvořák changed Dett's life. Called "Dr. Hoppe" in Dett's memory of him, he asked if Dett could arrange African American spirituals on the piano. After performing for him, Dett found himself on the receiving end of a strange request: "He urged me to come to Germany for study, leaving me his card which for years I treasured chiefly as a souvenir."[63] Dett was apparently stunned by the offer, but also dismissive of it. "Much of what Dr. Hoppe had said really did not greatly interest me," he remembered. "At that time there was little respect for Negro music or its possibilities."[64] Only later, after hearing the Kneisel Quartet perform Dvořák's music as a young student at Oberlin, did Dett begin to believe in the possibility of creating African American art music and that he could be the one to compose it.

This mysterious Dr. Hoppe might have planted two separate seeds into Dett's mind: first, to compose African American art music, and second, to travel to Central Europe to study. Going to Germany became a lifelong dream of Dett's, one he realized in 1932 when he took the Hampton Institute Choir to Central Europe on tour to perform his own choral music, much of it inspired by the music of Dvořák and Brahms.

The same decade Dett received an invitation to visit Germany, a teenaged Hazel Harrison began taking piano lessons with the German pianist Victor Heinze in La Porte, Indiana.[65] A former pupil of Theodor Leschetizky and Ignacy Jan Paderewski, Heinze lived in Chicago but came frequently to La Porte to give lessons. Harrison recalled that the first time he heard her perform, "he was very pleased; he had visions of me playing in Germany with an orchestra and he, Heinze, conducting."[66] From a young age, at Heinze's encouragement, Harrison entertained the thought of performing abroad.

Eventually, Harrison's dreams of concertizing in Europe became a reality. Following a recital in Chicago, Heinze introduced Harrison to her future piano teacher, the legendary concert pianist and composer Ferruccio Busoni. After listening to her play for him backstage after one of his concerts, Busoni said, "Now, little girl, you are very, very talented. Now, what I want you to do is this: I want you to work on technique. I want you to work on technique endlessly. In the meantime, I want you to finish your school and as soon as you finish your high school, let me know, because I want you to come to Europe."[67] And she did. With the help of Heinze, Busoni, and others, Harrison traveled to Germany, where she performed with the Berlin Philharmonic in 1904. Between 1904 until the outbreak of WWI in 1914, she lived in Berlin intermittently and studied with Busoni and other teachers.

Stories such as Dett's and Harrison's teach us about the immense transnational power of musical exchange. Central Europeans' cultivation of African American musical talent and their encouragement of these students to look beyond their locales for audiences and musical inspiration yielded rich new musical produce. It was surprising what turning outward to German-speaking Europe could quickly accomplish for African American musicians enduring white supremacy in the United States. Buoyed by their international exchanges with Central Europeans in the United States, African Americans, like the Germans they encountered, imagined other possibilities for Black musical expression.

Let us consider one last story, that of the young pianist Raymond Augustus Lawson witnessing the composer and conductor Gustav Mahler give one of his last concerts before his death. In residence in New York, Mahler visited Hartford, Connecticut, on a cold and snowy night on February 16, 1911, to perform orchestral works by Beethoven, Weber, and Liszt, and his own transcription of a Bach suite at Parsons Theatre. Lawson sat transfixed by the composer's conducting and was especially struck by "his playing of a Bach composition on the harpsichord while conducting the orchestra."[68] It is unclear, however, where Lawson sat in the concert hall. Would the racial politics of the day

FIGURE 5. A concert program advertising the soloists for Felix Mendelssohn's *Elijah* Oratorio at Boston Symphony Hall, 1915. The program states: "The Elijah Chorus, Dr. W.O. Taylor, conductor, will render Mendelssohn's 'Elijah,' Thursday evening, April 15th, 1915 at 8.15 o'clock at Jordan Hall." Courtesy of the E. Azalia Hackley Collection of African Americans in the Performing Arts, Detroit Public Library.

have forced Lawson to sit at the back? His writings indicate that he rarely missed an orchestral performance in Hartford in his sixty years of residence, which indicates either a sustained commitment in Hartford to admitting Black patrons to classical music concerts or a sustained transgression of racial order by Lawson and perhaps a few others. Nonetheless, on that snowy evening, Lawson attended a performance by a preeminent Central European composer and deemed it one of the most thrilling musical experiences of his career. Shortly after the concert, Lawson left the United States for Central Europe to further his musical studies.

African American engagement with the Austro-German canon made it possible for them to imagine themselves in another country altogether, far away from the racist strictures trying to define and restrict their actions and beliefs. Their future lay in the German musical past. The siren song of the Austro-German canon beckoned them to Europe, singing to them that they, too, could join a transatlantic chorus. To shed the skin of white supremacy and become the pinnacle of Black musical achievement would require going to Europe, a place of liberation in the minds of many Black Americans. Booking tickets on boats sailing to Hamburg, some African Americans finally began to make the dream of visiting the land of Bach, Beethoven, and Brahms a reality.

These artists arrived in Central Europe with a deep and intimate knowledge of German musical culture; once there, they sought out new and liberating spaces to grow and perform. Encouraged by their own teachers, who were either from Central Europe or who had studied there, they became part of what Paul Gilroy calls the Black Atlantic in their travels to and from Europe. Black classical musicians pursued a different musical solution to the problem of race's entrenched barriers. If the United States could not provide for their musical and intellectual growth, if the United States failed to protect them from the violence and oppression of racism, German-speaking Europe, the heart of musical universalism, might finally be the place where the powers of music could transcend racial discourse and defeat racial determinism.

CHAPTER 2

African American Intellectual and Musical Migration to the Kaiserreich

Upon embarking on the North German Lloyd steamship for Germany in 1887, the young violinist Will Marion Cook made a terrible discovery: "I was a rotten sailor." A recent Oberlin graduate, Cook was on his way to Berlin to study music. As the ship glided across the ocean, his body protested violently against the lurching motions it was forced to endure. In spite of his futile attempts to acquire sea legs, he wrote in his unpublished memoir that his trip to Germany was nonetheless "beautiful to [him]."[1] Cook, who later became a prominent figure in African American musical entertainment in the early twentieth century, studied violin at the Royal Academy of Musical Performing Arts in Berlin. A student of Frederick Doolittle at Oberlin, Cook was standing on that boat to Germany in part because he came to believe that he could not continue studying in the United States as a Black man. Before Cook embarked on his passage to Berlin, Doolittle had suggested that he matriculate at the University of Cincinnati College-Conservatory of Music. But the city of Cincinnati's recent reputation for racial violence—and the conservatory's reputation for not accepting Black students—did not inspire confidence in the young performer. After much discussion with Doolittle, and after raising money in Washington, DC, with the help of Frederick Douglass, Cook booked a ticket to Germany.[2]

Considering how sick the journey made him, one might expect Cook to have expressed regret for stepping onto the wretched boat. But breathing fresh air between bouts of nausea, Cook felt surprisingly relaxed and calm. As far as he was concerned, he "was getting away from prejudice, ignorance, [and] oppression, and on [his] way to a real land of promise." In retrospect, he understood that his statement might cause "European immigrants to smile at this idea which reverses the order of things," but, he continued, "Many Negroes have felt exactly as I did on leaving the U.S.A." Cook could not believe how well Germans treated him on board and once he landed at the port of Bremerhaven in Germany. Although he knew barely any German, once the ship docked, he recalled, "The conductors and everybody were so helpful, so polite, that I asked myself, 'Is this heaven?'"[3]

Was Germany heaven for African Americans? Many certainly thought so. They compared Germany and America in their writings and conversations: Could they have been able to live in the United States as freely as they lived in Germany? The answer was usually a conclusive no. In Germany, African Americans could stay in any hotel they wished, visit any restaurant or café, and enter an opera house with full confidence of admission. Many walked through the streets of Leipzig, Berlin, and other cities with a newly discovered confidence rooted in their sense of Germany as a liberated space. Their text-based archives—letters to family and friends back in the United States, student newspaper chronicles, and memoirs they wrote commemorating their experiences in Europe—confirm what many scholars have concluded about Black internationalism across the Atlantic: Europe appeared to offer African Americans a new cartography of hopes and dreams, a place where they could reimagine the ties that bound together race, culture, and nation.

This chapter examines the lives and musical experiences of African Americans in the Kaiserreich, focusing especially on how they navigated new musical worlds. African American musical experiences in Imperial Germany were shaped by the politics of Black longing or Black desire. In her book *Territories of the Soul*, Nadia Ellis states that Black migration sometimes has less to do with the particular destination of migration and more to do with Black desires to leave.[4] The title of the recent publication *Anywhere But Here: Black Intellectuals in the Atlantic World and Beyond* also makes this clear. Examining individuals and communities seeking better lives and realities for themselves "anywhere but here," the authors argue that the history of Black intellectual endeavors "gives us insight into the elaborate, and sometimes contradictory, processes of self-determination, identity formation, cultural preservation, and political consciousness."[5] Similarly, Robin D.G. Kelley posits that the concept of exodus in historical Black thought represented aspirations of Black self-determination and departure free from white interference. The term ultimately "provided Black people with a language to critique America's racist state and build a new nation, for its central theme wasn't simply escape but a new beginning."[6] And indeed, young African American men and women were eager to leave American shores and enter into what they believed to be a musical and cosmopolitan world in Germany. Their own longings and desires brightly colored their experiences attending concerts or taking music lessons in cities such as Leipzig, Dresden, and Berlin.

Even though Black desire for a better life determined much of Black travel and migration in modern history, Europe also held a particular attraction for Black people as a specific site of cultural exchange. The continent appealed to African Americans by offering a tantalizing zone of intellectual and cultural activity that they believed they could not find elsewhere. In *The Practice of Diaspora*, Brent Hayes Edwards argues that for Black people across Africa, the Caribbean, and North America, the European metropole "provided a special sort of vibrant, cosmopolitan space for interaction that was available neither in the United States nor in the colonies."[7] For a promising young Black artist or intellectual looking beyond America's shores for stimulation and growth, no place looked or sounded quite so appealing as the European continent.[8] Considered the most important site to participate in cutting-edge international discourse, Europe in the minds of many African American elites was the fountain of knowledge from which they could develop their intellectual faculties. As a dynamic site of knowledge production and as a supposedly more racially egalitarian environment, Europe, African Americans believed, offered them a safe haven in which they could learn and grow as thinkers and artists.

To get there, African American classical musicians used the same networks they had built in the United States. And their endeavors paid off: with the support of friends, teachers, and patrons, they joined musical communities in Leipzig and Berlin. While abroad, the social worlds they inhabited were dictated by the rules of classical music. Black classical musicians went through the rituals of taking sample lessons with potential teachers, auditioning for conservatories, studying with teachers, rehearsing for performances, and attending operas or concerts in their spare time.

While attending to the rigorous requirements demanded of all classical musicians, Black classical musicians also navigated the politics of race. The specter of Jim Crow haunted their daily lives, determining where they could live and with whom they could interact. Yet German musical culture also informed their own nascent racial politics, inspiring some to rethink the relationship between race and culture. Black musicians' experiences in German-speaking Europe were transformative in ways they had not expected.

Transatlantic Networking Comes to Germany

They came in droves. Steamers bound for Bremen or Vienna were full of Americans on their decks, determined to study classical music in Leipzig, Berlin, and Vienna. Ethel Newcomb, an assistant to the pianist Theodor Leschetizky, observed these boisterous pilgrims warily. "From the steamer chair one watched with curiosity these bands of aspirants, proclaiming loudly their different ideas and shouting that they were on the way to Vienna and fame," she writes.[9] To Newcomb, these incoming students knew nothing of the tests they would be forced to endure in Europe's most musical city, nor of the requirements necessary to study with a famous teacher.

But many Americans had arrived under a long-standing belief: only when they embraced the music of Germany could they themselves become better musicians in America.[10] More than five thousand American students studied music at German conservatories between 1850 and 1900. The Leipzig Conservatory of Music, founded by Mendelssohn in 1843, became the beacon of light attracting the most American students, with almost thirteen hundred students attending the institution in the second half of the nineteenth century.[11]

FIGURE 6. African American pianist Bertha Hansbury poses with her colleagues in Berlin, 1909. The back of the photograph states, "After her graduation from the Detroit Conservatory of Music, Bertha Hansbury studied in Berlin, Germany, for a year. 1909." Courtesy of the E. Azalia Hackley Collection of African Americans in the Performing Arts, Detroit Public Library.

Although it is difficult to state with certainty how many of these American musicians invading German conservatories were Black, some names and profiles exist in published sources and scattered about various archives. One of the first Black Broadway musicians, William H. Tyers, studied composition in Germany in the 1890s along with Will Marion Cook.[12] Cook's fellow violinist Felix Weir also resided in Germany in the late nineteenth century, perhaps at the encouragement of his German music teacher in Chicago. The violinist Ella Thomas studied at the Berlin conservatory in 1905, and William Kemper Harreld, also a violinist, studied in Berlin in the 1910s with Siegfried Eberhardt.[13]

A majority of the students who went to Central Europe were instrumentalists, and pianists outnumbered them all. Among the many Black pianists studying in Central Europe were Leota F. Henson, a niece of the Fisk Jubilee Singer Frederick Loudin, who studied in Leipzig in 1884, and Hazel Harrison, who took lessons with several teachers in Berlin intermittently for a decade (1904–14); Portia Washington also studied in Berlin from 1905 until 1906; Bertha Hansbury, a native of Detroit, studied in Berlin in 1910; Carl Diton studied with Edward Bach and Anton Beer-Walbrunn in Munich in 1910, and Raymond Augustus Lawson studied with Theodor Leschetizky and toured Germany between 1911 and 1912.[14] A young and enthusiastic pianist named Floyd Dunston wowed Leopold Godowsky in Berlin, where he studied between 1902 and 1903. "He was a great favorite with all the staid old German professors, who advanced him at once from the first year's work to the second, and the outlook seemed most brilliant."[15] Unfortunately, Dunston died in Berlin of typhoid fever before he could advance to the next step in his career. Eddie Moore, another budding prodigy who had studied piano in Stuttgart, also died in Germany in 1896.[16]

A few vocalists also attended music schools in Germany and Austria. The baritone J. Elmer Spyglass, a graduate of the University of Toledo Conservatory of Music in Ohio, moved to Germany in 1915 to study and perform, where he resided until his death in 1957. The tenor Sidney Woodward, who won the friendship of the famed opera singer "Madame" Lillian Nordica in 1892, studied at the Dresden Conservatory in 1896 and traveled around giving concerts in Germany, Austria, the Netherlands, Belgium, and Russia, and the soprano Annis Hackley, a sister of the soprano and political activist Emma Azalia Hackley, resided in Düsseldorf in the 1910s.[17]

Coming to Central Europe from the United States was no easy task, and procuring the necessary funds to travel and live abroad was a significant hurdle. African Americans performing in Germany on professional contracts naturally used their booking agents and managers to successfully purchase tickets on steamships to Germany and reserve hotel rooms. African American

FIGURE 7. A studio portrait photo of the soprano Annis Hackley, taken in Düsseldorf, Germany. The autograph on the front states, "With best wishes to Mr. Harreld. Düsseldorf, Germany. March 26, 1910." The back of the photo bears the printed statement: "Photogr. Atelier 'Elite,' Düsseldorf, Schacowstrasse 62. Telephon 1150. Crefeld, Hochstr. 62." In Hackley's handwriting, the text states, "I suppose you have quite forgotten me. I would have sent you a p.c. long ago but I did not [undecipherable] here to find you as I heard you were away until a few weeks ago [undecipherable] know if you read this or not. Send mail to this address and it will be sent on to me. Sincerely, A. Hackley. 6618 Vernon Ave. Mrs. Annis Hackley, Chicago, Ill." Courtesy of the E. Azalia Hackley Collection of African Americans in the Performing Arts, Detroit Public Library.

students used a variety of means to study in Germany. Some received scholarships from institutions in the United States; others relied on private donations and fundraising efforts from within Black social or musical worlds. In a 1934 interview for *Etude*, for example, the African American composer Nathaniel Dett marveled at the fundraising efforts of Emma Azalia Hackley. "Evidence of the powers of this extraordinary woman is the fact that she was able to establish and maintain 'foreign scholarships' by which she sent abroad two promising Negro students, Carl Diton, pianist, Clarence Cameron White, violinist, for extended study," Dett recalled. "So far as I know, this achievement has never been equalled [sic] by any member of my race and becomes all the more remarkable when it is remembered that this good woman was herself of limited means."[18]

Other students came to Germany with more money in their pockets and powerful networks at their disposal. During her stay in Berlin between 1905 and 1906, for example, Portia Washington relied on her wealthy father, Booker T. Washington, to take care of her expenses. After she had exhausted the travel funds he had given her, Washington received a loan from the German Colonial Society, an organization that had commissioned her father to help construct cotton plantations in its German colonial holdings in Africa; the society had provided her with support and a promise of guardianship prior to her departure.[19] Washington benefitted from her father's close relationship to German colonial officials to stay afloat in Berlin as a piano student. The fact that an African American woman had access to funds inaccessible to German colonial subjects speaks to the privileged position her family held in German society.

Letters of introduction were essential for musical networking in Germany and Austria, and Black students were not immune from this custom. Washington's teacher in the United States, Annie Peabody, had studied piano in Germany with Martin Krause, a Liszt protégé. Peabody wrote a letter of introduction to her former teacher, and after he agreed to hear Washington play, Washington sailed to Germany in the summer of 1905 on the *Germania*.[20] Writing from his residence in Munich in July 1911, the pianist Ossip Gabrilowitsch sent a quick note to Theodor Leschetizky, his former teacher and mentor in Vienna, to inquire about the abilities of Raymond Augustus Lawson, a Fisk student. A few days later, Leschetizky wrote back one line, stating, "I greatly enjoyed discovering in Mr. Lawson a fine talent on the piano."[21] Via telegram, Gabrilowitsch reached out to Lawson with his phone number and set up a trial lesson. Gabrilowitsch then became Lawson's teacher during his stay in Germany.[22]

Hazel Harrison's piano teacher in the United States, Victor Heinze, convinced the pianist Ferruccio Busoni to teach Harrison during her stay in Berlin in 1904. Later, in the summer of 1912, Busoni then wrote to the pianist Egon Petri to advocate for Harrison as a pupil:

> Miss Harrison . . . young as she is, is already an old acquaintance of mine. When I heard her play today (again, after six years), I was most pleasantly surprised. I am sure, she will awake your pianistic interest which I beg you to direct in favor of her studies.[23]

These letters, often exchanged between former pupils and their teachers, most likely made entry into the world of music instruction in Central Europe easier for Black students.

After settling into their homes in Germany, most students needed to audition to enter conservatories or to be admitted to a private studio. Rarely, it seems, did they experience rejection from formal study because of their auditions. Instead, most teachers identified the students' musical potential. Will Marion Cook's story in Berlin offers one such example. Upon arrival in Germany, he provided the customary letter of introduction from his Oberlin professor to a fellow musician and alum settled in Germany that set the course for his musical development in the city. First, the alum recommended that he study with the violinist "Herr Moser" (possibly Andreas Moser) before auditioning to the music school.[24] Cook took her advice and prepared his audition for the conservatory.

The resulting audition was a disaster. Playing a piece that was too technically demanding for him, he fell apart on the stage. "Crying and cursing beneath his breath, he tucked the violin under his arm and started to leave the podium," Marva Carter writes. He was ready to call it quits when "a deep voice asked him if he could play anything else. It was the master teacher and founder of the Hochschule, Joseph Joachim himself!"[25] Encouraged by Joachim's kindness and patience, Cook auditioned again, this time with Beethoven's "Melody in F," and earned a spot in the conservatory.

At her audition for Krause in Berlin, Washington decided on impulse to perform a recently published piece by the Black British composer Samuel Coleridge-Taylor, "Sometimes I Feel Like A Motherless Child," instead of the standard repertoire of something baroque, classical, and romantic.[26] The dean of the women's department of the Tuskegee Institute accompanied Washington to her audition in Europe, and reported back to the New York Times that "Prof. Krause was profoundly impressed and immediately accepted her as a pupil."[27]

Washington's choice to perform a piece from Coleridge-Taylor's 1905 *24 Negro Melodies, op. 59* is a striking one. When she auditioned, the piece of music had only recently been published. A larghetto in E minor, the piece moves slowly at the beginning but gradually builds in tempo and becomes a thicker texture as the melody repeats in variation. The apex of the piece arrives around two thirds of the way into the composition, when the melody returns with Rachmaninoff-like grandeur, full of crashing chords and booming octaves in the bass register of the piano. Coleridge-Taylor's piano piece takes a seemingly simple melody and makes it somehow dazzling and somber, a shiny musical mirage of loss and grief. Washington's prospective teacher might have never heard anything quite like it. He enthusiastically agreed to teach Washington, but by October 1906, Washington's fiancé had proposed to her and she had agreed to come back to the United States to marry. Much to the dismay of her teachers, Washington left Berlin a year before concluding her studies.

With high risk in coming to Germany came great reward. For students like Cook, studying at the conservatory greatly improved his musicianship. Under the tutelage of Joachim and other violin teachers, Cook writes, "I began to gain in technique all I had lost by beginning serious study of the violin so late in life."[28] Studying under such an esteemed violinist would have most certainly brought Cook great prestige and made him appear more valuable or marketable as a budding instrumentalist.

Indeed, perhaps the greatest reward from studying in Central Europe was financial. Endorsements from German teachers proved to be valuable advertisements for students when they returned to the United States. For example, pianist Carl Diton received two endorsements from his teachers in Munich that appeared in newspapers and advertisements before his concerts. The first, from Edward Bach at Bavaria's Royal Academy of the Art of Music, stated, "I am very glad to recommend Mr. Carl R. Diton most warmly for concert; a highly talented pianist whose technique is brilliant and whose feeling for form is very strongly developed." The second stated, "'Mr. Carl R. Diton is a very excellent pianist and can be highly recommended to perform anywhere.'— Anton von Beer-Walbrum [sic], composer, Munich."[29] Similarly, Raymond Augustus Lawson used Theodor Leschetizky's line—"Americans generally have technique; Mr. Lawson has poetry"—in his promotional materials as well.[30]

Tapping into transatlantic classical music networks, African American classical musicians partook in the customs and rituals of formal introductions, sample lessons, and auditions necessary to gain teachers and improve on their musical instruments. Safely anchored in classical music, they learned to move fluidly in their new educational environments and build upon their knowledge previously gained in the United States.

Avoiding Jim Crow in the Land of Bach, Beethoven, and Brahms

Mary Church Terrell hated Dresden. A young Oberlin student eager to study in Europe, she had come to the city in 1889 because she "had heard that the purest German is spoken in Dresden." But upon arrival, all she heard was English, mostly spoken by white Americans. "The city was full of Americans and English," she complained. "Wherever I turned on the streets, I heard my mother tongue."[31] Quickly realizing that a city full of white Americans "was no place for a colored girl," she moved to Berlin, which had been her top choice for study anyway.

Even though Terrell loathed Dresden, the city gave her one of her first and most lasting treasures in Germany: opera. "In Dresden I received my first taste of German opera," she gushed in her memoir, "for there the most noted singers were appearing at that time. I went alone, for it was never unpleasant for me to go anywhere unaccompanied." When she landed in Berlin, the opera became part of her daily life. She entered the opera house, she confesses, "twice and sometimes three times a week" to partake in the ritual of finding one's chair, sitting down, watching the curtain rise, and hearing the orchestra and singers narrate a musical adventure.[32]

Classical music had brought many to Germany, and it thrilled Black students like Terrell. But it could not shield Black students from their encounters with Jim Crow. In Germany, African American students experienced racial hostility from white Americans, even though they were no longer in the United States. Although few writings from Black classical musicians exist to articulate it, the memoirs of Du Bois, Terrell, and Cook detailing their experiences in Germany in the 1880s and 1890s provide a few glimpses into daily life.

In Germany, African American students had to find ways to live outside the shadow of Jim Crow. Du Bois recalled the difficulties of searching for housing—not because of white German discrimination but because of protests from white Americans. He cringed whenever a well-meaning landlord eagerly told him that new Americans were coming to stay in the building. "The landlord would hasten to inform me beamingly that 'Fellow Americans had just arrived,'" he shared in his memoir. Ignorant of American race relations, the landlord believed he or she was sharing positive news with their

Black tenant. But how Du Bois wished to avoid such confrontations! "If there was one thing less desirable than white 'fellow Americans' to me," he acerbically stated, "it was Black 'fellow Americans' to them."[33] In Berlin, white American women urged Terrell's prospective landlord to reject her as a tenant, much to the landlord's concern. Terrell did not take the apartment the landlord offered her despite the white Americans' protests, and, she wrote, "I learned afterward on good authority that my countrywomen would have made it decidedly unpleasant for me if I had gone to that pension to live."[34]

Life on the campus of a university or a music school might have also reinforced Jim Crow politics in the Kaiserreich. Cook discovered that he was not the only American student at the Royal Academy of Musical Performing Arts in Berlin during his stay. During his first year, eleven Americans attended the school of music, and his class of Americans almost doubled the next year, with nineteen students. With whom would Cook have felt safe enough to interact? The other American students represented all geographical regions of the United States, ranging from cities such as Santa Barbara and Oakland on the West Coast to New York and Washington, DC, on the East Coast, from southern states to growing industrial cities in the north like Milwaukee and Detroit. Cook leaves no indication in his memoir that he bonded with his fellow American peers. One might assume the opposite in some cases: he might have avoided female violinists like Curri Duke from Lexington, Kentucky, or Dora Becker from Galveston, Texas.[35] Interacting with white American women may have been out of bounds, even in another country.

White European students were not necessarily more welcoming. The British composer Ethel Smyth, recently popularized again as a feminist icon, shared racist sentiments about Black students while a student at the Leipzig Conservatory of Music in the late 1870s. In October 1877, for example, she wrote to her sister Nina, expressing her shock upon meeting her classmates. "My dear, there are two real live mulatos [sic] and one *nigger* here! The nigg negress (for she is of the fair sex) is by way of being a great dresser. Nature manages her hair of course (and I'm sure no art could manage it), but [she wears] long gold earrings and most skittish bonnets and . . . gloves on all occasions."[36] Smith's condescending comment about a Black woman's hair perpetuated transatlantic notions of beauty and whiteness by rendering the Black woman's looks inferior.

Networking with fellow Black classical musicians was most likely vital, whether that meant attending an opera together or hosting friends for tea, as William Kemper Harreld and his wife did for Hazel Harrison and Alain Locke.[37] Portia Washington's experiences give us a striking example of Black networking. She relied heavily on her friend and fellow pianist Harrison for advice on acclimating in Berlin. Both college-aged African American women, they shared the same Berlin landlady and most likely exchanged information on pianists and technicians in the city. Washington also hosted dinner parties for other African American musicians. At one dinner party she hosted in Berlin sometime between 1905 and 1906, Washington met the singer Abbie Mitchell and the two immediately became friends, being musicians of the same age and both Black women seeking success in a foreign country.[38] Washington fostered Mitchell's love of German lieder, and the two of them played together for fun frequently thereafter.[39]

Black students strove to find community outside of these friendships with other Black musicians, and musical spaces became especially important for facilitating cultural exchange and empowerment. In a concert hall, African Americans learned the dictum and decorum of German culture. But musical spaces were also important for their intellectual and social development. Going to the opera was one such socially transformative experience. The opera house, Terrell discovered, was an international meeting ground, a transnational site of exchange where she "became acquainted with the youth of many lands." Terrell and a friend of hers from Russia "usually attended the opera together and sat in the peanut gallery, which was frequented by students, from whose comments I learned much more about the operas and music on general principles than I could have acquired in any other way."[40] Historically, the opera house was also a space that reinforced class hierarchy. Ticket prices determined where people sat, which functioned to enforce social boundaries. But in this case, the student section was also a place of community building and friendship making. It was invaluable to Terrell because it brought her into contact with fellow students who shared their musical knowledge with her in the form of gossip, whispers, and informative comments.

Cook experienced a similar kind of camaraderie in his forays to hear the orchestra in Berlin. Living in the capital in the time of Paderewski, Joachim, and Hans von Bülow, he attended the orchestra, the opera, or smaller chamber or solo concerts. "In that time I had learned to love those hospitable, unprejudiced, pre-Hitlerite Germans, to worship Beethoven, Wagner, and Joachim." During a promenade concert at the philharmonic in Berlin in the late 1880s, Cook became friends with a young Jewish German American named Max Adler who told Cook what to wear to the orchestra ("a white shirt with a high collar or people will ignore you").[41] Orchestra halls and opera houses made for good mingling spots, and in these spaces African Americans met people they might not have otherwise encountered.

W. E. B. Du Bois's well-known musical experiences in Germany might be the most illustrative of how transformative Germany's musical culture could

be. As a young student in Germany attending performances of Weber's opera *Der Freischütz* or a Beethoven symphony, Du Bois arrived at an epiphany
that greatly changed his understanding of the world around him and made
him the global cosmopolitan many historians now call him. He discovered
that classical music was not rooted in white American values. In Germany, he
writes, "Even I was a little startled to realize how much that I had regarded as
white American, was white European and not American at all." He instead
confronted in Berlin what he considered to be the true origins of Western
high art and culture. "America's music is German, the Germans said; the
Americans have no art, said the Italians; and their literature, remarked the
English, is mainly English," he writes. "Sometimes their criticism got under even my anti-American skin, but it was refreshing on the whole to hear
voiced my own attitude toward so much that America had meant to me."[42] In
Germany, listening to Beethoven symphonies and going to Wagner operas,
Du Bois discovered that he could love and lay claim to the same cultural
works as white Americans but on different grounds. There, Du Bois discovered that high culture did not belong to white Americans any more than it
belonged to him. He could divorce his admiration for "the great masters"
from white Americans' veneration of the same musicians.

The musical experiences of Du Bois, Terrell, and other African American students in Germany were an important part of their process of self-
discovery and even self-liberation. Much to their surprise, African American
students discovered that the opera house or the concert hall in nineteenth-
century Germany functioned as a transnational space of social formation
that challenged what they had conceived of as possible. Listening to a choir
and orchestra perform Mendelssohn's "Jauchzet dem Herrn, alle Welt" was
more than a musical experience. It was akin to an awakening, one that had
first been rooted in the United States but later blossomed on German soil.
The trick was to figure out how to take these experiences and convert them
into tangible social and cultural change in the United States. For young students such as Du Bois wishing to adapt the cosmopolitanism of German
philosophers and musicians, the challenge was, Kwame Anthony Appiah argues, "to take its power without its parochialism—to steal the fire without
getting burned."[43]

Returning Home?

It was returning back home that was painful. As the waves lapped across the
sides of their steamships, taking Black musicians to the Caribbean, to South
America, or to the United States, people's moods slipped constantly between

states of excitement, gratitude, and longing, and feelings of dread or even terror. Homecoming, it turns out, was not a unidirectional experience. In fact, while many were fleeing Germany at the onset of WWI, Werner Jae-gerhuber, later known as the grandfather of Haitian music, was just arriv-ing. The son of a German American businessman and a mixed-race Haitian woman, Jaegerhuber fled to Germany when the United States invaded Haiti in 1915. He studied at the Vogt Conservatory in Hamburg and remained in Germany until 1937—when it became clear that he was not safe from Nazi racial persecution—and returned to Haiti.[44]

Some Black musicians simply refused to return home. The Jiménez Trio, an Afro-Cuban chamber group comprised of a father and two sons (violin-ist José Julián Jiménez, pianist José Manuel "Lico," and cellist Nicasio), first toured Germany in the 1870s. Most members of the Jiménez family refused to return to Cuba, settling down and raising families in Germany instead. José Julián unhappily returned to Cuba, but his son Nicasio settled in France and became a violin professor, where he died in 1891. Lico had a success-ful career in Germany; he performed for Wagner at the Villa Wahnfried in Bayreuth and also for Liszt in Weimar. He received warm praise from both.[45] The bright and clever young singer J. Elmer Spyglass simply left the world of classical music altogether, shrewdly realizing that he could have a financially solvent career in Central Europe as a Black entertainer of popular works. Others wandered off to Paris or London (like Frederick Loudin of the Fisk Jubilee Singers), renouncing their previous lives in the United States and committing to living abroad.

Others sat grimly in their cabins or moodily walked on the decks of their steamships sailing back to the United States. The ship's return journey was often gloomy, as people forcibly and bitterly readjusted to a racial order they had previously left behind. Awkward silence accompanied many. Leaving to go back to the United States in 1894, Du Bois bluntly wrote in his di-ary, "There are five Negroes aboard. We do not go together."[46] Returning to the United States in 1914 because war had broken out on the European continent, Hazel Harrison found herself on a ship with Alain Locke and the Harrelds, communing over their experiences in Germany and their intermin-gling joy and dread toward reentry to the United States.[47]

Perhaps the most shocking outcome of these return voyages to the United States was that some African Americans came back to American shores pass-ing as white. They used the long passage back to the United States to trans-form from Black men and women into socially acceptable white people who had just returned from European ventures. In his unpublished memoir, Cook recalls a fellow violinist named Ed Winn, the son of a barber in the town of

Oberlin and a rival of Cook's at the Oberlin Conservatory of Music. Cook writes, "Later Winn studied in Germany, returned to this country and, like [another Oberlin graduate] Hattie, passed for white."[48] A white plantation owner in Texas named Philip Cuney, the grandfather of the African American musicologist Cuney Hare, sent his mixed-race daughter Jennie to Madame Nichol's Institute for Young Ladies in Mannheim in the 1860s. Upon her return, Jennie passed into the white community and cut off all contact with her immediate family.[49] If Europe was a continent where anything felt possible for talented young Black men and women, such stories suggest that the United States was the opposite. Social rigidity and segregation shaped the lives of many African Americans in the United States, even as they worked hard to circumvent its damaging effects on their lives and to ensure that it did not limit their potential educational or musical outcomes.

African Americans who were not able to pass as white (or who chose not to) dreaded returning home. Why go? What good awaited them upon arrival? Terrell recounts trying to console a young African American student who did not want to return to the United States. Exceptionally gifted, he was nonetheless "listless" in Berlin. "When I urged this young man to avail himself of the marvelous opportunities and advantages he enjoyed," she writes, his response was despondent: "What's the use of my trying to do anything extraordinary and worthwhile?" His time in Germany had opened his eyes to how difficult his life would be upon returning to the United States. "A man must have some kind of racial background to amount to anything," he insisted. "What have we done as a race? Almost nothing. We are descended from slaves. How can you expect a people with such a background as that to compete successfully with white people?"[50] His lament to Terrell was an expression of transatlantic racist thinking he had internalized. He tacitly accepted the Hegelian idea that Black people were a "people without history," a race without accomplishments or intellectual and artistic achievements to justify their value as U.S. citizens.

Although Terrell tried to cajole this student in the throes of an existential crisis out of his feelings of defeatism, she acknowledged that he was not alone in such thinking. In the United States, African American travelers forlornly stated, Black people possessed little to no cultural value or cultural capital. They believed they were fighting a war for cultural advancement and socially equality in the United States with one hand tied behind their backs. In Europe, they could shake off their feelings of defeat, shirk off the burden of responsibility for their race, and live on a continent with no cultural expectations of them.

Even the few recorded incidents of overt racism by white Germans did not shake them. Rarely did African Americans admit to experiencing anti-Black racism in Germany. In the diary of the Fisk Jubilee Singer Ella Sheppard, for example, only a few jarring encounters appear in her account of daily life in Germany between 1877 and 1878. "During intermission they & others passed through the dining hall where we rested, stood looking at us curiously just as one would look at statuary & then passed on through the opposite door to make room for those in the rear to look," she writes. "Their look was quite new and amusing. Nothing vulgar or insulting—only like such as one would give while studying an object."[51] Perhaps to some Black musicians in Central Europe, being an object of curiosity was better than being an object of disgust. Appiah observes that for W. E. B. Du Bois, "There was plenty of race prejudice about, but, for a change, it wasn't personally directed toward him."[52]

Clarence Cameron White's 1908 article, "The Negro in Musical Europe," contains many of these arguments. His text makes explicit the convergence of Black longing, European cultural vibrancy, and musical universalism that dominated Black thinking during the late nineteenth and early twentieth centuries. The article cites the careers of Samuel Coleridge-Taylor, Will Marion Cook, Abbie Mitchell, Felix Weir, Portia Washington, Amanda Aldridge, Harriett Gibbs Marshall, Annis Hackley, Gustav Sabac el Cher (an Afro-German military musician whom Clarence Cameron White calls "a bandmaster of the German army"), and Rachel Walker, among others, as evidence of Europe's welcoming embrace of Black people. "As far back as 1862 the Afro-American made his appearance in Europe as music student," White writes. The fact that Harrison performed in Berlin and won praise from "Europe's most severe critics" and that the composer Harry Burleigh received warm applause from the king and queen of England "only goes to show that it is here more a question of fitness than of color." In Europe, White insists, "the Afro-American can at all times be sure of a respectful hearing—not as a curiosity but as an artist."[53]

Most daringly, White employs the rhetoric of universalism to argue for Europe's better reception of Black musicians over the United States. "On every side you find the European musician and music lover as well realizes that music is too broad and too universal to be circumscribed by the complexion of the skin or texture of the hair."[54] Clarence Cameron White implies that while classical music in the United States operated along rigid racial fault lines, Europeans understood that classical music was simply too universal to be debased by racism. In Europe, universalism transcended petty racism.

But did it? As we will see in the following chapter, German musical discourse did not reflect White's own claims. Rather, by the time of White's writing, classical music had become racialized in Europe. Indeed, what unified much of the writing on Black classical performers in the same era as White's essay was the belief that music was a legitimate category for racial analysis. It is possible, however, to hold both White's claims and the historical realities of anti-Black German racism in the same space. African American experiences in Central Europe illustrate how much they valued their experiences away from U.S. racism. At the same time, however, Central Europe also perpetuated its own growing discourse of music and Blackness in the nineteenth and twentieth centuries. What is clear in both African Americans' experiences in Central Europe and the way in which white Germans encountered them is that their privileged identity as Americans—just as much as their race—determined how they lived their daily lives.

What is so striking about African American students' interpretations of Germany as a liberating space is that it starkly counters other Black experiences in Germany. At the same time that African Americans were attending the opera, German culture had begun the racist practice of placing Black bodies and Black cultures in zoos, culture shows (*Völkerschauen*), and minstrel shows. For example, Will Marion Cook lived in Berlin during the first five years of German colonial rule in sub-Saharan Africa; Hazel Harrison performed with the Berlin Philharmonic in 1904, the same year as the Herero and Nama genocide, in which German colonial soldiers murdered thousands of Africans in German South West Africa. Existing side by side, then, are German discourses of race and Blackness and African American students' quests for better lives.

However much those students might have expressed ambivalence about their lives in the United States, their treatment in Germany nonetheless reflected their privileged, elite status as Americans. Their Blackness was still an American Blackness, which meant that as they walked down Unter den Linden in Berlin or visited the St. Nicholas Church in Leipzig, they experienced Germany quite differently from Black Africans, many of whom arrived to Germany either because of racist commercial ventures (human zoos, ethnological villages, etc.) or due to increasingly fixed colonial ties. Marveling at German racial egalitarianism in the era of culture shows, African Americans lived in different social worlds from Black Africans.

The absence of Black Africans and working class Black diasporic men and women from African American travel narratives during the era of German colonialism is itself a revealing fact. Scholars such as Brent Hayes Edwards, Jacqueline Brown, Tina Campt, and others have convincingly demonstrated that far too often, many Black diasporic writings are documents of African American hegemony.[55] As much as African Americans abroad may have wished to promote a budding Black internationalism, their own texts might have perpetuated what Campt calls "a discourse that refers not so much to a relation of equity than of hegemony."[56] Black Americans did not seek out Black diasporic peers as equals, nor did they see them as such. Rather, African Americans' published reflections of their visits to Germany far too often reveal a "hierarchy between the privileged African American traveler to Germany and the Black German subject," Maria Diedrich warns.[57] As privileged Black travelers rather than permanent Black residents, African Americans in Germany frequently omitted in their eyewitness accounts other kinds of Black diasporic experiences or dismissed them as peculiar. Instead, with razor-sharp focus, African American writings highlighted white German egalitarianism in order to indict white American racism.

American nationality in Central Europe came with its own privileges and powers, ones that perhaps even undermined Black Americans' anti-racism and global cosmopolitan visions of musical and racial harmony. It explains why Black Americans experienced Germany as a liberating space, a spiritual and musical fatherland, and a site of blossoming international friendships. Their nationality (and occasional wealth) also explains why they were more easily able to circumvent impending racial stigmatization in Central Europe while Black colonial Africans could not, and why they might have been ignorant (perhaps willfully so) of German anti-Black racism, which was tied to the violence of colonialism. Simply put, many Africans in Germany—placed on display in ethnological exhibitions throughout the German countryside or working in cities—could not join African Americans in singing Beethoven's "Ode to Joy."

We must draw the conclusion that these American travel narratives were not like those of other Black diasporic migrants to Germany. Their melodies of travel to Central Europe carried with them wealth, access, and knowledge that white Germans actively denied Black people from Africa. Their songs hummed different tunes of potential and progress, hymns of longing that were outside of the colonial project but tacitly affirmed it, in keys of hope and desire. Germans listened to them sing their tales in Central Europe. But how much did Germans comprehend what they heard? What, if any of it, could they or did they understand?

CHAPTER 3

The Sonic Color Line Belts the World

Constructing Race and Music in Central Europe

When José Julián Jiménez arrived at the Leipzig Conservatory of Music in 1854 to register for instruction, the administrators were so shocked by what they saw that they wrote down "colored" (*farbiger*) next to his registration form.[1] "Mister José Julián Jiménez, born on the island of Cuba," they recorded, had recently traveled from New York to Leipzig to study the violin.[2] Who was this man who had crossed an ocean to visit them? Why was he here? Jiménez received support throughout his twenty-year-long relationship with the Leipzig Conservatory of Music from music veterans such as Ignaz Moscheles and Carl Reinecke. He spent many years studying violin and, as his school records indicate, learning music theory, organ, voice, and composition to complement his training. But his registration file indicates that in this moment, the administration was more interested in delineating him from the other students according to his perceived differences rather than acknowledging shared commonalities. His racial difference was noteworthy enough for the registrar to mark down.

Jiménez performed frequently throughout Germany with his two sons in the 1870s. Yet the registrar's early act in 1853 of marking the musician according to racial difference foreshadows what followed over the next several decades. Considered extraordinary by some, derided as markedly unoriginal by others, African-descended musicians in Germany and Austria became a growing phenomenon that provoked comment, compelled documentation, and warranted extensive explanation and analysis. Musical demarcation along racial lines became an important leitmotif in Black musicians' lives across the Atlantic.

This book begins its analysis of Black musical performances in German musical culture in the latter half of the nineteenth century for two reasons. First, the numbers of Black musicians traveling to Central Europe grew substantially by the 1870s and 1880s as they tapped into greater transatlantic markets of cultural exchange.[3] Second, the mid-to-late nineteenth century, scholars argue, represents a shift or a departure from previous discourses on race and culture. While some Europeans had previously been engaged in humanitarian principles of egalitarianism or believed in Herderian evaluations of cultural difference, a generational shift in attitudes toward people of African descent between the 1830s and 1860s changed much of European thought. European rhetoric that had once promoted a universal brotherhood became displaced, Catherine Hall argues, "by a harsher racial vocabulary of fixed differences."[4]

German nationalism and colonialism in particular played a significant role in defining racial ideologies within German culture.[5] By the 1870s—the era of German unification—shared spaces for interracial solidarity had begun to erode as colonial interest in subjugating peoples in Africa grew. Indeed, the birth of German settler colonialism demanded that Germans publicly bind together Germanness and whiteness in relation to people of color and commit to promoting a fixed racial hierarchy.[6] Intransigent notions of inherent racial inequality, presented as natural, came to inform ordinary Germans' estimations of people of African descent.

Yet scholars have tended to divorce nineteenth-century German musical culture from these global developments. The worlds of Beethoven, Brahms, and Wagner, we imagine, had little to do with the projects of globalization, let alone with Blackness. By incorporating narratives of globalization and diaspora into German music history, however, I challenge these claims. It turns out that Black musicians occupied a whole host of positions in German musical culture, from orchestral instrumentalists and military musicians to opera singers and bandleaders. They performed everywhere, from the royal palace to Richard Wagner's surprise sixtieth birthday party.[7] And even the most elite music journals of the nineteenth century, including Robert Schumann's *Neue Zeitschrift für Musik*, reported on the musical activities of Black people.[8]

In this chapter, I argue that transatlantic notions of race informed audiences' listening experiences of Black classical musicians in Central Europe and, more specifically, gave them the tools to begin to articulate classical music as a white medium. In the late nineteenth century, the audience listening to Black classical performers linked racial (in)abilities to musical performance to reach astounding conclusions. Between 1870—the decade of German unification—and WWI, audiences began to find ways to hear Blackness in performers' interpretations of Bach, Beethoven, and Brahms. Central European listeners, then, constructed what Jennifer Lynn Stoever calls a "sonic color line." White Germans, as we will see, turned to the practice of racial listening to mark classical music as white and Black musicians as foreign.[9] Central European audiences relied on ever-shifting and -evolving notions of Black musicality to process their own sensory experiences.

I also demonstrate that white German formulations of Blackness and classical music were informed by the practices of classical music itself. The gulf that divided German racialized listening experiences was an aesthetic one: ideological assumptions about vocal and instrumental music informed listener's expectations of a Black musician's performance. As the writings of German Romantics such as E.T.A. Hoffmann made clear, vocal singing sat in lower estimation than instrumental music. Intimately tied to the body and to notions of bodily production, vocal singing could be listened to contradictorily as both an artistic practice expressing interiority and a natural, even primal act. By the late nineteenth century, it became a racialized act as well, one in which Blackness could be sonically located in a singer's biology. But white Germans not only heard Black voices in a racial key; they also racialized Black instrumentalists' musical practice as well. Their concert criticisms illustrate that a Mendelssohn piano trio or a Chopin piano concerto could also be understood as a sonically Black or white performance.

What also anchored German listening practices was the belief in the supremacy of their music. The assumption that Germans were the best music-makers was so prevalent that many African American musicians took notice of it. An entry from the diary of the Fisk Jubilee Singer Ella Sheppard illustrates the degree to which Germans believed they were superior musicians: "One of the ladies present—a princess, I think—asked me who our teacher was and remarked that we must have studied many years to be able to sing as beautifully together. Such perfect intonation she had never heard before—and she seemed surprised to find our Mr. director was not a *German* but an *American*."[10] How else, this German response implies, could the choir have achieved such excellence in their musicianship if they had not received their training from a German?

Regardless of the kind of performance a Black musician delivered, however, their physical presence created a pretext for some Germans to test out and sometimes reaffirm their own belief in their superiority over the supposedly lesser races. Discussions of Black musicians, whether in local newspapers or in scholarly journals, used their musical performances to re-affirm the cultural and biological inferiority of Black people in both Africa and in the New World, to flesh out German ideologies about the seriousness of German music, and to locate "authentic" forms of musical expression in the bodies of the performers themselves. Regardless of one's position within German society, Neil MacMaster writes, "underlying the colonial policies of left and right, of Social Democrats and Marxists, as well as Conservatives and Liberals, was an unquestioning assumption of Black inferiority."[11] Black cultural inferiority was assumed to be an unalterable visual and sonic fact, a necessary condition of modern life, and, increasingly, part of everyday life.

Or was it? The problem with Black performances of classical music was that they so often exposed the shoddy construction of these sonic racial de-marcations. Were Black classical musicians primitive people or could they be just as sophisticated as white people? To dare to answer that question meant addressing whether Black people were capable of creating and performing art music, which white Europeans had claimed as uniquely their own. Listen-ers had to reckon with a much wider scale of Black diasporic musical ability and talent than they were sometimes willing to acknowledge.

German music criticism, then, reveals the difficulties white Germans faced in coming to terms with the complexities of the Black diaspora. Ger-mans' shifting elision in terminology offers one illustration of this. Over the course of the nineteenth century, German employment of the term "Moor" dropped in favor of "Negro" to describe people of African descent, a change in vocabulary that represented a significant downgrade in position for Black people in German society. While "Moors" connoted "brave warriors, Chris-tian saints, and the riches of Africa," the term "Negro," Mischa Honeck, Martin Klimke, and Anne Kuhlmann argue, "alluded instead to a trading commodity; a childish, cheap, and unskilled hand."[12] Black performers often received both labels in concert criticism and advertisements, irrespective of their own backgrounds. The words used even to categorize Black people, then, were also undergoing constant revision.

Yet even with the transition from "Moor" to "Negro" in German thought, there was an occasional flattening of Blackness that presented Black people as static and monolithic. Germans often conflated different Black identities together in their accounts of Black musicians. To read reviews, one would think that there were no differences between African Americans, sub-Saharan Africans, and Afro-Europeans who had been born and raised in the Habsburg Empire or who had grown up as the children of Prussian servants.[13] Some-times white writers made little attempt to distinguish Africans in the Congo "in need" of civilizing from Afro-Cubans studying abroad. Occasionally, however, German concert criticism demarcated Black Americans as separate from other Black performers by virtue of their positions as formerly enslaved peoples. In these moments, the reactions of German listeners illustrated the potency of American notions of race from across the Atlantic Ocean.[14] Mostly, though, Germans' disavowal of diversity within Black cultures suggests the lengths to which German institutions and individuals were willing to go in order to sustain their fictions of Blackness.

German conversations about Black classical musicians, then, reveal the limits of musical universalism itself. In my first chapter, I illustrated how potent the siren song of German musical universalism had become to African American musicians and intellectuals. Hearing its call, they found ways to make the universality of classical music conform to Black cultural politics in white supremacist America. Singing its melody, they placed themselves on boats sailing across the Atlantic Ocean and imagined other musical worlds outside the confines of Jim Crow. Arriving in Central Europe, however, they found themselves participating (perhaps unwittingly) in a musical transfer of a different sort. But their presence in Central Europe meant that white listeners occasionally confronted the limitations of their own universalist musical aesthetic in an era of growing cultural and racial nationalism. By the early twentieth century, I argue, whiteness had become a necessary qualification for performing classical music.

All of these factors—Blackness, whiteness, Germanness; sight, sound, race, and culture—come together in the concert hall and in the opera house in nineteenth-century Central Europe. Scholars have seen these threads as separate for far too long, in part because German musical discourse, having erased Blackness from itself, presented them as such. But German musical culture was more global, messy, and entangled than its idealized self-presentation. Instead, it was part of the very projects of globalization, transnationalism, colonialism, and racism from which many of its listeners believed it was divorced.

Coming to Terms with the Black Diaspora: The Fisk Jubilee Singers as Musical Albatross

The Fisk Jubilee Singers did not perform classical music in Germany. Nor were they the first Black musical ensemble to travel there to perform. But they require our attention because their powerful status and prominent position as the first serious musical ensemble meant that they touched nearly all aspects of German society during and after their visit.[15] It is in their personal accounts and other documents that we see most clearly the contrast between

Black understandings of themselves and German expectations of Blackness, and that we witness some of the most dominant tropes Germans used to describe Black musicianship coming to light.

Arriving in Germany in 1877 to raise money for Fisk University, the choir sang songs such as "Steal Away to Jesus" and "Swing Low, Sweet Chariot" for ten months across the nation, performing in small Lutheran towns like Eisenach and Jena and in major cities such as Berlin, Cologne, and Stuttgart. At their concerts, royalty wept and audiences were left speechless. Their concerts in the Berlin Cathedral were filled to such capacity that two hundred people were forced to stand in the back to listen to them.

How German audiences discussed the Fisk Jubilee Singers became the pattern for German music criticism of Black musicians for decades. First, notions of primitivism colored much of their praise. The "primitive," Sieglinde Lemke writes, "was the antonym of discipline, order, rationality—the antithesis of 'civilized.'"[16] What made Black people primitive was not only their supposed lack of rational intelligence, but also their lack of a sophisticated culture from which to draw artistic inspiration and intellectual curiosity.[17] Culture—including music—fell along a racial fault line; high culture was by nature European, and Black diasporic cultures primitive.

By the late nineteenth century, the discourse of Black primitivism had become two-pronged, embodied in the primitive "natural peoples" (Naturvölker) on the one hand and in the Black popular entertainer on the other. The myth of natural peoples has its roots in nineteenth-century anthropology, when academics divorced non-European peoples from narratives of Western civilization and progress. "Cultured peoples" (Kulturvölker) were white and European, deemed civilized by their history and civilization. Natural peoples were usually non-European, often racialized as Black and Brown, whose supposed lack of history and culture made them suitable objects of anthropological study.[18] Constantly under a colonial gaze, natural peoples were the embodiment of the primitive in white European formulations because they failed to adhere to European hegemonic norms.

The caricature of the popular Black entertainer also functioned to reinforce white beliefs of Black primitivism. By 1896 the digest Der Artist reported that there were over one hundred Black entertainers living in Germany. Black minstrel shows and dances such as the Cakewalk "brought to the surface uncomfortable elements of the radical changes in Germany associated with colonialism, transnational capitalism, and the emergence of mass culture," Jonathan Wipplinger argues.[19] Mass culture made caricatures of Blackness more easily transmissible, and new markets, recognizing Black entertainment's increasing popularity, offered it as a modern, sometimes colonial, consumer good. A popular repertoire for Black ensembles in the 1870s and 1880s included spirituals and sacred songs from church, as well as "coon" songs, plantation numbers, and other "humorous" acts for German audiences.[20] Mixing together dance, comedy, and song, Black vaudeville shows presented African Americans as jovial tricksters whose appeal lay in part in their physicality as performers and dancers.

White German interest in seeing both "natural peoples" and Black popular entertainers perform for them had everything to do with their desire for a perceived Black authenticity. The impresarios of human zoos (*Völkerschauen*, literally "people shows") constructed environments that were meant to resemble the "natural habitats" of Africans so that white observers could take part in a fully immersive experience.[21] Black popular entertainers in Germany also emphasized their authenticity as "real" Black performers. The comedian Edgar Jones, for example, was a featured performer in numerous German playbills in the 1890s. German advertisements touted "the best Negro comic in the world," with print ads and posters that appeared on lampposts or billboards stating that Jones was a "wirklicher Schwarzer," or "real Black," unlike other imposter performers circulating in Germany at that time.[22] German audiences need not fear being tricked by a white performer in blackface, in other words, because they could see a Black performer for themselves.

The desire to see "real Blacks" may have been responsible for the high ticket sales for the Fisk Jubilee Singers' tour in Germany. Yet the Fisk Jubilee Singers' visual and musical presentation caused Germans to calibrate their expectations against what they experienced after leaving the venue. Straddling the line between the anthropological and the popular, the Fisk Jubilee Singers moved German audiences with the gravitas and religiosity of their musical performances. Their presentation of African American identity—which was genteel, Protestant, and imbued with African American respectability—confounded listeners, who had associated Blackness with an African primitivism. It was surprising for white German listeners to learn that there was more than one way to be Black.

One major difference between the Fisk Jubilee Singers and other Black performers was the location of their concerts: throughout their stay, the ensemble sang their sold-out shows in some of the most sacrosanct spaces in the nation, including the Berlin Cathedral and the Berlin Sing-Akademie. Where the Fisk Jubilee Singers performed mattered just as much as what they were performing. Unlike Black minstrels, who entertained listeners in cheap, popular venues or African "villagers" performing music in a human zoo, the Fisk Jubilee Singers sang their music in spaces usually reserved for

European high art musicians or for church choirs. These sacred locales elevated their artistry above other Black musical performances and demanded that listeners situate their songs on a higher musical plane. By the nature of the recital space in which the Jubilee Singers sang, German listeners unquestioningly accepted that their music was the most sophisticated, cultivated, and respected genre of Black diasporic music, even if it remained inferior to European art music.

German reviewers and audiences were also often surprised by their fashionable, Western-style dress. Sheppard's diary records an encounter at a reception in Berlin:

> [I] felt so keenly that a certain Countess' eyes were constantly fixed upon me that I could not help asking her in broken German, "What is the matter?"
>
> She, in equally broken English, replied: "Oh, I so astonished, you speak English—beautifully, and oh, you *dress*, like we."
>
> I replied, "Why, what did you expect me to have on?"
>
> She replied, "Oh, Africani, Africani."
>
> I suppose she expected us to have on only five yards of calico wrapped about us à l'Africaine.[23]

Clothing was a strong visual symbol of the civilizing mission and its ability to convert "savages" into Christianized subjects. For example, white European missionaries encouraged Africans to change their dress and conform to Western notions of beauty, culture, and behavior as outward expressions of their civilizational processes.[24] But the Fisk Jubilee Singers' dress may have also implicitly violated the supposed natural order of racial hierarchy by visually denying white audiences the opportunity to conceive of themselves as superior in dress and culture than people of African descent.

Not only did their style of dress surprise Germans, but the variety of skin tones among the singers was another source of astonishment. Nearly all of the concert reviews, stories, and biographical sketches on the Jubilee Singers mention at some point how varied in skin color the Jubilee Singers appeared. For example, a Berlin critic complained that the appearance of the Jubilee Singers did not meet his expectations. "One had imagined that these North American slaves would have a clearly Black appearance," the author explained, "[but] of the ten members represented from the society, only two appeared truly Black to the eye; the rest were more or less mixed, some so much so that their African heritage would not even be suspected on this side of the ocean."[25] *Die Post* also emphasized the diversity in appearance among these African American musicians: "We encountered there eight full-blooded negresses, one mulatto, and a light-colored mestizo, of whom only her hard, kinky hair betrayed her heritage."[26] Much like their racial mixture (perceived or real), Germans would attribute their musical mixture to European influence as well.

Even if the Fisk Jubilee Singers' appearances and mannerisms betrayed German expectations of Black people, audiences nonetheless turned to a variety of racist stereotypes to make sense of the ensemble's Blackness. Tellingly, three aspects of German music criticism illustrate how Germans determined the musical merits of the Fisk Jubilee Singers. The ways in which they listened for Blackness appeared in concert criticism for decades thereafter. First, German critics focused heavily on the perceived melancholia in African American music and musicians, a long-standing belief dating to at least the 1860s. German writers assumed that African Americans had adapted melancholia as a form of cultural and musical expression as a result of their history of enslavement. Music criticism often described the Fisk Jubilee Singers' music and performers as melancholic or "elegiac."[27] In so doing, they perpetuated a transatlantic belief that nature had turned African Americans into an inherently long-suffering people and thus made them better able to withstand oppression.

Second, reviews of the Fisk Jubilee Singers located Blackness in the ensemble's voices. Many listeners frequently described the singers' voices as "natural," implying that the singers were closer to nature than white Europeans. One reviewer stated, "They have beautiful . . . voices of a pure, healthy sounding timbre entirely free from those tricks ([and] artificialities) which we so often censure in European singers."[28] The critic's act of hearing their voices as pure, natural, and unspoiled by civilization perpetuated ideologies of primitivism, which praised the supposed advantage Black diasporic people possessed as a racial group somehow untouched by cultural development over more "developed" Europeans.

Music criticism also used animalistic language to describe the Fisk Jubilee Singers' voices in a manner that predates much historical scholarship. In an 1878 review of the choir, one critic states their singing sounds like "the scream of the persecuted and enslaved ones, and sometimes it is a wild shriek, corresponding to the hot blood of the Negro race."[29] The critic's description of their style of singing as "screams" and "shrieks" connotes instinctive and apelike noises. In so doing, the critic associated Black musicianship with unintelligible noise. Moreover, the phrase "hot blood of the Negro race" marked Black people as intemperate and uncivilized—long before German critics in the jazz age used similar phrases.

FIGURE 8. "The Jubilee Singers at the Sing-Akademie in Berlin. Drawn to life." Taken from the magazine, *Daheim* 14, no. 30, April 27, 1878, supplement: "Of the times—for the times." Courtesy of bpk Bildagentur/Staatsbibliothek zu Berlin, Stiftung Preußischer Kulturbesitz, Berlin, Germany, Newspaper Division/Art Resource, NY.

Third, German reception of the Fisk Jubilee Singers also illustrates that German music critics had already begun to espouse the notion that Black music could rejuvenate a failing Europe long before writers such as Ivan Goll ("The Negroes Are Conquering Europe") or Alice Gerstel ("Jazz Band") issued such declarations in the 1920s during the Weimar Republic. Reviews of the Jubilee Singers that appeared in even the most elite music journals suggested how Black music could be called upon to aid German art music in its improvement of itself. To the German critics, the "natural" sounds and supposedly simplistic musical abilities of the Fisk Jubilee Singers made the choir a perfect foil for critiquing German musical culture.

For example, one reviewer argued that Black music was exactly what a decaying European musical culture needed to revive itself. "We have much to learn from them," the critic said. "We with our old culture, with our classical achievements piled one above the other like some palatial structure, do not see that the foundation upon which the superstructure is raised is beginning to decay . . . in other words, we are losing sight of the primeval simplicity so excellently delineated by these Negroes."[30] The music of American slaves, in other words, could help German composers of art music rebuild their own foundation.

The most daring articulation of the belief that African American spirituals could contribute to Western art music came from the *Neue Berliner Musikzeitung*. Decades before Antonín Dvořák shocked classical musicians by telling composers of Western art music that African American folk music could serve as the basis for musical composition, the music critic of the *Neue Berliner Musikzeitung* made the same claim in his concluding remarks on the Fisk Jubilee Singers' concert:

> Hungarian music had to wait a few years before it could—through the efforts of Liszt, Brahms, and others—be made accessible to German friends of the arts and then positively influence German production. Should Negro music find an apostle with the same energy and talent as those found in Hungarian music, who knows if the music won't achieve a similar position in our musical life?[31]

Here, the reviewer directly ties African American music to Western art music in the most explicit and provocative terms. In the nineteenth century, Hungarian music, closely tied to Sinti and Roma music, represented a particularly romantic sensibility in Austro-German musical culture. Considered wild, rhythmic, modally adventurous, and inferior to German art music, it became a source of inspiration for German composers.[32] Hungarian music's beautiful primitiveness was something to be improved upon, teased out, and reconfigured. It was up to Austro-German composers to take on the challenge of writing in a Hungarian style without it overpowering their own music's classical roots. It is in this spirit that the critic of the *Neue Berliner Musikzeitung* offers the same backhanded praise of African American music. In spite of its exotic differences, and in spite of (or perhaps because of) its simplicity, the music of the Jubilee Singers could be appropriated into a larger German tradition.

What unifies much of the German discourse surrounding the Fisk Jubilee Singers in the 1870s is the belief that music was a legitimate category for racial analysis. The Singers' music offered a point of entry for scholars investigating folk music's ethnic, national, and regional musical boundaries, and it could inspire a new generation of German composers to approach music with fresh ears because of its primitive, childlike qualities. Listeners' praise of the ensemble as a potential source of inspiration to German musicians reveals a "primitivist modernist" aesthetic at work well before the 1920s, the era that scholars have traditionally assumed this discourse first came into existence. Never held up as equal to or even similar to Germany's strong choral musical tradition in the nineteenth century, the choral music of the Fisk Jubilee Singers resonated the most with listeners when heard ethnomusicologically and in dissonant, contradictory keys: modern yet primitive, childlike, simple, and natural yet strange and unfamiliar, the music of the Fisk Jubilee Singers was heard by Germans as an amalgam of sounds that could only have been produced by Black people in the New World.

As we will see below, reviews of Black classical musicians shared many of these tropes. Indeed, many of the same formulations of Black musicians—that they sounded different than white Europeans, that their appearances were confusing because they were not African—appeared in concert music criticism. However, instead of locating Blackness in supposedly Black sounds, listeners heard it in compositions by white European composers. Listeners used their writings to articulate evolving positions on the relationship between sight and sound, between race and culture, and between ability and authenticity. Classical music became a site where Blackness also had to be defined and made sense of, even if listeners used elaborate logistics to do it.

Will the Real Black Patti Please Stand Up?

Unlike most instrumentalists who came to Germany for formal training, Black singers who traveled to Germany came to advance their already established professional careers. The majority of Black singers who traveled to Germany were women. Part of a gendered phenomenon known as the

"Black Prima Donna," they toured around the United States, Europe, Australia, and New Zealand in the late nineteenth and early twentieth centuries. The women who traveled to Germany included Marie Selika (Williams), Rachel Walker, Jenny Bishop, Sissieretta Jones, Annis Hackley, and Abbie Mitchell, and smaller unknown female groups such as a "Negress Quartet" who performed in Germany and Austria in 1885.[33] Although it is unclear where and when Rachel Walker might have traveled to Germany and Austria, evidence suggests that, at the very least, she sang for the princess of Saxe-Coburg and Gotha and a countess of Baroda.[34]

Many of these women traveled under monikers such as "the Black Swan" or "the Black Jenny Lind," presenting themselves as a racial variant of a prominent white singer. One of the most popular titles was "Black Patti," a reference to the famed Italian singer Adelina Patti. A contemporary of the "Swedish Nightingale" Lind, Patti had a light, fluttering voice well-suited for operatic roles such as Zerlina or Lucia. In the 1880s and 1890s, Black women in the United States began to use the title "Black Patti" to gain followers. Flora Bergen, for example, called herself the "real Patti" in response to Jones's use of the title.

In the 1890s, two Black prima donnas traveled to Germany to much fanfare: Marie Selika and Sissieretta Jones, both of whom called themselves the "Black Patti" during their tours.[35] Both singers had trained with well-established classical musicians, performed difficult and technically demanding musical works, and used established entertainment managers to land contracts in Germany. Selika toured as part of a troupe called the African American Concert Company, sponsored by the popular entertainment manager William Foote.[36] Rudolph Voeckel, a German American, became the manager for Jones's German tour and for the rest of her career. Together they created the Black Patti Concert Company in 1894, featuring Jones and a variety of white and Black musicians, including the German-born pianist Felix Heinck.[37]

Marie Selika, dubbed "the Queen of Staccato," was born in Natchez, Mississippi, raised in Ohio, and moved to San Francisco in her early twenties to study music.[38] Selika toured intermittently throughout Europe beginning in the 1880s and continuing well into the 1920s.[39] After Selika wound through Europe during her second tour in 1891, the *Chicago Daily Tribune* reported in 1894, "It remained for the critics of Germany to complete her triumph. Everywhere in that country she was received with great enthusiasm."[40] She received numerous encores in Berlin and had to stop her program to perform her first aria again for the audience. The *Berliner Tageblatt* raved about the sweetness of her voice, its extraordinary range, "pure tones, her wonderful trills and roulades, her correct rending of the most difficult intervals" that won over

FIGURE 9. An 1899 poster of African American soprano Sissieretta Jones, also called "The Black Patti." Courtesy of the Library of Congress, Prints and Photographs Division, Washington, D.C. Collections: Posters: Performing Arts Posters.

amateurs and professional musicians alike that evening. "It is almost impossible to describe the effect of her voice," the reviewer gushed; "one must hear it to appreciate its thrilling beauty."[41]

The writer's effusive praise was not out of the ordinary. Throughout her stay in Germany, Selika appeared to earn adoration from even the most difficult critics. The Bavarian *Schweinfurter Anzeiger*'s reviewer reported in 1884, somewhat in a state of disbelief, "The audience was literally carried away by enthusiasm for the singing of this wonderful woman. Only once before has the city of Schweinfur [sic] been favored with so rare an opportunity of listening to so bewitching a voice as that possessed by this American lady, and that was on the occasion of the concert of the celebrated contest of Totto Luger, the opera singer of the Royal Court of Prussia."[42]

Most reviews did not comment on Selika's Blackness, aside from describing her as a woman with "coal-black hair."[43] Only later in the 1920s when Selika sang again in Germany did reviews mention her race. Her concert featured some art songs and a piece entitled, "Je suis Titania la blonde" from Ambroise Thomas's opera *Mignon*. In a press release for the upcoming concert, a German critic wrote, "Imagine, a Negro singer of such dark visage, in the role of the blond Mignon and attempting to sing the airy vocal polonaise."[44]

Jones, on the other hand, became a much more pronounced symbol of Blackness and of the Black prima donna to German audiences during her short stay in 1895. Born in Virginia to a carpenter and a washerwoman in 1869 and raised in Rhode Island, Matilda Joyner moved to Boston to study music, where she changed her name to Sissieretta Jones. Her voice quickly made an impression on managers and directors in the entertainment industry, and by 1888 she had already toured several major American cities.[45] The repertoire that Jones performed indicates that she was a well-trained lyric coloratura soprano. A clever marketer, she also sang many of the exact same songs in Patti's standard repertoire. Between 1888 and 1916, her standard pieces included excerpts from Verdi's *Rigoletto* and *La Traviata*, and she sang numerous art songs by French and German composers as well. Like Selika, Jones sang a rendition of the Swiss echo song—a piece of music designed to display a singer's vocal techniques—to great acclaim.[46] By 1895 Jones was secure enough financially and had a strong enough reputation in the United States to tour Europe. Like Selika, she used a German agent (in this case, a man named William Gottschalk) to set up her bookings in Berlin.

Biographies and other works about Jones that have sought to detail her time in Germany have relied on her scrapbook, located in the Schomburg Center for Research in Black Culture in the New York Public Library, and on translated reviews that appeared in the *Indianapolis Freeman* newspaper to investigate German reception of her. By not reading German print sources directly, they have missed a bigger story, for in actuality, Jones's title of Black Patti was contested during her entire stay.

It turns out that Berlin was embroiled in a war of divas in February of 1895. Two Black Pattis were competing against each other in the musical city at the same time: Sissieretta Jones and an unknown singer named Jenny Bishop. Little documentation exists on Bishop, the singer who usurped Jones's debut in Berlin that cold winter. One report from the *Detroit Plaindealer* in 1892 states that Bishop was a daughter of an enslaved woman who "picked cotton in Virginia," and that she was a specialist in "old plantation songs."[47] At Bishop's Berlin debut in mid-February as the "Black Patti," a few days before Jones performed, she sang mostly "Negro songs" to positive acclaim.[48] Other newspapers, such as the *Berliner Börsen-Courier* also described Bishop's musical performance as deeply empathetic, quietly moving, and melancholic.[49] In so doing, their criticisms tapped into the practice of associating African American musicianship with melancholia. Like countless other reviews of Black performers, one report concluded, "Thus Miss Bishop is not only a curiosity for the eyes, but also a welcome [sound] for the ears."[50] Bishop's appeal to white audiences was, like all Black performers, dualistic—both sonic and visual, always racially marked.

Nonetheless, the problem remained for German audiences that two self-fashioned Black Pattis were singing Italian arias and Swiss echo songs in Berlin at the same time. The city could only support one. "Both parties fight for the honor of holding the title, the real Black Nightingale," a writer at the *Berliner Intelligenzblatt* gossiped. West of the city at the Apollo-Theater one Black Patti (Bishop) sang, and in the north at the Wintergarten Varieté was another (Jones), who swore that she alone was the real one. "They both appear to be right," the author wrote in frustration, "because the one is as Black as the other, and the one sings so beautifully as the other."[51] What was the city of Berlin to do?

Jones's management agency went on the attack. The barrage of advertisements announcing her arrival in many daily newspapers and other promotional materials sought to undo the level playing field Bishop had created. One such promotional article on Jones appeared on February 17, 1895, in the popular daily *Berliner Börsen-Courier*, two days before her premiere. Called "How Sissieretta Jones was discovered," the story—a wildly fabricated and sensational tale—told of Jones's rise from a "simple Negro maiden" in Kentucky to a superstar. Years prior, at a festive celebration that the scientist Thomas Edison was hosting for President Grover Cleveland, the article begins, the partygoers heard a voice singing "whose smoothness and interiority immediately arrested everyone's hearts." At the sound of her voice, the crowd demanded to know who the singer was. Edison came forth boasting of Jones, holding a wax phonographic cylinder with her name on it. After hearing her perform, President Cleveland's wife took the young singer under her wing and found her a proper music teacher. She wanted to see "if [the teacher] thought it was possible for a Negress to learn how to completely overcome the unpleasant, strange, and unmelodic guttural sound [*kehllaute*] of her speech and become a perfect singer."[52] The teacher graciously agreed to this supposedly difficult challenge and discovered that "the Negroes have the finest musical ear." Two months after working intensely with the teacher, Jones debuted at the White House to great applause. She was a sensation, a "Black Patti in the White House!" the article advertised. She had come to Berlin only to discover that an imposter had been imitating her. "She looks sharp against [such] a worthless competitor, an obscure singer who has also taken the name of Black Patti," the writer sneered.[53]

The story is fascinating for all of the details it incorrectly shares as facts—and for its racial depiction of Jones's musicking body. No evidence exists that suggests Jones worked on a farm in Kentucky, as the article states, or that she knew Edison. Most striking, the German print source describes her voice as guttural. In so doing, the German source (even if it had been placed there by an American or by Jones herself) asserted that Black voices were sonically different from white ones. The article's claim of racial difference confirms Nina Sun Eidsheim's finding that listeners located a "fundamental physiological difference" in Black voices dating back as far as 1891.[54] By concluding that Black people have "the finest musical ear," the article also reinforced the popular transatlantic idea that Black people were inherently more musical than others. Lastly, the article's appearance in print journalism indicates just how seriously Jones took Bishop's claim to be the real Black Patti. Jones's success (financially and musically) depended upon eradicating the threat of another Black female singer's popularity.

When Jones stepped onto the stage at the Wintergarten Varieté on February 19, 1895, people were ready to finally hear the "real" Black Patti, as headlines indicate.[55] Her concert program was typical for a white soprano prima donna in the nineteenth century: Charles Gounod's "Valse Arietta," two American art songs, most likely an Italian aria by Giuseppe Verdi such as "Sempre Libra" from *La Traviata* (a standard in her repertoire), and "The Last Rose of Summer."[56] Unlike Bishop, she did not sing any African American spirituals or other "Negro music." In fact, the only African American composer to ever appear in Jones's standard repertoire over the course of her career was Will Marion Cook, and she only performed his music after she had returned to the United States and began performing vaudeville. Jones's concert tour is a reminder that only in the early-to-mid-twentieth century did it become customary for African American classical singers to perform African American art songs (usually spirituals) as part of their concert repertoire. Singers such as Roland Hayes and Marian Anderson popularized arrangements by classically trained composers Harry Burleigh and Nathaniel Dett in the 1920s and 1930s.[57]

In numerous articles on Jones's performance, reviewers praised her bel canto, an Italian vocal style of the eighteenth and nineteenth centuries that emphasizes a singer's light tone and flexibility. They also applauded her musical ability and excellent delivery. "It is not only the dusky complexion that is real about her," a reporter for the *Das Kleine Journal* marveled, adding, "The clear, full-toned voice, a soprano with range of two octaves, has the true ring."[58] Jones demonstrated a strong technique and vocal prowess on the stage that proved why she was a well-regarded singer of operatic arias.

Yet in order to praise Jones, critics felt compelled to minimize her Blackness in their reviews, even while they claimed (in the language of color-blindness) that her talent was "quite independent of color or nationality."[59] For example, many reviews stated that Jones's name was a misnomer, for she was not actually Black. The critic for the *Post* declared Jones's stage name inaccurate: "only half the name fits, but fortunately the better half. 'Patti,' we may rightly call her, although we protest against the adjective 'Black.' . . . The only thing 'Black' about her is the beautiful shining hair."[60] He was grateful that the Black Patti he had encountered was more (white) Patti than Black. Many reviewers squirmed over the use of the word Black to describe Jones, calling it an offensive and rude term. A critic for the *Berliner Börsen-Courier* stated, "[The] adjective 'Black' seems to us unnecessarily impolite."[61] All of these reviews imply that the characteristics and qualities of Blackness were somehow offensive in themselves. Their statements, and countless others, suggested that Jones's visual Blackness was better when minimized. Nana Badenberg writes, "The notion that white is to be understood as positive and Black as negative can be assumed to have come only from the perspective of a European, a light-skinned culture, even if it is not explicitly stated."[62] Blackness was deemed neither beautiful nor worthy of celebration to these critics; rather, it was something to be ignored if it could not be excised.

One way that music critics worked around Jones's Blackness was by making her biracial, stating that "only her full lips and the delicate brown tint of her complexion betray her mulatto blood."[63] A critic for the *Berliner Börsen-Courier* stated, "Miss Jones is evidently of Negro blood, but not alone of

Negro blood. She is a mulatto of bronzed complexion and pleasant expressive features, with full lips and high forehead and the bearing of a lady, even to the choice of her costume."[64] Skull shapes and sizes were critical forms of data collection within the emerging field of racial theory and anthropology.[65] Europeans and North Americans often assumed that Black people's lower foreheads (a myth) were physical evidence of their supposedly lower intellectual aptitude and ability. Describing Jones's "high forehead"—and coupling it with praise for her posture and dress—provided evidence to support the theory that she was mulatto, thus denying her the full extent of her Blackness in an effort to appease German audiences. As Kristin Moriah has observed, "In [Jones's] German reviews, an insistence on her lightness, or a denial of her darkness, seems analogous with praising her musical talent."[66] Her perceived white features therefore trumped any positive attributes her African forebears might have given her.

Critics also used chocolate to describe Jones and Bishop with high frequency. The *Berliner Morgen-Zeitung*, for example, called Jones an "imposing figure with a chocolate-colored tint."[67] Bishop, the "exotic singer" wasn't Black so much as "chocolate brown," according to the *Nationalzeitung*.[68] The *Berliner Börsen-Courier*'s critic mentioned Bishop's appearance to dismiss her moniker: "A twist: Miss Jenny Bishop actually has a chocolate-brown coloring," the critic writes, "and the epithet 'Black Patti' is therefore out of place."[69] Yet the association of chocolate with Blackness, Silke Hackenesch argues, "is not based on a vague similarity of some people's skin color to the color of an edible product. Instead, it is based on the imagination of 'dark people,' tropical places, and practices that produce chocolate." Advertisements and other products created a romanticized view of plantations in the New World and linked tropical fantasies of colonialism to the exploited racialized bodies that companies relied on for their colonial goods. "There is nothing 'natural' about the connection of certain brown and black products with the pigmentation of human beings," Hackenesch concludes.[70] Rather, the repetitive association of white Germans over time linked people of African descent to colonial commodities, steeped in discourses of exoticism and primitivism.

Many German music critics explained Jones's success by emphasizing the "naturalness" of her musicianship. These comments are a damning form of praise, for they imply that the singer's mastery was without thought or effortless, requiring no training or dedication. Reviewers from the *Norddeutsche Allgemeine Zeitung* and the *Kreuz-Zeitung* noted that the singer possessed "great natural gifts," which were revealed "in the easy, natural manner of her singing; there is no seeking for effect, only the endeavor to render music and text their true effect."[71] The critic in *Das Kleine Journal* also remarked that "the colored singer's voice has been well endowed by nature."[72] Their remarks on the "naturalness" of Jones's voice could have equally appeared in comments on the Fisk Jubilee Singers in the 1870s.

Jones returned to the United States armed with glowing reviews of her performance. With European accolades in tow, Jones garnered even greater audiences in the United States than she attracted prior to her trip. When asked upon her return to Berlin in 1895 by an American journalist if there was a difference in her reception by audiences in Europe and America, Jones responded: "Yes, a marked difference. In Europe there is no prejudice against my race. It matters not to them in what garb an artist come, so he be an artist . . . It is the artist['s] soul they look at there, not the color of his skin."[73] Jones's comment, like many other African Americans' statements about racism in Central Europe in the Kaiserreich, was more of an indictment against white American racism than it was a critical illustration of European racial terrain. Even if she never publicly stated it, German constructs of race nonetheless shaped their reception of her musical performances.

Debating Black Merit and Intelligence: Black Instrumentalists and German Music Criticism

Black instrumentalists posed a conundrum to German listeners. German-speaking Europe promoted the common misconception that instrumentalists were more serious, better trained, more intellectual, and more dedicated to high art than singers.[74] First espoused by German Romantics such as E. T. A. Hoffmann, this peculiarly German perspective insisted that instrumental music—symphonies, chamber music, piano sonatas, and the like—were more noble or pure musical genres than opera. German music critics also elevated instrumental music as a national treasure that showcased German intellectual and artistic superiority.

Central European musical discourse frequently denigrated Italian opera, and critics' assessments of singers denied these musicians recognition of their musical intelligence and rigorous classical training. Whereas instrumentalists could convey through their hard-won efforts a highly cultivated technique and musical intelligence, singers could only instinctively grasp the primitive and easily accomplished nature of singing and therefore could not necessarily commit themselves as thoroughly to a higher understanding of music.

This musical reasoning came to the foreground in discourses on music and virtuosity and it also took on racial meaning in reviews of Black musicians.

Black singers such as Jones and the Fisk Jubilee Singers received praise for the "naturalness" of their abilities and for qualities in their manner of performing that German audiences assumed they inherently possessed. But rarely did Black singers earn applause for their musical acuity.

Black instrumentalists, however, posed a different set of questions and challenges, since their decision to pursue instrumental music rather than vocal music supposedly revealed the seriousness of their purposes and their musical intelligence. Reviews of the Jiménez Trio, the Afro-Cuban violinist Claudio Brindis de Salas, and the African American pianist Hazel Harrison highlight how some German listeners used race as a category of analysis in their concert criticism. In different ways than with Black singers, German music critics confronted classical music's whiteness by virtue of assessing the technical abilities of Black instrumentalists.

The Jiménez Trio offer us the first example of how Black instrumentalists could be listened to on racial terms. Jiménez came to the Leipzig Conservatory of Music to study in 1853.[75] Thirteen years later, in 1869, Jiménez's two sons joined him in Leipzig to attend the same school. Nicasio studied the cello and his brother José Manuel "Lico" studied piano. Their jury exam recital programs and registration records in Leipzig illustrate the rigor of their training. Taking lessons with some of the most prominent teachers working in Germany at the time, including Moscheles, Reinecke, and Ferdinand David, they performed with Leipzig's Gewandhausorchester and joined small chamber groups.[76] The music that the Jiménez brothers chose to play, and the music that the Jiménez Trio as an ensemble later performed, was almost entirely German.

The *Musikalisches Wochenblatt* and *Neue Zeitschrift für Musik* both reported regularly on students' recitals (they were open to the public), and thus offered comments on the two brothers' student recitals in 1870 and 1871. Lico, the pianist, was pretty good. He had "good musical sense" and supportive technique. But Lico's cello-playing brother, Nicasio? He was stunning. The very first review of him, in the *Neue Zeitschrift für Musik*, states that he played the Georg Goltermann cello concerto "with a mastery that created general astonishment." The critic could not believe Nicasio's "beautiful, captivating tone, paired with his lyrical execution," nor could he offer enough vociferous praise for how Nicasio was able to "playfully overcome the most difficult double stops and the fastest passages" with a "purity and conviction in intonation." He had, in short, "all of the qualities of a splendid cello virtuoso."[77] Other reviews in the *Musikalisches Wochenblatt* confirmed the critic's account: keep an eye on this student, the reviews said, for his intonation, warm tone, and brilliant technique were the stuff of musical legend.[78]

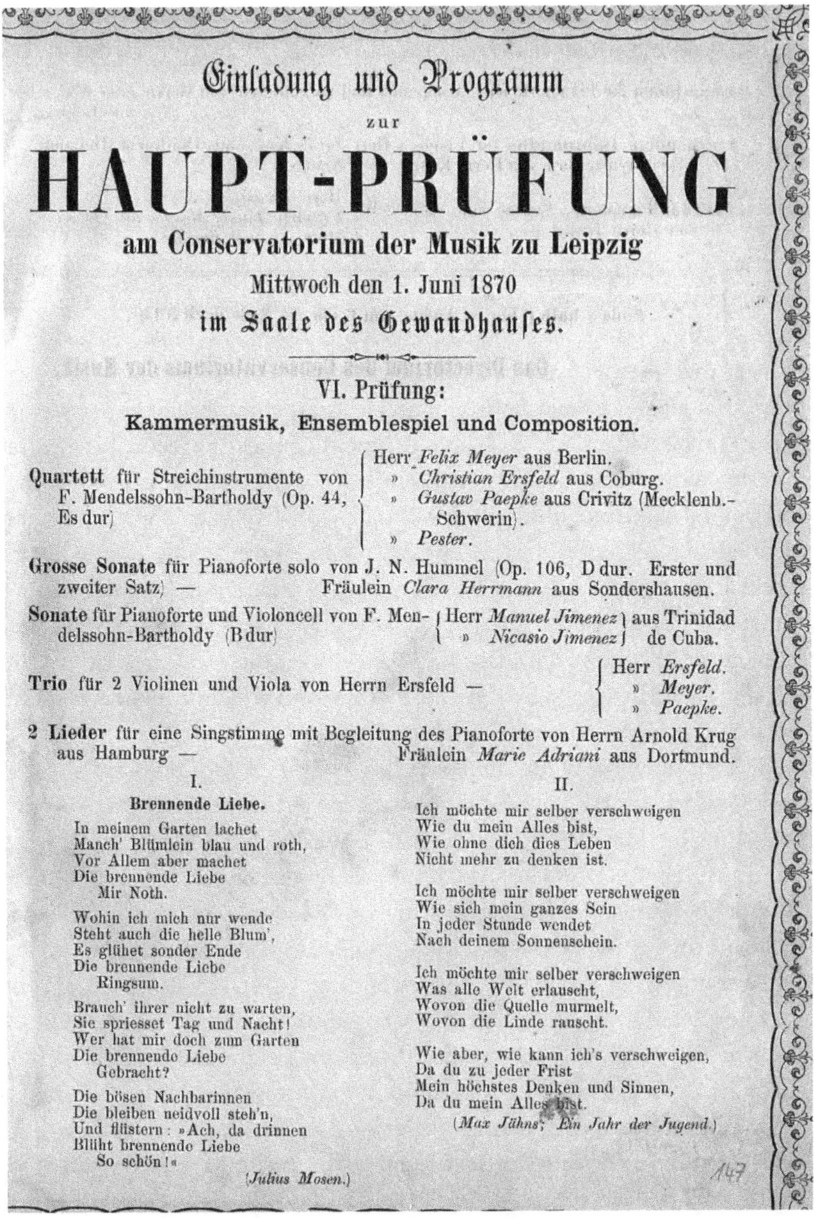

Einladung und Programm

zur

HAUPT-PRÜFUNG

am Conservatorium der Musik zu Leipzig

Mittwoch den 1. Juni 1870

im Saale des Gewandhaufes.

VI. Prüfung:

Kammermusik, Ensemblespiel und Composition.

Quartett für Streichinstrumente von F. Mendelssohn-Bartholdy (Op. 44, Es dur)

    Herr *Felix Meyer* aus Berlin.
    » *Christian Ersfeld* aus Coburg.
    » *Gustav Paepke* aus Crivitz (Mecklenb.-Schwerin).
    » *Pester.*

Grosse Sonate für Pianoforte solo von J. N. Hummel (Op. 106, D dur. Erster und zweiter Satz) — Fräulein *Clara Herrmann* aus Sondershausen.

Sonate für Pianoforte und Violoncell von F. Men- { Herr *Manuel Jimenez* } aus Trinidad delssohn-Bartholdy (B dur)   { » *Nicasio Jimenez* } de Cuba.

Trio für 2 Violinen und Viola von Herrn Ersfeld —
    Herr *Ersfeld.*
    » *Meyer.*
    » *Paepke.*

2 Lieder für eine Singstimme mit Begleitung des Pianoforte von Herrn Arnold Krug aus Hamburg — Fräulein *Marie Adriani* aus Dortmund.

I.

Brennende Liebe.

In meinem Garten lachet
Manch' Blümlein blau und roth,
Vor Allem aber machet
Die brennende Liebe
    Mir Noth.

Wohin ich mich nur wende
Steht auch die helle Blum',
Es glühet sonder Ende
Die brennende Liebe
    Ringsum.

Brauch' ihrer nicht zu warten,
Sie spriesset Tag und Nacht!
Wer hat mir doch zum Garten
Die brennende Liebe
    Gebracht?

Die bösen Nachbarinnen
Die bleiben neidvoll steh'n,
Und flüstern: »Ach, da drinnen
Blüht brennende Liebe
    So schön!«

(Julius Mosen.)

II.

Ich möchte mir selber verschweigen
Wie du mein Alles bist,
Wie ohne dich dies Leben
Nicht mehr zu denken ist.

Ich möchte mir selber verschweigen
Wie sich mein ganzes Sein
In jeder Stunde wendet
Nach deinem Sonnenschein.

Ich möchte mir selber verschweigen
Was alle Welt erlauscht,
Wovon die Quelle murmelt,
Wovon die Linde rauscht.

Wie aber, wie kann ich's verschweigen,
Da du zu jeder Frist
Mein höchstes Denken und Sinnen,
Da du mein Alles bist.

(Max Jähns, Ein Jahr der Jugend.)

147

FIGURE 10. A studio recital concert program for students at the Leipzig Conservatory of Music, dated June 1, 1870. Featured are the Afro-Cuban musicians Manuel [Lico] Jiménez (piano) and Nicasio Jiménez (cello), who performed Felix Mendelssohn's Cello Sonata in B-flat Major, op. 45. Courtesy of Hochschule für Musik und Theater "Felix Mendelssohn Bartholdy" Leipzig, Hochschulbibliothek/Archiv.

Between 1872 and 1875, the Jiménez family toured across Europe as the Jiménez Negertrio, performing in at least fifty-six different cities.[79] Outside of the confines of their familiar home of Leipzig, away from friends, teachers, and critics who knew them well, they faced a greater variety of responses to their musicianship. One vein of reviews applauded the players for performing works from the Austro-German canon (especially Liszt, Schumann, Mendelssohn, and Louis Spohr) with "noblesse" and artistry. Their training at the Leipzig Conservatory of Music was on full display for audiences to hear, and many applauded their musical choices and execution. The trio astounded audiences in Aachen in October 1875, for example, and the local critic's praise, reprinted in the *Neue Zeitschrift für Musik*, indicates just how moving the ensemble could be. Lico demonstrated his "technical mastery, musical intelligence, and sensible handling" of the music, and he knew how to restrain his passion in a measured manner to perfectly execute his musical phrases on the piano. Nicasio possessed "impeccable technique, a pithy tone, and tasteful execution of his phrases," and José gallantly led the trio through Mendelssohn with great understanding.[80] What the ensemble seemed to be especially known for was its intonation, even in different spaces and weather climates. They were comprised of a solidly good pianist with a better cellist (even negative reviews the ensemble received over the years stressed that the cellist was excellent), led by a violinist father who very much knew what he was doing and was in control of the ensemble.

Yet race nonetheless featured into the reviews of the trio. Critics found the appearance of the Jiménez Trio distracting at best or abhorrent at worst. One critic, for example, found the pianist Lico's "black fingers, hopping up and down [on the piano keys] . . . sufficiently grotesque."[81] In an 1873 review of the Jiménez Trio's performance of Schubert and Schumann lieder arrangements, music by Chopin, and Liszt's fantasy on Verdi's *Il Trovatore*, the reviewer noted, "At first glance, it may appear peculiar, almost comic, to hear the interpretation of works (besides Chopin) of German masters skillfully performed by Negroes."[82] Grotesque, strange, or bizarre, the Jiménez Trio did not look like classical musicians to these critics because they were Afro-Cuban.

One striking feature of concert reviews of the Jiménez Trio is their refusal to locate the trio's national identity in Cuba, the Caribbean, or even simply in the New World. Written in a style that smacked of the colonial civilizing mission, a short report in the *Musikalisches Wochenblatt* on the Jiménez brothers' student recitals simply called them "natives [*Eingeborene*] who have come to Leipzig to receive their artistic civilization."[83] Much like how converts were baptized or converted to Christianity, the Jiménez Trio, too, had come to Central Europe to receive the blessings of musical civilization.

Many reviews did not conceive of the ensemble as Afro-Cuban but rather as African. One critic for the *Neue Zeitschrift für Musik* stated that it had been "interesting" to watch "three sons of a wholly southern race of people render [music] in the spirit of Bach, Beethoven, and Chopin."[84] A critic for the *Musikalisches Wochenblatt* misidentified the group as Ethiopian, stating that "From a cultural-historical standpoint, it is certainly impressive for us to think that the Ethiopian race has already conquered German music."[85] Life in Germany would be turned on its head if, in the future, one could hear "Beethoven's Symphony no. 9 performed by court musicians of the Sultan of Wadai."[86] Although the passage drips with sardonic language, it nonetheless speculates about a world in which Africans had conquered German music. At first a fantasy, Fatima El-Tayeb argues, white German fears of Black people conquering Germany became a growing concern.[87]

What became implicit in reviews of the Jiménez Trio was that music critics tacitly understood classical music as a white genre of music—until the ensemble performed it. At one of Nicasio's student recitals in Leipzig, a critic commented that Nicasio's virtuosic cello-playing, beautiful intonation, and excellent bowing technique were so good that even "many of his white colleagues" were permitted to be jealous of him.[88] Nicasio played as well as—if not better than—a white student, thus demonstrating that classical music did not belong to white people.

While critics might have disagreed over some interpretive or technical aspects of the Jiménez Trio's performances, they nonetheless heard the performances as legitimate concerts of classical music. The flashy sonic acts of the violin virtuoso Brindis de Salas, on the other hand, were anything but. From the beginning of his career in Central Europe, Claudio José Domingo Brindis de Salas Garrido (or, simply, Brindis de Salas) caused waves of excitement with his outrageous playing style and bombastic personality. Settling in Germany in 1880 and residing there until 1900 when he moved to Buenos Aires, Argentina, Brindis de Salas became a mirror reflecting German conversations about Black masculine musicality in the Kaiserreich. Like the Jiménez Trio and others, he traveled with other Spanish-speaking musicians, with white Americans, with women, and with Central European Jews when he toured Germany.[89] He performed many difficult pieces, including Mendelssohn's Violin Concerto, Beethoven's Romance in F Major, Henryk Wieniawski's Polonaise, and a Niccolò Paganini violin concerto.

The manner in which dozens of newspapers in Germany reported on Brindis de Salas gives us a whiff of the sensational. He was, according to different reports, an African violinist, the son of a Negro colonial officer stationed in Madrid, a native-born Martiniquais, and the grandson of an African

Negro chieftain who had been sold into slavery and sent to Cuba. In the most patronizing version of the latter story, an African warrior chief died while en route to Havana, Cuba, and his son (Brindis de Salas's father) was placed in the house of a Cuban gentleman who loved him so much that he eventually granted him his freedom and provided him with an education. This particular biography perpetuates a violent myth of the "good slave owner" because it praises the supposed Cuban gentleman for his magnanimity instead of recognizing the horrors of slavery to which Europeans subjected Africans. What seems to be clear from these different reports, however, is that from a young age, Brindis de Salas exhibited "the makings of such an excellent musician that his father had to send him to the Paris Conservatory."[90] He trained with the violinists Charles Dancla and Hubert Léonard in Paris, he was supposedly the last student of Ferdinand David, and he earned accolades from the kings of Spain, Portugal, France, and Germany.[91]

It is still unclear what about his legacy is verifiable. Sometimes called the "Black Paganini," Brindis de Salas was, according to different reports, given the French Legion of Honour, made a baron by Kaiser Wilhelm II, and married to a German noblewoman. "He was covered with orders," the violinist Ovide Musin gossiped later in his 1920s memoir, "and when the old Emperor William of Germany gave a dinner at the palace to which de Salas was invited, and on his being presented to the Emperor, the latter exclaimed: 'He is more decorated than I am.'"[92] It is true that different newspapers called him a "Chevalier" by 1882, which implies that he had most likely received some honors or awards.

One example of Brindis de Salas's musical activity that illustrates his unique musicianship is his frequent performance of the Austrian violinist and composer Heinrich Wilhelm Ernst's showstopping Othello Fantasy as the concluding piece on his concert program. The fantasy is a medley that takes musical excerpts from acts 1 and 3 of Gioachino Rossini's opera Othello. Full of tricky double, triple, and quadruple stops, harmonics, and difficult bowing, it is not a work for the faint of heart.[93] Playing the piece in tune is an Olympian feat, especially since some passages require the violinist to move quickly back and forth from a triple stop on the bottom register of the violin to the absolute top of the register. Ernst had earned a reputation as the heir to the infamous violinist Paganini, whose musical compositions stunned (and enraged) audiences in Europe for their extreme technical difficulties.

In playing this musical work, Brindis de Salas demonstrated that he also followed in the same tradition as other virtuosic violinists. Yet picking a work on the theme of Shakespeare's Othello might also suggest an awareness of his own Black masculinity. He might have chosen it to capitalize on how audiences perceived him. Or it might have been a defiant gesture, a wink, or a nod. The figure of Othello, after all, was well known in European cultural productions in the mid-to-late-nineteenth century through performances of the character by Ira Aldridge, the African American Shakespearean actor. It might have been one of the most recognizable and potentially uplifting symbols of Black masculinity during Brindis de Salas's European career.

But were Brindis de Salas's musical performances any good? "Claptrap," the *Musical Times* called his playing in Darmstadt in April 1885. Pure "claptrap." The reviewer uttered one of the most damning statements one could proffer of a musician in the nineteenth century: "He is a virtuoso rather than an artist." The reviewer complained, "The tone he produces from his instrument is devoid of power, yet his technical abilities are truly marvelous."[94] Brindis de Salas seemed to represent everything reprehensible about the world of virtuosic performance in the nineteenth century.[95] A critic for the *Allgemeine Musikalische Zeitung* registered his complaints in the opposite direction. Brindis's technique was atrocious. "Not only notes but whole bars" were razed by Brindis de Salas's haggard playing during his performance of Paganini's Violin Concerto, and the audience had been forced to endure his plodding the whole night. "Mr. Brindis should keep his fingers away from Beethoven," the reviewer condemned. "He doesn't understand him."[96]

The most dismissive critics brought race to the center of their analysis: the only reason why audiences had been enthralled with Brindis de Salas was because he was Black. Right after declaring Brindis de Salas unfit to perform the music of Beethoven, the reviewer homed in on why there had been such an overwhelming commotion for him at the recital. "Understandably the applause was monstrous," the reviewer dismissed, "because it's not every day that one sees a Moor play the violin."[97] It is remarkable, a reviewer for the *Musikalisches Wochenblatt* wrote, that Brindis de Salas had drummed up such a furor in the city of Berlin unlike anything the reviewer had seen in some time, because he was not very good. "The great excitement for Brindis de Salas," the author concludes, had more to do with "appearance than with accomplishments."[98] In Vienna, a similar remark: it was only because of his "interesting dark skin color" that the "Negro violinist" had won over his audiences. "Today," the writer scorns, "there are dozens of violin virtuosos at the same midlevel position in their technique and intonation."[99]

Above all, critics enjoyed describing Brindis's Blackness. Daniel Jütte argues, "Brindis virtually dropped—to use an image from Heinrich Hoffmann's children's book *Der Struwwelpeter*—into an inkpot of the journal and came out blacker than he'd ever been."[100] The *Heidelberger Zeitung* called him "a real full-blooded Negro" and several other concert reviews contrasted his dark skin color against the whiteness of his fellow performers (one critic called him the direct "antipode" to his fellow performer, the noted Spanish violinist Pablo de Sarasate).[101]

Others instead saw Brindis de Salas as mixed race, but with dominant African features. A critic for the *Stuttgarter Neues Tagblatt* came to the conclusion that Brindis "is not solely of Negro blood, for his mother belonged to a mixed race, while his retreating forehead, wooly hair, bulging lips are a wholly unmistakable Negro-type inherited from his father."[102] The reviewer's 1882 article indicates how much stereotypes of Black bodies—wooly hair, big lips—had entered German musical culture and had been influenced by scientific racism. Jones was able to escape her Blackness by virtue of her supposedly high forehead; Brindis appeared in music criticism as a caricature of a grotesque Black man.

Not everyone, of course, spoke of Brindis de Salas in such dismissive and scathing tones. Some defended him. They admired his "exceptionally gifted artistic nature," his "clean and beautiful" tone, elegant bowing, and solid technique.[103] Yet even those who sought to defend Brindis de Salas did so on racial grounds. His style and manner of playing, they argued, "are proof that the highest musical talent can be found also in the Black race and that the bounds of cultivation are not so narrowly drawn as people commonly accept."[104]

How much Brindis de Salas's musicianship could be attributed to his race became another point of contention. Some critics painted his and other Black instrumentalists' playing style as somehow ineluctably Black. A German music critic described Joseph White, for example, as "an entirely Black violinist . . . in whose playing lives the entire fervor of a still untapped natural peoples."[105] Decades later, the Black German oboist and conductor Gustav Sabac el Cher received similar criticism when a writer for the *Deutsche Zeitung* complained that "in his conducting he cannot escape the distinctively nigger style of dance movement."[106] In his memoir, Ovide Musin remembers discussing Brindis de Salas's style of playing with his music teacher, Léonard. When Musin asked Léonard why he allowed Brindis de Salas to play differently, Léonard supposedly replied, "He plays like a Negro—the difference in nature; if he were to play as you do, it would not make any impression."[107] Musin and possibly Léonard believed that Brindis de Salas's playing style was a natural, instinctive, and inherent expression of his Blackness.

Yet other critics heard nothing Black in Brindis de Salas's performances. For example, the same Stuttgart critic who loved Joseph White for "sounding Black" on the violin was disappointed to discover that Brindis de Salas offered nothing inherently Black in his musical style. His playing was good, the critic wrote, but "remarkably, we discovered straight away [that there was] very little in his playing that we understood to be of his race."[108] The question of whether Blackness could be located in instrumental music is strikingly similar to German debates about the supposedly different nature of Black singers' voices. Both discourses turned to biological racism to delineate sonic racial difference in Black musicality of whatever kind, vocal or instrumental.

German racial constructions of Black instrumentalists reached an apex in concert critics' responses to Hazel Harrison in 1904, the first Black woman (and most likely first Black musician) to perform as a solo instrumentalist with the Berlin Philharmonic. Their reviews of her performance indicate how much listeners had come to rely on race to understand Black performances of classical music. A student of Ferruccio Busoni and Egon Petri, Harrison offered much of the usual fanfare required of a professional pianist at the time. Her May 1904 concert program, for example, reveals that she played six Chopin etudes, Schumann's Piano Sonata in G Minor, and a Bach Prelude and Fugue before concluding the evening with two pieces: Moritz Moszkowski's fiery *Caprice Espagnol* and an arrangement of Johann Strauss, Jr.'s, waltz *Tales from the Vienna Woods*.[109]

Harrison's accomplishments won her an opportunity to perform with the Berlin Philharmonic on October 22, 1904, making her the first Black woman to perform with the ensemble. She played Chopin's Piano Concerto in E Minor and Edvard Grieg's Piano Concerto in A Minor. Only a few reviews of Harrison exist. Many newspapers simply chose to ignore her performance. The reviews of Harrison that do exist focus on both her race and her gender as significant musical problems that she had to overcome in order to perform the music of white male composers.

Gendered language runs through music criticism of Harrison. Since at least the early nineteenth century, European music critics gendered instrumental music's repertoire, arguing that "stereotypically masculine qualities of athletic bravura, interpretative and physical power, and showmanship" were requirements to perform much of it.[110] In the estimation of many (male) critics, very few female pianists could rise above their gender to properly execute and interpret classical music. For example, in the case of the pianist Clara Schumann, Alexander Stefaniak writes, critics argued that she was able to perform her husband's music so well because she could "make her own subjectivity recede, projecting only the male composer's work."[111] It was necessary to male critics, in other words, for women pianists to overcome their gender in order to give convincing musical performances.

Harrison apparently failed this challenge. Some critics praised her technique, calling it "smooth and fluid."[112] "She plays with clean, accurate technique and a delightful touch," a Berlin reviewer writes, "and her reading revealed a true musical nature."[113] However, most listeners seemed to think she lacked the rigor to see the whole concerto through, and one critic suggested that her "careless use of pedal" destroyed the piece's clarity.[114] Walther Pauli complained that "her performance was flat and expressionless" because she lacked physical power.[115] Although it is impossible to gauge the veracity of these comments, they nonetheless suggest a gendered viewing of Harrison's musicianship by implying that Harrison lacked (masculine) robust properties to properly execute a rigorous concert program.

Not only did critics discuss Harrison in a gendered manner but they also picked apart her racial appearance. As with reviews of the Fisk Jubilee Singers, Brindis de Salas, and the Black Pattis in Berlin, German critics debated the use of the term Black to describe Harrison. Most reviews did not call her Black or a Negro at all, but concluded that Harrison was biracial. "This is the first time a colored girl has ever played in Berlin," observed one critic, "and the first time I've ever heard a mulatto in a serious composition in public."[116] As a supposedly mixed-race woman, these reviews state, Harrison offered listeners something exciting and new in classical music, overturning their assumption that most Black musicians belonged to the realm of minstrelsy or vaudeville.

Her race was also used to explain the qualities of her performance. For example, one critic concluded that Harrison was able to convey the "beautiful melancholy of Chopin," because "melancholy is a characteristic of the young woman's race."[117] In so doing, the critic attributed her performance not to her talent, hard work, or musical intellect, but to a quality perceived to be inherent in African Americans. Harrison had nothing to do with her own musical accomplishments.

This same reviewer's praise of Harrison also relied on white supremacist ideas of Black primitivism to assess its merits. The critic states that her performance was remarkable because "the colored race has thus far done nothing worth mentioning in music."[118] His comments thus reinforced the Hegelian notion that Black people stood outside histories of intellectual, cultural, and technological progress. Michelle Wright rightly points out that these formulations were always paradoxes: "[Black people's existence] is constantly denied any role of importance, and yet its implied inferiority is the crux of Europeans' arguments for their ostensibly self-evident superiority."[119] In other words, upholding assumptions of Black primitivism was necessary for European critics such as Harrison's to maintain the white supremacist ideology that German musical culture was superior.

FIGURE 11.   A portrait photo of the African American pianist Hazel Harrison, undated. Atlanta University Photographs, Atlanta University Center, Robert W. Woodruff Library.

The critic also attributed any Black success to white help. "Our best Negro songs are not the product of the Black race, but of that white genius, Stephen C. Foster, and a freak like Blind Tom [Thomas Wiggins] does not count, because he is not a musical nature, but simply a marvelous imitator," the critic continued. White intelligence and white cultivation were behind any Black accomplishments. Black people could not create, only imitate. Yet Harrison's performance indicated to this critic that perhaps Black people were almost ready to enter the realm of high art. Like reviews of the Fisk Jubilee Singers, Harrison's performance represented the potential Black people possessed to overcome their supposed cultural backwardness and enter into Western civilization. Rarely, however, did Black musicians ever seem to meet that goal. Yet for those who understood Black musicianship as this critic did, Harrison symbolized the potential successes of racial uplift, achieved only through white intervention and musical schooling that allowed her to rise above her race's musical inadequacies.

The critic concludes his review by reformulating the question of whether nature or culture was responsible for Harrison's musical performance. Is Harrison "a musical prophet arisen among the colored race, like Booker T. Washington, to show by her example what others can do if they will try," he asked, "or is it the Caucasian blood in her veins that is doing the work, for she is not a full blooded Negress?"[120] In other words: was Harrison successful in the concert hall because of her cultural upbringing or because of some inherently perceived whiteness?

Both theories are deeply flawed. First, the writer's supposition that Black musical success was (potentially) attainable through hard work negates the fact that Black musicians had been performing serious concert music in Germany since at least the 1870s—and it ignores the history of earlier generations of Black musicians such as George Bridgetower, a Black violinist and composer who was one of Beethoven's contemporaries and friends in the early nineteenth century. It also dismisses any African American musical achievement in the United States and Europe prior to Harrison's performance as meaningless or a byproduct of Black laziness.

Second, the reviewer's alternate theory that Harrison's performance succeeded because of the "Caucasian blood in her veins that is doing the work" reinforces white supremacy and biological racism. In this formulation, Harrison simply had to have been born mixed race in order to successfully perform this music. The critic's comment extols a different kind of "one drop rule" than the one that plagued American racism. If "one drop" of African ancestry made a man or woman ineluctably Black in the United States, the critic in this case suggests that Harrison's theoretical "one drop" of whiteness rescues her from Blackness' lamentable musical inferiority. Moreover, the critic revises the transatlantic trope that Black people have a "natural" musical ability by instead insisting that, for classical music, Blackness was not enough to interpret the sophisticated works of the "great masters." Whiteness was, in this estimation, a necessary qualification to perform classical music.

What is especially striking about these comments is that they appeared during an era in which growing fears of miscegenation became more pronounced in German society. In German colonial South West Africa, for example, the administration enforced a strict one drop rule that relegated all children born of white German men and African women to the status of African "natives."[121] Unlike Harrison, they were not protected by their white blood. Indeed, El-Tayeb writes, "'mixing' between the Black and white race was condemned as 'unnatural' and disastrous not only for the offspring itself, but for all mankind."[122] Yet reviews of Harrison, Jones, and the Fisk Jubilee Singers suggest that white ancestry was responsible for "rescuing" these Black musicians from themselves.

While scholarship has focused heavily on constructs of race in discourses of the voice, instrumentalists have often escaped our historical analyses. Yet reviews of Black instrumentalists in the nineteenth and early twentieth centuries also illustrate how listeners perceived of racial difference in instrumental concerts. Many of the same racial practices found in white German music criticism of Black singers such as the Fisk Jubilee Singers or Jones also worked their way into a performance of something as supposedly benign as a cello sonata or a Grieg piano concerto. In no genre or repertoire of music were Black musicians able to escape white music critics' evaluations of them in ways that did not reinforce anti-Black assumptions of racial difference. Their perceived Blackness—or invisible whiteness—could always be attributable to their musical performances, for good or for ill.

Black Belonging, White Silence, and Racial Synesthesia

In 1909, five years after Harrison's debut with the Berlin Philharmonic, a stormy colonial debate reached parliament about a Black musician named Gustav Sabac el Cher—the son of an African man and a German woman who had joined the Prussian military and served as bandleader. Eduard von Liebert, a member of parliament and the former governor of German East Africa, brought to parliament's attention a shocking fact: Black musicians were currently serving in the German military.[123] "It has come to my attention—and I wish it weren't so," von Liebert lamented, "that a Prussian cavalier regiment has a Negro for a drummer and a Prussian infantry regiment has a Negro for—I don't know, for a Kapellmeister or a drumming major." If Black musicians were indeed part of the German military, then their presence would be an egregious transgression because the commanders would then have "absolutely no racial feeling and absolutely no racial pride."[124] Von Liebert charged, "I would like to see a Briton or an American subordinated to a colored man—this is unthinkable! It would end in rebellion and mutiny."[125] He concluded, "We know too well the good and the bad sides of the Ethiopian race and they should not be permitted to be placed above or near our own soldiers."[126]

Gustav Sabac el Cher, born and raised in Berlin and a former student at the Royal Academy of Musical Performing Arts in Berlin, had actually sued and won against a newspaper the year before for proliferating such slander.[127] But Von Liebert's comments only a year later demonstrate the terrible growing power of white German definitions of Blackness, whiteness, and Germanness in music. Von Liebert denies any possibility that Black musicians such as Sabac el Cher—who had German citizenship—could ever be considered German. Much like concert reviews of Black performers, many of which dismissed any lurking assumption that Blackness and Germanness could combine, von Liebert's remarks make it clear that a Black person had no business in German settings.[128]

German reception of Black classical musicians, appearing intermittently from the 1870s through the 1910s, illustrates that constructs of Blackness, whiteness, Germanness, and music were not peripheral to German musical culture in the nineteenth century but rather very much at its center. Listeners heard the music of the great masters in a racial key and dictated their interpretations of Black performers accordingly. Racially unmarked for so long, classical music became an audible signifier of a white, European culture (against a supposedly primitive, non-European one) only when listeners were forced to think about classical music's racial alternatives.

The legacies of German concert criticism in this regard have been profound. First, the presentation of Black classical musicians as a strange but temporary phenomenon, outside the bounds of the world of German music, ensured that their performances would not survive in established narratives of German music history. The German press's refusal to comment on Harrison is an especially informative case study. Their silence implies that they considered Harrison's performance to be nothing more than a fleeting moment, unworthy of commemoration. In refusing to create a written record of her performance, newspaper editors and writers ensured that such performances would be forgotten in Germany once they left living memory. Figures such as the Jiménez Trio and Harrison have become ghosts to us, even though they had strong relationships to institutional figures (Wagner) and musical institutions (Berlin Philharmonic). Art music's Black musical past was never public because it was never meant to be public. Always marginalized or treated as anomalies, Black classical musicians' experiences in

Central Europe are a historical lesson in the conjoined forces of racism and nationalism in Central European music.

Second, German concert criticism suggests in general the power of synesthesia. The aesthetic pleasure that a listener derived from a sonic encounter had to be explained in visual terms. The defined or well-articulated relationship between sight and sound was of course something that already existed in German musical culture. As Nicholas Cook argues, in their quest for "pure music" listeners tried to divorce sight from sound by the mid-nineteenth century, darkening concert halls in order to supposedly hear sounds better. Such activity, he warns, "is always an indicator that ideology is at work."[129] The notion that what listeners saw could determine what they heard, I argue, took on a racial dimension in the nineteenth century as audiences made sense of perceived visual differences embodied by Black performers. This relationship between sight and sound, so often relegated to the realm of "Black music," greatly affected classical music as well.

Relatedly, wittingly or unwittingly, Central European audiences practiced a form of colorism in their reception of Black performers. Sometimes they attended a performance because they wanted to see a performer who was "fully Black." Other times, they praised a Black musician such as Jones or Harrison for their bronze or "chocolate brown" appearance. In reality, what audiences saw in front of them was more varied or mixed than they had anticipated. Yet frequently German music criticism indicates a hierarchy of Blackness that worked in close proximity to the performer's perceived whiteness (or lack thereof). Hence, a concert critic could believe that because Harrison appeared biracial, she was able to perform classical music. Sight and sound worked in tandem in nefarious ways.

Third, the rhetoric of the civilizing mission ideology, of saving Black people from themselves through classical music, meant that audiences found it difficult to acknowledge Black merit independent of white magnanimity. Brindis de Salas's family was "saved" by white Spanish plantation owners, Jones was plucked from obscurity by Edison, and even Harrison's redeeming virtues as a performer could be explained by her perceived white ancestry.

In sum, Black musicians' performances of classical music in the nineteenth century were not free from the politics of race. German musical culture did not abstain from the transatlantic project of anti-Black racism. Classical musicians and critics in Central Europe formed their own definitions of Blackness in relation to music, even as they applauded Black performers for appearing on their stages.

PART II

1918–1945

CHAPTER 4

Blackness and Classical Music in the Age of the Black Horror on the Rhine Campaign

Even before Roland Hayes stepped onto the stage in the Konzerthaus Berlin's Ludwig van Beethoven Hall in May of 1924, Berlin residents had already begun to express their outrage. Prior to his arrival that night, some Germans had protested his appearance in front of the American Embassy and called for his concert's cancellation. In fiery letters to German newspapers, they argued that his presence onstage would remind Germans of the "Black Horror on the Rhine," a derogatory term referring to the stationing of French colonial troops from North and West Africa in the occupied Rhine region of Germany after WWI. Numbering approximately eighty-five thousand at their height between 1920 and 1921, the soldiers drew the ire of contemporary white German men and women, who spread racist, highly sexualized, propagandistic images depicting Black men raping white women to denounce what they deemed to be a Black invasion on German soil.[1]

Because of German outrage, the American consul general warned the young Hayes, who was in Prague that summer studying German lieder, not to visit Germany until the Allied army occupation had withdrawn from the Rhine region. International newspapers picked up on the furor of Berlin locals and reported about the potential scandal his Liederabend posed. As a precaution, Hayes traveled to Berlin from Pilsen, Czechoslovakia, with a few Czech friends to make his arrival look less conspicuous. Once in the glittering capital, he discovered that he had not been banned from performing in the city and he arrived at the prestigious Beethovensaal the night of his performance with no difficulties.[2]

Nonetheless, when a visibly nervous Hayes arrived onstage to perform, he heard the sounds of booing and jeering from the audience. As parts of the crowd roared against the sight of him onstage, he began to softly sing the Schubert lullaby, "Du bist die Ruh." His performance quietly won over the audience, and, according to multiple reports, the crowd's roar quieted to a still silence. After the last notes of Schubert's lied had floated through the concert hall, the audience burst into applause. By the end of the evening, the Konzerthaus boomed with boisterous praise for this African American tenor from rural Georgia.

Hayes's story that May of 1924 encapsulates so many of the changes that shaped Black classical musicians' performances in the interwar era and how audiences listened to them. Prior to WWI and the collapse of the Habsburg and German empires, Black classical musicians were an exotic sight in Central Europe but not necessarily a threatening one. If anything, their performances were sonic spectacles signifying a changing global terrain during the first era of mass entertainment. Not anymore. Following the destruction caused by WWI and the high rise of inflation that debilitated the economies of a greatly reduced postcolonial Germany and a newly formed postimperial Austria, audiences in German-speaking Europe began to treat Black classical musicians as a threat to Austro-German culture.

What is important to understand is that constructs of Blackness had not, in actuality, changed that drastically in the period after WWI. In fact, there was more overlap in cultural discourses of Blackness between the late nineteenth century and the interwar era than scholars have thus far assumed or discussed. From the 1880s through the 1920s, scientists, scholars, and artists consistently assumed that Black cultures were inherently more primitive than European high culture, and mass culture and visual culture depicted them as such. German and Austrian audiences frequently relied on the same racist notions of Black bodies, sounds, and cultures, steeped in colonialist and white supremacist ideologies, to interpret the Black performances they were witnessing. Black American popular culture, now in the form of jazz instead of the cakewalk, was still to German minds a tantalizing, exotic product made by outsiders and consumed by a white audience that cultural critics frequently denounced as wild and reckless. Moreover, listeners continued to assume that Blackness and Germanness were two separate and even incompatible markers of identity, even when performances muddled them together sonically. In the same vein, listeners continued to racialize classical music itself as white. Continuities abound, then, in how audiences understood Black bodies and Black cultures between the late nineteenth and early- to mid-twentieth centuries.

Although attitudes might not have changed that much, the consequences of listening to a Black performer had altered considerably. Against the backdrop of the stationing of French colonial troops and the Black Horror propaganda campaign that followed, Black classical musicians arriving in Germany found themselves in an economic climate of both unimaginable riches and extreme poverty. Their dynamic careers in Germany and Austria represented to a large array of listeners both the immense new opportunities and tragic pitfalls of their transatlantic age. Embodied in their performances was a variety of new experiences and realities with which audiences were forced to contend. Black classical musicians and their listeners were part of an ever-moving kaleidoscope of social, economic, and political changes that shaped Austro-German musical culture. They represented what Moritz Föllmer calls the "multiple modernities" that were able to coexist in the interwar era.[3] Indeed, this multiplicity was part of what defined interwar Central Europe.

The constantly changing statuses of Black musicians as symbols of success and opportunity on the one hand and racial degeneracy and anxiety on the other fit neatly into Central Europe's constantly changing cultural topography after WWI. "The Weimar Republic," Peter Fritzsche argues, "remains compelling not because of the glimpses of social democracy and social welfare it offers, but because its public life was formed so forcefully by the sense that nothing was certain and everything was possible."[4] With the instability of Weimar Germany, in other words, also came opportunity.[5]

Building on the scholarship of cultural historians of interwar Central Europe, I argue in this chapter that out of the economic, social, cultural, and political instability of interwar Central Europe emerged two distinct historical realities: first, that African American classical performers had never had so many opportunities to perform in German-speaking Europe. While many white German and Austrian musicians could only attract half-filled halls, African American concert singers routinely offered sold-out performances.[6] Because of the relatively low cost of living in Central Europe, the newly emergent social networks of Black performers, their heightened new cultural status as Americans, and the benefaction of a powerful white patronage network comprised of wealthy aristocrats who advocated for their careers, Black musicians became international superstars in a manner that was frankly impossible before WWI. But Central Europe's instability also meant that Black classical performers had never before experienced so much vitriol or so many threats of violence. The new reality of Black bodies in some of the most elite musical spaces now represented to some everything that was wrong with the new postimperial states of Germany and Austria.

Hayes's Liederabend in Berlin demonstrates how both historical realities functioned at the same time and in the same space. He had arrived on the stage in Berlin in part because of the support of white Central European teachers, patrons, and friends, some of whom quite literally drove him across the border to ensure his safe arrival in Germany. He had spent the previous twelve months studying the German lied in Vienna and Prague because of both a Black network of singers and a white patronage system that had connected him to the proper teachers for his voice type and repertoire. Hayes then used his connections and financial advantages to perform in an elite German musical space previously unavailable to Black musicians. Yet his debut was mired in the violent politics of anti-Blackness that increasingly dominated German musical culture. For the first time—and not the last—German-speaking audiences interpreted a Black musician's performances of German music as a threat to the German nation.

The fact that such provocative racial performances occurred in the world of classical music contradicts popular perceptions of interwar jazz-age Europe and its associations with the avant-garde.[7] Yet, Karl Christian Führer warns, "Our understanding of Weimar culture is incomplete without a grasp of broader patterns of cultural production and consumption, and skewed if it does not take into account the conservative tastes and the forces of tradition which also characterized it."[8] In his book *The Rest Is Noise*, Alex Ross makes a similar point, arguing that "the automatic equation of radical [musical] style with liberal politics and of conservative style with reactionary politics is a historical myth that does little justice to an agonizingly ambiguous historical reality."[9] Historians have frequently relied on the same narrative device to analyze the history of the Weimar Republic: the notion on the one hand that the political sphere was always reactionary, antidemocratic, and lurching from crisis to crisis, and the belief on the other that Weimar culture was a vibrant site of experimentation and liberalism. In so doing, Jochen Hung writes, their scholarship reinforces "the narrative of cultural experimentalism against the backdrop of democratic breakdown."[10]

Such is the case of Black performances of supposedly bourgeois, static, and—perhaps to some—boring classical music from the Austro-German canon in the 1920s and 1930s. Instead of finding reactionary and culturally stuffy politics in the world of classical music and liberalism and progressivism solely in jazz or avant-garde music, we see a wide variety of responses to Black classical musicians across many different political perspectives and social positions. Black classical musicians garnered support from well-known leftist activists, including high-ranking members of international communist parties, but they also drew praise and unending support from aristocrats, conservative newspaper columnists, and bourgeois listeners. And Black classical musicians could also face hostility from these different audiences as well.

If anything, Black performances of Schubert and other composers illustrate that the Austro-German canon was an especially potent powder keg in the transatlantic twenties, precisely because of its institutional history, claims to national identity, and performative promises of transformation. German and Austrian state funding of musical affairs frequently reinforced the notion that they were "nations of culture" (Kulturnationen) whose responsibility was to provide for the cultural needs of their citizens.[11] One would not expect an economically destitute German state, in the aftermath of a destructive, years-long war, to immediately start providing financial support to over thirty opera houses.[12] Yet the fact that state regimes financed orchestras, opera houses, and concert halls in the name of national unity is an illustration of how much classical music reigned over cultural life in the interwar years. Black musicians' entry into the world of classical music in Germany and Austria made the relationships between politics and culture, race and national identity, and music and locus even more potentially explosive.

This chapter examines the arrival and treatment of Black classical musicians in Central Europe from the mid-1920s until the mid-1930s, focusing on how Black musicians created opportunities for themselves in spite of constantly shifting political terrain. They faced some of the most hateful tropes and rhetoric in Central European history, which I discuss below. Yet they also formed some of the most powerful networks and allies to launch their careers, even after Hitler came to power in 1933. Instead of performing in Germany, Black musicians increasingly used their networks to live and perform in Austria, slowly migrating southward by 1932. The social and cultural consequences of anti-Black racism, however, continued to mire Black musicians' live performances and careers. Their profound economic successes and their volatile audiences, both hostile and adoring, were two sides of the same coin in interwar Central Europe.

Black Horrors, Jonnys, and Josephines: Tropes of Anti-Blackness in Central Europe

The title of Ivan Goll's 1926 article—"The Negroes Are Conquering Europe"— says it all: during the interwar era, Black musicians had begun to pour into Central Europe from the Caribbean, North America, and Africa in unprecedented numbers.[13] In comparison to the Kaiserreich, Weimar Berlin and

Red Vienna had become hotbeds, some denounced, of Black popular entertainment. Popular shows such as the Chocolate Kiddies, La revue negre, and
Black People Revue sold out quickly in both capitals, and Black entertainers brought to German audiences new dance crazes such as the Charleston,
the Shimmy, and the Foxtrot.[14] Reflecting on his experience in Berlin in the
1920s, the African American journalist Roi Ottley guessed that there might
have been approximately three thousand Black people in Germany in the
1920s.[15] That does not, of course, include groups or performers who only
passed through Central Europe to tour, such as the Hampton Singers or
the Fisk Jubilee Singers, who traveled to Germany in the 1920s. Yet Goll's
headline also reflected growing anxiety over what Germans and Austrians
perceived to be an ever greater presence of people of African descent on
Central European soil.

What Black classical musicians faced in the interwar era that had not been
part of Black experiences before WWI was a new and even violent antagonism toward their performances. With the so-called boom in Black bodies
and cultures in German-speaking Europe after WWI caused by the stationing of Black troops on German soil and by the "jazz invasion" of Black diasporic musicians, many German-speaking nationalists became alarmed that
there were more Black people in Europe than ever before. They argued that
Black people, whether they were entertainers such as Josephine Baker or
African migrants working in the docks, were invading and destroying German culture. Jonathan Wipplinger argues, "It is important to think through
how discussions of the Black presence in the occupation zone functioned in
the context of Berlin's modernist interest in Blackness and American popular
culture."[16] The fact that Black performers began to travel through Central
Europe during the same time span as the Black Horror propaganda campaign and its aftermath is worth noting. Central European discourses of anti-
Blackness took on an air of anxiety as politicians and citizens alike decreed
that Black people threatened to destroy white Europe, whether through acts
of sexual violence, racial mixture, or cultural hybridity.

In newspapers, private correspondence, and public speeches, German and
Austrian citizens and politicians repeatedly invoked three symbols of the imagined racial and sexual threat posed by Black people to explain why they were
protesting against or advocating for Black classical musicians in the interwar
era: the Black Horror on the Rhine, the "Jonny" figure from Ernst Krenek's
1927 opera, *Jonny spielt auf*, and Josephine Baker. There were, of course,
other Black tropes and figures in Germany and Austria during the transatlantic twenties. The Chocolate Kiddies, the first Black troupe to tour Central Europe after WWI, drew impressive crowds to their shows, and Black

entertainers such as Ruth Bayton earned almost $200,000 a year in Berlin, according to gossip in newspapers. But nonetheless, stereotypes of the Black Horror, Jonny, and Josephine took on lives of their own that lasted beyond their initial appearance. Audiences uttered these three particular tropes like curses in their denunciations of Black cultural labor—including Black classical musicians—and its supposedly harmful effects in German-speaking Europe.

The first striking example of how this supposed Black threat to German culture loomed over society in the interwar era was the Black Horror propaganda in the early 1920s. The Black Horror threat—and, more important, the cries of hysteria from white Germans about it—placed Blackness in a negative and threatening light. Coming from several countries and regions in Africa, including Algeria, Morocco, and Senegal, and stationed in the Rhineland area of Germany from 1919 to 1924, these French colonial troops originally went unnoticed in the German media during the first year of their occupation.[17] But by the early 1920s, the scandal of the "Black shame" ("Schwarze Schmach") had reached every corner of German society. Germans created organizations dedicated to protesting the presence of African troops. There was, above all, a sexualized nature to the Black Horror campaign, as propagandistic posters warned that Black male soldiers would take white German women against their will.[18] Sexually graphic images circulated in print and on coins depicting grotesque Black men on the verge of raping innocent white women. Often caricatured as anthropoids, Black troops appear animalistic in these images and unable to control their own desires.

At the heart of this campaign was a commitment to affirm a racially exclusive definition of the German nation as white. This nationalist and racist self-understanding can be traced back to the nineteenth century.[19] For decades, the historian Tina Campt argues, "Germanness [was] equated with purity and superiority, while racial mixture represented dangerous forms of impurity, pollution, and inferiority."[20] Under colonialism, scholars argue, the German body came to represent something pure, biological, and white that needed protecting from foreign (Black) elements. White German racial and sexual anxieties, located in their depiction of Black and white bodies, was part of a larger discourse that reached back to before WWI.

But the global nature of the war and its outcome on German society greatly changed the political nature of this conversation on racial miscegenation and cultural impurity. Prior to WWI, German debates about racial mixing occurred mostly in their African colonial territories or were focused on what was occurring in those territories. The question of whether children born of white German men and African women in the German colonies could claim German citizenship had become a subject of debate and eventually legislation. After WWI, however, German fears of Black people mixing with white Europeans had reached home. The German body was now under threat by the presence of Black soldiers on German soil and, just as important, by the offspring these soldiers produced. Campt writes, "Unlike the stereotypes that preceded it, the Rhineland Bastard is the first representation of a *domestic*, German-born Black 'native.'"[21] Because of the presence of African colonial soldiers in the Rhineland (which reminded white Germans of the economic, social, and political consequences of the war) and because of the growing fears stoked by racist German nationalists, the Black Horror campaign symbolized white Germans' first confrontation with Black claims to German soil and citizenship.

Ultimately, the Black Horror trope worked to foster an "us vs. them" dichotomy that depicted the civilized and cultured German at the mercy of the savage and primitive Black man. Letters to the editor, opinion pieces, and propagandistic pamphlets and speeches repeatedly expressed the sentiment that French colonial soldiers were a threat to Germans because they were unable to comingle with enlightened white Europeans. Their savagery and primitivism threatened to ruin, dilute, or degrade European civilization. Writing for the *Grenzland Korrespondent*, for example, one journalist argued, "The 'Black Horror' is not only a disgrace for Germany. It is much more. It represents the desecration of white culture in general."[22] The journalist thus linked Germanness to whiteness. "The reputation of the European culture is in danger," in other words, because "savages" were overseeing a cultured people.

Ironically, most of the Black troops had left the Rhine region by 1921. The only troops still stationed in Germany after 1921 were not Senegalese or from other regions of sub-Saharan Africa, but rather from the North African countries of Algeria and Morocco. And although the number of supporters in the propaganda campaign declined, Iris Wigger argues that "the stereotype of the 'Black shame' remained popular and present in German society."[23] But their real identities did not matter to perpetrators of the Black Horror propaganda, nor could they compete against the myth of the pitch-black African soldier.[24] The frightening image of a lurking Black man circulated widely, and the perceived threat of Black savagery infiltrating white European culture remained at large throughout the interwar period. The image of Black troops on the German Rhine became the symbol of dark savagery at its worst in post-WWI Germany. Propagandists optimized the troops' Blackness to create fear and panic among the populace in an attempt to mobilize citizens against this invasion of foreigners.[25]

What also posed a potential racial threat to German culture was the arrival of jazz to Germany and Austria. Audiences heard and saw performers of jazz in sexual and racial terms. Like the African troops stationed along the Rhine, jazz musicians served as a locus for German anxiety over racial mixing. Their rhythmic gyrations and the physicality of their dancing tempted listeners to move their bodies in ways deemed sexually daring. Naked, wild, and dancing "with their senses" instead of their minds, Black entertainers, in Ivan Goll's estimation, offered Central Europeans sexual liberation.[26]

One figment of the Central European imagination in particular embodies Central European anxieties about jazz, race, and sex in the interwar era: the character Jonny from Krenek's 1927 opera, *Jonny spielt auf*. By the late 1920s, the figure of Jonny personified in crude form Central Europeans' imaginings of Black jazz musicians. Jonny, an African American musician living and performing in Europe, was, in the words of Wipplinger, "an amalgam of competing ideas about African Americans and their music."[27] With his banjo (an obvious musical signifier of American folk and lowbrow music), his colloquialisms, and his jovial and capricious manner, Jonny represents an impish womanizer with ebony-dark skin and bright white teeth. He is constantly trying to win a "new white girl" while hopping around on his numerous adventures and escapades, and he seems to dance through life shirking any responsibility and ignoring any hardship that might befall him.[28]

The Jonny character represents a highly sexualized Black man who carelessly engages in affairs with white women. Like the Black Horror figure, Jonny is also ultimately proof that Black men are sexually deviant, perhaps diseased, and that they ultimately cannot be trusted.[29] In propagandistic posters, music, and literature from the 1920s and 1930s, white women who associated with these potently sexualized Black men were often depicted as either whores or victims, depending on whether the women were perceived to be active or passive participants. In many ways, the trope of the sexually active Black man turned whiteness into something that needed protection and defending.

Although Krenek's jazz opera first premiered in Leipzig and had a long and successful run throughout Germany, it became associated with scandal and degeneracy after its premiere in Vienna in February 1928. Viennese nationalists and pan-Germanists, for example, demonstrated against what they called the desecration of Viennese high culture. Similar to the degenerate art exhibit that appeared a decade later, they condemned both Black people and Jews for desecrating Central European high culture. "To the Viennese! Our opera house, the first site of art and culture in the world and the pride of all Viennese, has succumbed to Jewish-negroid perversities. . . . Christian

Viennese men and women, artists, musicians, singers, and antisemites appear in measure and protest with us against this unprecedented cultural shame in Austria."[30] Both the Jonny figure and the Black Horror were egregious scandals to some, for they threatened to impurify the German body racially and culturally.

If Black men were reduced to threatening soldiers lurking in the shadows or to roguish Jonny figures sleeping with white women, then Black women in popular entertainment, embodied in the figure of Josephine Baker, offered Austrian and German audiences a different type of fantasy: a chance for white heterosexual men to finally unleash or liberate their sexual desires.[31] Black women entertainers in interwar Austria and Germany gave audiences permission to fantasize about exotic and erotic sexual encounters with people of African descent without the threat of violence that they associated with Black masculinity. As the historian Nancy Nenno argues, women like Baker "successfully mitigated the German popular fear of primitive sexuality associated with the 'Black Horror.'"[32] Entertainers such as Baker, Bayton, and dancing girls in ensembles such as the Chocolate Kiddies and the Black People Revue offered viewers a different type of Black exoticism, one linked to primitivism and deviance in a similar manner to Black male sexuality, but one that listeners instead found unthreatening.[33]

The complicated character of Baker, who toured Central Europe in 1927 and 1928, powerfully illustrates the gendered division in white German and Austrian responses to Black sexuality. Described as "childlike," "wild," "primitive," "lascivious," "savage," and "beautiful" in the European press, Baker embodied many of the contradictions embedded in the fantasized image of Black women. No other figure has come to represent Black female sexuality in twentieth-century Europe quite like her. Her provocatively nude public performances, combined with her scandalous and numerous love affairs offstage "served as a notorious advertisement for the unbridled, voracious sexuality attributed to, and expected of, the Black woman since the Hottentot Venus," Nenno writes.[34] Intentionally playing with colonial tropes dating back to the nineteenth century, Baker mixed the "primitive" with the "modern" and in so doing danced on the line between Black agency and white sexual desire.[35] Similar to Goll's racialized and sexualized description of Black dancers in "The Negroes are Conquering Europe," white German and Austrian critics fixated heavily on her body. After attending her revue in Berlin, produced by the African American entertainer Louis Douglas, the artist and journalist Ottomar Starke stated, "Her bottom, with all due respect, is a chocolate semolina flummery of agility, and she is rightly proud of this gift of nature."[36] The use of chocolate imagery to describe the bodies of Black women thus continued to prevail in Weimar German discourse.

Both desired and abhorred, Baker seemed to create furor wherever she went. Her stay in Vienna in 1928 is especially illustrative of how her mythology as a highly sexualized Black woman provoked a debate about race, sex, and German culture. Baker arrived in Vienna in February 1928 to stage her revue "Black on White" ("Schwarz auf Weiß") only shortly after the opera *Jonny spielt auf* had closed, causing the second scandal tied to Black sexuality in a short manner of months.[37] Upon her arrival in Vienna, opposition to Baker became fierce and swift. Led by Anton Jerzabek, a popular Christian Socialist and founder and chairman of the Anti-Semite League (Antisemiten-bund), Austrian Hakenkreuzlers (often times university students) and far-right demonstrators protested against what they perceived as another racial defilement of their city.[38] Defending Viennese values, they argued that they needed to "save Vienna from the Negro shame."[39] Cartoons and other images that appeared in Viennese daily newspapers portrayed Baker in the nude, often in sexualized positions or dancing enticingly with Viennese men.[40]

Those who defended Baker usually sang her praises in a racial key. In a letter to the editor of the *Illustrierte Kronen-Zeitung*, a man named Ganst Höllwerth wrote in favor of bringing Baker to the city and told citizens to stop being so outraged. She wasn't that special, after all. "If it really matters, you could dunk our female entertainers in a chocolate factory and achieve the same effect. But they wouldn't have the same full, beautiful lips and the charming smile . . . I believe that there are better things to do than stand for hours at the train station waiting for the Negress to show up [to harass her]."[41] Again, critics clung to the language of chocolate to describe Baker. Moreover, by suggesting there was no difference between Baker and white performers, the critic refused to recognize Black creativity as distinct or unique from what white Central Europe already had to offer. Even some of Baker's biggest advocates, including Count Adalbert Sternberg, who defended Baker in Viennese parliament, relied on racist notions of Black authenticity and dance to argue in favor of her appearance. Sternberg, for example, told his colleagues that "whites don't know how to dance. Only Blacks conserve in dancing its human and sacred quality."[42] Much like in the nineteenth century, listeners believed that Black people possessed innate qualities that made them gifted with dance and song, thus denying them agency in their own cultural productions.

The most fascinating rebuttal of Baker's enemies appeared in an editorial in the *Illustriertes Wiener Extrablatt*, and it directly connected Austria's complicated history of empire, American racism, and global white supremacy to Viennese reactions to Baker. The author writes:

> If Austria were a country with a big colonial territory in the tropics, with lots of colored peoples, then one could perhaps better understand this resistance against the appearance of a colored woman at a Viennese theater. Americans and Englanders have a high contempt against peoples of other colors because they created this belief in the superiority of the Anglo-Saxon race over foreign colored people. But Austria doesn't have any colonies and therefore it doesn't appear to have a reason to look down upon other people on this planet. For the Austrian, it is possible for the mulatto or the Negress to simply be a human being like any other.[43]

In the author's telling, both Habsburg and post-Habsburg Austria lacked a historical connection to global exploitation and colonialism that would warrant holding such a racist position on Baker's performance. White Anglo-American racism relied heavily on their belief (a false one, the author implies) that white people were better than people of color. But Austria, standing outside of a global history of colonialism and racism, did not need to participate in such racial constructions.

A few ideas appear in vivid color when we step back to consider the three tropes of anti-Blackness that were so prevalent in German-speaking Europe in the aftermath of WWI. First, all three tropes fixate on Black sexuality and center around the deep insecurities of white men in both Germany and Austria and the vulnerability (or lack thereof) of women, depending on their race. Second, the tropes all illuminate the fear of collapse or ruin—and both Austria and Germany were newly formed states born after the collapse of their empires. Each trope touches on fears of cultural and racial invasion, whether through France and its empire or through Americanism in the form of jazz and Baker. Lastly, it is worth noting that two of the dominant tropes center on music. By the 1920s, Black musicians had become powerful icons of a new age. Caught in an entangled cultural web in the post-WWI era, Black figures became signs that audiences relied on to orient their world.

Black Networking, White Patronage, and the Birth of the Black Classical Celebrity in Central Europe

Shortly after listening to the soprano Anita Patti Brown perform in Los Angeles in April 1921, a German Jewish socialist named Louis Michel wrote a letter of support to her that appeared in the *Chicago Defender*. In the letter, he invites the soprano to come to Germany so that her "conquering genius" could finally be fully admired. "As a German-Jewish-born admirer," he writes, "I wish you a much broader future than you can ever attain in America, where even in the higher realms of art, injustice-forming derelicts are drawing race lines and color bars."[44] Michel's letter implies that while white Americans refused to recognize Black talent in classical music, Germans—the real listeners and tastemakers—did.

A similar article appeared in the same outlet in 1928, this time written by an African American doctor who had just returned from a long medical residency in Germany and Austria.[45] "Why go to Europe," Wilberforce Williams asks, especially if the United States also has its own rich cultural institutions? Because in the United States, he writes, "there are libraries, art galleries, museums, and music halls of a cultural nature where people of color are not welcomed, nor even admitted."[46] Yet in all of his travels to the continent, he had not once seen a poster stating that Black people were unwelcome in a public or private residence. In Germany and Austria, art was for all. For these reasons, he had made Central Europe his destination for his medical residency.

These two letters, one from a German-Jewish émigré in America and the other from an African American doctor returning from Vienna and Berlin, offered the same tantalizing, shimmering fantasy: go to Central Europe. There, outside of the United States, African Americans could find empowerment and success beyond their wildest imagination in the concert halls. Both letters carried semblances of truth. The poverty of German-speaking Europe, the wealth of American backers, the prestige of Central European aristocrats, and the financial savvy of concert management agencies meant that African Americans enjoyed unprecedented access to elite social circles and concert halls.

WWI cracked open a Pandora's box of anti-Black rhetoric, rooted in the newly formed and insecure postimperial states of Germany and Austria. But WWI and the interwar era it birthed also made it possible for Black classical musicians to enjoy new opportunities to perform in some of the most sacred spaces in Austro-German musical culture. For the first time, Black classical musicians enjoyed celebrity status in Central Europe. Their concerts (and the audiences who followed them around) granted them fame and money beyond their wildest dreams.

As before WWI, Black classical musicians' careers in Central Europe were greatly shaped by what they sang, where they sang it, for whom they performed, and how they appeared onstage. They were, like the singers before them, respectable spectacles who garnered the favor of their audiences because of what they performed and the musical culture surrounding it. The genre they performed gave them access to institutions and teachers that were not available to Black popular musicians, for example, and like the Fisk Jubilee Singers or pianists such as Hazel Harrison, they continued to dress in upper-class fashion, now including tuxedos and fashionable gowns, for their audiences.

Yet WWI had changed their circumstances abroad greatly. African Americans were ready and able to take full advantage of new platforms to perform on, new management agencies to represent them, and new patrons willing to support them. In fact, in the interwar era, African American performers such as Hayes outearned many of their fellow native German and Austrian classical musicians. By May 1924 Hayes had come to understand how much of a commodity he was in the classical music market. Writing to the African American intellectual Alain Locke in April 1924 from his hotel in Prague, Hayes gushed, "Dear Boy, my life is so beautiful and satisfying now that my cup of joy remains perpetually at a state of overflow. I never expected to have been so happy in this life as the success of my work (which is my meat and drink) has brought me."[47] Two weeks later and still in Prague, a now-confident Hayes wrote to a new manager in the United States, "You will never book me anywhere nor with anybody or organization that is not anxious for my services. This thought also gives place to my saying—most emphatically—that I wish only to sing in important and conveniently accessible centres on my next tour . . ."[48] Clearly, Hayes understood his rising value following his Central European tour.

One of the reasons for Hayes's financial successes—one of the reasons why he could perform in sold-out venues and demand outrageous sums of money—was his network of white patrons. They provided financial advice, offered introductions to sought-after teachers, hosted Black classical musicians in their homes, and bought expensive, front-row seats to their concerts. "His excellency" Juliusz Jan von Twardowski and his wife (also friends with Locke), for example, provided Hayes with a lawyer, Dr. Pieta, who gave him financial and legal counsel in Central Europe—in consultation with the Twardowskis.

Yet Hayes, like the baritone Aubrey Pankey and other Black musicians, also provided something in return. Through their friendships, Black classical musicians often shared with curious Central Europeans their experiences as Black men and women in the United States. In so doing, they promoted their politics of racial uplift and anti-racist struggle that came to define the global interwar era. Because of these relationships and because of the networks that formed in Central Europe around Black classical musicians, those musicians thrived in markets hostile to many others. Their status as elite musicians meant that they offer a fascinating case study of how Black diasporic musicians and their social relationships functioned in the transatlantic jazz age, one that is altogether different from that of Black popular musicians.

What Black classical musicians participated in and practiced was often a form of Black internationalist cultural politics.[49] It was of immense importance to form alliances with international communities outside of the United States. Their lives and careers on- and offstage were often imbued with the same spirit of Black cosmopolitanism, internationalism, and sometimes even Black activism—even though musicians such as Marian Anderson often avoided engaging directly in political conversation, and even though the music Black classical musicians performed was not "Black music."[50] It was important for Black classical musicians to find allies on their side, not because they implicitly believed white Germans or Austrians offered solutions to their problems but rather because the problems of American racism pushed them to join a world beyond American shores and to consider American racism a regional and local problem.[51] Away from the United States, Black classical musicians such as Pankey and Hayes found in their white audiences, patrons, and allies comfort in the thought that not all white listeners were like white Americans.

Black classical musicians' lives offstage in Germany and Austria were similar to those of other Black performers abroad in that they promoted the importance of resisting anti-Black racism and recognizing Black artistry. Peering into the social worlds of Black musicians in 1930s London, for example, Marc Matera demonstrates that "Black musicians often developed close ties to Black pressure groups in the city" who used antiracist and anticolonial causes as occasions for Black organizing and music-making.[52] Like Black jazz musicians in Europe, Black classical musicians also became intimately involved in their new social environments. Through their new alliances, they participated in meaningful cultural exchange about the values of classical music and the importance of disavowing anti-Black racism. Similarly, Black classical musicians in Central Europe also created their own Black networks, often articulating the problems of American race relations to white Germans and Austrians and in so doing sharing what they believed were its solutions.

But the social world of classical music—steeped in prestige and bourgeois or even aristocratic respectability—meant that Black classical musicians created entirely different careers for themselves in interwar, jazz-age Europe. In the 1920s especially, Black classical musicians enjoyed the benefactions of aristocratic and wealthy patrons and the enthusiastic support of elite classical musicians in Vienna and Berlin like never before. They enjoyed having sold-out concerts that placed them in popularity above other white European and American performers, including other native Germans and Austrians. It is important for us to consider, then, how Black classical musicians' careers, experiences, aesthetics, and lives differed both from those of white classical musicians and from those of Black popular musicians in the interwar era.

In the interwar period, unlike any time before, Black classical musicians became elite musical celebrities. They traveled, resided, and performed in spaces that remained off-limits to the vast majority of Black people in Central Europe.[53] Colonial African migrants, many of whom had been in Germany for decades or were the children of colonial African migrants, were in economically precarious situations throughout the Weimar period, for example. Lacking German citizenship papers as former colonial subjects, they lived in a liminal space that made them permanent residents of Germany but ineligible to receive state unemployment benefits as German citizens. Some worked in unskilled or menial jobs as porters, doormen, or waiters. Over time, more turned to performance on whatever terms as a way to make a living. Black workers who had trained as mechanics or who had first come to Germany as teachers now found themselves dancing in a revue or performing in a jazz band.[54]

Black classical musicians, however, did not ever experience such dire circumstances. Where they resided offers just one example of how differently they led their lives. Some, such as Josephine Harreld, daughter of the African American violinist and former Berlin resident William Kemper Harreld, stayed in one of the top hotels in Salzburg for a summer while at the Mozarteum University Salzburg. Hayes resided for a summer in a villa owned by a Bohemian countess in Prague, and Anderson lived with the aristocratic von Erdberg family in the well-to-do neighborhood of Charlottenburg in Berlin.[55] With the advice and aid of his friends in Vienna, Hayes also considered purchasing a villa in the Austrian countryside.[56]

Additionally, Black concert musicians often employed classical music management agencies to book them prestigious music venues. Both Anderson and Hayes became shrewd in dealing with these agencies abroad. In Hayes's case, he experienced both the highs of having concert agencies compete for his attention in cities such as Prague and Budapest and the lows of being swindled by one small concert management firm who had sent him to Graz and Karlsbad but then refused to fully pay him.[57] After that incident, Hayes, through the advice of the Twardowskis, became savvier in his financial dealings. Although Hayes worked with the legendary Borkon management agency in Berlin in the 1920s, for example, his biographers write that

"Roland got the word out that he was not under the exclusive representation of any continental European management." At least five different music agencies tried to convince Hayes to let them promote his concerts in Europe, and he was happy to let them all fight with each other for the opportunity to represent him—and present him with the most lucrative contract.[58] By 1924, the *New York Times* reported, Hayes was earning $100,000 per year.[59] Anderson also had different agencies competing against one another to book her concerts in Europe. One of the reasons why Anderson hastened to return to Europe from the United States in 1933 was because her Swedish concert manager Helmer Enwall offered her an unheard-of contract of sixty arranged concert bookings. Under his management, she sang over one hundred concerts in Europe in a twelve-month period.[60]

Black classical musicians also appeared differently in marketing materials than jazz musicians—or white classical musicians. Dressed in gowns and tuxedos, their promotional photos suggested decorum and modesty. But their Blackness created an added excitement and novelty in the era of jazz. They were respectable spectacles who promised concert halls good money during an era rife with inflation, and agencies pitched them as such. They promoted performers such as Anderson and Pankey as "Negro singers" who could provide both the traditional German lieder that audiences desired and something new but still respectable in the form of Negro spirituals, which they considered to be a form of African American folk music. For example, advertisements that appeared in newspaper ads or on poster placards frequently highlighted or showcased a musician's Blackness, calling musicians such as Roland Hayes a "Negertenor," Pankey a "Negerbariton," and Robeson "Der Negerbaß".[61]

In advertisements for Hayes's performances that littered newspapers in Vienna and Berlin, the texts also made it clear that both Hayes and his accompanist were Black. That might be in part because of Hayes's own commitment to keeping a Black pianist with him throughout Europe (he alternated between two: Lawrence Brown, who toured with him in London, and William Lawrence, who performed with him in Berlin and Vienna). In a letter to his concert management agency, Hayes writes, "I am glad you have understood the necessity of my bringing my own accompanist, Mr. William Lawrence, who is also a Negro and an unusual accompanist. I ask only that you do for him (after he arrives and begins his work with me) what you would have done for the pianist you might have engaged there."[62]

Rarely did these advertisements mention the singer's nationality—either because it was assumed knowledge or because it did not matter as much as the singer's race or both. The one exception to this labeling practice was

Anderson, who initially received the label "Negersängerin" but by 1936 only appeared in advertisements with her full name. She had become a big enough sensation to no longer need an explanation or introduction.

Concert halls and managers also heavily emphasized the performances of African American spirituals that always appeared at the end of a concert program for Black concert singers. African Americans also gave countless interviews with the press, where they informed them about African American spirituals, which they referred to as a form of art song.

The experiences of Black classical musicians differed radically from those of Black jazz musicians or African colonial migrants because of their relationships with their teachers. The continuing German nature of American music conservatories meant that teachers in the United States still maintained a belief in the supremacy of Austro-German music. Many also maintained connections to Central Europe, which they used at the behest of a student as they had done for earlier generations of Black musicians. In 1929, for example, a young woman named Princess Mae Richardson studied harp at the New England Conservatory of Music with the Austrian musician Alfred Holy. Impressed by her performances, the teacher helped her prepare to study in Austria for the year, most likely using his own connections to procure her a teacher abroad.[63] Other instrumentalists also found teachers in Central Europe, including the Fisk alumnus Warner Lawson, the son of Raymond Augustus Lawson, who had himself studied in Germany in 1911. Warner studied with Artur Schnabel after receiving a degree in music literature from Yale in 1929. Roy Tibbs, another Fisk and Oberlin alumnus, studied in Vienna between 1934 and 1935 while on sabbatical as the head of the piano department at Howard University.[64] Rudolph Dunbar studied with Felix Weingartner in Vienna in the 1920s.[65] Teachers were vital to the careers of many Black classical musicians abroad. Anderson's teacher, Raimund von zur Mühlen, for example, introduced her to teachers and patrons in Berlin. Hayes's teacher in London, George Henschel, most likely introduced Hayes to his Viennese teacher, Theodor Lierhammer, in 1923.[66]

Lierhammer's studio might be one of the most striking cases of a Central European teacher working with Black musicians. Lierhammer appears to have taught at least half a dozen Black male singers in the 1920s and 1930s in Vienna. Born to Polish and Austrian parents in Austria, Lierhammer became a respected singer of German lieder in Vienna.[67] He was an old veteran in the world of German lieder by the 1920s: he had trained at the Vienna Conservatory and sung lieder under the baton of Felix Weingartner, and Richard Strauss and his wife had personally requested that he perform Strauss lieder in concert.[68] Lierhammer lived in London as a professor of singing at the Royal Academy

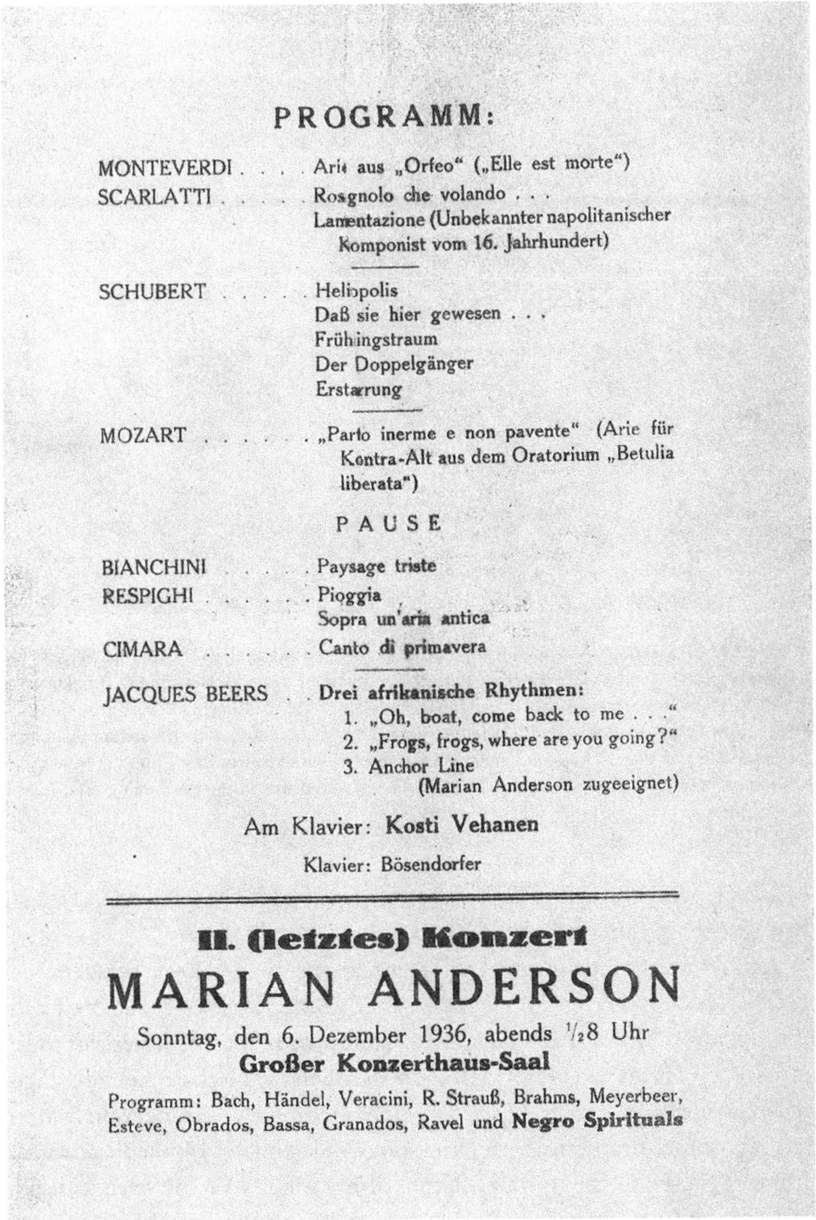

PROGRAMM:

MONTEVERDI . . . . Arie aus „Orfeo" („Elle est morte")

SCARLATTI . . . . . Rosgnolo che volando . . .
Lamentazione (Unbekannter napolitanischer
Komponist vom 16. Jahrhundert)

SCHUBERT . . . . . Heliopolis
Daß sie hier gewesen . . .
Frühlingstraum
Der Doppelgänger
Erstarrung

MOZART . . . . . . „Parto inerme e non pavente" (Arie für
Kontra-Alt aus dem Oratorium „Betulia
liberata")

P A U S E

BIANCHINI . . . . . Paysage triste

RESPIGHI . . . . . . Pioggia
Sopra un'aria antica

CIMARA . . . . . . Canto di primavera

JACQUES BEERS . . Drei afrikanische Rhythmen:
1. „Oh, boat, come back to me . . ."
2. „Frogs, frogs, where are you going?"
3. Anchor Line
(Marian Anderson zugeeignet)

Am Klavier: **Kosti Vehanen**

Klavier: Bösendorfer

II. (letztes) Konzert

MARIAN ANDERSON

Sonntag, den 6. Dezember 1936, abends $\frac{1}{2}$8 Uhr
Großer Konzerthaus-Saal

Programm: Bach, Händel, Veracini, R. Strauß, Brahms, Meyerbeer,
Esteve, Obrados, Bassa, Granados, Ravel und **Negro Spirituals**

FIGURE 12. Marian Anderson's concert program from Zurich, Switzerland, September 25, 1935. Courtesy of the Marian Anderson Papers, Kislak Center for Special Collections, Rare Books, and Manuscripts, University of Pennsylvania, MS 200, Box 179, Folder 8459.

FIGURE 13. The African American tenor Roland Hayes and his teacher Sir George Henschel in England in 1921. The label on the back states: "For: Roland Hayes, 58 Allerton St., Brookline 46. From: Mary Armstrong Melvin, 100 Boylston Street, HA 6–0413. Chatting in the sunlight are Roland Hayes, now a famous tenor, and Sir George Henschel, first conductor of the Boston Symphony Orchestra, in this picture taken in England around 1921 when Hayes was a pupil of Henschel." Courtesy of the E. Azalia Hackley Collection of African Americans in the Performing Arts, Detroit Public Library.

of Music, where he most likely became acquainted with Henschel, Hayes's first teacher in Europe.[69]

Lierhammer's most prominent (and perhaps most beloved) student was Hayes. Through Hayes, for example, Lierhammer became acquainted with the world of African American art song and with African American musicians. After Hayes had performed a few spirituals for Lierhammer, the singer fell in love with the genre. "I vividly remember his astonishment on hearing me sing some Aframerican [sic] folk songs," Hayes later recalled, "an astonishment caused by the spiritual affinity of my songs with the spirit and style of the great German master [Bach]. 'But you have it all there,' he assured me; 'it is the same language.'" African American spirituals, like Bach or Heinrich Schütz's cantatas, Lierhammer told Hayes, met "on the common ground of purpose, feeling, and fitting form," and shared the same musical poetic style and religious spirit.[70] Even after Hayes finished his musical instruction with Lierhammer, he would visit his former teacher often in his home on Fasangasse whenever he returned to Vienna from then on, and corresponded from afar as well.[71]

But Hayes was not Lierhammer's only Black student. For example, Lierhammer later taught John Payne, a friend of Hayes. Payne and Joseph Edwin Covington, who had performed as a vocalist with the Southern Syncopated Orchestra, an ensemble specializing in ragtime music and popular songs, both lived in Vienna in 1929 and studied voice with him, as did Pankey in the early 1930s.[72] It is possible that Hayes introduced Pankey to Lierhammer, because, according to the *Neue Freie Presse*, Hayes was responsible for discovering the young baritone.[73] Black singers' reliance on Lierhammer suggests a stable Black network built around one teacher in Vienna.

When it came to forming their own Black networks, Black classical musicians rarely chose to socialize with Black popular musicians. Instead, they socialized with each other. Many Black classical musicians first networked with each other in London before arriving in Central Europe. Hayes and his pianist Lawrence Brown had first found contacts in London, including aristocratic white patrons, then later shared those with Anderson. Josephine Harreld lived an exciting summer in Salzburg in 1935. She befriended the soprano Anne Brown (who later originated the role of Bess in Gershwin's opera *Porgy and Bess*), who asked Harreld to accompany her on one of her recitals. A witness to Anderson's Salzburg recital of 1935, Harreld met the singer backstage after her recital and introduced herself as William Kemper Harreld's daughter. "Josephine?" Anderson replied, "I never would have known you!"[74] Anderson asked Harreld to send her greetings to her parents back in the United States, then invited her to her hotel room to visit. Harreld visited Anderson several times that summer, writing home to her parents that the two had "chatted like two schoolgirls for a long time" over lunches and breakfasts in the city. Harreld also spent her free time touring around Vienna with Roy Tibbs and the singer Frank Harrison that summer. Together they saw "Beethoven houses, the Schubert house and museum, St. Stephansdom . . . memorials to many musicians, the opera, the hotel where Wagner stayed, and a dozen other remarkable sites."[75]

Above all else, however, the careers of African American classical musicians differed greatly in the interwar era from those of popular musicians because of their patrons. Artists, musicians, writers, and aristocrats from Germany, Austria, Hungary, and Czechoslovakia formed the majority of friendships that singers such as Anderson and Hayes acquired abroad. They represented an elite musical world to which a new generation of African American performers had access. Black classical musicians also enjoyed enthusiastic support from some of the most famous classical musicians, ranging from Bruno Walter and Arturo Toscanini to the Mahler singer Sara Cahier, and they benefitted economically, socially, culturally, and musically from the committed patronage of wealthy German-speaking and white American aristocrats and artists. Patrons arranged for different figures in society to come to their homes for tea, so that they might hear Black singers such as Anderson or Hayes perform lieder. Cleverly, these white patrons also frequently invited over agents from management firms who might be willing to represent these budding young singers. After hearing them sing at an aristocratic patron's salon, elite agencies placed Black performers in venues usually reserved for top orchestras and singers.

What differentiated Central European support for Black classical musicians in the interwar era from before might have been the identities of the patrons. White evangelical and aristocratic patrons—tied to British and German royalty—had supported the Fisk Jubilee Singers in the 1870s, for example. But in the interwar era, Jews, ethnic minorities, and people of color from the global south formed the closest bonds with African Americans, confirming Wipplinger's argument that German Jews stood at the center of African American cultural production and exchange in Germany in the 1920s and 1930s.[76]

In Vienna, Hayes and Locke befriended Jewish musicians and Bohemian or Eastern European aristocrats such as the pianists Theodor Leschetizky and Ossip Gabrilowitsch (both of whom had taught the Black pianist Raymond Augustus Lawson in the 1910s), Jakob Wasserman, the famed writer Arthur Schnitzler, and von Twardowski. Anni Schnitzler, Arthur's daughter, was part of the management agency promoting and booking Hayes's concerts, but it is clear from their exchange of letters that she and Hayes were also friends. In one letter, Anni teases him: "What are your plans for spring and summer? Where are you going to stop first in Europe? And are there going to be another 100 recitals in U.S.A. next season, poor man? Or are you going to sing 250 times?"[77]

Many women were financial backers and social brokers of Black classical musicians. For example, the white American opera singer Edyth Walker wrote to Hayes in 1926 expressing her disappointment that he wouldn't be singing again in Munich. "One lady said she would walk four hours to get anywhere to hear you! That means much for a woman of society!"[78] "Women of society," to use Walker's phrase, comprised a significant source of support for Black classical musicians in the interwar era. They arranged salons and hosted teas, lunches, and small private performances with exclusive, invite-only audiences. Anni Schnitzler, for example, put Hayes in touch with an agent in Denmark via her own piano teacher, Severin Eisenberger, who had attended one of Hayes's concerts and loved it.[79] Vilma Jurenkova, a pupil and assistant of Leschetizky, also wrote to Hayes to ask him about his concert in Vienna in October 1923, suggesting to him that she could get the main correspondent of *Musical America* to attend. She invited him over for tea where, she promised, he would meet "very nice people who are very interested in your concert!"[80] Countess Marguerite Hoyos had been so moved by a performance by Hayes that she attended in Vienna that she wrote to her friend Countess Bertha Henriette Katharina Nadine Colloredo-Mansfeld to suggest that they meet in Prague for Hayes's next concert in October 1923.[81] Countess Colloredo-Mansfeld spent the summer of 1924 teaching Hayes German literature, history, and poetry.

But Hayes also socialized with leaders from the Global South. For example, he visited with the Liberian ambassador Momulu Massaquoi at the Liberian embassy in Berlin, along with other notable Black figures such as Paul Robeson, Alain Locke, and Langston Hughes.[82] Hayes and Massaquoi may have bonded over their earlier careers as students in Nashville, Tennessee—Massaquoi at Central Tennessee College and Hayes at Fisk University, albeit a decade later. Backstage after his recital in Berlin in 1924, Hayes met Suhasini Nambiar, the first female member of the Communist Party of India, wife of A.C.N. Nambiar, an Indian nationalist who spent most of his career in Europe garnering support for Indian independence, and sister of the feminist political activist Sarojini Naidu, who was the first female president of the Indian National Congress. "During my stay in London, Miss Douglas has very often spoken to me about you," she writes to Hayes in a letter inviting him and William Lawrence, Hayes's accompanist in Vienna, over for dinner at her home in Wilmersdorf on Prinzregentenstraße. She continues, "A few of our musician friends, mostly German, are also anxious to have a word with you and are waiting to hear from you." Hayes's connections with global leaders illustrate the varying and diverse social worlds Black classical musicians chose to inhabit.[83]

White American patrons were also important interlocutors for Black classical musicians. Arguably one of the most important women and musical figures to mentor African American concert singers in Germany and Austria in the 1920s and 1930s was Sara Cahier, an American-born contralto tapped by Mahler to perform at the Vienna State Opera House in the early twentieth century. Under Bruno Walter, she gave the world premiere of Mahler's "Lied von der Erde" in Munich. When Hayes came to Berlin in 1924, for example, she and her husband wrote to him privately inquiring about his Liederabend and gave Hayes two tickets to hear her perform in *Lohengrin* at the Prussian

State Opera in Berlin.[84] They asked in return for three tickets for Hayes's concert in Berlin.

Because Cahier had also been on the faculty at the Curtis Institute of Music in Philadelphia, Marian Anderson's hometown, she also became acquainted with Anderson through their mutual friend, a physician and avid music lover named Charles Hirsch. An acquaintance of Kosti Vehanen, Anderson's accompanist, Cahier worked with Anderson for an entire summer in Jáchymov, Czechoslovakia, strictly on Mahler lieder. Cahier used her status and privilege as a wealthy white American woman and prestigious Mahler singer to invite elite audiences to hear Anderson perform in her home and also introduced Anderson to Gertrude Moulton in Austria.[85]

Gertrude Moulton played a pivotal role in Anderson's career. Like Cahier, Moulton hosted a tea for Anderson at the Grand Hotel de l'Europe in Salzburg (the same hotel where Harreld resided that same summer) after her celebrated Liederabend, where she invited many of the most established figures in classical music in the 1930s to attend—including, of course, Cahier. Harreld gossiped in a letter home to her parents, "Bruno Walter, Felix Weingartner, Erich Kleiber, Lotte Lehmann, . . . and Toscanini were there and were simply carried away."[86] Following a Salzburg recital that

FIGURE 14. A photograph of (L:R) Sara Cahier, Kosti Vehanen, and Marian Anderson in Salzburg in 1935, taken by Erika Gast. Courtesy of the Marian Anderson Papers, Kislak Center for Special Collections, Rare Books, and Manuscripts, University of Pennsylvania, MS Coll 198: vol. 3, p. 13, items 1–2.

Moulton hosted, Walter arranged for Anderson to perform with the Vienna Philharmonic.

There were a variety of reasons why patrons, listeners, and friends supported Black classical musicians. Some white Americans, such as Cahier and the poet Louis Untermeyer, were deeply critical of American racism. Cahier expressed her commitment to supporting the endeavors of African American musicians in an opinion piece she wrote for a Berlin newspaper, which later found its way into Hayes's hands. Echoing the sentiments of African American musicality that went back to Dvořák, Cahier argued that only African Americans, an oppressed people, had any kind of musical talent or potential in the United States. Cahier wrote that "America was hard soil" for musical genius. "The trouble was," Hayes recalled, "that the American people did not have to have music to live. Only amongst the Negroes, [Cahier] thought, could music be said to be a spontaneous accompaniment to the ordinary circumstances of living." Cahier then pointed to Hayes's musical career to further her argument.[87]

Although Cahier's views were in many ways reductionist by reaffirming the notion that African Americans were a distinctly musical people, her actions as a supporter of Hayes's career were bold, especially in light of white American racism—even in Europe. Indeed, the specter of Jim Crow continued to affect social relationships in Europe. Hayes, for example, had been kicked out of a hotel in France after white Americans had complained about him being there.[88] In 1920s London, Lord and Lady Astor had to reassure a very nervous Hayes that he was welcome at their home after he learned that the couple had invited some white Americans from Virginia. Prior to the white Southerners' arrival, Lady Astor told them that Hayes was their esteemed guest and that if the white American couple were unhappy about it, they would be asked to leave.[89] A decade later in 1935, Josephine Harreld also experienced bullying from white American students at the Mozarteum University Salzburg. Like African American students had discovered generations before her, white Americans were not a reliable source of allyship abroad.

Not only were more white Europeans coming into contact with American culture in the global 1920s and 1930s but they were also coming into more contact with American racism. Indeed, European support for African Americans often went in tandem with their denouncements of American society. Well before the Nazis came to power, Meredith Roman writes, "US racism was identified in the Soviet Union as the most egregiously horrific aspect of capitalism, and the United States was represented as the most racist country in the world."[90] Stories of lynchings, Jim Crow laws, and unjust trials such as the Scottsboro boys trial proliferated in European news media, including

German-speaking presses. By the early 1930s, protest movements such as the global campaign to clear the names of the Scottsboro boys were central episodes in the formation of global racial politics in the 1930s.[91] Many patrons and friends of Black classical musicians responded to these developments with horror. Applauding African American concert performers sometimes functioned as a symbolic gesture of protest against American racism and a proclamation of what they believed to be a universal brotherhood.

Black cultural politics—in the form of racial uplift, political organizing, and creative expression—were part of Black classical musicians' lives off stage. Some, like Anderson, avoided discussing the politics of race in the United States, choosing instead to perform the politics of racial uplift through singing African American spirituals. Yet others, Aubrey Pankey or Paul Robeson, were outspoken Marxists by the late 1930s. Hayes's private correspondence offers another example of Black cultural politics and intellectual exchange with Central Europeans. He frequently disseminated pamphlets and books to German and Austrian friends and patrons on Black history and culture. Writing to Walter White, a leader of the NAACP, from Paris in 1924, Hayes asked White if his forthcoming book would be available in French and German translation, for he wished to disseminate it abroad. "I have already distributed the pamphlets you gave me among my aristocratic and interested friends who tell me that they will order it," Hayes writes.[92]

Three different letters from friends in Vienna to Hayes in 1926 indicate the immense cultural impact Hayes's dissemination of materials had among his Central European friends and patrons. In February 1926, Anni Schnitzler wrote to Hayes to thank him for sending her Alain Locke's new book, *The New Negro*, in the mail from the United States when he had been home on leave. She had asked him for reading recommendations the last time he was in Vienna, and he had delivered: "I think that book *The New Negro* is as complete an answer to all my inner questions as it is possible today," she writes.

> I can say that I *read* it, I really *study* it. And I am glad to see that through you I knew a great deal already. Mr. Locke's article, "The New Negro," is *very* fine and extremely well written. Everything he says is so *very* right and his manner of expressing things is such a very noble one. I liked him so much when I met him in Vienna two years ago. I instantly felt that he was an exceptional man.[93]

A month later, she also wrote to thank Hayes for sending her poetry by Countee Cullen. "The other day I received your parcel: Countee Collen's [sic] volume, "Color," and was very glad to receive it . . . Don't you think that some of his poems might have tempted [composer] Hugo Wolf to compose them?"[94]

It appears that Hayes sent out multiple copies of Locke's edited book, *The New Negro*, one of which landed on the desk of Hayes's attorney and financial adviser, Dr. Pieta. In a lengthy letter to Hayes, Pieta writes that he was ashamed to admit how little he knew about Black struggles as a white man. "[It] was you, Mr. Hayes, who first showed me and so many others how little the outward appearance tells us of the inner life of your people," he writes, "and how much that is beautiful and ideal you and your race are able to give to the world."[95]

These comments capture exactly the kind of simultaneity that Föllmer and others have argued dominated Central Europe in the interwar era. Pieta's remarks illustrate the developing political consciousness among Central Europeans of white American racism, even while denunciations of the Black Horror or Baker dominated German-speaking cities such as Vienna. White patrons' enthusiastic support for Black classical musicians, coupled with the familiar concert hall environment in which these musicians performed and the established management agencies representing them, made it easier for German audiences to continue supporting Black musicians even during the wave of anti-Black propaganda. Thus, the unique and elite social networks in which Black classical musicians operated make it possible for us to see more clearly how some of the very same audiences who denounced jazz could also adore musicians such as Roland Hayes or Marian Anderson.

In this environment, the careers of Black classical musicians expanded beyond any previous capacity. Their status as elite musicians and even as celebrities placed them in spaces inaccessible to many Black jazz musicians and African colonial entertainers and on par with many other white classical musicians at the time. Yet their experiences as Black men and women and their political positions meant that they shared similar perspectives with other African Americans abroad on the values of Black networking and the goals of anti-racist work at home and abroad. Their racial positions ultimately set them apart from white classical musicians in how they navigated their lives and careers in Central Europe and how audiences and patrons treated them.

German-speaking audiences admired Black classical musicians and Black jazz musicians for different reasons. White German and Austrian listeners could support Black classical musicians because what and where they performed made them respectable. The genre of music and the culture associated with it had opened doors for Black classical musicians in ways that other genres could not. Audiences took note when prominent musicians such as Walter attended Black musicians' concerts—which functioned as a form of endorsement. Accordingly, the public granted Black classical musicians the

most favor and admiration because of their institutional affiliations, patronage networks, and the genre of music they performed.

Sitting in on Hayes's debut in Vienna in 1923, Locke said as much. His essay, written for the African American media outlet *Opportunity*, is a veritable
Who's Who list among musical elites and also a testament to these politics of
racial uplift. Locke writes that Hayes's concert was so thrilling that listeners

> missed [Maria] Jeritza's annual leave-taking of the Opera to attend; that
> Madame [Sigrid] Arnoldson Fischoff, the primadonna who has sung
> with the greatest tenors of two musical generations . . . requested an
> Italian aria as an encore and declared it 'perfectly sung'; that the cre-
> ator of the role of Parsifal declared very generously that he would
> have given half his career for such mastery of the mezza-voice; that
> occasional Americans of the foreign colony spoke with pride of 'our
> American artist' whom until recently they could never have heard
> without condescension and, in some parts of our country, proscrip-
> tion and segregation.[96]

In Locke's essay, the politics of racial uplift and the power of white elite
support are all wrapped in one. The growing power of the audience in shaping the careers of Black classical musicians was beginning to have an immense effect. If during the Kaiserreich white audiences of Black classical
musicians were largely unknown, now during the interwar era they were
making themselves known. Attending Black concerts became a performative
statement, and in so doing, white musical elites endorsed Black classical musicians like never before. Not only were Black classical musicians worthy of
teaching; as the presence of white elites in sold-out concerts suggested, they
were now worth listening to as well.

Anti-Black Backlash on the Concert Stage

Nonetheless, Black classical musicians were not immune from the mounting
anti-Black politics of the day. "Between 1925 and 1933," Christine Naumann
argues, "no year passed without manifested nationalist opposition to African American performers."[97] And while musicians from England or France
also faced resistance to their performances, Susann Lewerenz points out that
Black entertainers faced not only xenophobia but also racist attacks.[98] The
figures of the Black Horror, Jonny, and Josephine endured throughout the
1920s and 1930s, and although Black jazz musicians and African colonial migrants most likely bore the brunt of racist antagonism, Black classical musicians faced it as well.

Hayes's career in Central Europe offers a striking example of how essentialized notions of Black people wound their way into audience reception of Black classical performers. The fact that Hayes, an African American tenor, became associated with the Black Horror campaign provides an example of how race trumped nation in white German-speaking Europe. Protestors erased Hayes's American citizenship in order to make him into a Black man (vaguely defined) who threatened white Europe. Their claims baffled Hayes, who wrote, "I refused to believe, however, that they would hold me, a private Negro citizen of the United States, responsible for the presence of French-speaking Africans . . ."[99] Yet white Germans continued to associate Hayes and other African American musicians such as the Four Black Diamonds with the stereotype of French colonial troops stationed along the Rhine.[100]

Even when critics or protestors acknowledged his American identity, they weaponized it as a way to discredit his performances. An open letter published in a Berlin newspaper that asked the American ambassador to forbid Hayes from performing "called for the prevention of a certain calamity: namely, the concert of an American Negro who had come to Berlin to defile the names of German poets and composers; a Negro, the writer said, 'who, at best, could only remind us of the cotton fields of Georgia.'"[101] Black musicians, including American classical musicians, had nothing to offer civilized white Germans.[102]

In addition to being a Black Horror on the Rhine or an American Negro picking cotton, Hayes also became a Jonny character in the German imagination. Print media and visual culture made Hayes into a Jonny entertainer in many different ways. First, like the Jonny character in Krenek's opera, German and Austrian audiences associated Hayes with greed and money. As Alan Lareau points out, in Krenek's opera, money is the only thing powerful enough to lure Jonny away from women.[103] Press characterizations of Hayes also emphasized his ruthless desire for capital. They decried him as a wealthy foreign artist who was profiting from German demands to hear beautiful music and taking away money from local German artists. Unlike real artists, who exist only to serve art, Hayes was a greedy and manipulative Black trickster who thrived on deviance and manipulation.

At the heart of this characterization of Hayes as a greedy Black entertainer was a miscommunication in Berlin in 1926. The event caused the audience that had supposedly fallen in love with Hayes in 1924 to turn against him two years later. Hayes earned the ire of concertgoers for apparently refusing to perform at his own concert until the seats were filled. Appearing in gossip columns in both Germany and Austria the day after, the story of his hour-long delay on the concert stage was subject to many calls of denouncement. Though he was scheduled to sing at 8 p.m., newspaper columnists gossiped that Hayes had apparently looked out into the audience prior to his performance, saw that it was empty, and "climbed into his car and drove off." A frustrated audience sat waiting while the concert board had to search for him and cajole him into performing for the crowd, which he did an hour later. "The audience remained confused and disconcerted, for the concert board hadn't even bothered telling the audience a white lie [to appease them]."[104]

In Hayes's memoir, he claims that he had performed late out of protest because his manager had withheld his concert fees. But the damage had already been done. Berlin residents had paid money to hear him perform, and they left the concert hall feeling betrayed. Newspapers such as the *Wiener Morgenzeitung* reported, "During his appearance on the podium, the Negro received hisses from a part of the audience."[105] (The choice of noun—"the Negro"—is striking in the last sentence. Pointing out his Blackness worked to reinforce German biases against foreign musicians as greedy entertainers who only performed for money, not for the purity of their art.) Newspapers in several major cities, including Hamburg, Berlin, and Vienna, caught wind of this resentment and cast shame on Hayes with headlines such as, "The Naughty Negro who would not sing until he heard the money ringing in the till," and, "The Negro tenor who was mad because the concert hall was not sold out."[106]

Hayes's financial drama only added more intensity to ongoing debates that Black musicians were taking jobs from German musicians and that they were ungrateful for all of the professional opportunities Central Europe offered. "The contortions of these exotic guests has not any connection with art and culture," complained a right-wing German newspaper. "German artists who have undergone long years of training are starving, while troops of colored performers are getting enormous salaries."[107] African American performers were detrimental not only to German art and culture but also to the German economy, some Germans protested. Hayes was no longer a cultivated artist who strove to create art instead of earn money; he had become a greedy Black entertainer just like anyone else, motivated by money and lacking in culture or civilization.

Like the Jonny character, not only was Hayes ruthless in his desire for money, but he was also lustful for white women. The Viennese began calling him a womanizer, claiming that he "won the confidence of all women's hearts."[108] Reporting on Hayes's sexual appeal to women, one journalist wrote, "They had regular wars here to secure tickets to his concerts. The women here almost killed each other in order to get into the concert hall to hear and more importantly to see the Black singer."[109] Gossip columnists intimated that Hayes had been having affairs with several women, and the press attributed to him the same sort of heightened male sexuality that was often attributed to Black men in Germany and elsewhere in the 1920s and 1930s. One newspaper, for example, gossiped that "the public must not be surprised if, after [Hayes's departure], they were to see Black babies wheeled through the Ring in coroneted prams."[110]

Multiple presses also picked up on a brewing scandal as well: Hayes had begun having an affair with a countess in Vienna.[111] The sheer mention of Hayes's association with Viennese aristocracy brought a whiff of scandal to the city. The Viennese daily newspaper *Die Stunde* mentioned that Hayes had become engaged to "a central European princess," while other newspapers specifically linked him to Countess Hoyos and later reported his engagement to a countess from the Colloredo-Mansfeld family. [112] When Hayes returned to the United States in the late 1920s, he left in part because he was frustrated by critics who were so fixated on his skin color and sexuality that they were unable to talk about anything else.

For Black women, the primary trope with which they had to contend was Baker. The figure of a scantily-clad dancing Baker dominated European culture and determined the treatment of Black women in Germany and Austria. For example, Fasia Jansen, an Afro-German woman who survived the Nazi regime, recalled in an interview how Baker was one of the few symbols of Black womanhood for her as a child. "I always wanted to be a dancer," Jansen told Campt, "and my [white German stepfather] was crazy about Josephine Baker."[113] In a letter to her parents in the summer of 1935, Harreld, a student at the Mozarteum University Salzburg, writes, "[Anderson] and Josephine

FIGURE 15. A cartoon appearing in the Baltimore African American newspaper, the *Afro-American*, on January 8, 1927, depicted the scandal of Roland Hayes's affair with a Viennese countess. Courtesy of the AFRO American Newspaper Archives.

Baker are certainly the outstanding Negro celebrities here. I hear more about them than about anyone else. In fact they are the *only* ones that one hears of. Several people say I look like Josephine Baker! They think they are paying me a magnificent compliment when they say that."[114] Harreld's irritation at being compared to Baker of course reveals her own respectability politics as the daughter of wealthy professors who had also traveled to Europe before. Yet her comment also illustrates the ubiquity of Baker's image in Central Europe at the time, years after the entertainer had left.

Yet other Black women offered alternative models of Black womanhood in Central Europe in the interwar era. Trying to combat the stark image of Baker as a Black jezebel conquering Central Europe, the German Jewish journalist Anna Nussbaum published an essay in *Der Tag* in 1928 called "The Afro-American Woman" ("Die afro-amerikanische Frau"). While applauding Baker, Florence Mills, and other Black women entertainers, Nussbaum also intentionally presents counterexamples to the overpowering image of Baker in her essay. She brings in Phyllis Wheatley, the nineteenth-century opera singer Marie Selika Willams, the Harlem Renaissance poet Georgia Douglas Johnson, and the sculptor Meta Warrick Fuller as examples of respectable Black women who also created high art. Even though Black women are doubly burdened by their identities in the United States and face varying forms of discrimination, Nussbaum argues that "there are today women of the African race in America who work as physicians, nurses, and teachers; and in political, industrial, and art life, with success."[115]

Anderson represents the strongest counterexample to Baker in Central Europe. A devout Protestant, Anderson especially drew countless life-long committed fans, in part for playing the role of the anti-Baker. Arriving onstage in elegant, expensive, yet modest-looking gowns, she exuded primness, sincerity, and artistry. Her sartorial choices were never supposed to distract the audience from the serious purpose of her art. Where Baker was wild and outrageous, Anderson was modest and humble. While Baker indulged white male fantasies of erotic primitivism, Anderson performed a bourgeois, Victorian, pious, modest, respectable womanhood with what many considered to be graceful elegance. She became a perfect foil for German-speaking audiences who denounced jazz but still wished to claim a kind of racially harmonious cosmopolitanism. She was, in short, the most acceptable and respectable Black commodity in Central Europe.

She had achieved this image in part through her networks, patrons, and management agencies, who presented modest images of her to the public. Newspapers gossiped about her arrival to different German-speaking cities and the aristocratic patrons and teachers who met her at the train station, where she always appeared in modest dress stepping off the train. Images, produced and disseminated by management agencies, certainly presented her in this manner. Lotte Meitner-Graf, a legendary photographer to musical celebrities, took a series of photographs of Anderson in Vienna, which Anderson most likely used for promotional materials.

In one such image (figure 16), Anderson appears youthful as she gazes upward past the camera, her hands clasped in prayer. The photograph offers no hint of scandal, but rather a highly stylized image of an innocent young maiden. In another (figure 17), she is demure, dressed fashionably yet modestly and turned slightly away from the camera, revealing only her profile.

Anderson did not disavow her identity as a Black woman. Rather, she frequently tied her identity as an African American woman to her religious identity as a pious Christian. In interviews with the press, she frequently instructed listeners to hear the beauty and religiosity in African American spirituals. Steeped in racial uplift, intentionally quiet on the matter of Black politics in the press, she instead emphasized what she deemed to be the values of African American culture through her performances of songs such as "My Lord, What A Morning."

The almost unending flow of fan letters, love letters, and marriage proposals to Anderson that fill her archive attest to the level of celebrity she had reached by August 1935. Harreld gossiped to her parents in August 1935 that "there is a Baron following Miss Anderson around. The men are crazy about her. She does look grand."[116] But unlike Baker, Anderson's public image (and private persona) always emphasized her moral purity and humility in addition to her beauty. Most important, Anderson also became a Black woman against which Central Europeans could compare others. In contrast to the irritation she expressed at being compared to Baker, Harreld did not mind being mistaken for Anderson. One day, while walking around Salzburg, she was stopped by a woman who asked if she were Anderson. She joked in a letter to her parents, "I may have gained ten pounds but I evidently have not grown six inches . . . I have not tanned that much. I was very flattered, however, and told her so."[117]

Anderson became a powerful image of Black womanhood that stood in direct contrast to European media portrayals of sexually loose Black women, as embodied by Baker, even as Baker tried to fight her own image as sexually lascivious. When Baker appeared onstage in Vienna in March 1928 in a long, cream-colored gown singing African American spirituals, critics and audience members asked why the city had made such a big fuss over her. The *Wiener Zeitung*, arguably one of the most influential daily newspapers in Vienna, attempted to correct the image: "After seeing Ms. Baker, one realizes

FIGURE 16. Marian Anderson studio portrait photograph taken by the legendary Viennese photographer Lotte Meitner-Graf, 1934. This is just one of over eighty photos taken together in collaboration; the majority of the images depict Anderson looking youthful, modest, and pious. In this one, Anderson's hands are clasped tight, as if in prayer. Marian Anderson Papers, Kislak Center for Special Collections, Rare Books, and Manuscripts, University of Pennsylvania, Ms. Coll. 198: vol. 2, p. 19, item 1.

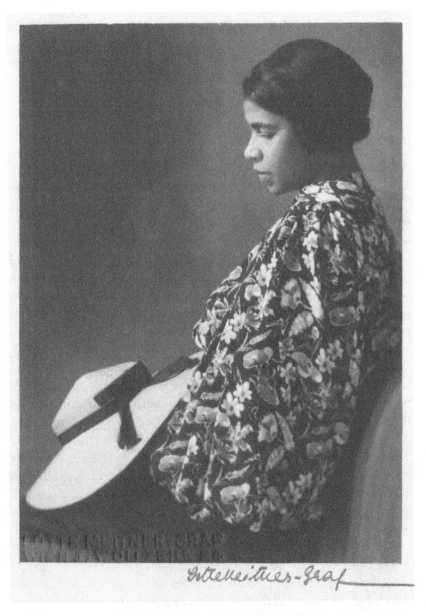

FIGURE 17. Marian Anderson studio portrait photograph taken by legendary Viennese photographer Lotte Meitner-Graf, 1935. In this image Anderson appears youthful and fashionable in her floral-print ensemble and braided hair. Marian Anderson Papers, Kislak Center for Special Collections, Rare Books, and Manuscripts, University of Pennsylvania, MS 198: vol. 3, p. 28, item 2.

that there wasn't a more fraudulent and evil trick in how she was publicized: as the daughter of a wild bushman. In reality is she such an expressive, distinguished, tender, and if not beautiful then certainly charming young woman."[118] The gendered politics of respectability and racial uplift in African American culture became an important tool for Black women resisting white modes of sexualization and fetishization in interwar Central Europe.

The Promises and Pitfalls of Music-Making in Interwar Central Europe

When Anderson decided to go to Europe in the late 1920s, she had reached an impasse in her career in the United States. "I was going stale," she writes. "I had to get away from my old haunts for a while; progress was at a standstill; repeating the same engagements each year, even if programs varied a little, was becoming routine; my career needed a fresh impetus, and perhaps a European stamp would help."[119] Like many other Black musicians, the promises of European success—and, just as important, European validation—pulled Anderson abroad and into a new social world of European art music. Going to Europe also meant more to Hayes than financial gain. "I wasn't so interested in the money," he insists in his memoir. "I was intoxicated by the fact that I hadn't broken through [in America]." Frustrated with constantly bumping up against glass ceilings in the United States, Hayes decided to leave altogether.[120] For many talented Black performers, Germany and Austria offered them the promise to realize their full potential and find affirmation of their musicianship.

However, Germany and Austria also became a site of anti-Black racist backlash to their performances. Enraged by the so-called "Black Horror on the Rhine" and by the popularity of Black entertainers real and imagined (such as Jonny and Baker), white audiences protested against Black musicians in greater numbers than before WWI. At the same time, other listeners supported and endorsed Black classical musicians with greater substance and verve than before WWI.

The experiences of Black classical musicians on- and offstage highlight the complexities of anti-Blackness and social opportunity in interwar Central Europe. In spite of his various aristocratic backers and music teachers, Hayes became a symbol of the Black Horror and Jonny in German-speaking Europe. In fact, one could argue that it was because of his newly acquired wealth, earned from his concertizing in Central Europe, that he drew the ire of audiences angered by a Black man's success on the stage.

Anderson's story offers us an example of the gendered nature of audience reception in the age of the Black Horror campaign. Both she and Hayes shared the same networks and patrons, both becoming popular Black classical celebrities unlike anything Central Europe had witnessed before—yet she escaped the most severe anti-Black criticism. In part because of her own self presentations as a modest, pious, anti-Baker, and in part because of the gendered response from her fans, Anderson was simply not a threat to Central European audiences in the way that Hayes was. She nonetheless also attracted romantic offers from white Central Europeans, but her gender, public persona, and private life were safeguarded from these racial and gendered relations.

Regardless, Black classical musicians had to manage their careers within the shifting racial terrain of the 1920s and 30s. Sometimes, like the Black Horror case, their Blackness was right at the center of protest, regardless of their American nationality. At other times, their nationality as Americans was precisely how they earned the favor of the very same people who denounced the supposed Black Horror threat in Germany.[121] Constantly faced with white audiences' ever-changing and kaleidoscope views of them, Black classical musicians learned how to navigate the Central European marketplace with remarkable flexibility. Their rise to the status of celebrity indicated the social and economic possibilities afforded to Black classical musicians at the time. They stood apart from Black jazz musicians socially because of what they performed, and they also maintained different and wealthier careers than many white classical musicians because of their race. In Weimar Germany and Red Austria, Black classical musicians could be adored or loathed for the exact same things on completely different grounds. What they could no longer be, however, was ignored.

"There is a horde of white people who believe that Negroes can or should only sing hymns, spirituals, and jazz," the Black writer Ernest Rice McKinney wrote in 1932. "It has taken some pretty long and arduous work on the part of Roland Hayes, Marian Anderson, and say, Hazel Harrison, to convince whites that Negroes had, or ought to have, any adaptability for Chopin, Beethoven, or Bach."[122] In part because of their powerful networks and careers in Central Europe, Black classical musicians had finally broken through into a greater transatlantic world to prove that Black people could also claim the music of Bach, Beethoven, and Brahms. But how convinced were white audiences of their performances?

CHAPTER 5

Singing Lieder, Hearing Race

Debating Blackness, Whiteness, and German Music
in Interwar Central Europe

Issued decades after Roland Hayes's death in
1977, the album *The Art of Roland Hayes* (1990), compiled by the Smithsonian Collection of Recordings, features a smattering of different songs from
his recording output between 1939 (at age fifty-two) and 1967, when he sang
Beethoven's "Trocknet nicht" for his eightieth birthday at the Isabella Stewart Gardner Museum in Boston, Massachusetts. The album does not represent the African American tenor in his prime. The great irony of Hayes's
career as the first successful Black concert tenor is that he—unlike other successful Black concert singers such as Marian Anderson and Paul Robeson—
did not issue any records until he was in his fifties. It shows. The voice we
hear seeping through our speakers sometimes sounds unstable and raspy. It
wavers too much. It has difficulties sometimes turning around the curves of
a musical phrase.

But what this recording teaches us is how Hayes cultivated his vocal technique and developed his own art of expression. In his most well-known song,
Schubert's "Du bist die Ruh," he manages to sustain a soft and consistently
fluid voice in his upper register. Singing "Du bist die Ruh / der Friede mild"
all in one smooth phrase, he expertly rolls his *r* in the word *Friede* and fades
away at the end of the word *mild*. When he sings, "Ich weihe dir / voll Lust
und Schmerz / zur Wohnung hier / mein Aug und Herz," he articulates the *h*
in *weihe* and carefully separates at the end of the stanza *Aug* from *und* using

a glottal stop. Listening to Hayes sing Schubert is to partake in a lesson in musical decision-making. The choices he makes throughout the duration of the lied were thought out in advance and well executed live, even if his voice sounds to our ears more tired than we would wish. The voice itself still has the same feathery soft smoothness that audiences came to love, even though it was never a booming one.

How Hayes comes across on this recording, and how listeners in the 1920s understood him, is as a Schubert singer. Recognizing the musical conventions that singers have employed to perform Schubert for decades, Hayes tapped into them, using his education and musical training to sound like a Schubertian singer. His diction—how he articulates in his recording of "Du bist die Ruh" phrases such as *zur Wohnung*, his narrowed vowel *e* in the word *Schmerz*, his lack of diphthong in the word *mein*—as well as his dynamic control and musical sentence construction are markers of his excellent and famous musicianship.

Of course, Hayes wasn't the only Black concert singer applauded for faithful and thoughtful interpretations of German lieder. Anderson's 1946 recording of Schubert's "Der Tod und das Mädchen," also one of her most popular numbers, highlights her own musical tastes and ideas at work. Breathless, hurried, and anxious at the beginning, her singing encapsulates the terror and fear of the maiden meeting the eerie figure of Death.

But it is the musical choices she makes in taking on the role of Death that brought her acclaim as a lieder singer. Sung at half the speed of the Maiden's text on the same note (D4) throughout, Anderson urges the Maiden, "Gib deine Hand, du schön und zart Gebild." The text does not get in the way of Anderson's controlled singing, even as she articulates the consonances in the line. The last phrase, "Sollst sanft in meinen Armen schlafen," slows down even further as Anderson warms her sound while sinking to a low D3 on *schlafen*.

In this chapter, I offer close analyses of two Black musicians and their shape-shifting performances of German lieder in Vienna, Salzburg, and Berlin in the interwar era: Hayes (1887–1977) and Anderson (1897–1993). In these case studies, I examine the singers' attempts to master the German lied, a process they undertook because of its influential position and multivalent function in German concert life. Lastly, I consider local reactions to their performances of German lieder and, relatedly, German culture. As we will see, audiences' responses were varied and even contradictory. But, I argue, regardless of the range of their opinions, they all processed their musical experiences through a racial filter. Some German listeners applauded Black singers for "becoming white" on stage through their masterful interpretation of a Brahms lied and welcomed them as honorary Germans. Others insisted that they had heard Blackness in the music of Schubert simply because the performer was Black. None of the positions, ranging from glowing to skeptical to even downright hostile, eradicated notions of racial difference. On the contrary, they all upheld them. Even when in direct opposition to one another, white listeners relied on the category of race to form their aesthetic judgments. Audiences routinely resurrected racial barriers in response to Black performers' musical attempts (intentional or otherwise) to undo them. White listeners' struggles to come to terms with Black musicians' performances are proof that musical reception was not a passive experience but rather an active process whereby racial categories were being worked out and renegotiated in interwar Central Europe.

Why the German lied? Why were musicians committed to spending so much time to learn this body of repertoire in particular? A composition usually written for voice and an accompanying instrument or group of instruments, the lied became a central focus of German music in the nineteenth century and a ritualized element of German concert life in the twentieth century.[1] If music is the most German of the arts, then the German lied is arguably the most German of genres in music history. "The fact is," Richard Taruskin states, "that only two important musical genres were actually German in origin, and one of them was vocal."[2] The German lied is so German, he argues, "that it has retained its German name in English writing."[3] Indeed, in one of Hayes's unpublished writings praising the lied, he too reinforced German lieder's musical hegemony. "The reason we have come to use the German word rather than the French (*chanson*) or the Italian (*canzone*) or any other," he writes, "is because the Germans, in a very special way, were able to retain and improve a national quality in this form of musical expression."[4] Karl Christian Führer's meticulous research on radio programming in Weimar Germany, for example, demonstrates that the Liederabend dominated classical music programs in Leipzig and nearby regions more than symphonies, chamber music concerts, operas, or oratorios.[5]

Yet its highly ritualized performance tradition, embodied by the Liederabend (or voice recital) gave the genre an internationalist bent by the 1920s. "The classical vocal recital," Laura Tunbridge argues, "became a performative nexus for identifying as belonging to a certain race or nation while simultaneously demonstrating one's command over a number of different languages and styles."[6] The Liederabend's challenge in the interwar era was to see if the singer could become a musical shapeshifter, a mystical medium of different styles, affects, and manners of expression from across time and space.

Ultimately, the lied offered the same paradox that lured other musicians to German art music of the modern era: it was universal in its appeal but also local and intimate as a form of musical expression. Audiences and performers also believed the lied—a genre of music accessible for singers at all levels to learn—to be imbued with the essence of Germanness because it captured sentiments of ardency, simplicity, and desire. It was understood that one must master the German language and spend years immersed in the culture of the lied's musical homeland (German-speaking Europe) before one could expect to capture the feelings and sentiments that many cherished in these highly prized musical works. Many international musicians strove to execute the German way of singing and to create the German sound, but, according to the native ears of Austrians and Germans, most performers fell short.[7]

A cherished body of music, known for its intimacy and expressivity and beloved for its familiarity, the lied proved to be the most provocative as a form of national, racial, and gendered performance. Unlike opera, which relies on costumes, makeup, and set design (in addition to the music and libretto) to create characters, the German lied repertoire has many nameless and purportedly universal or raceless characters that African Americans could play. Arguing that they should be judged based on the purity of their performance alone, not on the particular character (Aida, Othello, Carmen) they had been assigned to perform, African American concert singers could assume different racial and national forms.

What white audiences in Central Europe had not expected, however, was that African Americans would take on these many kaleidescopic forms so well. Although African American musicians had traveled to Europe before the interwar era, the majority had performed Black popular music, like Josephine Baker, or sung African American spirituals, like the Fisk Jubilee Singers. As I discussed in chapter 3, Black singers who traveled to Germany and Austria before WWI, such as Sissieretta Jones, had not specialized in German music either, preferring instead to sing Italian arias or American parlor songs. In the interwar era, however, Black concert singers committed themselves to the study of German music in a manner that was simply unprecedented in the history of Black musicianship in Europe. In fact, it was precisely due to their rigorous study and meticulous execution of German lieder that African American concert singers rose to celebrity during the so-called transatlantic jazz age.

Ultimately, what German reception of Black concert singers teaches us is that race was the primary filter through which listeners interpreted Black performances of the Austro-German musical canon. On the basis of their listening practices, critics determined whether a singer's performance met the standards not only of Austro-German musical culture but also of cultural citizenship. Black performances of lieder suggested that cultural identities had the power to supplant racial ones and that Germanness was something that could be mastered through performance and study, rather than biological inheritance through whiteness. Upon hearing Black musicians perform, white Central Europeans confronted the provocative reality that their identities were not stable categories passed down genetically but were transmutable through the very act of performance. Critics, audiences, and even Black performers' closest friends and allies in Central Europe reconstructed the sonic color line anew in response to these racially transgressive performances. Their constructions remained remarkably constant, even after the Nazi seizure of power and Engelbert Dollfuss's establishment of an Austrofascist state in Vienna in 1933, demonstrating a strong consistency in attitudes toward Black voices across a shifting geopolitical terrain. Black classical musicians could be loved or loathed for singing German lieder, but the notion that their voices sounded either "white" or "Black," German or un-German, could not be uprooted.

A Black Steiner: Roland Hayes as a German Lieder Singer

The son of formerly enslaved parents from the Deep South, Roland Hayes was, Jeffrey Stewart writes, "the first African American vocalist to challenge the color line in modern concert singing."[8] He first fell in love with European art music as a student at Fisk, and along with Marian Anderson, he started a tradition of African Americans performing and excelling in their studies of German lieder that continues to this day. Hayes spent much of the 1920s in Europe learning lieder before making his career in the United States. In an essay for the *Musical Courier*, Hayes writes, "It is true that I had learned about vocal technique in America, but I had to travel to Europe to learn about music."[9]

To make his dreams of becoming a lieder singer come true, he moved to Central Europe in the early 1920s. "I was determined to establish myself throughout Austria and Germany as a singer in the great lieder tradition," Hayes shares in his memoir.[10] Settling in Vienna in the fall of 1923 to study with the accomplished Polish baritone Theodor Lierhammer (for "coaching in the Viennese tradition"), Hayes sought to immerse himself in Vienna's robust musical life.[11] He admired the "Musikstadt der Welt" and how much the city's cultural life centered on music. He focused carefully on studying the works of "Vienna's own musician," Schubert, and built up a repertoire from that composer's six hundred lieder in addition to learning songs

FIGURE 18. A photograph of African American tenor Roland Hayes aboard the German steamship the North German Lloyd, undated. A stamp on the back states, "Bordphotograph, R. Fleischhut, D. Bremen, Norddeutscher Lloyd, Bremen." Courtesy of the E. Azalia Hackley Collection of African Americans in the Performing Arts, Detroit Public Library.

by Brahms, Beethoven, Schumann, and Wolf.[12] In mid-April 1923, Hayes's agent booked him his first engagement in the city of Vienna—a city he described as "jealous for the interpretation of his songs"—and he finally had his chance to prove to the Viennese that he was a worthy practitioner of German lieder.[13] His concert program comprised seventeenth- and eighteenth-century pieces, followed by the music of Schubert, Wolf, and Brahms.

The relationship Hayes developed with Lierhammer in Vienna played a critical role in his own musical development. Lierhammer, who spoke six languages fluently, preached the gospel of the German lied to all of his students. In a rare interview that appeared in a 1904 article for the *Etude* magazine, called "Dr. Lierhammer and the German Lied," he articulated his pedagogical philosophy and musical commitments. "To me," he confessed, "the lied is the highest level of the singer's art." And no composer was better at composing lieder than Schubert. "The most simple lieder are the most difficult ones; and those that we deem childish and unaffected are the hardest to interpret correctly . . . Schubert's melody is always beautiful and simple, but most difficult to reproduce. What Mozart is to opera, that is Schubert to the lied."[14]

Lierhammer's unorthodox approaches to singing might explain why Hayes and his teacher bonded so closely. First, Lierhammer was insistent that "foreigners" could sing the German lied. He highlighted singers outside of German-speaking Europe who he believed had mastered the German lied, like the Polish soprano Marcella Sembrich, whom he called a paragon of legato singing. Second, Lierhammer and Hayes might have worked well together because Lierhammer already harbored a deep suspicion of singers who tried to sing repertoire that was bigger than their voices. The best voices for lieder singing, Lierhammer argued, were not even that loud or commanding: "The greatest liedersingers [sic] of our time were not vocal giants." It was more important to learn how to sing piano and legato ("And legato must be finely distinguished from slurring, which is a most reprehensible habit," Lierhammer countered) than to try to develop a voice that was bigger than it actually was.[15]

Hayes had a small voice. He was an expert in singing softly, creating vocal coloring, and shaping vocal lines with minute detail. Like Lierhammer, Hayes also remained adamant throughout his career that the best way to learn German lieder was through the music of Schubert. "I like the Schubert music for the quality which suggests improvisation and spontaneity, and for its highly colored, imaginative feeling," he explained in his memoir. "It lends itself to emotional re-creation and can be made to sound endlessly fresh and inspired."[16] Hayes's training in 1920s Vienna with Lierhammer fit perfectly with his own vocal abilities and perceptions of German lieder.

Perhaps for those reasons, when Hayes premiered on the European continent, he stunned Viennese critics. Although he was to their minds unmistakably foreign—one critic described him in primitivist terms as "a small, agile Negro with crisp hair, thick lips, and shining white teeth"—to some, his expert execution of German lieder suggested a cultivation far removed from what they imagined to be his primeval Blackness.[17] Hayes's diction, pronunciation, and lyricism were apparently evidence of that great Austro-German musical tradition that many believed created a unique German sound. A critic for the popular newspaper *Wiener Allgemeine Zeitung* wrote, "No German could sing Schubert with more serious or unselfish surrender. Do not imagine that it is sufficient to be white to become an artist. Try first to sing as well as this Black man did."[18] His observation is a remarkable example of what critical race theorists call marking/unmarking in historical discourse. This author critiqued the popular assumption that one had to be white in order to be an authentic singer of German lieder. The critic admitted that he too had assumed that classical music and German national identity were anchored in whiteness—until he heard Hayes sing. Thus, the critic's comments revealed "the invisibility of whiteness as a racial position," as Richard Dyer describes it, for only after Hayes had performed the German lied did the music and its performers become marked in racial terms.[19] But much to the critic's surprise, he discovered that German musical identity was not irrevocably bound to whiteness after all. The relationship between appearance and sound, between race and culture, could be severed.

Hayes's performance in the spring of 1923 was the first of many that challenged audiences' notions of what constituted authentic performance practice. Following his successful debut in Vienna, Hayes embarked on a tour through Central Europe that took him to Graz, Budapest, Karlsbad, and Prague. Hayes credited Countess Colloredo-Mansfeld with helping him learn how to sing lieder with authority. Together in Prague they read definitive biographies of historical German figures including Johann Wolfgang von Goethe, Friedrich Schiller, and Otto von Bismarck, and played through the music of Bach, Handel, Mozart, Schubert, Schumann, Beethoven, Brahms, and Wolf.[20] The countess suggested numerous changes to Hayes's performance style that also transformed his singing. From her he learned to elongate or double the consonants on specific words (such as the *l* in *liebe*), thus giving him a more authoritative grasp of lieder performance practice.[21]

Following his time in Prague, Hayes headed to Berlin in May 1924 where, as I discussed in the previous chapter, he subdued an angry crowd with his performances of lieder. Much of Hayes's success in Berlin has to do with his choice of repertoire. His decision to begin his Liederabend with Schubert's

"Du bist die Ruh" turned out to be the best possible choice for that moment for several reasons. First, singing softly forced the crowd to stop shouting at him in order to hear him. Second, the lied's sweetness, warmth, and quiet (the primary dynamic markings are pianissimo) were disarming; its performative qualities did not present Hayes as a threatening stranger. Rather, the piece gave the opposite impression: the performer of "Du bist die Ruh" sounds gentle and patient. Third, "Du bist die Ruh" was one of Schubert's more well-known lieder, and its comforting familiarity may have also helped subdue Hayes's audience.

What Hayes offered the crowd on that evening in 1924 was ultimately something intimate, familiar, and beloved. Expecting scandal, exotic curiosity, minstrelsy, and indecency (which they associated with Blackness), the audience encountered a soothing, simple, and beloved Schubert lied. Instead of sounding like other African American singers of spirituals and popular music, Hayes resembled musically the native German-speaking performers the audience was accustomed to hearing.

After their initial resistance, most Berliners were impressed by how expertly Hayes had mastered the German lied. Several newspapers called him a "true artist" who had captured the feeling and sentiment of German lieder with breathtaking accuracy and warmth. In the right-leaning nationalist newspaper *Deutsche Tageszeitung*, the musicologist Hermann Springer called Hayes a "Negro who shows dedication in singing Schubert and Brahms for us in the German language."[22] The seriousness of Hayes's musical purpose found approval in Berlin. In fact, it was "specifically in these songs by Schubert, Schumann, Brahms, and Wolf that one noticed that Roland Hayes is a real artist, not just a singer but rather a musician," wrote a critic for the conservative German People's Party (DVP)-backed *Deutsche Allgemeine Zeitung*.[23] Like the critic for the *Wiener Allgemeine Zeitung*, the writer claimed that real artistry was located in the purity and universality of German music. In their eyes, Hayes had transitioned from being a Black entertainer to a more "universally" appealing artist of classical music.

Hayes's extensive classical vocal technique and training especially earned the admiration of several critics. "Without any exposed effects, [Hayes] builds his voice from the inside out," praised the *Deutsche Tageszeitung*.[24] "His voice isn't big," observed *Der Tag*, "but has a rather pleasant sound and is very well cultivated, so that all of the [voice's] shading was effortlessly at his disposal."[25] Nearly every review of Hayes's performance used words such as "cultivated" and "smooth" to describe Hayes's voice. "Mr. Hayes," wrote the critic for the more liberal *Berliner Tageblatt*, "possesses . . . a magnificent mezza voce; he masters the whole falsetto, the head voice, which he [sings] in piano as if [from the belly], with great skill . . . It remains admirable what his teacher was able to make out of him."[26] The critic's implication that Hayes's successes as a vocalist came almost entirely from his German teacher perhaps made his performances more palatable to readers. The writer located genius elsewhere, outside of Hayes himself.

It was obvious to many listeners that Hayes was a foreigner, but they marveled at how he had been able to mask that foreignness. The *Deutsche Allgemeine Zeitung*'s critic remarked that the range of feeling (*Gefühlskreis*) that made German Romantic music unique had to be a foreign sensation to Hayes, yet "one was astonished to hear with what depth of expression and understanding for the specific voice he sang lieder such as Schumann's 'Nussbaum' or 'Ich hab im Traum geweinet' and Schubert's 'Nacht und Träume' or 'Die Forelle.'"[27] The well-loved, conservative cultural feuilleton *Berliner Börsen-Zeitung* agreed: the critic Siegmund Pisling praised Hayes's performance in the sold-out hall warmed by "an African heat."[28] Pisling wrote:

> A Moor who sings Schubert, Schumann, Brahms, and Hugo Wolf in German without much of an accent is worthier of listening if he can feel the spirit of the German lied. And Hayes gets it. How he sings Schumann's "Ich hab' im Traum geweinet"! A Black man! A couple of white singers could learn a lesson from him.[29]

Pisling's use of the word Moor is especially striking because it harkens back to earlier histories and mythologies of Black migration. While the moniker "is an ambiguous, multivalent term whose meaning could differ significantly according to time period, language, location, and other contexts of use," Arne Spohr argues that it nonetheless carried "colonial and racist connotations."[30] Here, however, Pisling used it to distance Hayes from his middle passage diasporic Blackness and conjured up instead a much older image, giving Hayes's supposedly foreign allure an exotic, otherworldly time and locale.

Regardless of the nature, degree, or location of Hayes's foreignness, many Berliners believed that he had accomplished something almost unimaginable: he had somehow learned to "penetrate the spirit of the German lied" and possessed the ability to perform with "so much ardency [*Innigkeit*]" required to interpret German music.[31] Hayes's lieder performances "were in a gentle, flawless German with so much ardency, sung with such deep and true sentiment" that many listeners left the Konzerthaus's Ludwig van Beethoven Hall convinced of Hayes's musical genius.[32] But, as one critic surmised, "The listeners, who perhaps had expected vaudeville, soon became aware that here, real and very serious art was speaking to them."[33] Real art, the previous quotation implies, was German art, and few singers of any nationality could truly master it. Yet Hayes, as an African American, had been able to. Following this concert, an American studying music in Berlin greeted Hayes backstage and said, according to Hayes, "Goddamn it . . . put it there! This is the first time I have seen the Germans admit that good art can come out of America."[34] Both diasporically Black and quintessentially American, Hayes's twoness, as Du Bois called it, played an important role in his acceptance in Central European society.

Hayes performed in Vienna one last time before returning to the United States, and the "Musikstadt der Welt" welcomed him back. An admirer and patron wrote to him afterward, gushing, "I very rarely saw our public so enthusiastic and you really deserved it!"[35] Following his recital on October 8, 1925, a review in the *Neue Freie Presse*, a popular liberal newspaper, demonstrated how critics depicted Blackness and German lieder as antagonistic opposites:

> A Negro who sings Beethoven, Schubert, Brahms in their original language, and—dare we (almost) say it—also in the musical original language! [His] phrasing, expression, soulfulness are the attributes found in the spiritual and intellectual expression of the lied that we hear in native German lieder singers. The voice, while not always untinged by foreign resonances, encounters its best [quality] in an eminently cultivated, fabulously light connection between the falsetto and the head register . . . Sometimes, you begin to think that you're listening to a Black Raval, other times, a Black Steiner . . . Yet [this is] by all means an eminently remarkable appearance that captured and held the listener's attention.[36]

To the reviewer, Hayes is a musical contradiction. As with other Black singers, Hayes received nicknames that made him a Black variation of a white performer, including the "Black Raval," in reference to the Vienna Court Opera lyric tenor Franz Raval; the "Black Steiner," in reference to the popular Austrian concert singer Franz Steiner; and the "Black Caruso," in reference to Italian operatic tenor Enrico Caruso. He is foreign, yet musically expressive in a natively German way. He comes from a primitive or primeval culture, but he sings Beethoven, Schubert, and Brahms in their original (German) musical language. Descriptions of his Black body imply that Hayes should have been more comfortable in the world of dance and Black popular music, yet he had proven himself capable of the kind of "spiritual and intellectual expression" that normally only native singers of the lied could articulate. Many became convinced that Hayes was a musical chameleon, a cultural chimera who had firmly established his credentials as a twentieth-century lied singer through his mastery of the appropriate performance practice tradition.

Marian Anderson and the German Lied

One of the most famous singers of the twentieth century, Anderson launched her career in German-speaking Europe studying and performing German lieder. Regarded as "most decidedly a Handel-Schubert singer," Anderson possessed a cultivated voice that many believed emoted best when singing religious works, especially Schubert's "Ave Maria," Handel's "Begrüßung," and Bach's "Komm, süßer Tod."[37] She resided in Central Europe intermittently throughout the 1930s and became an overnight international sensation after her debut at the Salzburg Festival in 1935, where Toscanini said she had a voice heard "once in a hundred years."[38]

Anderson's primary motivation for studying in Europe had little to do with cultivating her vocal technique; rather, she sought out German teachers in the United States, England, Berlin, and Vienna who could coach her in the lieder repertoire.[39] Like Hayes, Anderson began seriously studying German lieder in England before journeying to Germany. In 1927, Anderson asked Hayes's accompanist Lawrence Brown to find her a reputable teacher in London, and Brown convinced the German concert singer Raimund von Zur Mühlen, a celebrated lieder singer and former student of Clara Schumann, to teach her.[40]

Anderson's time with the aging yet highly respected tenor and vocal pedagogue was brief but productive. Anderson recalls singing Schubert's lied "Im Abendrot" for Zur Mühlen in one of her early lessons, and he was not impressed.

"Do you know what that song means?" he demanded.

"Not word for word," I said, "and I'm ashamed that I don't."

"Don't sing it if you don't know what it's about."

"I know what it's about," I explained, "but I don't know it word for word."

"That's not enough," he said with finality.[41]

Following this encounter, Zur Mühlen gave Anderson a book of Schubert lieder in German and suggested that she learn "Nähe des Geliebten" for the following lesson. According to Anderson, he intentionally gave her a copy of Schubert lieder that did not provide any English translations, thus forcing her to translate and study the text carefully. For her next lesson, she was expected to provide a line-by-line analysis of the text, an aspect of her musical training she carried with her for the remainder of her career.[42] Anderson's training in Europe shaped her approach to the repertoire of German lieder and the art of singing itself. Her accompanist Kosti Vehanen recalled, "When Miss Anderson arrived in Europe, her programs were conceived in typical American form. A number of composers, some quite unimportant, were on them. Miss Anderson's first coach in Berlin suggested many other songs in an effort to acquaint the newcomer with different types."[43] She began to focus on understanding the cultural and intellectual significance of the body of lieder that European audiences sought out.

Anderson gave three recitals in Berlin in 1930. First, she performed lieder and African American spirituals in the Bach Hall at the Konzerthaus.[44] Following her success there, she performed for a private gathering hosted by her patron and teacher, Sara Cahier. Finally, she gave a recital at Berlin's Friedrich Wilhelm University (today's Humboldt-Universität) for prospective managers interested in signing a contract with her.

In her memoir, Anderson recalls that she walked onto the stage in the Bach Hall that October feeling intimidated by the native German speakers who comprised her audience. "I was about to sing before a German public," she writes, "a group that would be alert to every subtlety of its own language and would probably know most of the lieder by heart. It gave me a strange feeling." Her accompanist Michael Raucheisen appeared frightfully nervous, and rightly so: in the audience were some of the most elite members of Berlin's musical community, including the pianist Artur Schnabel. But when the reviews began to appear in German newspapers a few days later, Anderson was pleased to discover that the majority of them were glowing.[45]

As in the reviews of Hayes's performances, critics could not seem to describe Anderson's sound without discussing her physical appearance. In Anderson's case, her skin color was interpreted in a gendered manner. While critics often reported that Hayes was "dark-skinned," Anderson just as often became a light-skinned biracial woman under their gaze.[46] At her Salzburg debut in 1935, one critic even described her as a "mulatto." "Wearing a white, long, low-cut silk dress, with a huge flower in pale red at her cleavage," he writes, "she looks as if she had sunbathed too long in Africa." This Salzburg critic denied Blackness in Anderson's appearance. "As far as a white person is entitled to a judgment of taste," he continues, he found her pretty and lively, "with inky black hair, beautiful bright eyes, and moving facial expressions."[47]

Anderson's supposedly exotic looks earned the attention of most reviewers, but her deft skill and handling of German lieder were what impressed the majority of them. Taken aback by the conviction with which she sang lieder, Rudolf Kastner, music editor at the liberal *Berliner Morgenpost*, wrote, "This

FIGURE 19. Marian Anderson studies a musical score with pianist Kurt Johnen. Marian Anderson Papers, Kislak Center for Special Collections, Rare Books, and Manuscripts, University of Pennsylvania, 198: volume 1, page 36, items 1–2.

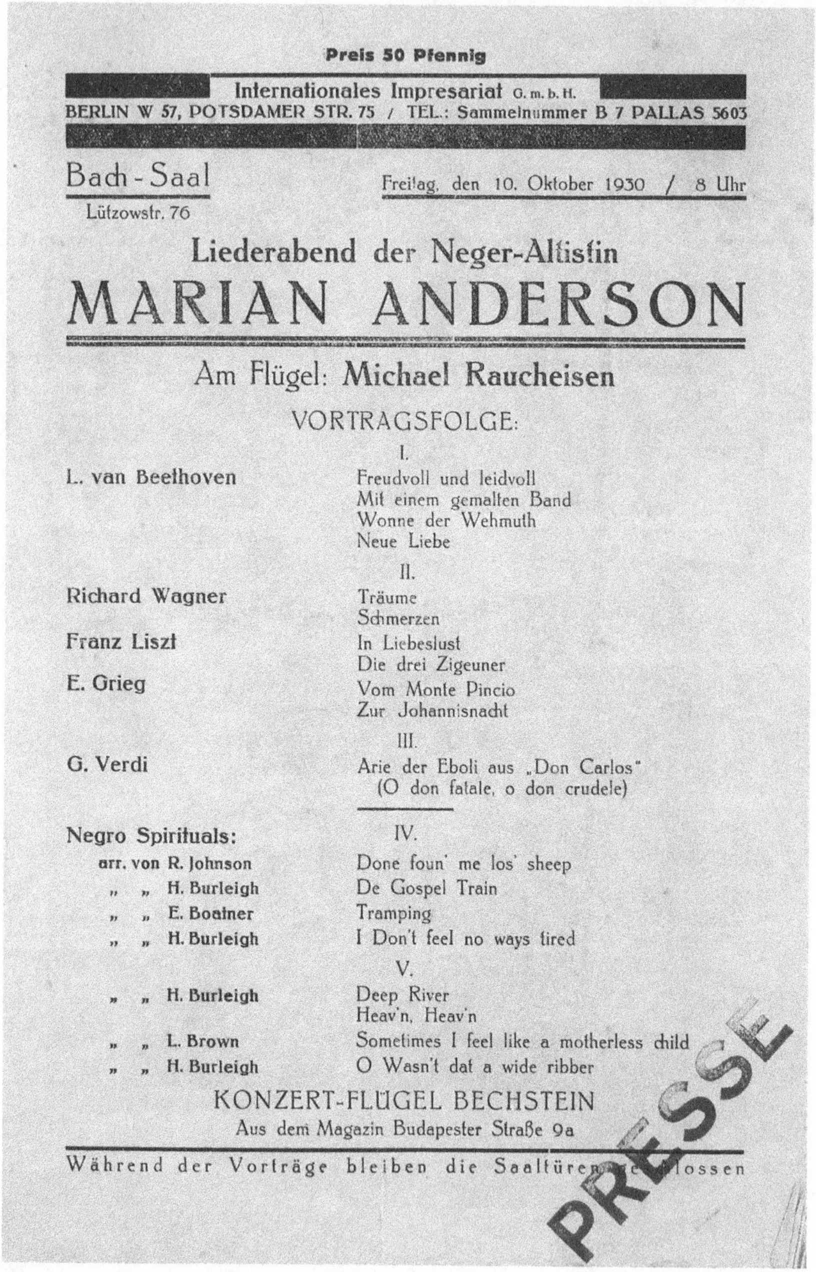

Internationales Impresariat G. m. b. H.
BERLIN W 57, POTSDAMER STR. 75 / TEL.: Sammelnummer B 7 PALLAS 5603

Bach - Saal   Freitag, den 10. Oktober 1930 / 8 Uhr
Lützowstr. 76

Liederabend der Neger-Altistin

MARIAN ANDERSON

Am Flügel: Michael Raucheisen

VORTRAGSFOLGE:

I.

L. van Beethoven   Freudvoll und leidvoll
                                Mit einem gemalten Band
                                Wonne der Wehmuth
                                Neue Liebe

II.

Richard Wagner   Träume
                                Schmerzen

Franz Liszt   In Liebeslust
                                Die drei Zigeuner

E. Grieg   Vom Monte Pincio
                                Zur Johannisnacht

III.

G. Verdi   Arie der Eboli aus „Don Carlos"
                                (O don fatale, o don crudele)

Negro Spirituals: IV.

arr. von R. Johnson   Done foun' me los' sheep
  „   „ H. Burleigh   De Gospel Train
  „   „ E. Boatner   Tramping
  „   „ H. Burleigh   I Don't feel no ways tired

                                V.

  „   „ H. Burleigh   Deep River
                                Heav'n, Heav'n

  „   „ L. Brown   Sometimes I feel like a motherless child

  „   „ H. Burleigh   O Wasn't dat a wide ribber

KONZERT-FLÜGEL BECHSTEIN
Aus dem Magazin Budapester Straße 9a

Während der Vorträge bleiben die Saaltüren geschlossen

PRESSE

FIGURE 20. The program for Marian Anderson's Berlin recital, October 1930. Marian Anderson Papers, Kislak Center for Special Collections, Rare Books, and Manuscripts, University of Pennsylvania, MS Coll 200, box 178, 08532. Used by permission.

remarkable woman sang German lieder at that, with a nonchalant command of style, a language so meaningfully accentuated, [and] with convincing musicality."[48] Indeed, Anderson's mastery of German was so complete that critics in Germany and Austria asked her repeatedly in public interviews how she came to speak German so well. By the end of her residency in Vienna in 1937, listeners joked that her accent was so local that she occasionally lapsed into Viennese dialect; she admitted that she occasionally had to remind herself to speak high German.[49]

Her linguistic mastery over the poetry and her musical mastery over the score made her a phenomenon. The critic at the *Deutsche Allgemeine Zeitung* marveled at Anderson's feat in the Bach Hall:

> Imagine this: [she is] a member of the Black race, an artist through and through, and she began her evening with lieder from Beethoven, continued with songs by Wagner, Liszt, and Grieg (all sung in German) . . . And she sang these German lieder—above all those by Beethoven—with such a mature understanding, so soulfully inspired and deeply musical; you don't hear something like this every day.[50]

Anderson continued to earn praise for her authoritative performances of lieder in Central Europe during the 1930s. In Salzburg in 1935, critics admired the "genuine German maiden-like feeling" with which she sang Mahler's "Die Urlicht [sic]."[51] "What a lovely rebuttal to [these] false racial theories!" cried a critic for *Das Echo* after her performance in Vienna in November of the same year. "Have you ever heard Schubert [sung] more joyfully, more 'Schubertly' than from this Negress, who thoroughly enchants us with this almost northern breath . . .?"[52] The most affirming praise of Anderson's abilities came by the end of her residency in Central Europe. After her concert with the Vienna Philharmonic in June 1936, a critic for the daily apolitical *Neues Wiener Journal* wrote, "It might surprise you that Marian Anderson comes to us as primarily as an interpreter of German classical music; but whoever has heard her sing Schubert, Schumann, or Brahms once knows that she is on utterly convincing terms with German musical art."[53]

The Germanness of Anderson's musical interpretations was especially impressive, a few critics surmised, because her Blackness could have so easily thwarted her Liederabend's success. Many reviews applauded Anderson for having cleverly walked this racial tightrope and for overcoming the limitations that her race must have surely imposed on her talent. Indeed, a critic for the *Neue Freie Presse* in Vienna reported, "When one chats with the famous Marian Anderson, one can, in spite of her dark brown tint, occasionally forget her exotic heritage."[54] In admiring Anderson's elegant, sophisticated, and spiritual renditions of Bach, Handel, and Schubert, some critics claimed that they were looking past her Blackness, even though her race had most likely drawn some of them to her performances in the first place. Attempts to ignore or forget her Blackness illustrate Patricia Williams's observation that "performance becomes a vehicle through which the Other is seen and not seen."[55] Initially drawn to her because she was exotic and foreign, audiences in Germany and Austria came to adore Anderson because they believed that she embodied the characteristics of German music when she sang. A *New York Times* reporter in the audience marveled that the Viennese had "reached the point of accepting practically without challenge her sovereign interpretations of Schubert, of Wolf, of Mahler—in short, of masters whom they usually concede to foreigners only with all manner of hair-splitting and reservations."[56] Anderson was no longer a foreigner; on the stage, in concert dress and singing German lieder, she became one of them.

Black Bodies, White Souls

The problem remains, however, that both Anderson's and Hayes's Blackness—demure, subdued, and minimal in the case of Anderson or wildly primeval in the case of Hayes—posed a stumbling block to many listeners enjoying these performances of German lieder. However entranced some critics were by their stunning renditions of Schubert lieder, they nonetheless could not imagine Anderson or Hayes as both Black and capable of expressing the German spirit. Instead, these critics encouraged listeners to erase the singers' Blackness and make them white. At the end of an interview with Hayes in 1925, for example, a reporter for the *Neues Wiener Journal* suggested that Hayes "appears to have a white soul."[57] A separate headline on Anderson articulated the same kind of race-crossing: "The Negro Singer with the White Soul."[58]

Both Hayes and Anderson had to stop being Black in the listener's imagination in order for them to accept the performers' remarkably compelling renditions of German lieder. Many critics felt compelled to expunge anything foreign or alien about the performers before they could accept the validity of their musical interpretations. For example, a Hamburg newspaper insisted that Hayes's race had disappeared during his Liederabend: "Color bleaches under the rays of art, and what remains is man."[59] Only after Hayes's color had been (metaphorically) bleached could the critic see Hayes for the true artist that he was. In fact, one journalist proposed that future listeners close their eyes when they heard him sing: "[To] avoid being disturbed by the Negro's gaze, a wise fellow shuts his eyes during the singing, which then focuses one's concentration."[60] Hayes's Blackness was a distraction that demanded

a solution for white listeners to hear properly: severing the relationship between sight and sound. The popular *Wiener Zeitung* also erased Anderson's
Blackness in order to make her Viennese. "In the city of Vienna," the critic
writes, "Marian Anderson is a foreigner no longer." She had become "not
a Black but rather an artistic sensation" capable of convincingly rendering
some of Austro-German music's greatest works.[61] A top critic from the Viennese *Mittags-Zeitung* offered similar praise of Hayes: "Not as a Negro, but
as a great artist, he captured and moved the audience."[62] Such statements,
made in earnest, offer yet another example of how the practice of un/mark-
ing in music criticism functioned. In both cases, music critics assumed that
whatever was Black could not also be universal and that what was universal
could not be tainted by ethnic particularism, leaving whiteness untouched
and unspoken. Until Anderson's departure in 1937, listeners attending her
sold-out Liederabende insisted that they were not frequenting her concerts
simply because of her exotic background. "The artistry of Anderson," one
critic assured his readers, would have existed "if the singer were white."[63]
Her mastery of the German lied made Anderson any white singer's equal.
She was worthy of attention not because of her race but in spite of it.

What is going on here? Why did listeners insist on seeing Anderson and
Hayes as white? Dubbing Black classical musicians "Negroes with white
souls" went beyond erasing, dismissing, or downplaying their Blackness. In
a musical context, that phrase tacitly affirmed the whiteness of classical music. Behind musicians' claims to German art song's universality and pure
artistry lies a racialized view of the music itself. By insisting that Hayes's and
Anderson's souls were white, listeners were then able to adopt them into
the world of cultivated German music and make them honorary members
of German culture. The term "Negro with a white soul" granted listeners
the ability to recognize Black concert singers' artistry while simultaneously
reinforcing the popular assumption that other forms of Black expression had
none. Thus, when a newspaper described Anderson as "The Negro Singer
with the White Soul," they reassured listeners and readers that her interpretations were trustworthy and culturally valid.[64] In this moment, one can see
how listeners aligned Black musicians' appearance with their musicianship.
Because they *heard* Anderson and Hayes as German and therefore as white,
listeners felt compelled to *see* them as white as well.

Critics often painted Black concert singers in stark contrast to Black jazz
musicians in order to elevate them to the status of a white European concert singer. For example, after Hayes's last performance in Vienna in October 1925, the critic at the *Neue Freie Presse* wrote, "What [could be] a greater
contrast to such brutal, 'Black' music [than] songs of astonishing European

trimness like those of Roland Hayes!!" [65] The *Berliner Allgemeine Zeitung* also
set up a contrast between Black minstrel entertainers and Hayes:

> The Negro as a world-class borrower or master robber are fading sen-
> sations. The nigger as a clown-eccentric, voluntarily and lucratively
> submitting himself for the grinning pleasures [of his audience]—
> [performing] an everyday variety number—at the mercy of [their] feel-
> ings of racial superiority. But a Negro tenor with a sufficiently intrigu-
> ing program [comprised] of the most tender flowers from Schubert,
> Schumann, Brahms, and Wolf's artistic garden? . . . Yes, something
> different is possible. [66]

When African American baritone Aubrey Pankey sang in Vienna in November 1931, he received similar praise: "A Black man," Robert Konta of the *Wiener Allgemeine Zeitung* writes, "who sings Schubert and Richard Strauss with
overwhelming intensity of feeling and forms them into great unforgettable
experiences. He is a boon for our period where one is very easily inclined to
see in all Negro musicians mere jazz band clowns. There are evidently Black
men who are messengers of culture at its greatest."[67]

These reviews exploit racist stereotypes of the Black entertainer. Clown-
like, insipid, brutish, and smirking, the aggressively masculine Black musician
functions as a straw man against which critics can praise the Black concert
singer. But in doing so these critics did not elevate Black performers. Rather,
pitting clownish jazz musicians against Black concert singers devalued both
kinds of performers and performances. There were no celebrations of Black
musical talent or accomplishment on the musicians' own terms. Instead, the
Black musician either fulfilled the Central European stereotype of Black musicality or was rescued from it by virtue of art music's near-magical properties of uplift and transcendence.

Hayes knew the public consistently tried to erase his Blackness and he was
quite frustrated by it. While traveling through Paris in 1924, Hayes confessed
in a diary entry that he knew his Blackness was a catalyst of some kind,
sparking listeners to work through their ideas of race and music. "Although
I know my face to be Black," he wrote,

> I am persuaded that the Spirit's choice of my body to inhabit has some
> specific purpose . . . I am not pleased when I am told that my being
> Black does not "matter." It does matter, it very much matters. I am
> Black for some high purpose in the mind of the Spirit. I must work
> that purpose out. [68]

Wishing neither to be absorbed into the world of whiteness nor relegated solely to the world of Black music-making (high or low), Hayes sought acceptance as both a Black man and an interpreter of German lieder. Classical music was universal, many claimed, but as Hayes's and Anderson's stories tell us, audiences tacitly understood it to be a white medium.

White Music, Black Sounds

Many critics applauded Black concert singers for becoming white on stage, but others heard their performances as fundamentally Black anyway, despite the lack of any racial music signifiers. Sometimes critics relied on theories of cultural and biological racism to explain what they understood to be a faulty musical interpretation, attributing a performer's supposed inadequacies to an insurmountable cultural and intellectual gulf that no amount of effort or training could bridge. For example, the influential Viennese music critic and editor Julius Korngold remarked of Hayes "that from each phrase, though technically perfectly rendered, a primitive sort of feeling wells up."[69] After hearing Hayes sing, the critic Elsa Bienenfeld complained, "He sings over the expression of the words. As if African intelligence could not follow the German line of thought. But he has the expression of the melody. That may be his instinct."[70] Unlike the journalist at Hayes's Berlin recital who credited his teacher for Hayes's convincing performance—and not Hayes's own efforts—Bienenfeld perpetuated the longstanding myth of Black musical talent as "natural" or "inherent" and therefore untrainable, being incapable of intellectual adaptation or evolution. Both refused to recognize the musician's agency in and capacity for the proper study and interpretation of lieder.

But concert criticism went beyond musical interpretation or linguistic fluency and extended to the nature of sound production itself. The music, they argued, *sounded* Black, despite the fact that it was a Schubert lied. This approach routinely functioned to refute the singer's claims to be a professional musician trained in Western art music. To these critics, Black performers had no place in Central Europe, no matter what they sang or performed. Their Blackness was immutable and ever present, manifesting in the ways in which their bodies produced sound. Trapped by their own biology, by their own racial and cultural limitations, and unable to transcend their bodies' limitations, they were forever doomed to imitate but never actually produce Germanness.

Black concert singers were, of course, capable of producing Black sonic effects akin to those that exist in popular music. "In popular genres," Eidsheim writes, "vernacular languages and pronunciation styles are used to tag performers with social distinctions."[71] A singer's unique wail or hum can purposely function as a marker of their identity and refer to a particular historical tradition in singing. But classical singers largely eschew individual style in favor of adherence to strict musical conventions of diction, timbre, and tone.[72] After all, all European-trained singers deliberately followed the stylistic conventions dictated by Western art music. If listeners claimed to have heard Blackness in the voices of African American singers, we are left to draw one of two conclusions: either there were indeed fundamental biological differences in Black singers' vocal production, or the distinction between Black and white singers in interwar Europe lay, as Eidsheim writes, "beyond the sound itself."[73] Some listeners in the 1920s insisted that they heard a fundamental difference in sound. Listening with a racial ear, music critics relied on the long-established transatlantic belief that Black vocal difference was located in the timbre of the singer's sound. The notion that Black American voices sounded different from white voices had existed in the United States since at least the 1890s, when the American trade paper the *Phonogram* wrote that "Negroes [record] better than white singers, because their voices have a certain sharpness or harshness about them that a white man has not."[74] But interwar era concert music criticism provides evidence that such views had traveled across the ocean.

Often German and Austrian critics compared Black concert singers' voices to their skin color, creating a racialized form of sensory alignment in which the sound of the singer's voice matched their visual appearance. Listeners described their voices as sounding like the colors black, purple, or blue—all dark hues. In 1930 the *Vossische Zeitung* wrote that "[Anderson's] complexion is not altogether Black, but she has a dark, blue-black voice which she handles with artistic accompaniment and taste. . . . Sonically her voice sounds somewhat unusual to our ears, exotic: but we readily take a fancy to its appeal."[75] The critic for the daily *Berliner Morgenpost* admired her "purple sonority" which the critic found fitting for a contralto.[76] In Vienna in the mid-1930s, critics compared the darkness of Anderson's tone to the darkness of her skin color. For example, one Viennese critic wrote, "The dark, soft tone of her voice works so well with [her] African skin color."[77] In Salzburg, another stated that Anderson possessed "a dark voice, brown like her skin."[78] Others praised her "soft, dark, alto voice" and gushed about "the marvel of this dark woman, this dark voice!"[79] In 1935, a critic for the *Salzburger Volksblatt* complained that her deep and dark voice's "negroid coloring" made it difficult to hear any resonating overtones. "The voice goes down deeply as a very dark contralto, and [then] up surprisingly high[, reaching the range of a] soprano.

Where does this little chest find such power?"[80] Like those of other Black singers in interwar Austria and Germany, Anderson's voice became black like her race, an audible marker of her racial difference.

White American and white European singers who were Anderson's contemporaries, however, faced no such criticism. Indeed, in examining their reception it becomes clear how the practice of racial un/marking shaped critics' listening practices. At first glance, all contralto voices described in print media appear to share similar features: their low range meant that critics frequently used adjectives such as "dark" to describe them, regardless of the singer's race. But that is where the similarities stop. German and Austrian reviews of white contraltos such as Gertrude Pitzinger, Sigrid Onegin, and Margarete Matzenauer emphasized color and tone with less specificity than they did with Anderson. Their voices were "big," "warm," or "glorious" (*herrlich*), they could have wide ranges, they could sound masculine, and they could sound like a church organ or a cello obligato. But rarely did critics assign a particular color or hue to a singer's voice, and they never related vocal color to the singer's appearance (hair color, eye color, skin color, size, shape, etc.).

Rather, what made these white contraltos' performances praiseworthy was their ability to control their voices, not necessarily the timbre of the voice itself. Pitzinger, one critic lauded, possessed "a secure, functioning feeling of style, that she used to meet each lied composer's characteristic tone, a natural and convincing style of artistic expression, and a fresh, musical joyfulness."[81] About a decade before Anderson arrived, her mentor Cahier received praise from Austrian critics for being "in full command of all the rules of singing." After hearing her "bring forth a captivating pianissimo and then in the next blink of an eye yield a shocking fortissimo," the audience knew that she was a true connoisseur of the lied.[82] The Jewish American contralto Sophie Braslau was one of the most well-known American performers in the 1920s. After her performance in Berlin in 1925, the critic Otto Steinhagen stated that Braslau's "phenomenal" voice was "an alto of astonishing resonance, a seldomly heard depth and power therein that at times reminds one of a manly register. But then come the highs of a mezzo-soprano, likewise the full power and expression-rich elasticity."[83] Power, control, technique, and the conviction of one's artistic expression were the markers of a white contralto singer's success to the ears of Austrian and German music critics.

In addition to describing the voices of Anderson and other Black singers as dark, listeners also frequently called them guttural, as if they were more primal than white voices. For example, the *Wiener Zeitung* wrote, "The gutturalness of [Anderson's] expression lends her organ the timbre of an Italian viola."[84] "Sometimes," wrote another Viennese critic, "the sound rounds further in the back of her throat—is that due to her English mother tongue or is it actually because of her foreign blood?"[85] Even Hayes's high tenor could not prevent the Viennese music critic Balduin Bricht from gendering and racializing it, describing it as a "somewhat guttural expression of a tenor voice with a feminine resonance."[86] When Pankey, a baritone, performed in Salzburg in 1932, he was also criticized for sounding Black. His style of singing was said to be too different and exotic to offer German listeners anything of value. His voice, which the critic described as lacking in color, was "different natured from that of Europeans. It sits very far back and is very guttural. Obviously, this has to do with the Negroid formation of the mouth."[87] When Pankey performed in Berlin in 1924, a critic at the *Berliner Tageblatt* articulated what he believed was so special about the Black voice:

> That which we love about the voices of a people so young at heart and in touch with nature—the smooth, unspoiled sound, the sophistication that does not allow for any unaesthetic, flat, or violent sound to emerge—Mr. Pankey possesses to a large degree. In his case also, his empathic understanding of our language, tone, and sentiment. Schubert's "Wanderer," concluded with "Nacht und Träume" in deep resignation, couldn't have been rendered more impressively.[88]

In contrast, some listeners championed other Black singers' voices precisely because they thought their voices lacked the guttural quality Black musicians were supposed to naturally possess. For example, when Kosti Vehanen first heard Anderson perform at Berlin's Friedrich Wilhelm University with the concert manager Rulle Rasmussen, they discussed her voice using language similar to that of critics. Vehanen recalled that Rasmussen observed,

> "I think she is a marvelous pupil with a beautiful voice; but evidently she has much to learn."
> [Vehanen replied,] "I don't know. I think the voice is well placed, without the guttural tone that most Negroes have."
> "I don't mean the voice," Rulle replied. "I mean the expression, the interpretation."[89]

These debates about singers' voices—purple or brilliantly light, guttural or more cultivated—reveal that audiences often relied on biological notions of racial difference to understand a performance of classical music. Their criticisms of singers' voices and behaviors assumed that there were essential qualities to their performances—biological and cultural—that were not only fundamental to their musicianship but could not be overcome through musical practice, cultural immersion, or linguistic training. To these listeners, their Blackness was irredeemable, permeating everything it touched—including classical music itself, which supposedly had little to do with race.

Dropping the Act

German and Austrian audiences were willing to grant Black singers unequivocal authenticity in one repertoire: African American spirituals. In spite of their different and even oppositional stances on Black concert singers, most music critics concluded their reviews by praising the performers for their heartfelt and homegrown rendition of songs such as "Sometimes I Feel Like a Motherless Child" or "Go Down, Moses." Here, finally, after a long evening of performing Germanness, Black singers supposedly dropped the act to reveal their "true selves." Their true selves were apparently not German or European at all. Neither did critics locate Black authenticity in a contemporary, vibrant, bustling, transnational, and transatlantic Black diasporic society; instead, they firmly planted Black singers in nineteenth-century antebellum America. African American spirituals were, in many listeners' minds, authentic musical expressions of life in the antebellum Deep South, and audiences praised them accordingly with repeated calls for encores. *Die Stunde*'s reporter wrote that although Pankey sang German lieder well, the "best that he gave us, however, was definitely in the native spirituals."[90] The critic for the *Berliner Tageblatt* stated that Hayes closed out the evening with songs that were "sung as on the plantation."[91] At one of Anderson's last concerts in Vienna in November 1937, the audience loved her performance of spirituals so much they demanded that she perform several of them twice.[92] Although Central European audiences might have thought that they were listening to local and humble expressions of formerly enslaved Black peoples, musicological scholarship suggests otherwise. African American concert performers frequently arranged spirituals for white American and European audiences.[93] Hayes's performance of African American spirituals in Central Europe sounded very much like European art songs; for one recital in Berlin in 1925, for example, Hayes orchestrated his arrangement of spirituals for harp and strings instead of using the piano.[94]

A few critics warned against emphasizing African American spirituals over German lieder in evaluating the performances of Black concert singers. Although the music critic for *Das Echo* loved Anderson's performance of spirituals such as "He's Got the Whole World in His Hands," he nonetheless pushed back against the popular opinion that African American spirituals were her best work. "It would be an injustice, however, to only emphasize these songs," he stated. "Seldom has Schubert been sung with such a sense of style and relatability."[95] The critic for *Die Stunde* agreed: "When she sings, her Schubert is the most authentic and best Schubert, and the spirituals move us as if they originated from the Danube and not the Mississippi."[96] Unlike performances by Robeson or Hayes, which critics praised for transporting the audience to a southern plantation or the Mississippi River, Anderson's Liederabend was fully Viennese, in this critic's estimation, for even her spirituals reminded audiences of themselves.

African American Liederabende functioned as sonic experiments in Central Europe where audiences tested out the relationship between race and sound in classical music during an era of increased transatlantic Black migration and travel. Audience constructions of whiteness and Blackness tell us that race was not only a visual experience but also a sonic phenomenon in German musical culture. Using their "listening ear," audiences sought to determine what they were seeing and hearing in the Austro-German canon along racial lines. They revisited their definitions of Blackness and whiteness in response to Black performers' musical erasures of the Black-white binary that dominated transatlantic discourses of race, nation, and culture in the twentieth century.

But African Americans' masterful musical game of mimicry vs. authenticity, which allowed them to be at once Black and German on stage, always relied upon the audience to play along with them. The shared, liminal space of the concert hall was, ultimately, a temporary one. Audiences left in the wake of the Liederabend relied on two particular modes of racial listening. Some chose to call Black singers white, which by proxy associated Germanness with whiteness. Others insisted that something foreign or alien, located in the Black body, had impinged on a Black musician's ability to produce German sounds, thus sonically marking their performances as irredeemably un-German. Race was ultimately the filter people used to understand performances of repertoire from the Austro-German canon. A fixed, false dichotomy guided their complex listening processes: Blackness or Germanness. Both categories remained, in sobering daylight, two separate spheres on opposite poles.

CHAPTER 6

"A Negro Who Sings German Lieder Jeopardizes German Culture"

Black Musicians under the Shadow of Nazism

In the summer of 1935, Salzburg was a battle-ground. Over three hundred people had gathered inside the ballroom of the Hotel de l'Europe one heady August afternoon in defiance of the Salzburg Festival's administration. Rumor had spread of a dynamic young Black singer with a gift for singing Bach, Handel, and Schubert who had been denied the right to perform at the festival. Backed by a small but supportive set of patrons, this Black woman by the name of Marian Anderson had shown up to the alpine city anyway. The audience at her first concert did not even fill the main concert hall of the Mozarteum building, but enough of them were so impressed by what they heard that they told others of the evening's success. Determined to see the singer's successes come to fruition, a wealthy white American woman named Gertrude Moulton set about organizing an afternoon teatime for hundreds of listeners with the fortitude of a military general.

"Seldom have I seen an audience like the one that came to hear Miss Anderson," Anderson's accompanist Kosti Vehanen later shared in his memoir.[1] The Archbishop of Salzburg sat in the front row in priestly dress, announcing his support for her and his rebuke of the Festival's wrongdoings in the most visual manner possible. If the archbishop was concerned that Anderson would be left wanting of an appreciative audience, he was mistaken: before the end of the afternoon, Anderson had earned so many accolades from prominent musicians that she became an international superstar virtually overnight.

Although many Americans today know Anderson as the woman who sang on the steps of the Lincoln Memorial in 1939 in defiance of the Daughters of the American Revolution, her performative politics began earlier than that, in Nazi Germany and fascist Austria. By the end of her stay in 1937, Anderson, like other Black musicians, had become a lightning rod in the world of classical music. Those who opposed her decried the presence of Black musicians in German musical life. Her supporters presented her as a champion of musical brotherhood and unity in the face of oppression. Against the backdrop of two right-wing, nationalist, racist, and fascist states, listeners became embroiled in a war about Black musicians and whether or not they belonged in Austro-German musical life.

Throughout the 1930s, this chapter argues, two competing notions of German music were at war with one another. One interpretation, in effect since at least the early 1920s, praised Black classical musicians as evidence of art music's transformative powers. As I demonstrated in the last chapter, critics frequently lauded Black musicians for supposedly overcoming their race to present near-faultless interpretations of the German music. Through

FIGURE 21. Marian Anderson and her accompanist Kosti Vehanen at the Mozarteum building in Salzburg in August 1935. Kislak Center for Special Collections, Rare Books, and Manuscripts, University of Pennsylvania, Ms Coll 200, UPenn Ms. Coll. 198: vol. 3, p. 9, item 2.

the powers invested in German music, Black classical musicians were able to shed their racial identities to become proper musicians, which listeners implicitly raced as white.

The other interpretation, however, was less welcoming, more hostile, and growing in popularity: German music needed defending against outsiders. Speaking before parliament in Berlin in 1923, Hermann Schuster of the far-right German People's Party (DVP) offered up the paradox that has been at the heart of German musical discourse for decades:

> Music is the most German of all our arts. None has emerged as specifically from our cast of mind as has music. At the same time, music is the art most capable of serving propaganda for us abroad. It is at once the most German and the most international of the arts, and is best able to contribute to the restoration of our honor and esteem in the world.[2]

What drew outsiders to German music was the very reason it needed protection from them: its universal greatness.

By 1932, protecting Austro-German music required violence. In fact, the 1930s can be distinguished from the 1920s (and before) by the increasingly extreme position those on the far right took against Black classical musicians. For many, what had once been considered "universal" now only belonged to some. It had been bad enough for Black jazz musicians to perform, they believed, but now the public was willing to consume their own music performed by members of a primitive race. Black musicians performing classical music specifically became a source of racial shame that demanded a violent response. The voices of mobs in protest, the sounds of booing and hissing, and the cries of "niggering!" (*Vernegerung*) became over time the most piercing sounds in concert halls and opera houses. Their cacophony drowned out the increasingly desperate calls of fellow audience members for unity in diversity.

Far-right condemnations of Black classical musicians reveal a growing challenge to the wide-ranging attitudes and experiences that the 1920s had ushered in. If before numerous possibilities and opportunities were open for social or cultural pursuit, by the 1930s a diversity of modernities—the plurality of experiences, affectations, sentimentalities, and perspectives—could no longer be tolerated by leaders of the far right. German solutions to the supposed crises of the interwar era called for unity, clarity, and decisive action—even across different ideological positions.[3] Unsurprisingly, the majority of solutions offered in response to the "problems" posed by diversity were in actuality what the historian Moritz Föllmer calls "homogenizing visions of change."[4] Nationalists in particular offered to purge society of difference and the messy complications that came with it "for the benefit of those deemed 'Germans' and at the expense of those deemed outsiders."[5]

Attaining a single, unified modernity—a "better" modernity, in the words of the historian Jochen Hung—required cleansing German culture of diversity of any kind, including in classical music.[6] It became increasingly difficult for orchestras to justify performing the music of Jewish composers such as Mendelssohn and Schoenberg; Jewish musicians went to rehearsals only to discover they had been barred from performing. The only way to purify the body again was to purge it of its supposedly alien elements. By the late 1930s, a majority of Black musicians had fled Central Europe. Those who stayed behind—Black Germans and African colonial migrants—faced persecution, violence, and even death.

Ironically, however, the demand for Black musicians never died, even if the far right had hoped it would. Their ongoing popularity is a reminder that while the years 1933 and 1934 may have represented a political shift, the 1920s still had lingering cultural and aesthetic effects.[7] The Nazis, Pamela Potter argues, neither desired to eradicate entire cultural trends wholesale, nor were they capable of it. "The exclusion of certain people (Jews, Communists, and others) may have been carried out with shocking thoroughness," she writes, "but it did not necessarily lead to the eradication of their artistic influences."[8] Even during WWII, German radio programs broadcast the music of Louis Armstrong, Duke Ellington, and Benny Goodman and simply concealed their names.[9] Throughout Nazi Germany, Susann Lewerenz argues, the state paradoxically employed Black musicians and entertainers from the former colonies and from within Germany to further Nazi colonial propaganda and to appeal to ongoing demands for "exotic" entertainment.[10]

Anderson's own experience fending off offers from German agencies after 1933 bears this out. One agency in particular seemed keen to track her down: knowing she would be performing in nearby Poland, the agency asked if she couldn't stop by Berlin for a day. Although, she writes, "I was not eager to appear in the Germany of those days," her manager posed an outrageous sum of money to the agency and "offered Berlin a single date." If they wanted Anderson, in other words, they were going to have to take the date or leave it. The Berlin agency eagerly accepted it, including the high fee to have her perform. "There was only one other question—was Marian Anderson an Aryan? My manager replied that Miss Anderson was not 100 percent Aryan. That ended the correspondence."[11]

In the case of Anderson, the agent's comments tell us that the desire for international superstars still existed in Nazi Germany, even if the agent in question claimed to be unaware of Anderson's race. The desire to employ international artists (and artists of color), was still strong enough to compel the manager to inquire into the status of Anderson's tour in Central Europe, even knowing that there might be a negative outcome to the inquiry. But everyone involved eventually came up against a legal barrier to her performance that they could not work around. Unlike recordings by foreign artists, which still circulated in spite of Joseph Goebbels's ban on them, the visuality of Anderson on a German stage could not be managed.

Like other Black musicians, Anderson hoped that if Nazi Germany couldn't hire her to perform, Austria would. Indeed, the majority of Black performances of classical music in the 1930s took place in Austria, not in Nazi Germany. The pianist Josephine Harreld spent the summer of 1935 in Salzburg, and the contralto Marguerite Wood attended the same institute a year later. Wood lived in Salzburg, Vienna, and Milan until WWII forced her to return to the United States.[12] In Vienna, the pianist Roy Tibbs visited the famous Beethoven memorial with other Black classical musicians in the city. Even the advent of the Nazi state did not prevent some African Americans from popping over into Germany to attend the Bayreuth Festival or catch an opera in Munich. But by the late 1930s, performing while Black in German-speaking Europe became an increasingly dangerous experience.

In this chapter, I examine the fight for the soul of Austro-German music in Central Europe, using the performances of Black classical musicians and their experiences in Central Europe to access German and Austrian attitudes toward race, gender, and nationality in the tumultuous decade of the 1930s. There were both violent protestors against and ardent defenders of Black classical musicians in the 1930s, all the way up until the annexation of Austria in 1938. At the heart of each reaction—for or against Black musicians— was the unshakeable belief in the supremacy of the Austro-German musical canon. Even Austrian conservatives who were against annexation nonetheless expressed their position as one of "German—Austro-German—cultural superiority," the historian Michael Steinberg argues.[13] In Germany and Austria, audiences for and against Black musicians turned to the universality of German music to explain why someone should or should not be permitted to perform the music of Bach, Beethoven, and Brahms. But regardless of their position, the universalizing promises of German music died when Black classical musicians could no longer be protected from white violence.

From Protest to Riot: Aubrey Pankey's Liederabend in Salzburg, May 1932

Whenever Black musicians performed German music on German-speaking soil they were playing with fire. Even when Roland Hayes faced adversity for performing in Berlin in 1924, one strain of criticism fixated on the outrageous audacity he had to sing German lieder in particular. "While he may understand modern music," the critic writes, "it would be impossible for him to interpret the cultured works of German poets, since he speaks out of the soul of his aboriginal people. We decline to have this section of works by Mozart, Bach, Handel, and Schubert presented by this Negro."[14] The root cause of German anger, according to this perspective, concerned the performance of German music itself. The notion that Black performances of German music were themselves an affront in their own right became the bedrock of anti-Black critiques in the 1930s.

Hayes's now-legendary debut in Berlin in 1924 began with boos and hisses and ended with applause and even adoration. But Aubrey Pankey's 1932 premiere in Salzburg ended with a riot. There to perform the music of Schubert, Richard Strauss, and other German composers, the African American baritone instead found himself fleeing under police protection from Nazi rioters who demanded the Mozarteum cast out the performer. Pankey would later describe that evening as one of the most terrifying ordeals he had ever experienced as a concert artist.[15] Pankey's Salzburg Liederabend became a moment when anti-Black thinking led to violent action, marking the first time that Black classical musicians faced a violent mob that could not be assuaged by tone of voice or the quality of one's musicianship. Organized protests against Pankey demonstrate that there was no longer any circumstance acceptable under which a Black singer could prove himself worthy of performing German music.

Born in Pittsburgh, Pennsylvania, Pankey studied music at the Hampton Institute in Virginia with the noted composer, pianist, and choral conductor Nathaniel Dett.[16] He continued his training at Oberlin Conservatory of Music in Ohio and at Boston University before leaving in 1931 to study in Europe. Between 1931 and 1940, he lived in Germany, Austria (where he studied with Theodor Lierhammer in Vienna), and France. His first recital took place on November 17, 1931, in Vienna: a promotional advertisement listed him as a "Negerbariton" hosting a Liederabend in the small music hall.[17]

Pankey's Liederabend in Salzburg the following May did not go well. Discovering where he was to perform, Nazis in Salzburg placed flyers throughout the city on the day of his premiere, "asking the people not to enable a Negro to take the daily bread of German artists."[18] In this way, the reaction to Pankey's performance echoed that of Hayes in Berlin in that both performances symbolized foreign artistry in German culture and non-Aryan artists taking money from the deserving German workforce of musicians. Much like antisemitic Viennese posters against the Black popular entertainer Josephine Baker and the opera *Jonny spielt auf* that linked jazz to Jewish degeneracy, the flyer also decried both Jews and the "Negro spirit" for inculcating German culture with their racial poison.[19] The preservation of German culture was at stake. It was time, the Nazis announced, to defend the city against this racial threat.

In anticipation of the protestors, the police closed down the Mozarteum building's ticket booth well before the concert to prevent lines from forming. They also stood on the steps and in the halls of the house and ensured that it was only possible to enter the building with an admission ticket. Plain-clothes detectives lurked in the hallways, looking for suspicious activity. Pankey was able to sing without protestors entering the building. But they waited outside for him, shouting and singing nationalist songs. They tried repeatedly to storm the building but were blocked by the police.[20]

Two detailed records exist documenting Pankey's performance, both in the right-leaning *Salzburger Volksblatt*. The first is a concert review written by an unnamed critic. The second is an opinion piece that appeared the following day. Both are damning in their analysis of Pankey's performance, and both utilize nearly all of the discursive tropes available to Austrian and German audiences in the 1930s to make Pankey an inferior musician because of his race. The writer of the first essay published in the *Salzburger Volksblatt* begins:

> I don't know. Whenever you see a Negro, you get the feeling that he has a quiet longing for his grasslands. If he doesn't laugh frantically and show his shiny teeth, there is something strangely indifferent in his features. You believe him right away that he—in the true sense of the word—feels utterly out of place in Europe.[21]

What made the "Negro" out of place was his reliance entirely on his monotonous physicality to entertain his audience. In contrast, "The white [man], especially the German, is moved more by his emotions; his music is more melodious and spiritually deeper." Black people, on the other hand, "love uniformity, in which only forced rhythms bring an expression of joy."[22] Nothing about this critic's opening statements are original; rather, his criticisms rely on the same worn-out descriptions that portray Black musicality as primitive, simplistic, and almost ritualistic.

The critic had little to say about Pankey's performance of classical music. He noted that Pankey had "supposedly come by his education in Vienna," a phrase that cast doubt on Pankey's training. But Pankey's voice, due to his "negroid mouth formation," was unable to produce sounds pleasing to European ears. "For our taste," the author writes, "the voice lacks in color especially in piano, the ability to modulate, and shading . . . When this voice dampens, it sinks into a tender but monotonous gray." Reproducing the stereotype of Black performers as melancholic but not intellectual, the critic concludes, "[Pankey's] Schubert was the most successful where the music was tragic."[23]

Although he doubted that Black performers ultimately possessed the sophistication and inherent qualities found in German music to conquer German lieder—"There is hardly any need to fear that the Black race will also annex the German lied after conquering the dance hall"—he nonetheless applauded those who had protested against Pankey's Liederabend that evening and encouraged others in the future to "act out against this pollution through Nigger music." Their reactionary efforts, he promised, would ensure "the regeneration of German culture."[24] In order for Germany to undergo a full cultural renewal, racial transgressions like those that Pankey had committed must be stopped.

The anonymous opinion piece that appeared the day after the aforementioned review was even more aggressive. The writer of it warns that the demonstration against Pankey's recital that Monday was simply a taste of what was yet to come. Only a fraction of the followers of the Nazi party and other right-leaning parties that had participated in the demonstration were in attendance, he argued, and many more were equally committed to safeguarding Salzburg's "cultural goods" and "national dignity" in the wake of foreign invasion.[25] He commended the rioters for disrupting what was an utterly disgraceful act: a Black musician performing German music.

The opinion piece offers a rigorous rejection of German musical universalism. On the one hand, the author applauds the German-speaking lands for music so beautiful that it appealed to a broad audience: "When the German lied has so much appeal that everyone around the world sings it, and when thus also baptized Negroes sing it (such as 'Stille Nacht, Heilige Nacht'), then the German spirit should rejoice in this rather than negate it."[26] He also praises the city of Salzburg itself as an example of German music's intrinsic greatness: it hosted the greatest festival in the world that attracted visitors dedicated to pursuing art.

But, the writer argues, it is precisely because of German music's greatness that Black people should not be allowed to perform it. Black performances of German music represented a form of racial miscegenation. Salzburg, the greatest musical city of the world, "should not allow a Negro to sing, let alone [to sing] German lieder, and Schubert lieder at that." The critic stated that he understood and sympathized with African Americans' history of suffering, and that their progress in American society was to be commended. Referencing *Uncle Tom's Cabin*, he writes, "There was a time when every

German soul had human compassion for the poor, tormented slaves who were abused and exploited by whites." But what Pankey and other Black musicians wished to do was akin to racial mixing. Their eagerness to devour German music endangered whiteness itself. Blackness and Germanness were simply inhospitable to one another, and attempts to bring them together through musical performance were themselves racial transgressions. The conclusion of the author's piece is quite clear: "A Negro who sings German lieder jeopardizes German culture." The path that Germans must choose, however unpleasant it might appear, demanded that they use political and even violent methods to protect German art and culture.[27]

Looking back on his ordeal in Salzburg, Pankey told the *Chicago Daily Tribune*, "I thought I was in some of the southern sections of the United States when I heard the mob. I never expected this in Europe."[28] The irony of finding Jim Crow practices of public behavior in Central Europe did not escape other Black musicians caught in the growing crossfire of a cultural battle for the German soul.[29]

Unfortunately for Pankey and others, threats of violence against Black musicians never dissipated in the 1930s. Black performances of German music became, to far-right ears, a sonic form of racial miscegenation, which could only be understood as a threat to the German nation and a danger to the future of the white race. More white Germans called for the removal of Black lives, cultures, and experiences from German spaces.

Those Who Fled and Those Who Stayed: The Black Exodus from Central Europe

Pankey's harrowing ordeal was not enough to deter other African American musicians from performing in Central Europe in the 1930s. Nor was it enough to change the minds of some African Americans who continued to insist that life in Central Europe was more glamorous, less harmful, and more racially harmonious than that in the United States. Both before and after the establishment of the Nazi racial state in 1933, some African Americans continually upheld their belief in a Germany without racial prejudice. In so doing, Robbie Aitken writes, they "consciously presented idealized and romanticized visions of a Germany in which there was a lack of color prejudice."[30] Their comparative frameworks reflected their own desires to indict the United States' long history of white supremacy, which outweighed their willingness to acknowledge the realities of anti-Blackness on the ground in Central Europe.

Frank Smith—an African American doctor like Wilberforce Williams and Ossian Sweet, both of whom lived in Vienna in the 1920s—found the Viennese to be unfailingly polite and steeped in a culture of decorum and aristocracy, and he similarly placed Central Europe in comparison to the United States in his writings. "Since leaving the States," Smith shared, "I have never heard a rough or profane word used by a policeman."[31] Many interpreted the absence of white American anti-Black violence abroad to mean that Central Europeans were more affirming and racially progressive than white Americans.

Writing from Vienna in 1929, the journalist J. A. Rogers scoffed at the notion that African Americans faced discrimination in Europe. He writes:

> As to color prejudice [in Europe], it is hardly necessary to say that it does not exist. I have said already so many times that one may travel every part of the European continent and, instead of meeting it, meet only what seems special attention just because one is colored, provided he keeps away from white Americans. Color prejudice is a form of American insanity that the European cannot understand; instead of finding the Negro repulsive as the American pretends, the European finds him attractive and seeks his company. And that is why every colored American should try to save enough money to make at least a brief trip to Europe. It will give him a new vision of life that will certainly repay the cost.[32]

Even as fascism in both Germany and Austria became an increasingly present reality, African Americans continued to uphold these beliefs. In 1936, the Wagnerian W.E.B. Du Bois made a pilgrimage to the town of Bayreuth in Nazi Germany—shortly after the Olympic games in which the African American sprinter Jesse Owens had famously competed—because he had "an interest in the development of the human soul and for the spirit of beauty, which this shrine commemorates and makes eternal."[33] Like a pilgrim in the Holy Land, Du Bois reported to the *Pittsburgh Courier* that he had taken his seat in the Bayreuth opera house, waiting to partake in a once-in-a-lifetime ritual: listening to Wagner's operas in Bayreuth. The event would last from approximately 5:00 until 10:30 p.m., and "nothing," he assured readers in his newspaper column, "not even meals, interrupts this sacrament."[34]

But something did disrupt his religious rite as he prepared to transcend into a realm of unknown human expression and thought. Sitting in the seat in front of him, also waiting for the thick, velvet curtain to rise, was a wealthy white American. Oblivious to Du Bois's presence, he boasted about his wealth and social status to his friend, bragging about booking a table at a restaurant right next to the Wagner family. Such behavior, Du Bois thought, was appalling and arrogant, embodying the worst aspects of class and race on both sides of the Atlantic. Even more than that, Du Bois fumed, it went against "what Richard Wagner lived to teach."[35] This white American was incapable of grasping Wagner's message to the world: that we should reject superficiality in all forms and instead strive to depict and understand the earnest struggles of all mankind.

It is striking that Du Bois's complaint focused not on Nazism or on German anti-Black racism but on a white American man. Du Bois, like other African American writers, frequently ignored or dismissed anti-Black racism in Germany or the experiences of other Black diasporic populations abroad in order to highlight the benefits African Americans received in traveling through Central Europe. "Subsumed under the hegemonizing and generalizing designation 'Negroes in Germany,'" Maria Diedrich writes, "Black Germans in these African American narratives of the German '30s and '40s are relegated to a diasporic periphery at best." Rather, mentions of anti-Black racism, Diedrich argues, were "balanced, if not silenced, by individual public voices like those of Locke, Du Bois, and [the African American journalist John] Welch, who continued to compare their personal experiences as African Americans in Germany to their everyday lives in the United States— and found life in the United States deficient, relentlessly dangerous, and humiliating."[36]

Josephine Harreld, studying piano performance and conducting at the Mozarteum University Salzburg in the summer of 1935, also shared little about her experience interacting with white Austrians and Germans. The only experience of racism she shared came from white Americans. International students at the Mozarteum were Harreld's closest friends because white Americans refused to talk to her. She confided to her parents, "The root of the trouble is three girls . . . They have become very thick and are the sophisticates of the group. They feel that I have overstepped my bounds by entering into conversations at the table and by acting like a reasonable human being."[37] Although Harreld normally sat at another table at lunch, one day her seat was occupied by a guest and she was forced to sit at their table. The three white American girls removed themselves from it. "Jane [a young white woman from Smith] says that her family has Negro servants. So for that reason she cannot overcome her prejudices."[38] Harreld's retort was mired in the class and respectability politics that her family espoused. "So have I!" Harreld told a student who had witnessed the racist act of discrimination, "And furthermore, I have had white servants as well."[39]

Not once in Harreld's letters home to her parents that summer in Salzburg does she mention Nazism or fascism in Germany or in Austria. In fact,

Harreld seemed to have no qualms about popping over to Munich, a few hours' train ride away from Salzburg, to visit the National Theatre Munich in 1935.

The downplaying or dismissal of anti-Black racism by African Americans in Central Europe was rampant. Worse, a kind of victim blaming and colorism seeped through the pages of the few reports on the diversity of Black experiences in Central Europe, when they appeared at all. Rogers insisted that any signs of anti-Black prejudice in Germany that existed had been caused by the presence of Black Africans from either France's present or Germany's former colonies. Rogers had listened to "the Negroes in Berlin" complain about experiencing white violence or hatred and ultimately rejected it. "[Their complaint] may be true, but I find it hard to believe it, because all with whom I came in contact were so spontaneously friendly."[40] Worse, Rogers blamed Black Africans for their maltreatment. "I also saw Negroes, *very dark ones*, in places and generally doing things they would not be permitted to do in America."[41] Rogers's comment reflects his own colorism and biases against African migrants.

Carter G. Woodson's remarks on Black jazz musicians in Nazi Germany were even more vicious and downright violent. The historian and founder and editor of the *Journal of Negro History* applauded Hitler for casting jazz out of Nazi Germany. "There was nothing racial in this effort," Woodson insisted. "Self-respecting Negroes are welcome in Germany." Rather, Woodson writes, "Hitler set a noble example in trying to preserve the good in civilization. Would to God that he had the power not to drive them for [sic] one country into another but to round up all jazz promoters and performers of both races in Europe and America and execute them as criminals. Negroes must join in such a crusade."[42]

Woodson's caustic comments completely ignored the increasingly difficult situations in which Black musicians found themselves. Following Hitler's placement as dictator, some African American entertainers struggled to gain employment from familiar haunts or acceptance in musical circles in Germany particularly. Some, like Lillian Evanti, hosted Liederabende in Germany shortly after Hitler had assumed power. But others often paid a terrible price for staying and performing in cities such as Salzburg or Berlin. Jules Bledsoe, a Viennese favorite, had difficulty finding work in post-1933 Germany: his concert manager had attempted to arrange a concert in Berlin for him after the ban against foreign artists was in place but to no effect. Paul Robeson spent about twenty-four hours in Berlin on December 21, 1934, which was ample time to convince Robeson and his family to leave as quickly as possible. Essie Robeson, Robeson's wife, later recalled their arrival at the Berlin Friedrichstrasse train station and how Robeson's dark skin drew attention. A white woman, outraged and affronted to see a Black man in Berlin, marched over to uniformed policemen on the platform to complain. Essie wrote in her diary that they felt as if a lynch mob were about to attack him. It was, Essie wrote, "a terrible feeling of wolves waiting to spring," the following day as they boarded the train to Moscow. "For a long time after the train moved out of Berlin, Paul sat hunched in the corner of the compartment staring out into the darkness."[43] Like Hayes and Pankey, Essie Robeson drew a comparison between the Jim Crow South and Nazi Germany, finding them to be less dissimilar than she had expected.

By the late 1930s, all African Americans were advised to leave the European continent as quickly as possible. William R. Tatten, an orchestral leader who had been a member of Will Marion Cook's orchestra, publicly urged African Americans to get out of Europe in 1938. Interviewed by the African American paper *New York Amsterdam News*, Tatten said, "I advise Negroes to stay out of Europe altogether unless it is absolutely necessary to go over there."[44] Although Tatten, who had returned to the United States from Vienna in October 1936, claimed that he offered his advice not because he was concerned about the treatment of Black people in Europe, but because of oncoming war, his message does not sound entirely truthful, especially when one considers his own trip back to the United States. Tatten had originally traveled to Germany to perform with Cook's Southern Syncopated Orchestra, then onward to Switzerland and Czechoslovakia, where he led several all-white jazz-influenced orchestras. Tatten settled in Berlin in 1930, where he organized his own ensemble to perform at the Haus Vaterland, the Hotel Esplanade, and the Princess Restaurant in Berlin; he later recalled being in Germany when Paul von Hindenburg was elected president. Tatten was still in Berlin when the Nazis came to power, and he was forced to flee to Budapest. There he formed a Hungarian orchestra that went on tour with him to Vienna, and from Vienna he returned to the United States.[45]

There remains no discernible pattern of how and why Black musicians left or sometimes fled Europe to return to the United States. In some ways, their departures remain as invisible or unrecognizable as their entrances into Germany and Austria. Some musicians' exits were relatively uneventful. Other musicians, such as the Fisk piano professor William Allen, fled under duress: Allen had been in Poland to study with Egon Petri (Hazel Harrison's former teacher) during the summer of 1939, and fifteen days before the invasion of

Poland, he received notice from the Dutch Embassy that he should pack his bags and return to the United States immediately.[46]

The opera singer Caterina Jarboro reported her terrifying 1939 journey back to the United States from Europe in true dramatic fashion. When Germany invaded Poland in September, Jarboro, who had been performing in opera houses in Europe since 1934, had been engaged to perform in Poland near the Soviet border. She apparently had to leave all of her luggage behind, fleeing to France before returning to the States. "Because of the war situation," a reporter for the *New York Amsterdam News* writes, "Mme. Jarboro had to cancel engagements previously scheduled directly in the war zone and along the frontier." " 'No more,' explained the diva, 'shall I be able to sing in Germany, Czechoslovakia, Lithuania, Poland, Austria—all countries to which I have returned year after year for engagements.'"[47] Jarboro's remarks that she could no longer find work in Germany, Czechoslovakia, Austria, and other countries explains why so many African American musicians continued to reside in German-speaking Europe until the late 1930s. In the United States, they had few opportunities to perform with major opera houses or symphony orchestras. As long as European opera houses and orchestras—no matter how big or small—were willing to take them, African American classical musicians could earn money in their profession.

Jules Bledsoe also returned to the United States from Germany on a German cruise liner in 1938, arriving in April on the SS Bremen of the North German Lloyd line. He was somewhat apprehensive about booking a ship out of Bremen, but he explained that it was the only boat that would get him to the United States in time for his other engagements. Bledsoe told a *New York Amsterdam News* reporter in 1938:

> My trip was extremely pleasant, although I got the feeling that this might have been because the Germans want to impress foreigners that the Nazi program is being misrepresented. . . . Whereas in former days, many Negroes could be seen on the streets of Berlin, none are now in evidence, foreign or otherwise. The German people, at heart, I believe, like Negroes, but because of Nazi dictatorship, which preaches intense nationalism, they must practice race hatred for political reasons.[48]

The African American journalist Roi Ottley, however, was less forgiving of German mistreatment of African Americans. He counters Bledsoe's more positive impressions of life in Nazi Germany. According to Ottley, a young Black German teacher named Mary Ann was accepted to study at Berlin's Friedrich Wilhelm University (today's Humboldt University) and live in the

student residence halls. She left the United States, Ottley writes, with warnings ringing in her ears:

> "Germany! Child, are you crazy!" . . . "You can't go there. Don't you
> know what they're doing to the Jews!" . . . "Something dreadful is sure
> to happen!" . . . "With all of Europe to see why do you want to go
> there!" . . . "In his book, *Mein Kampf*, Hitler calls the Negro a 'half-ape,'
> and says it's 'criminal foolishness' to train him. You don't think you'll
> be allowed to go to school there after that, do you!"[49]

Mary Ann went anyway, stubbornly believing that things weren't as they
seemed, but within a few months of living in Germany she asked her parents
to bring her back to the United States. She spent her last few days in Berlin
living in fear.[50]

Although it is unclear how many African American musicians and entertainers fled German-speaking Europe right before war broke out in 1939,
what remains remarkable is how many musicians continued to eke out a
living in Central Europe prior to the outbreak of war. They lived and performed in these hostile spaces long after the Nazi racial state had enforced
rules to encourage their departure and long after German nationalists in
Austria expressed their desire to cast them out. Only war could convince
some African American musicians to leave, and by then it was often too late
for them to escape. For Black Germans and African colonial migrants, the
situation was even worse since they had little choice but to stay.[51] Like other
racial minorities in Europe, many were captured and sent to concentration
camps in Central and Eastern Europe.[52]

The Last Woman Standing: Marian Anderson in Austria, 1935–37

By November 1937, a few months before the Third Reich annexed Austria,
Anderson had become a polarizing figure. She was most likely the last remaining prominent Black musician in the city, and her Liederabend that
month symbolized either the universalist ideals of classical music at a time
when popular support to repress these ideals was at its apex or the downfall
of German music at the height of a cultural crisis, depending on the listener.
What Viennese reception of Anderson teaches us is how much the city had
become divided over its musical, national, and racial future in the months
leading up to the annexation. As we will see, critics' praise of Anderson carried overtones of desperation and fear: they held her up as a beacon of light

in a time of darkness and insisted that she represented the beauties of universalism in an era of extreme nationalism and racism.

Anderson's concerts were always politicized, including her most famous 1935 Salzburg Festival concert. In fact, Anderson's first trouble with right-leaning gatekeepers of German music began there. Anderson had settled permanently in Vienna in the fall of 1934, having spent the summer in Germany working with Sara Cahier exclusively on the music of Mahler. Little evidence exists about her stay in Nazi Germany that summer, but the little she has said echoes reports from other Black musicians: it must have been profoundly uncomfortable, even frightening. In Vienna, she set about trying to prove her merits and woo Viennese audiences with her singing. "To sing and be accepted here [in Vienna]," she later shared, "meant another milestone in the direction I had always hoped to go."[53] At her first concert at the Wiener Konzerthaus in Vienna, she won over the crowd with her lieder interpretations, especially of Bach's "Komm, süßer Tod." She made such an impression on the audience that Dr. Waitz, Archbishop of Salzburg, approached her after the concert to ask if she could give a charity concert in the Salzburg Cathedral at the Salzburg Festival.

But then Salzburg, near the Austrian-German border, had become a contested site of Nazism by the early 1930s. Jewish intellectuals such as Stefan Zweig had stopped visiting, and a few years later Toscanini would resign from the festival in protest. The last time a Black musician had performed in the city—Pankey—he had been chased out of town. The invitation offered to Anderson to come to Salzburg and perform, and the consequent debates about that invitation, articulate the varying positions on Anderson that listeners took up in the 1930s. The questions of whether the universalizing message of German music applied to everyone and whether music could and should transcend racism and nationalism became more urgent throughout Anderson's career in Austria. Anderson's performance in Salzburg in 1935 was at that time the greatest musical test of these competing ideals.

The test failed. The administration soundly rejected Anderson's petition to perform at the Salzburg Festival: "According to your wish I hereby answer your two letters of March 29 and April 24 as well as that of Dr. Hohenberg that there can be no question of Marian Anderson [singing in the festival] since earlier experiences firmly speak against it."[54] Baron Heinrich Puthon, the president of the Salzburg Festival committee, professed ignorance of her request to perform and claimed that there was simply no room for Anderson in the festival because all of the performances had been scheduled months earlier.[55] No matter how many impresarios and prominent musicians protested on Anderson's behalf, the Salzburg Festival would not budge.

Anderson's concert manager Helmer Enwall wrote to the Viennese manager Wilhelm Stein in outrage over this incident, accusing the festival of flat-out racism. "When every summer singers of different nationalities appear in Salzburg, and when Marian Anderson is known throughout the world as one of the finest and most distinguished lieder singers and interpreters of Schubert, Mahler, Brahms, and others, all the more must we be given a reason why permission has not been granted," he writes. "[I wonder] whether it is perhaps her dark complexion?"[56] The Salzburg Festival prided itself on being open to different nationalities but in reality was not welcoming to different races.

Anderson chose to sing in Salzburg anyway. Perhaps pressured by international elites, the Salzburg Festival eventually relented and let her perform at the Mozarteum building—albeit unattached from any of their own activities. Within minutes of her landing in the alpine city of Mozart, gossip swirled around Anderson. The Austrian and German media reported that the "Salzkammergut [region] was streaming with the thrilling sensation" of this "exotic nightingale" in a grey-pink dress.[57] Her friend and accompanist Vehanen reflected later that within a few days of being in Salzburg, "Enough prominent people were there for the news of Marian Anderson's artistry to spread around; soon her name was on everybody's lips. She had quietly gained the attention and the confidence of the influential musicians."[58]

On the day of her second recital, Anderson performed for a nearly sold-out house filled with some of the most prominent members of Austria and Germany's musical life. In his memoir, *Between the Thunder and the Sun*, the American journalist Vincent Sheean provided an eyewitness account of hearing Anderson sing in Salzburg, and the list of attendees at Anderson's recital he provides is a roll call of Europe's classical music elites. Moulton had organized an afternoon concert for almost four hundred people at the Hotel de l'Europe, including the Archbishop of Salzburg, "Toscanini, [Lotte] Lehmann, [Bruno] Walter, and practically all the other musical powers of Salzburg."[59] In many ways, their attendance at Anderson's recital was a political act. By gathering to hear Anderson sing, they hosted their own demonstration against the Salzburg Festival and publicly indicated that they were willing to defy, annoy, or alienate those who saw Anderson's presence as unsavory.

According to her private notes, Anderson sang a combination of baroque and Romantic pieces that afternoon. She began by singing the popular Henry Purcell aria, "When I Am Laid in Earth," followed by Doménico Scarlatti's "Se Florindo è fedele" and Handel's "Ah! Spietato!" Her Schubert pieces were "Der Tod und das Mädchen," "Die Forelle," and "Die Allmacht." She sang

Brahms's "Die Mainacht" and Mahler's "Irrlicht" and "Rheinlegendchen" as well. Having just returned from Finland, where she worked with the composer Jean Sibelius, a mentor of hers, she sang two of his pieces, "Die Libelle" and "War es ein Traum." She concluded with four African American spirituals: "Deep River," "Crucifixion," "Lord, I Can't Stay Away," and "Heav'n, Heav'n."[60]

Audiences found Anderson's recital moving, thoughtful, emotional, and most pleasing to Austrian and German ears. She received numerous encores, and at the Archbishop's insistence, Anderson had to repeat Schubert's "Ave Maria" for the audience. At the end of one of Anderson's spirituals, Sheean observed, "There was no applause at all—a silence instinctive, natural, and intense, so that you were afraid to breathe. What Anderson had done was something outside the limits of classical or Romantic music."[61]

After the concert, Toscanini and Walter came backstage and thanked Anderson personally for her performance. Toscanini told Cahier, "What I heard today one is privileged to hear only once in a hundred years." Vehanen clarified the significance of Toscanini's statement further: "He did not say the voice he heard, but what he heard—not the voice alone but the whole art."[62] In other words, Anderson's entire artistry and her entire mastery of German music had impressed Toscanini.

Anderson's decision to perform under growing opposition and hostility became one of the defining features of her long career. Although she had not been able to perform as part of the Salzburg Festival, she nonetheless won her battle to create public spaces for listeners to hear her sing. Her pattern of showing up to perform in the face of considerable protest and administrative pressure to relent only strengthened over the next few years.

For example, in June 1936, a few short months before the Berlin Olympics in Nazi Germany, Anderson performed again to adoring crowds and in the face of much opposition—this time violent. Singing with the Vienna Philharmonic at the behest of Bruno Walter, Anderson performed Johannes Brahms's Alto Rhapsody as part of an all-Brahms evening.[63] Walter's insistence on collaborating with Anderson on Brahms was not only aesthetic; it reflected his own politics as a German Jew who had been forced out of the Berlin Philharmonic in 1933 with Hitler's rise to power. Throughout his time with the Vienna Philharmonic, he made no attempts to hide his loathing of the National Socialist movement. In his memoir, he writes in visceral prose, "Hitler was made chancellor and the Nazis set the Reichstag building afire. The gates of hell had opened."[64]

Throughout the 1930s, Bruno Walter worked with several Black classical musicians either in private lessons or in public concerts. Prior to inviting Anderson to perform with the Vienna Philharmonic, for example, Walter had already performed with Hayes in New York City on March 26, 1925. Showing his "willingness to explore repertoire that was foreign to him," Hayes writes, Walter conducted Hayes in a performance of excerpts from Bach's St. Matthew's Passion and orchestrated arrangements of African American spirituals.[65] When Hayes returned to Vienna in 1926, Walter sought him out again to perform with the Vienna Philharmonic for October, but Hayes had already decided to return to the United States for a few concerts.[66] In 1935, prior to Anderson's Salzburg debut, Walter had also started teaching conducting to Josephine Harreld.[67]

For his collaborative work with Anderson and others, Walter received angry promises of violence from Austro-German nationalists. Throughout the 1930s, protestors threw stink bombs into the Vienna State Opera House and other musical venues to decry the "degenerate" and "debased" music that they believed had infiltrated these spaces. In Walter's memoirs, he recalls Vienna's descent into terror and anxiety as the Nazis began to assume more cultural influence and political power. It became all the more necessary to resist and defy those who professed through violence to be reclaiming German culture.[68] But the news that Walter had engaged Anderson to sing with the Vienna Philharmonic brought him a death threat so severe that Vienna's police were called in to help.[69] When Anderson stepped onto the podium with Walter to sing Brahms, plainclothes officers watched from the shadows.

The concert fostered a daring and defiant spirit of community among her Viennese supporters. And nearly all of the reviews in the Viennese media—none of which appeared in right-wing presses—were unanimous in praising the quality of musicianship that had been on display that evening. "What would Brahms have said?" read several headlines the day after the concert, as if suggesting that Vienna was living in truly modern times to be hosting a Black woman in the Musikverein. *Die Stunde*, marveling at Anderson's performance, asked "What would [the poet Goethe] have said to such a beautiful song sung from the mouth of a Black woman . . .?"[70]

What Anderson's singing symbolized to some in late 1930s Vienna was the power of musical universalism in spite of German nationalism and racism. Much to the horror of Austrian Nazis, for example, the *Neues Wiener Journal* concluded their review of Anderson's June 1936 concert by stating, "But who dares formalize what is so much larger than this: understanding, the brotherhood of two races [performing] in character of the music?"[71] Anderson's debut with the Vienna Philharmonic represented the aspects of German music that nationalists wished to see buried: its universalism, its ability to bring musicians of different races together for the purpose of performance. Music could stand for brotherhood and equality in a Beetho-venian sense in a city that was becoming increasingly hostile to such ideals.

By late 1937, though, just over a year after Anderson's Vienna Philhar-monic debut, it had become increasingly difficult to maintain and uphold these optimistic beliefs in the face of a growing and unified opposition to them. In November 1937, Anderson hosted another recital in Vienna, and the Viennese knew it would be her last. Growing concern from her family, friends, and supporters back in the United States coupled with mounting social unrest and political upheaval in Vienna led Anderson to leave the city. Her swan song in the city of Vienna—one last Liederabend—sold out the large Musikverein Hall days before her appearance. The *Neues Wiener Jour-nal* reported, "We have not heard Marian Anderson, the incomparable Ne-gro singer, in Vienna for over a year. Her reappearance proved the extent to which the Viennese concert audience had taken her singing to their hearts; the large Musikverein Hall was sold out to the last row."[72]

At her farewell concert, with her accompanist Vehanen at her side, An-derson sang music that the Viennese loved best: the lieder of Schubert, Wolf, Handel, and other German composers. She also offered them a trio of Si-belius lieder and several African American spirituals, which the audience

FIGURE 22. Marian Anderson in Vienna, 1930s (figures unidentified). Kislak Center for Special Collections, Rare Books, and Manuscripts, University of Pennsylvania, Ms. Coll. 198: vol. 8, p. 19, item 5.

demanded she sing repeatedly.[73] Critics nearly unanimously agreed that Anderson had never sounded better; she was at the pinnacle of her artistry. One
dedicated follower at the *Neues Wiener Journal* noticed a stark transformation
from her 1934 arrival in Vienna to her last recital in 1937: "During the time
of her absence, she has become visibly and audibly more mature," he writes.
No more did listeners see a "gangly creature with big burning eyes on the
podium, but rather a woman, beautiful and aware in her own way, a priestess
of her art."[74]

Again in universalizing tones, critics sang the praises of Anderson's ability
to remind Vienna of its shared humanity, even while pointing out the supposed foreignness of her musicianship. "[The] triumphs of her expressive
presentation are greater [than the foreign sound of her voice] since they are
testimony of a moving, very emotional heart," the critic for *Das Echo* writes.
"And therefore Anderson in the end virtually ensures the opposite effect of
the exotic, of the bizarre; *she proves how the human heart speaks intelligibly
to everybody.*"[75] Similarly, the critic for *Die Stunde* spoke of Anderson in the
language of universal human rights: "*[Her concert] makes those people happy
who have not yet given up their belief that all men are equal.*"[76] Anderson's final
farewell was a musical testament to Austrian liberal ideals in the wake of
ongoing right-wing nationalist assault.

Anderson's concertizing in Central Europe then became imbued with
more than just musical and aesthetic meaning in the late 1930s. A symbol to
many of the aspirational goals of racial equality, universal brotherhood, and
harmony among nations, her Liederabende brought out growing divisions
between nationalists and defenders of a cosmopolitan Central European
culture. Anderson faced continual opposition from nationalists, National Socialists, and other ideologues who prided themselves on protecting German
culture from foreign invasion. But other listeners also adored Anderson for
the same reasons her enemies detested her: she represented the possibilities of racial harmony through the shared and cherished action of musical
performance. Leaving only a few months before the annexation of Austria
by the Third Reich, Anderson became a ghost whose elegant image haunted
the city of Vienna well through the postwar era, where her performance of
Schubert's "Nacht und Träume" became the swan song of the city's past,
wedged into people's memories.

Black Departures and White Reckonings

Writing to the *New York Times* in 1942, a Viennese expatriate residing in the
United States named George Kugel reflected on a concert he had attended

in 1932 or 1933, "before Vienna had awakened to the acuteness of the Nazi menace." Explaining that a fight broke out in, of all places, the Musikverein Hall, because of the performance of "Negermusik," he recalled:

> After [the ensemble played] the blues, hoots and cries of "Negermusik!" and "Pfui!" from the few Nazi provocateurs [at the] back of the orchestra stalls soon developed into a free fight, in the course of which the rowdies were ejected. Little did we realize that incidents like these, which we minimized then—they were repeated nightly at Josephine Baker's performances too—were all part of the Nazi master plan: to lump all exotic, advanced art—"Stravinsky, Picasso, Schoenberg, Alban Berg, Kandinsky, Marian Anderson, whatever it might be"—together as "negroid" and discredit it as unworthy of the Aryan.[77]

Anything "negroid" needed to be expunged from German musical culture, ranging from Baker to Schoenberg to Anderson. Black performers and their musicianship had come to stand for racial miscegenation, commercialism, and sexual deviance. Protesters against this rhetoric, however, attempted to move singers such as Anderson away from these racist discourses (even while they sometimes reaffirmed them through their interpretations of Anderson's musicianship) and fought hard to create a harmonious space for Anderson and other Black classical musicians amid the overwhelming hostility toward anything deemed "negroid."

But in the fight to determine who had the right to perform in Central Europe, Black musicians lost. African American classical musicians in particular fled or were pressured into leaving Central Europe by the late 1930s, labeled "degenerate" and poisonous by the National Socialist press. These musicians were entirely capable, the National Socialists assured German speakers, of creating only the worst kind of racial pollution. The Nazi state would work hard to ensure that Black cultures and people would be eradicated in Europe.

The Nazi state followed through with their avowal to cleanse Europe of its Black presence. In December 1943 a letter from the African American entertainer Evelyn Anderson Hayman arrived at the offices of the *Chicago Defender* for publication in their "Swinging the News" section. She had written to Chicago from a concentration camp in Germany. "Dear Swinging," Hayman writes, "I was formerly with Lew Leslie's Blackbirds (1929) and wish to be remembered to all my friends. I have been interned here for more than a year. I am in a very nice camp and have it very good here. The wife and two daughters of Freddy Johnson, the pianist, are here also."[78] Sending Christmas greetings to friends and loved ones in the United States, she signs her letter from Post Tettnan[g], Germany. Held against her will at a concentration camp near Liebenau, Germany, occasionally able to sneak in items such as lipstick from the Red Cross, Hayman represents the terrible consequences and outcomes of being a Black musician in Nazi-occupied Europe, the very thing Anderson had come to fear. Living in Paris, like many other Black musicians, Hayman had ignored several warnings about Nazi invasions. And like other African American musicians who had chosen to stay on the outskirts of Central Europe, she soon found herself experiencing the full terror of Nazi racial policy.

Although Nazi German actions against Black musicians were inconsistent and minimal in comparison to their organized attack against Jews, they nonetheless indicate the dangerous sincerity behind their efforts to eliminate racial difference in Europe. After being interned in a concentration camp for eight months, the popular jazz trumpeter Valaida Snow arrived back to the United States in ill health, underweight and frail. She had been living in Denmark conducting an orchestra when Nazi Germans arrested her. Her experience in the camp was terrible: regularly whipped, beaten, and called a "Black pig," she became malnourished after living on a diet of three potatoes a day for over six months.[79]

Even inside Nazi concentration camps, the demand for Black musicianship continued. Arthur Briggs, a jazz trumpeter, spent four years in a concentration camp near St. Denis, France, playing "Better Days Will Come" on his trumpet. Rudolph Dunbar, a classically-trained conductor who participated in the rebuilding efforts of postwar West Germany, was shocked when he first met Briggs to see how much Nazism had ravaged him and others. Dunbar also made sure to record how concentration camps expected Black musicians to perform Black music for them. The commandant, for example, ordered Briggs to join two other Black musicians in the camp, "Gay Martins from West Africa and Owen Macauly, a colored youth who was born in England," to sing "Negro spirituals."[80] Dunbar left his meeting with Briggs with the growing realization that no one had been spared by the evils of German racism and nationalism, not even talented African American musicians. The supposedly harmonious and universal world of classical music could not liberate anyone from racism's destructive power.

There was one surprising and lasting outcome of this divisive climate in the 1930s that manifested after 1945. Many of those very same Central European musicians who had attended Anderson's concerts in Central Europe eventually fled to the United States. There, they trained a new generation of Black students in classical music, and this generation would later return to Central Europe after the demise of the Nazi racial state. The opera singers Marion Freschl and Lotte Lehmann, for example, both of whom had witnessed Anderson's Salzburg recital in 1935, were adamant that they wished to support Black vocalists in the United States. They worked with and supported singers such as Camilla Williams, Shirley Verrett, and Grace Bumbry, all of whom broke racial barriers at major opera houses in Central Europe after 1945. The legacies and impact of Anderson, Hayes, and other Black classical musicians would live on—just not in the ways audiences in the 1930s might have expected.

PART III

1945–1961

CHAPTER 7

"And I Thought They Were a Decadent Race"

Denazification, the Cold War, and (African) American Involvement in Postwar West German Musical Life

In the summer of 1953, at the age of sixty-eight, William Kemper Harreld, a violin professor at Morehouse College, recorded in his diary his various travels through Germany and Austria. His journey was both a musical pilgrimage and a homecoming of sorts, for he had been a violin student in Berlin in the 1910s. Later, he had lived vicariously through his daughter, Josephine Harreld, while she spent the summer of 1935 taking piano lessons at the Mozarteum University Salzburg; he received her reports of listening to Marian Anderson sing in Salzburg and trekking across the border to visit the National Theatre Munich. One can hear the enthusiasm and feel the almost dizzying excitement bordering on panic humming in diary entries written during his return trip to Central Europe as he visited violin shop after violin shop in Vienna, loving each one more than the next, walking down Mahlerstrasse (which he underlined as if in disbelief: "Mahlerstrasse") near the Vienna State Opera House, attending rehearsals of a Mozart horn concerto at the Mozarteum building, and purchasing tickets to attend the Bayreuth Festival.

As much as Harreld's trip was a musical return to Germany and Austria, it was also an introduction, for much had changed in the decades since he had last lived and performed in the land of Bach, Beethoven, and Brahms. The geopolitical landscape of Germany and Austria, for example, had altered considerably. A few snippets in his diary—"Russian Zone!"—highlight the Iron Curtain's growing shadow over Germany and Austria, which had been cast early after the war but had only become starker after the Berlin Airlift in 1948. In Vienna he watched Russian steamships sail down the Danube and in Heidelberg, enjoying the good weather, he encountered "refugees from behind Iron Curtain. And Americans."[1]

In fact, everywhere Harreld went, he marveled at the sheer number of Americans crowding Germany and Austria. Most likely repeating a fact he had heard from someone in Heidelberg, he noted that the number of Americans in the city had "grown from 8,000 to 120,000 since [the] war."[2] What impressed him strongly was not only the presence of white American soldiers everywhere but also the sheer number of African American soldiers living freely and traveling through the German countryside when off duty. Indeed, there may have been no stronger or more noticeable difference of this new, postwar Germany to Harreld than the presence of Black Americans everywhere he went. He counted three Black troops in a station restaurant in Bayreuth, followed around a "Negro painter" in Cologne, and spent a pleasant boat ride with another Black soldier along the Rhine who eventually disembarked in Koblenz.

Much had changed since Harreld had last had the pleasure of riding on trains roaring across the German landscape. The United States had become a superpower and an occupying force whose political, cultural, and social interventions shaped much of postwar West German society. African American troops stationed in Bavaria, Baden-Württemberg, Berlin, and Hesse spent the early decades in postwar West Germany and Austria living like conquerors and victors. In the fictional story *The Last of the Conquerors* (1948), the African American author and veteran William Gardner Smith writes, "Many Black Americans came alive for the first time in the ruins of Berlin . . . Members of a victorious army, they found respect and consideration for the first time—but from their former enemies."[3] Gratified to be away from Jim Crow in the United States and on their military bases, African American soldiers escaped into German daily life. "In fact," Maria Höhn and Martin Klimke write, "soldiers were able to develop deeper relationships with the civilian population in Germany than they had during the war in Great Britain, France, or Italy, because once hostilities were over military units tended to remain in a particular locale for extended periods. They thus established day-to-day routines that fostered their connections to the local community: for example, attending local church services, dances in village pubs, as well as performances in the theaters and opera houses of Germany's bombed-out cities."[4] Harreld's short notes of experiences such as his aforementioned Rhine river cruise record this new reality for African Americans and the Germans they encountered.

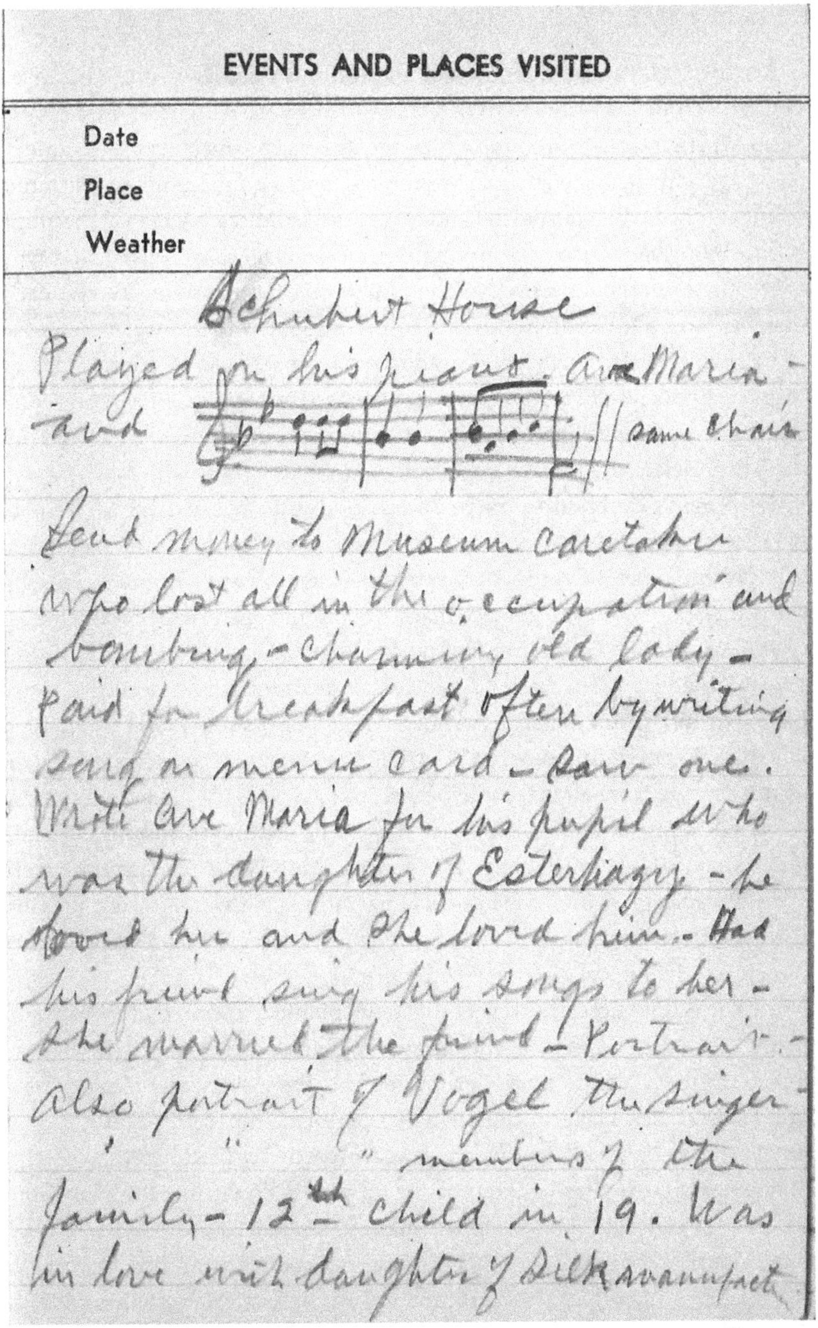

Date

Place

Weather

Schubert House

Played on his piano — Ave Maria — and [musical notation] same chair

Gave money to Museum caretaker who lost all in the occupation and bombing — charming old lady — Paid for breakfast often by writing song on menu card — Saw one. Wrote Ave Maria for his pupil who was the daughter of Esterhazy — he loved her and she loved him. Had his friend sing his songs to her — she married the friend — Portrait — Also portrait of Vogel the singer — " " " members of the family — 12th child in 19. Was in love with daughter of silk manufacturer

FIGURE 23. An entry from the travel journal of the Morehouse College violin professor William Kemper Harreld, June 1953. He played two Schubert melodies on Schubert's own piano in Vienna: "Ave Maria" and the "Rosamunde" theme, which appeared in many of Schubert's works. The version Harreld documented in his travel journal entry is most likely from Schubert's Entr'acte no. 3 in B-flat Major, a piece of incidental music for orchestra. Josephine Harreld Love Collection, box 27, folder 31. Courtesy of the Spelman College Archives.

Yet the fact that the man recording these short bursts of prose had lived in Germany before—trailed two decades later by his daughter's own stay in Salzburg and Munich—reminds us of the degree to which intergenerational cultural exchange linked people's experiences across time. Another example, stranger still, is the unusual life and career of the African American baritone J. Elmer Spyglass, who was among the local villagers in Schwalbach who came out to greet American soldiers liberating Germany during the early hours of postwar Germany. Once a young student who had traveled abroad to Germany in the 1910s upon graduation from Toledo's Conservatory of Music in Ohio, he had simply never returned to the United States, living comfortably instead with his wife in the German countryside even throughout the Third Reich.[5]

Both men's experiences might appear odd to us because they fail to adhere to the zero hour (*Stunde null*) mythology, which constructs a neat and tidy chronological division between pre- and postwar Germany. In contrast, these experiences connect Black bodies and Black experiences across twentieth-century Germany. The notion that Germany started over after 1945 with a clean slate has endured its fair share of challenges from historians like Rita Chin, Heide Fehrenbach, Atina Grossmann, and Geoff Eley, who have forcefully argued that "1945 did not and could not represent an absolute rupture from all that came before." Nonetheless, within the discourse of race and race thinking, they have observed, "assumptions of the Stunde null remain largely unchallenged."[6] Incorporating William Kemper Harreld and Elmer Spyglass into our historical narratives of twentieth-century Germany punctures myths of Black-white encounters on German soil and blurs our clean teleological divisions even more.

At the same time, however, the new political context of West Germany created new political meanings for Black performances of classical music. In the wake of Nazi German defeat, the American military relied greatly on Black classical musicians to perform important cultural labor on West German soil. In this chapter I present two case studies of this phenomenon—the Berlin debut of the Guyanese conductor Rudolph Dunbar in 1945 and the US State Department–sponsored tour of George Gershwin's opera, *Porgy and Bess*, in 1952—while acknowledging that there were many others. In both of these examples of Black classical musicians on West German stages, moments of rupture and continuity shaped German musical and cultural life.

The first performance of note took place only a few short months after Hitler committed suicide and the Nazi state fell apart, when the American authorities invited Dunbar to lead the Berlin Philharmonic in one of their first concerts under occupation powers. Both American and German audience members perceived an irony in the US authorities engaging a Black musician to teach the Germans how to supposedly become more civilized. It was as if the world had turned upside down, according to some reports, if those who were supposedly uncivilized (that is, Black diasporic peoples) could instruct the Germans on how to finally be civil.

The second case study finds the American military again relying on Black musicians to instruct Germans, albeit this time for self-congratulatory and hypocritical reasons. Responding to Soviet propaganda that depicted American institutions as deeply racist, the US State Department sponsored a tour of George Gershwin's opera *Porgy and Bess* to Europe in 1952 to celebrate their racial progress and to demonstrate to the world the importance of democracy. Here, too, currents of anti-Black racism run through the production and reception of a cast that included internationally renowned singers such as Leontyne Price and William Warfield.

In the case of both performances, the American military acknowledged that they were dependent on Black classical musicians to contribute to historical, political, and racial discourses in a manner that neither white American classical musicians nor Black jazz musicians could satisfy. Only Black classical musicians offered the technique and musical rigor that the American military believed would impress German audiences and the right racial background to morally shame them for their failures. From the American perspective it also was an added advantage that in the process Black classical musicians provided much-needed evidence to support the fragile myth that the United States was a place that embraced racial difference.

Yet within this new political context, historical continuities in German racial listening practices nonetheless persisted. However much Harreld was right to document the changing geopolitical situation surrounding him in 1945, we will see that cultural notions of race, music, and talent in Germany remained stubbornly entrenched in historical notions of Black authenticity. Perhaps the problem was that the American bodies performing cultural ambassadorship abroad were never just read as American bodies, even if American authorities frequently presented them as such. Rather, German expectations of Blackness—Black sounds, musicianship, and talent—anchored in decades of racial and musical discourses informed their own listening practices, even while they sometimes strove to listen differently.

The ultimate irony here is that American efforts to engage with Germans in the world of Western art music often reinforced to Germans their own musical superiority. "In trying to determine just what kind of break the Stunde null amounts to in German musical identity," Celia Applegate writes, "we inevitably encounter in both institutional and individual memories the continual reappearance, like some hardy perennial, of the image of music in the ruins."[7] German musicians and German music emerged out of the early decades of the postwar era relatively unscathed and untouched by either the politics of denazification or the politics of the Cold War in part because of American admiration for the Austro-German musical canon. And Blackness and Black people remained stubbornly outside of German musical culture, even while new occupation powers sought to integrate them into Germans' musical experiences.

Rudolph Dunbar and the Paradox of Performing Denazification in West Germany

Less than three months after the fall of the Third Reich, on July 20, 1945, the writer and anti-Nazi activist Ruth Andreas-Friedrich recorded a most remarkable encounter with Dunbar in her diary:

> In the evening, an American artist sought out [conductor Leo Borchard]. A Black man. He is as beautiful as a panther, and more passionately interested in Bach and Beethoven than most Germans. He has traveled the world, given concerts in countless countries. "They flock to my concerts," he said and looked at us with the eyes of [Persian King] Ahasuerus, "not because they want to hear my music, but because they want to hear how a Negro makes music. We are the most disregarded people in the world. Even more disregarded than the Jews, right?" And again he looks at us with the eyes of Ahasuerus. "Or the Germans." Is it a victor standing before us, in his elegantly tailored American uniform, beautiful like a panther, and passionately interested in Bach and Beethoven? Suddenly, we are all embarrassed in front of one another. Until [Borchard] bends down to place his scores on the shelf, pulls out a Bach cantata, and hands it to his beautiful guest. "If you would like to have it?"[8]

Her account captures all of the tensions and complexities surrounding German engagement with Dunbar while also illuminating Dunbar's own agency in facilitating conversation. What dominates Andreas-Fischer's passage is her own racial fascination with the conductor, whom she twice calls "beautiful as a panther." His eyes gleam, he appears elegant in his uniform, but nonetheless her animalistic description implies that there is something not only exotic but potentially powerful and dangerous about him.

His power might stem from the word she uses to describe him—"victor." Like many other Germans who met him, Andreas-Fischer mistook Dunbar for an "American" in her diary when he was from British Guyana. Associating Dunbar with the US Allied forces was not entirely inaccurate, however, as his own "elegantly tailored American uniform" suggests. Nonetheless, Andreas-Fischer calling Dunbar a "victor" represents a significant shift in international relations that occurred after the collapse of the Third Reich. Perhaps for the first time in German history, the appearance of Black soldiers garnered respect (albeit some of it hostile) instead of outrage. Unlike after WWI, when French African colonial troops stationed on the Rhine inspired a racist, far-right propaganda campaign of protest against interracial relations, the African American soldiers who landed on German soil, passing candy to children, cigarettes to men, and stockings to women, became conquering heroes. Part of their newfound power came from the fact that they were Americans. "Like the British and French," Höhn and Klimke write, "Germans also viewed Black soldiers first and foremost as Americans or Yankees—as conquerors who wore the uniform of the victor nation—and not as 'Negroes.'"[9] In the words of William Gardner Smith, "[The Germans] were racists, but we were conquerors and the look in their eyes was respect."[10] Wearing American uniforms, Black men, including Dunbar, tapped into a new power previously unavailable to them, which Andreas-Fischer's diary entry documents.

Yet Dunbar excites Andreas-Fischer not only because of his ties to a rising global superpower. Andreas-Fischer was apparently so struck by Dunbar's interest in German composers that she recorded it twice in the same paragraph. Here, Andreas-Fischer reconfirmed the long-standing myth that Black people were far removed from German music. She harbored the same assumption that would later inform how music critics and audiences interpreted Dunbar's performance that September. Yet her account also reveals to us a musician operating in the full knowledge of what white European audiences expected of him. By stating that audiences attend his concerts "not because they want to hear [his] music, but because they want to hear how a Negro makes music," he illustrated an astute awareness of European demands for Black bodies on stage.

Lastly, Andreas-Fischer's diary entry also suggests how quickly Black people became involved in a complex triangulation between Germans and the growing silence about the Holocaust, a theme I explore at length in the next chapter. In Dunbar's encounter with Andreas-Fischer and her colleagues, his quip about victimization and the Holocaust ran so deep that her colleagues' primary response to it was silence. In a room full of white Germans, Dunbar stated that Black people "are the most disregarded people in the world. Even more disregarded than the Jews, right? Or the Germans." While the first reference points to the Holocaust, the second appears to mock Germans' own narratives of victimization, which presented them as the primary victims of Nazi aggression as opposed to its beneficiaries. Dunbar's comment, which questioned Germans' sense of victimization, made his German acquaintances so uncomfortable and "embarrassed in front of one another" that eventually Andreas-Fischer's colleague, Borchard, changed the subject by handing over a Bach cantata "to his beautiful guest."

Dunbar was quite the figure to break the racial barrier at the Berlin Philharmonic that fall. Although his debut with the Berlin Philharmonic has appeared in a few historical accounts, his own biography and perspective on his debut has tended to disappear from our narratives documenting the performance, even though he was the primary agent of it. A classically trained clarinetist from British Guiana (his manual, *Treatise on Clarinet Playing*, published in 1939, still sits on the shelves of many music libraries), Dunbar left the Caribbean to attend the Juilliard School in New York City in the 1920s. Following his career in New York, he studied music under Felix Weingartner in Vienna, eventually leaving for France, where he became highly involved in the 1930s Paris musical scene.[11] As WWII raged, he offered concerts with the London Philharmonic Orchestra in 1942 and L'Orchestre de la Société des Concerts du Conservatoire in Paris in 1945.[12]

Yet Dunbar's musical pedigree, while impressive, only presents one side of his multifaceted life. He spent a majority of his adulthood challenging anti-Black racism and promoting a Black diasporic worldview. As a war correspondent and journalist for the Associated Negro Press, he reported frequently to newspapers in the United States about atrocities the Nazis had committed against Black people. In an article for *Tempo* titled "News from Paris," for example, Dunbar shared personal stories of his encounters with musicians who had experienced Nazi crimes firsthand. He wrote an article for the African American newspaper and civil rights outlet the *Chicago Defender* in September of 1944, titled "Trumpet Player Briggs Freed after Four Years in Nazi Camp near Paris," which documented Arthur Briggs's account of the horrors of the Nazi regime.[13]

It was precisely his commitment to Black internationalist politics that had driven much of his musical activities during WWII and inspired him to include William Grant Still's *Afro-American Symphony* in his Berlin concert. Dunbar was an outspoken critic of the British empire and praised by the Black Marxist George Padmore, among others. His concerts in England and France during WWII debuted works by different Black composers such as

Coleridge-Taylor and Still.[14] He also used his performances with the London Philharmonic Orchestra in April of 1942 to "raise funds for Britain's colored allies," an act that reveals Dunbar's support for pan-Africanism. His own feelings of ambivalence toward European imperialism may have stemmed from his experience in the United States. In an article for *Time* a year after his Berlin Philharmonic debut, Dunbar told the reporter, "[The British] want to say, 'Look what we have done for Dunbar'—but it is not the British who have done it for me, it is the Americans."[15] For these reasons, Dunbar may have readily identified with the American mission to denazify Germany and to extend greater cultural influence over Europe more broadly.

As proof of his own Americanism and commitment to denazification, when Dunbar walked onto the stage to conduct the Berlin Philharmonic at the sold-out Titania Palast in Berlin, he proudly wore his war correspondent's uniform.[16] Indeed, the act of wearing his military uniform for a musical performance also suggested the strong tie between musical performance and politics, making him appear very much like the "victor" Andreas-Fischer claimed that she had seen before her. Before the concert began, Dunbar first led the audience in a performance of "The Star Spangled Banner"; some Germans stood, others remained seated. That evening, he conducted Weber's *Oberon* Overture, Tchaikovsky's Symphony no. 6, "Pathetique" in B Minor, and the German premiere of Still's *Afro-American Symphony*.

While Dunbar had his own reasons for conducting the Berlin Philharmonic, the American military had theirs. In the immediate aftermath of WWII, the United States and the Allied forces writ large sought to restructure German society and culture in the hopes of eradicating Nazi ideology from civilians' everyday lives. The denazification process also extended into German musical life. The Allied forces in Germany recognized that restructuring German cultural life would contribute to the broader goals of reeducating Germans. John Bitter, a US Army official and a central figure behind the reorganization of the Berlin Philharmonic, recalls, "I said to myself, now the war is over, now I would like to help rebuild the good Germany: that of Beethoven, Schiller, Goethe, and Brahms. One cannot always continue to conduct war."[17] Rebuilding the "good" Germany meant offering both punishments and rewards. To that end, the Allies rigorously blacklisted composers, conductors, and musicians, and their decisions often caused controversy, such as the 1946 trial of the famed conductor Wilhelm Furtwängler. They prohibited Germans from singing "German military music, or . . . German or Nazi anthems, in public or before any group or gathering"; they promoted performances of previously banned German composers such as

FIGURE 24. Wearing his US military uniform, the Afro-Caribbean conductor Rudolph Dunbar conducts the Berlin Philharmonic at the Titania Palast in Berlin in September 1945 in one of the orchestra's first concerts after WWII. Courtesy of Getty Images.

Mendelssohn; and they prosecuted and blacklisted German musicians who had actively participated in the Nazi regime.[18]

However, American efforts to denazify German musical culture were always stymied by their dualistic nature. Constantly walking a precariously thin line between punishment and rehabilitation, between authoritative governance and the promotion of cultural democracy, between shaming Germans for departing from their supposedly exceptional past and desperately desiring to project themselves as the Germans' cultural equals, the American military undertook an uneven, arbitrary, and sometimes contradictory process of cultural renewal. In *Settling Scores*, David Monod writes that postwar West German musical life endured "the complex, confused, and often contradictory efforts of the American authorities to punish musicians for the things they had done in the Third Reich while establishing the foundations of a democratic cultural life." The American military was always trapped between two conflicting goals, he writes: "punishment and freedom, or, put another way, control and democracy."[19] Ultimately, the United States oscillated between policies of modest restraint and harsh adjudication, all the while hoping they might convince Germans to see them as their cultural peers.[20]

Perhaps wishing to see themselves as Germans' musical and cultural equals, the American occupiers fixated on musical institutions that they could control, the Berlin Philharmonic being one of them. The placement of Leo Borchard at the helm illustrates how quickly Allied forces sought to break with the past. An anti-Nazi activist who had participated in underground resistance movements in Berlin, Borchard was banned by Nazi officials from performing music after 1935 because they deemed him "politically unreliable." After the war, he became the poster child for the "good German musician," and he led the Berlin Philharmonic and the Prussian State Opera from May 1945 until his untimely death at the hands of an American officer that September, just a few days before Dunbar's debut.[21]

Although it remains unclear how he had come to know Dunbar or why he had chosen to invite him, it was Borchard's invitation that brought Dunbar on stage to conduct the Berlin Philharmonic at the Titania Palast—with the approval of the American authorities.[22] It appears they eagerly welcomed this musical event because it so readily aligned with their own goals. Prior to and after Borchard's death, the American military sought to place a non-German musician at the podium of the Berlin Philharmonic for political reasons. "By installing a foreigner as principal conductor of the Philharmonic," Abby Anderton argues, "American authorities hoped to dispel any lingering Nazi claims of German cultural superiority once and for all."[23] It became important to showcase to the German public that "outsiders" were also capable of producing musical greatness.

Although Dunbar only performed as a guest conductor, his debut not only fulfilled the American mission of installing a foreigner but it also functioned to remind Germans of their racial crimes. It mattered greatly to American officials that a Black man was conducting. As in other areas of the postwar occupation, what American authorities sought was to both punish and encourage, and in matters of race their strategy was no different. Although Heide Fehrenbach is right that official denazification rarely stressed the problems of racism, nonetheless in matters of music they occasionally made symbolic gestures in such directions. The American military wished to project to ordinary Germans an idealized image of the United States as a nation more racially inclusive than Germany, and to that end, they sponsored musical performances by musicians whom the Nazis would have denounced.[24]

Above all, American authorities believed that the prestige of Black classical musicians demonstrated that Americans had succeeded in race relations where Germany had so clearly failed. Recalling how Nazi Germany had banned Marian Anderson from concertizing "because of the color of her skin as a Negress," American authorities insisted on using Black musicians to symbolically denounce Nazism, announce the arrival of a new global order, and present themselves in a better light.[25] To that end, Eric Clarke, the head of the music branch in the Western zone in the mid-1940s, declared that Black classical musicians such as Anderson and Dorothy Maynor were among "the best assets in the reorientation of Germans."[26] US Brigadier General Robert McClure also welcomed the arrival of African American musicians to Germany on these grounds.[27]

At the behest of American authorities, Marian Anderson did indeed return to Germany in 1950, giving two sold-out shows—one in Berlin and one in Munich—to adoring crowds. Like Dunbar, Anderson performed to a 2,000-person crowd of Allied soldiers and Germans at the Titania Palast in Berlin, and her audience cheered for her so much that she had to devote "half an hour after her formal program to bows and encores," including several spirituals and German lieder.[28] Following Anderson's recital, US Army General Maxwell D. Taylor hosted a reception in celebration of Anderson, with invited guests from the other Allied powers, including the British general G. K. Bourne.[29] While much of the repertoire that she performed that night consisted of standards dating back to her stay in Germany in the 1930s—Schubert's "Der Tod und das Mädchen" and "Ave Maria," for example—the pomp and circumstance surrounding her Berlin reunion were wildly different this time. Attended by Berlin patrons (many of whom still fondly recalled her stay in Germany decades prior) and military generals, Anderson's Liederabend had greatly changed its meaning in Germany's postwar context.

African American classical musicians held a unique position that made it possible for them to become important cultural symbols to American authorities and Germans who heard them. Here, their identities as both Black *and* classical musicians came into play. Take, for example, the US Information Control Division's insistence on having "top-rank American Negro vocalists give concerts in Germany."[30] African American vocalists like Anderson, singing on German stages in full-length gowns, were subtle weapons of denazification. According to Timothy Schroer, the Allies believed that "if Germans could hear talented African Americans performing artistic works capably, they could be convinced that Blacks were not racially inferior."[31] Black classical musicians could shame Germans into seeing the error of their ways. As classical musicians, they embodied all of the privilege, prestige, and respectability that American authorities needed to try to impress Germany while also providing racial symbolism. Both parts of their identities—being African Americans and being well-trained practitioners in Western art music—were necessary for this unique kind of cultural labor.

Jazz music and rock and roll only went so far in positively changing German impressions of the United States, in part because of their associations with the vernacular and popular culture. Similarly, white American classical musicians did little to strike a blow at German racial attitudes. Moreover, to many white German listeners, white American classical musicians offered watered-down variations of their own white European singers, thus reinforcing their belief in the superiority of German music. Black classical musicians, however, represented a vibrant, effective geopolitical tool—if wielded properly. They could remind Germans that Americans, too, excelled in the world of classical music and that the United States was not a cultural backwater after all. But their Blackness could also be wielded to instill in German society a new vocabulary of racial acceptance. They represented all the promises and possibilities of universalism following an era that had so vocally rejected those principles. Black classical musicians, then, promised to be a vital part of the American military's agenda to rehabilitate German musical culture.

The American military certainly interpreted Dunbar's performance in September 1945 in these terms. The Allied Control Council, the organization responsible for overseeing cultural events in Germany, approved his request to perform at Borchard's behest because they saw it as "a valuable step in wiping out racial prejudices."[32] American newspapers covering the event promulgated this view of German musical and racial rehabilitation repeatedly in their growing mountain of publications on Dunbar in Berlin. *Time*, for example, wrote, "US occupation authorities were all for [Dunbar's performance], though their interest was more in teaching the Germans a lesson in racial tolerance than in Dunbar's musicianship."[33] The American occupation forces laid the foundations for this lesson as early as possible. In an article titled "Berlin Gets Hep to Classics via Negro Conductor," a journalist for the *Chicago Defender* writes, "The hall which once rocked with the race-hate strains of Nazi 'Horst Wessel [Song]' was rocked with the rhythms of Composer William Grant Still's *Afro-American Symphony*."[34]

Yet the American solution to use Black musicians to denazify West Germany was always overshadowed by the fact that the American military was itself a deeply racist institution. Höhn and Klimke write, "It was ironic that this rigidly segregated and deeply racist army took on what commanders called 'the most important job ever undertaken by the United States,' namely, the reeducation and democratization of the defeated German foe."[35] There was, perhaps, no greater irony in hiring Dunbar to teach the Germans a "racial lesson" than the fact that the American military was also enforcing racial segregation among their own troops stationed in West Germany and attending Dunbar's Berlin debut. Black musicians were also not free from Jim Crow harassment overseas. For example, when Anderson performed in Munich, white Americans protested because she stayed at the Hotel Excelsior, a hotel run by the US Army.[36] Although she had arrived in Munich as a cultural ambassador of the United States, her own stay at a military-run, predominantly white hotel became mired in the very same racist politics that the authorities were hoping her performances in Germany would publicly disavow.

If the practice of racial and musical denazification was complicated (to say the least) on the American military's side, the end results were even murkier on the German one. The American military's open admiration for German music coupled with its severe punishment of musicians who had complied or collaborated with the Nazi regime meant that the responses of Germans to American interrogations of their musical pasts was one of flat denial.[37] If German musicians were supposed to have learned something from their Nazi past, it is unclear just what, exactly, that was.

Worse, throughout the course of denazification, the majority of musicians simply returned to their positions, having escaped any meaningful conversation on their relationship to Nazism. Virtually all of the members representing Germany at UNESCO in 1953 had been prominent musicologists and composers under the Nazis.[38] The failure of denazification meant that the process of rehabilitating and internationalizing German music happened far too quickly. Joy Calico argues against the "persistent image of the FRG [West Germany] as the postwar utopia for modernist music." Instead, she writes, we see in the case of the music critic Hans Schnoor "a former Nazi music critic, rehabilitated in name only, resisting the Allied-led, modernist musical remigration with the familiar rhetoric of National Socialist journalism."[39] Instead of disrupting German musical life, the American occupation and denazification effort ensured that much of it continued in its previous guises and forms.[40]

The fact that these representatives of German music slipped past denazification efforts and back into postwar musical life suggests a greater thread of continuity between Nazi and postwar Germany than historical narratives had earlier granted.[41] Rather than breaking from the past, many musical figures simply learned how to hide from it. Thus, German music's central and sacred function to German culture remained unsullied. The belief—promoted by German exiles and adopted by Allied forces—that Nazi intolerance had nearly destroyed Germany's great musical tradition covered a whole host of sins.[42] German musical exceptionalism remained as firmly in place after the war as it did under Hitler.

German musicians' narratives of their own Nazi pasts manifested in their relationship to Dunbar in ways that are strikingly similar to what scholars such as Priscilla Layne, Katrin Sieg, and Angelica Fenner have observed in their research on race and denazification. In short: Germans used Dunbar's visit to avoid culpability and to flee responsibility for their actions through the experience of emotional catharsis. German listeners stated that they had experienced emotional and intellectual epiphanies in Dunbar's presence and finally learned to embrace African American music. After a lesson in syncopation from Dunbar during a rehearsal of Still's *Afro-American Symphony*, the first flutist of the Berlin Philharmonic purportedly said to Dunbar, "Now at last I understand your American jazz."[43] There are two things that are striking about this observation. First, Still's 1931 *Afro-American Symphony* actually had little to do with jazz. In fact, Carol Oja argues that the composition showcases many features of musical modernism from the 1930s, fitting into the sonic world of composers such as Edgard Varèse, Ruth Crawford, and Aaron Copland while using African American folk melodies and blues idioms.[44] Moreover, Still's *Afro-American Symphony* is just that—a symphony, not a piece of jazz music. Yet the flutist's remarks illustrate a greater assumption or misrecognition of different African American musical styles and traditions.

Second, it also reveals a new postwar mental logic at work. The flutist implies that because of Dunbar, he'd had a revelation that upended his previous ways of thinking under the Nazis. Musicians such as this flutist discovered that they had been "duped," in other words, and thus saw themselves as victims of Nazi cultural politics. Similarly, several American newspapers reported that after hearing the Berlin Philharmonic's musical performance, "an old German in the audience, looking at Dunbar, remarked to his wife: 'And I had thought they were a decadent race.'"[45] In these moments of cultural exchange, Germans claimed to have discovered that they were mistaken and were the victims of conspiracy.

Music criticism, slowly rearing up again in the summer of 1945, offers us perhaps the most potent way in which we see postwar logic developing so quickly after the fall of the Nazi racial state. It is no wonder that Dunbar's 1945 performance created German headlines that practically screamed in capitalized letters that "A NEGRO CONDUCTS BERLIN PHILHARMONIC." Although presented in the guise of a break from the past, German rhetoric nonetheless smacked of historical continuity instead of cultural rupture. Dunbar, like many other classical musicians, was a German Romantic musician at heart. He routinely expressed what German journalists called a "strong empathy for German Romantic music" and enjoyed exhibiting his deep knowledge of it.[46] In an interview Dunbar gave to the *Allgemeine Zeitung*, he emphasized his love for the German masters: "I love Beethoven, Brahms, Wagner, and the counterpoint of Sebastian Bach. When I come back from Paris, I hope above all to be able to conduct a Brahms symphony."[47]

Yet his love for German music was at odds with music critics' views of him as a Black man.[48] The *Berliner Zeitung*'s comments on this "musical sensation" reveal precisely the same combination of admiration and surprise that one encountered in earlier generations of reviewers. "He knows the scores, their forms, their commands," one reviewer was willing to admit. "Naturally, he doesn't execute European music well enough in our views. But it is shocking enough what he is still [able to] radiate."[49] In the critic's estimation, Dunbar, a British subject and student of Felix Weingartner, "naturally" lacked the ability to conduct European art music. These comments could have very well appeared in the 1920s and 1930s to describe Roland Hayes or Anderson, or even in the nineteenth century to describe the Jiménez Trio. Over and over again, the notion that a person of African descent could exhibit mastery of European art music ran afoul of German music critics' deep skepticism.

Typically, music critics determined that Dunbar was the most "in his element" conducting Still's *Afro-American Symphony*, even though Dunbar was not African American. *Der Morgen* praised Dunbar for familiarizing German audiences with a well-known American composer whose symphony embodied the "typical sound and style of the New World."[50] *Die Neue Zeit* wrote that Dunbar had "built a bridge between two continents" with the *Afro-American Symphony* and gave audiences a piece of music full of life.[51] The *Afro-American Symphony* conducted by Dunbar embodied "the folk songs and other tunes that interpret the lives of [Dunbar's] people—Still is a Negro like Dunbar."[52] Such a statement flattens Blackness to a problematic degree. Furthermore, it illuminates how white Germans in postwar West Germany "often *failed to see* the individuality of Black people and the differences between them . . . [I]n many cases [white Germans] contributed to solidifying the nexus of skin color and culture and—mostly as *unintended consequences*—contributed to the process of racialization," Moritz Ege writes.[53] Here in September 1945, at a performance celebrating a new racial and musical era, the same racial logics were already being played out. Dunbar was not a US citizen at the time of his performance, proving that his perceived Blackness mattered just as much if not more to both the producers and audiences of his debut than his nationality. His authority over African American music, like his assumed knowledge of jazz, was never questioned.

The ways critics described the music echoes prewar assessments of African American music. The *Allgemeine Zeitung*, for example, described the

Afro-American Symphony as sonorous, soulful, and rhythmic.[54] Some of the movements had a certain "homesickness," the critic for the *Allgemeine Zeitung* explained, then informing his readers that this was characteristic of the blues and African American music in general. The lively scherzo created the "excited mood of a Negro meeting [i.e., church revival]," and the finale captured the sentiments of the traditional African American spiritual, a genre with which many German audiences were already familiar. The critic noted, "Especially when this piece was played one naturally felt how deeply connected Dunbar is to it [the work], and here we ought to admire the Philharmonic Orchestra above all, who had immersed themselves into this foreign world."[55] Moreover, the press consistently referred to Dunbar as the first American conductor to perform with the Berlin Philharmonic since the war had ended, even though he was British Guyanese and had lived in London since 1931.

One measure of Dunbar's success, however, might be in the large number of Black conductors who followed him, for his debut established a working blueprint for how these later performances would go. In fact, West Germany in particular became something of a "promised land" for African American conductors, who benefitted from the American military's insistence on using them to denazify Germany, thus suspending American racial norms in order to do so. Take, for example, the Seventh Army Symphony Orchestra, the first and only symphonic orchestral ensemble ever formed under the supervision of the US Army. In 1955, Henry Lewis, an African American bassist who had been on the Los Angeles Philharmonic's roster until he joined the military, began his tenure with the ensemble as their assistant conductor.[56] However, after receiving recommendations from Hans Hörner, conductor of the Stuttgart Philharmonic, and Fritz Mareczek, conductor of the Southwest German Radio Symphony Orchestra, Lewis became the orchestra's principal conductor in March of 1956.[57] The interracial ensemble, with a Black conductor in tow, fit with the American authorities' vision of itself to a tee. The orchestra functioned as a well-respected ensemble in Germany while also adhering to the American authorities' message of racial acceptance, and the US Information Service (USIS) promoted it heavily in Germany.[58] In a report from Bonn to Washington DC, one official wrote, "The virtuosity and musical ability of the orchestra, coupled with a soldierly and yet free and easy bearing, made a great impression and changed not a few preconceived German opinions regarding cultural efforts and achievements in the United States."[59] From the US Army's perspective, the ensemble successfully proved that the United States could carry the same heavy cultural weight as the citizens they were trying to reeducate.

Frustrated with American musical institutions, other Black conductors went to Europe because they were afforded more opportunities to perform and study than they were in the United States.[60] Conductors such as George Byrd, Dean Dixon, James Frazier, Everett Lee, and James Anderson DePriest recognized in interviews that these unique opportunities to use their training and mastery as serious conductors in West Germany also allowed them to fulfill the role of cultural ambassador.[61] Dixon became a fan favorite in Germany and Austria, touring in both countries in the 1950s and 1960s.[62] Later, Paul Freeman, an Eastman School of Music alumnus, studied at the Berlin State School of Music (now UdK) through a Fulbright fellowship program before launching his career as a successful conductor as well.[63] Another student of Berlin's State School of Music, Isaiah Jackson, made his debut conducting the Vienna Symphony in 1970, for example, instead of with an orchestra in the United States.

Black conductors could be roped into claims of fairness and equality in German orchestras. K. H. Ruppell, the music critic for the *Süddeutsche Zeitung*, defended German orchestras against the claim that they favored German music by mentioning Black American conductors such as Dixon instead. "It is my duty to voice a protest against [the critic] Martin Bernheimer's accusation that the Munich press is indulgent toward German composers and performers and that it snobbishly misunderstands certain non-German works," he wrote to the *New York Times*. "We would rejoice," he counters, "if Dean Dixon, an American conductor who is very popular in Munich, would introduce us to important works of American composers at the Musica Viva concerts in Munich."[64] His sentiments that Germans had accepted Dixon as a convincing interpreter of classical music in the 1950s had some merit. Conductors such as Lee and Dixon were able to acquire lengthy contracts with regional orchestras in Europe, something unavailable to Black conductors in the United States for decades.

Yet the racial listening politics of Dunbar's debut cast a shadow over Black conductors in Germany and lasted for decades. Roughly fifteen years after Dunbar's performance, another Black conductor was unable to escape it. In August 1959, the African American conductor George Byrd debuted with the Berlin Philharmonic conducting an all-European program: Brahms's Symphony no. 2 in D Major, Boris Blacher's *Paganini Variations*, and César Franck's *Symphonic Variations*. Newspapers in both the United States and in Europe incorrectly reported that Byrd's debut with the Berlin Philharmonic was the first time a Black conductor had performed with the ensemble, forgetting Dunbar's appearance fourteen years earlier.[65] The Austrian newspaper *Neues Österreich*, for example, reported in their story, titled "Black

Director for the Berlin Philharmonic," "George Byrd from Brooklyn is the first Negro to conduct the Berlin Philharmonic orchestra."[66] How quickly Dunbar's own debut had been erased from public memory.

Moreover, critics spun the same racial logic that they had produced for Dunbar into the way they understood Byrd's performance with the Berlin Philharmonic. Most concert reviews found a way to highlight Byrd's Blackness. A critic for *Der Kurier*, for example, stated that "As a conductor George Byrd presented himself as a congenial, erudite, and imaginative Negro who takes music very seriously."[67] The critic's praise perhaps implied that Byrd was the exception rather than the rule for Black musicians. Another music critic's praise relied on the same kind of cultural and biological racism that had informed music criticism for decades: "Byrd, the colored [conductor], brings the instinctive, enchanting musicality of his race. His musicality proves itself even with the Brahms symphony."[68] Because he was Black, Byrd was supposedly more naturally "musical," a term the critic never fully defined.

I bring up Byrd's own debut with the Berlin Philharmonic so that we may reconsider Dunbar's. The latter's performance was potently symbolic for it represented an extreme racial and cultural change in just a short amount of time. Audiences and critics were aware that Dunbar's debut was a test case for German democracy and for race relations in light of recent events. Indeed, Heide Fehrenbach argues that when it came to Black-white relations in the wake of the Holocaust and Nazism, postwar German officials were obliged "to confront and counter persisting racial assumptions underlying notions of national belonging, and to do so under the bright light of international scrutiny."[69] Both German and American audiences heralded Dunbar's debut as a triumph. But historical distance provides us with another perspective. Dunbar's performance offered a moment when myths about Black musicianship were confronted only to be renewed, and German music—and those who played it—retained its innocence. Even at one of the most powerful moments in German history—the immediate aftermath of WWII—a Black musician's performance was unable to overturn decades of lingering notions of Black musicality in German culture.

Porgy and Bess and the Cold War in West Germany

At least with Dunbar's performance in Berlin in 1945, German audiences and the American military who sponsored the event interpreted the performance in the same light. They both understood—tacitly or explicitly—that Dunbar's debut represented a change to the national, political, racial, and musical order. The US State Department's sponsoring of an all-Black production of Gershwin's *Porgy and Bess* in 1952, however, represented a cornucopia of competing ideologies that never quite managed to align, even while both the Allied forces and the German and Austrian audiences at the performance walked away declaring the feat a musical success. The message that the United States had hoped to send to Berlin and Vienna, one that they believed portrayed the United States in a positive light, became reread or misread once it reached European shores. While German and Austrian audiences applauded *Porgy and Bess* as a successful American cultural export, they erroneously believed that it accurately depicted a deeply local, Black diasporic community. Their praise for the African American characters and performances raises doubts over the efficacy of American musical interventions abroad.

As the Cold War began to heat up in the 1950s, the US State Department began to employ art music as a tool of cultural diplomacy in global politics, somehow missing the irony of using music's supposed political neutrality as a tool of propaganda.[70] As Emily Abrams Ansari argues, "the war had convinced many Americans that military and ideological intervention in foreign affairs could benefit both American objectives and global stability. The only way to defeat the most wicked enemies, many Americans now felt, was to counter them with the power of good."[71] Implicit in this assumption, however, was that only the "right" kind of music had the cultural weight necessary to overturn negative influences.

Classical music was an especially potent geopolitical strategy for American authorities because of its long European history and its associations with art instead of entertainment.[72] In particular, American officials believed that classical musical offerings were effective abroad because they understood them to be both simultaneously national and universal—"national," Danielle Fosler-Lussier writes, "in that a single example of art could be understood as representing some characteristic of the United States as a whole; universal in the sense that people abroad should be able to interpret the music, like it, and evaluate it much as the senders would."[73] American perceptions of themselves as good, even innocent, in their support of music has been a lasting trope, especially in a German context.[74]

The potential problem with Cold War involvement in music-making was that the organizers frequently misunderstood the power of musical representation and audiences' perceptions of it, unable to recognize that, as Fosler-Lussier writes, "the seeming simplicity of musical diplomacy was an illusion." She continues, "Whether or not people acknowledged it, mediating music—moving it across space and time—changed its meanings."[75]

Especially in the case of *Porgy and Bess*, it becomes startlingly apparent just how little the opera's organizers in 1952 were able to control the opera's messaging once it left American soil. Its fractured and duplicitous significations were difficult enough to contend with in the United States, but the opera tour's managers had even less control over the opera's meanings once it left America's shores and traveled to Europe.

The American-sponsored tour of the opera, led by the Broadway director Robert Breen and the American National Theater and Academy (ANTA), was probably doomed from the start, for the opera itself had been mired in its own longstanding controversies well before it traveled across the ocean in 1952. Originally premiering in 1935 in New York City, *Porgy and Bess* follows the stories of its African American title characters, who live in a small coastal fishing village in South Carolina. Porgy, a crippled beggar in the fictional African American town of Catfish Row, falls in love with Bess, a prostitute and drug addict involved with a dangerous criminal named Crown. After Crown flees Catfish Row to escape arrest charges for murder, Porgy takes Bess into his care and the two develop an intimate relationship. Shortly thereafter, however, the police question Porgy's involvement in Crown's criminal affairs and throw him in prison. Upon his release, he discovers that Bess has left him for the drug dealer Sportin' Life. The final scene of the opera depicts Porgy resolving to leave Catfish Row and find Bess.

One of the primary contradictions embedded in the opera itself lies in its moniker, "an American folk opera." Naomi André argues that none of the terms—"American," "folk," or "opera"—were clear even in the 1930s when Gershwin first composed *Porgy and Bess*.[76] Sometimes compared to Alban Berg's *Wozzeck*, the opera borrows from numerous operatic traditions, thus musically representing what Gershwin hoped would be America's "vast melting pot."[77] Gershwin saw it as a hybrid between Romantic opera and "lowbrow" folk music, for he used some African American musical expressions as the basis for his operatic composition. "If I am successful," he once wrote to a friend, "[*Porgy*] will resemble a combination of the drama and romance of *Carmen* and the beauty of the *Meistersinger*."[78] Using Wagnerian leitmotifs (the popular theme "Summertime" occurs four times in the opera, for example), late-Romantic harmonic language, and rich orchestration, Gershwin's musical style firmly placed the work into a Western musical tradition. Yet even in the 1930s, Gershwin's designation of African American "folk" music within the genre of opera meant that the opera already contained multivalent meanings long before its Cold War tour.[79]

When the US State Department announced their decision to sponsor a production of *Porgy and Bess* in Europe, many Americans reacted unfavorably to the news. One problem that many people expressed at the time (and that continues to be a problem today) concerned the music itself. Many heard the musical numbers in Gershwin's opera—including children's songs, call and response choruses, religious prayers, and shouts—as nothing more than highly stylized musical stereotypes of African American life. The American musicologist Richard Crawford, for example, called Gershwin's musical compositions in the opera an example of "fakelore," for Gershwin confessed that he had composed all of the so-called African American spirituals in the opera himself.[80] Whatever sounded like African American folk music, in other words, had been the invention of this white, Jewish American composer. Gershwin had been inspired by his short trip to South Carolina to listen to African American communal singing, but in fact he did not use any music created by African Americans themselves.

Even the presentation of the Black musical idioms in *Porgy and Bess*—if we choose to call them that—reinforces a musical hierarchy. Richard Middleton argues that in *Porgy and Bess*, "Black idioms are encased, put in their place, by the style, orchestration, and structural conventions of late-Romantic opera." Moreover, "while 'Black' idioms are fine for Eden," Middleton writes, "grown-up emotions like personal love require the manner of European late Romanticism."[81] At various points in the opera, Gershwin drops the act, so to speak, and uses the musical language of European art music to portray complex emotional processes, thus implying that African American folk singing (loosely defined) was incapable of adequately representing them.

In the 1950s, both white and Black critics also objected to the subject matter of the opera. White, mainstream presses hesitated to endorse the tour for concern that the opera put America's handling of race—what one *Washington Post* critic called a "ticklish situation"—in a poor light.[82] In numerous African American circles, the greatest criticism of the opera stemmed from Gershwin's depiction of African Americans, which many found delusional at best. Langston Hughes openly lamented the State Department's sponsorship of this production in an opinion piece for the *Chicago Defender*. Why, Hughes demanded, could not the United States have sponsored a play "depicting Negroes as clean, well-behaved citizens, some even educated, some of the women as well dressed as whites, some of the men not crapshooters?"[83] In his view, Gershwin's decision to write about gambling crapshooters, drug addicts, and ignorant, pious villagers framed African Americans in the most negative of terms.

From the perspective of ANTA, who produced the opera abroad, the value of sending *Porgy and Bess* to Europe had everything to do with Gershwin and his music. By the 1950s, Gershwin epitomized the ideal American composer both within and outside the United States. The composer recalled an earlier decade of American travel to Europe in the "transatlantic twenties" before WWII, to which lively works such as *An American in Paris* (1928) testified. And it was in Berlin in 1926 that Gershwin had offered his European debut of his now-famous *Rhapsody in Blue*. His music quickly conjured up images in many listeners' minds of American vibrancy, syncopation, and musical experimentation within safe musical forms.

Not only was his music quite accessible to everyday listeners but American authorities also thought that the figure of Gershwin—an American icon—was politically safe to send abroad, unlike Aaron Copland and other composers. Ansari argues most forcefully in her book "that it was a particularly American experience of the Cold War, especially the influence of anti-communism, that led American composers to stay quiet about the influence of politics upon stylistic choices."[84] In this increasingly volatile climate, Gershwin was a safe and reliable choice to represent American cultural and musical values abroad.

Although the opera remained controversial throughout much of the twentieth century, few could deny that Gershwin's magnum opus was the first widely recognized American opera, one that successfully entered the musical canon and took its place in the operatic repertoire. By the time that it traveled to Europe in 1952, it was one of the only large-scale musical works widely acknowledged as a distinctly American cultural product.[85] In the harsh, brilliant light of Cold War American politics, *Porgy and Bess* gleamed brightly as a sparkling jewel worthy of representing American culture, if for no other reason than the fact that it had entered an operatic canon that had for centuries been dominated by French, Italian, and German operas. It was with this perception of the opera that the State Department readily encouraged its tour to Vienna and Berlin.

Yet there was another, more glaring reason why the State Department was eager to perform this work abroad. By the 1950s, it had become necessary to find effective means of combating the USSR's acerbic and accurate accusations of deeply institutionalized racism in the United States. In 1951, the US State Department acknowledged that "no American problem receives more widespread attention . . . than our treatment of racial minorities, particularly the Negro."[86] Although the USSR had pointed out American racial problems since the 1920s, during the Cold War, race and foreign policy became inextricably linked.[87] In 1946, for example, Secretary of State James Byrnes engaged in a skirmish with the USSR over voting rights in the Balkans. After protesting that the USSR was denying the rights of some of its citizens to vote, he received a short retort: "the Negroes of Mr. Byrnes" were denied the same rights. To numerous officials, that statement was "a checkmate of the first order."[88] The United States' woeful racial inadequacies were in the spotlight on the world stage and had the potential, as many saw it, to become the largest stumbling block in the nation's world policy. In sending African American performers abroad, the United States hoped to challenge international opinion of American society.

Although the United States sent a variety of jazz musicians and popular entertainers, Black classical musicians were also an important part of the global mission. Their investment in African American musicianship abroad during the Cold War led the United States to bring numerous musicians to tour Europe. The pianist Natalie Hinderas, for example, gave a recital for Radio Free Europe (five German radio stations whose sole purpose was to fight communism and broadcast their shows across the Iron Curtain) in Munich in 1957, and she performed on a sponsored tour through Vienna, Munich, Heidelberg, and Stuttgart.[89] African American choral director Jester Hairston also received sponsorship from the US State Department, as did the singer Elwood Peterson, who, after studying in Aachen in 1957, went on several USIS-sponsored tours. The flutist Dorothy Handy toured Germany in 1955 with the USIS. The Hall Johnson Choir, known for their performances of African American spirituals, also toured West Germany, performing in West Berlin's famous anticommunist Berliner Festwochen in 1951. Henry Blackmon, a singer, also performed in Germany on behalf of the USIS, and the opera singer Helen Phillips, sponsored by the US High Commission's Speakers and Artists Bureau, gave a thirty-concert tour in West Germany.[90] These musicians, and many more who performed in Germany as well, offer us a glimpse into the extent to which Black musicianship permeated West German postwar musical life as a result of the American government's initiatives to bring African American musicians to Europe.

Musicians make for unlikely and sometimes unwilling diplomats. A constant tension between politics and performance hummed in Cold War musical exchanges, especially since many musicians insisted that they simply did not care about politics and were only abroad to perform. Nonetheless, they performed the highly visible role of Americans abroad whether they recognized it or not.[91] From them audiences were supposed to learn what ordinary Americans were like, for better or worse. The two lead singers for the tour, the soprano Leontyne Price and the bass-baritone William Warfield, especially endured the harsh glare of an international spotlight that followed them around and speculated on a budding romance between the two of them.[92]

Away from the production, the cast of *Porgy and Bess* also assumed the roles of cultural ambassadors. In this case, however, the ensemble was fully aware of the racial politics of their performances offstage, seeking through their dress and comportment to redress Soviet depictions of African Americans as victims of racial injustice. One cast member remembered, "We always looked well when we went out. . . . We went in our evening gowns and our mink stoles."[93] Another cast member, Joy McLean, sardonically noted, "We surely didn't feel or look oppressed when we emerged from the theater."[94] Dailies such as *Bild,* a gossipy Berlin tabloid, marveled at these "dark-skinned performers" and mentioned how well dressed the performers were offstage.

The US State Department encouraged these views and told the performers to "keep in mind what you'd like your folks at home to read in the press about what you say."[95] The production, Ellen Noonan argues, saw "the performers as representatives of a different, but no less authentic, type of educated, accomplished, professional African American—in short, precisely the community members that [*Porgy*'s author] DuBose Heyward had written out of his fictional portrayal of Black Charleston."[96] In other words, in the eyes of the State Department, the African American musicians were more important for what they symbolized to European audiences than they were for the characters they performed on stage. It mattered more *how* they performed than *what* they actually sang. And it also mattered how well they dressed offstage in comparison to the costumes they wore on it.

As a result, African American opera singers were more reliable for American self-promotion than jazz musicians such as Louis Armstrong. Already reared in musical institutions usually reserved for white elites, they offered the respectability and the racial optics that the US State Department desperately needed in the wake of a growing civil rights struggle. Several performers also hosted Liederabende as part of their "goodwill" endeavors, including Irving Barnes and William Warfield, who wooed patrons in a Viennese *Rathskeller* with his performance of Richard Strauss.[97] Americans argued that the production of *Porgy and Bess* offered Germans the opportunity to encounter classically trained, highly talented African American musicians of high operatic quality.

When the opera headed for Berlin, it debuted on September 16 to sold-out crowds.[98] In Berlin, musical dignitaries such as Walter Felsenstein, the director of the Komische Oper in East Berlin, were in attendance, a sure testament to the opera's musical importance abroad. Felsenstein had requested two tickets to the performance in a letter addressed to the production's personnel, stating, "It [is] essential that I should familiarize myself with this production as well as the opera."[99] He was not the only East German in attendance. Although the East German press was notably silent on the Berlin production, East Germans did attend the performances. When the State Department discovered its popularity among residents of East Berlin, they

FIGURE 25. African American opera singers William Warfield and Leontyne Price, the leads of the US State Department–sponsored touring production of George Gershwin's *Porgy and Bess*, stand in front of the German Reichstag building in Berlin, Germany, September 18, 1952. Photo by Keystone/Hulton Archive/Getty Images.

ordered that East German currency be accepted at face value instead of the usual exchange rate of five deutsche mark to one US dollar.[100]

If the American authorities had hoped that German audiences would marvel at the professionalism of the cast and crew and ignore the content of *Porgy and Bess*, they were severely mistaken. In fact, the impressions that German audiences formed of the musical work stood in direct opposition to American interests. Berlin critics heralded the opera not as an American musical work—countering the US State Department's firm vision for it— but as a "Negro" opera above all, broadly defined. In 1954, Breen tried to correct this misconception. He commented to a press agent, "I notice that phrases 'Negro opera' and 'Negro troupe' and such are being used again by the press. . . . All through the last European tour we strongly emphasized to the press that *Porgy and Bess* must be referred to only as 'an American opera' or 'American troupe.'"[101] Nevertheless, Breen's wish for Germans to see *Porgy and Bess* as an American opera went unheeded, to which numerous articles and reviews can attest. Germans found the perceived Blackness in the performers, in the story, in the music itself, and in this staging alluring.

In its opening description of the opera, *Der Kurier* explained to its readers, "*Porgy and Bess* is an excerpt from the life of a Negro fisher and Negro harbor worker," as if the opera had presented facts instead of a fictional tale.[102]

Worse, music criticism conflated the two aspects of the tour that the authorities wished to divorce—the relationship between the African American performers and the characters they played. Many attendees believed that the singers were able to perform their roles so well because they were supposedly portraying parts of themselves and their history. Their remarks confirm Mari Yoshihara's argument that when singers of color take on roles in the operatic repertoire that supposedly look like them, audiences frequently do not divorce the identity of the singer from the role she has been cast to perform.[103] Similarly, in the German case, listeners conflated Black singers with their operatic repertoire.

Most German-speaking critics repeatedly remarked that it seemed so easy for the singers to slip into their roles. One critic noted, "A particular characteristic [of this opera] is the fact that everybody plays himself, but a fascinating surprise is the truthfulness with which the various figures are shown. Never before has one encountered such a style in Berlin."[104] *Der Kurier* also praised the opera's cast members in the same way, probably much to the horror of Langston Hughes: "The actors do not appear to be acting but just playing their own lives."[105] The critic from the *Süddeutsche Zeitung* praised the musicians in a similar manner, while also highlighting their Blackness, writing that "the dark-skinned guests performed as if it weren't a musical play with prescribed roles, but a piece of their being."[106] Another reviewer in Vienna's *Die Presse* made similar comments, mentioning that performances of *Porgy and Bess* by all-white casts prior to this one (in Copenhagen and Zurich) had failed because "the piece is so rooted in an American foundation, and in the milieu of the Negro, that it can only be effectively performed with Negro power."[107] In their estimation, only Black people could tell this authentically Black tale, for the two were one and the same.[108]

By describing the opera and its effects as a natural and effective form of operatic storytelling in which the actors simply played themselves, German critics reinforced pre-1945 stereotypes of African Americans. Instead of dispelling myths about Blackness, West Germans perpetuated them. Numerous reviews echoed the same primitivist sentiments toward African Americans that had thrived during the jazz era of the Weimar Republic and even during the Kaiserreich: African Americans were "hot-blooded" musicians whose music comprised "wild shrieks" that correlated to their fiery and passionate natures. One criticism from *Der Kurier* captures these underlying beliefs very well: "the voices are admirable. It is simply wonderful how the voices fall from a screaming high pitch into a rich normal voice again. Every tone and every movement is full of discipline."[109]

At the end of the tour Harvey Kellerman, an American liaison for the Berlin Cultural Festival, declared *Porgy and Bess* a "triumph" in Berlin. "Well-meaning friends advised against it," Kellerman stated. "So did prominent members of the American Black community, who feared that German or even any European audiences were not ready to appreciate the message."[110] But, Kellerman concluded, *Porgy* had surpassed everyone's expectations and transcended the international and political fray. In a letter to Breen, one American general personally thanked him for serving his country through art:

> It is through operations such as *Porgy and Bess* that World War III can be won without a fight. This means that you are saving lives and keeping our country free with every performance. Perhaps the thought that you are in the true front lines of the next war will help you to endure the many hardships and inconveniences which I know your work entails.[111]

President Eisenhower called the opera one of his Cold War "secret weapons," claiming it fulfilled his directive to go "forth and demonstrate that Americans too can lay claim to high cultural and artistic accomplishment."[112] The musicians in the production also received praise for their musical intellect and sophistication, and the American press credited them with dismantling lingering European stereotypes of the oppressed Negro. Following the opera's run in Europe, the US State Department later sent productions of *Porgy and Bess* to Africa, Asia, and South America.

Although the American government may have convinced Germans that *Porgy and Bess* deserved praise and accolades as a work of high art, the opera's subject matter and how the German public chose to discuss it allowed Germans to perpetuate myths of "the Negro." In 1956, for example, a journalist with the *Journal and Guide* argued, "Foreign audiences are seldom aware that *Porgy* does not deal with the present, they do not know that the music is not genuine Negro art. . . . While I was in Europe last summer, I had many heated discussions on the subject, but could not explain away the 'authenticity' of life as depicted in *Porgy*."[113]

Yet Afro-Americanophilia continued to thrive in West German musical circles.[114] While German audiences often expressed indifference to American modernist music, African American art songs continued to be wildly popular.[115] Black musicians, regardless of background, were still sought to perform. At the request of the German government, for example, the highly-regarded African American pianist Sylvia Lee (who worked at the Bavarian State Opera) taught African American spirituals to German choruses for seven years.[116]

Musical works such as *Porgy and Bess* and Still's *Afro-American Symphony* are only a few examples of West German demand for African American music.

In fact, German demand for African American art music and its practitioners became a frequent reference point in ongoing debates about the casting of African American performers thereafter. Following a contentious debate over the African American mezzo-soprano Vera Little's debut as Carmen at the Deutsche Oper Berlin in 1958, a writer for the *General-Anzeiger Wuppertal* commented directly on what the critic believed was a strong preference for African American singers. "The Berliners," the critic begins, "have a bias toward Negro voices. The *Porgy and Bess* ensemble celebrated triumph; Dorothy Dandridge as Carmen Jones is still unforgettable. All the more reason to be curious about Vera Little, who was announced as the Black Carmen from the USA."[117] The music critic Gerhard Wandel also held up Berliners' preference for African American musicians. "Particularly within the last few years," he writes, "Berliners have taken a shine to exotic guests. Just recall *Porgy and Bess*, [the dancer and choreographer] Katherine Dunham, and more recently, the dance group, 'Brasiliana.'"[118]

While Cold War officials applauded themselves on their successful launching of Black performances in Europe, for Black classical musicians their time abroad took its toll on them. Confessing privately to her manager Sol Hurok about the stresses of being a cultural ambassador, Anderson shared, "I was told beforehand that this tour would be strenuous, but I do not believe that anyone realized how strenuous. For, the world situation being what it is, there were things required of me as a Negro, as a representative of my people, that would not be required of someone else."[119] Placed in the unique situation of representing American high culture and its aspirations of entering a universal art music canon while also tasked with the greater burden of overturning well-founded Soviet criticisms of American white supremacy, Black classical musicians had the most to gain and to lose in these moments of cultural exchange. No one else could fulfill this dual function better than them. Because of their tour abroad, Price and Warfield became international superstars in high demand for years. Yet the musical performers and cultural diplomats were ultimately incapable of correcting gross misidentifications of African American life in German public discourse, even while displaying their classical training and excellent vocal technique.

The Return of Musical Blackness

American investment in German musical life after WWII was substantial and would be sustained for decades, yet the American relationship to German audiences was far more complex than government funders might have understood. German audiences never read American bodies as simply or uniquely American, a fact that the American military either sought to control in their favor or worked to deny. The politics of Black bodies in German musical spaces was no less complex, even if American organizers might have hoped otherwise. Rather, Black classical musicians frequently functioned as signs for older racial and musical logics that predated 1945.[120] In the case of German music and its legacies, the intellectual and cultural traditions that had undergirded public concertizing and listening for decades remained firmly in place, unable to be dislodged.

At the behest of the American forces, a new, postwar West German musical life quickly embraced Black performers on its stages in an unprecedented manner. Yet a closer look reminds us how drastically and quickly a new context can produce new cultural meanings while nonetheless producing or reproducing the logic of race. The question of what musical Blackness could or should look and sound like after 1945 did not dissipate after the establishment of two German states in 1949, nor after the Allied forces ended their occupation of West Germany in 1955.

Indeed, the next chapter takes up where Allied forces left off, by exploring how West German musical institutions and their listening publics—now free from Allied interference—produced, managed, and understood racial and gendered musical performances in the 1950s and 1960s. West German opera houses were especially eager to initiate public conversations on the changing meanings of music, national identity, and coming to terms with Germany's past, and they frequently employed Black opera singers to do so. West German questioning of the relationship of Black classical musicians to German musical culture did not lessen once the American authorities withdrew a significant portion of their troops. Rather, these questions took on a new sense of urgency when a new, younger generation of Germans began to ask them instead.

CHAPTER 8

Breaking with the Past

Race, Gender, and Opera after 1945

When the African American violinist William Kemper Harreld traveled around Austria and Germany in the spring and summer of 1953, he not only recorded the presence of African American troops on German soil. He also proudly shared his life-changing experience participating in one of the most important events in German musical culture: the Bayreuth Festival. Nestled comfortably in his seat inside Wagner's opera house, Harreld watched the curtain rise for one of the first operas that Bayreuth had been allowed to stage since the Allies shut down the opera house in 1945. "Bayreuth Festival Haus orchestra hidden from audience," he marvels. "Perfect singing-acting. Wonderful ensemble. Exceptional excellence in strings. Wagner's two grandsons manage fine in Bayreuth."[1]

Harreld's humor shines through in that last, modest statement, which conceals as much as it reveals in its judgment of the new directors of the Bayreuth Festival, Wieland and Wolfgang Wagner. When Harreld attended the Bayreuth Festival, Wagner's two grandsons had begun their transformation into new leaders of the opera world, taking on the almost insurmountable task of tackling one of the most contentious opera composers in German history—and only two years after the opera festival had been permitted to open again to boot. A site that had featured prominently in Nazi celebrations, the Bayreuth Festival transitioned under the Wagner brothers to one of the most daring and innovative spaces for operatic performances in postwar Central Europe.

Narratives of postwar West German and Austrian cultural life frequently present Anglo-American actors as the primary agents of change. In the wake of the Holocaust and the Nazi racial state, the Allied powers, often led by the American military, had pursued policies to drastically alter how German musical culture functioned. But West German and Austrian producers and consumers of culture were also capable of initiating their own conversations on cultural transformation and renewal without any Allied meddling. Especially in the world of opera, their forays into aesthetics and politics had little to do with what Allied forces thought of them. In fact, one of the greatest postwar controversies involving race, music, and German national identity occurred under the direction of the West German opera director Wieland Wagner—not because of American influence.

Opera directors may have been unconcerned with Allied politics but they did not lack agendas. Many figures, including Wieland Wagner, Walter Felsenstein, Carl Ebert, and Götz Friedrich, considered it their political responsibility to drastically alter opera and sever it from its previous Nazi-inflected ties. Through the works that they produced, they engaged in lengthy debates about race, national identity, the legacies of National Socialism, and the role of high culture in the public sphere, all while reconsidering the very purpose of high culture and its social responsibilities.

In this chapter, I argue that despite these opera directors' desire to modernize opera houses, longstanding notions of Blackness shaped both the production and reception of operas featuring Black singers in postwar West Germany and Austria. Opera directors and conductors hired Black singers to demonstrate that their opera houses were once again international and now even racially inclusive. At the same time, however, the ways in which they presented Black bodies on West German and Austrian stages often reinforced longstanding tropes of Black sexuality and racial differences that contradicted their own claims. Audiences, in turn, responded to these new and provocative performances by continuing to use race as the barometer for their interpretation of an opera production. If Black opera singers performed in exotic operas, the majority of listeners heralded the performer for bringing authenticity to the role. However, if Black opera singers performed in so-called white roles, audiences claimed that the performance was unconvincing. Because they relied on a singer's race and gender to make sense of exotic operas, this methodology failed them when Black singers took on operas by Mozart and Wagner.

Against the backdrop of these operatic performances, different processes were at work disentangling society from the recent Nazi past. In Austria's case, breaking away from what had been a "Greater Germany" became an important, immediate action spurred on by their new geopolitical context as a neutral territory within an emerging Cold War. If before 1938 Austrians thought of themselves as the "better Germans," after 1945 they no longer thought of themselves as Germans at all. In West Germany's case, breaking from the Nazi past was an important performative gesture that cultural institutions initiated to demonstrate that they had moved forward into a better future. Both West Germany and Austria sought to transform their perceptions of themselves. Musical performances featuring racialized bodies were critical to their endeavors.

But using Black musicians to disentangle the Nazi past was a difficult and contradictory process. Austrian and German anti-Blackness shaped and determined the actions of both opera directors and the audiences who attended their stagings. Both the production of racial difference on stage and the reception from audiences suggest that Blackness remained an ever elusive and problematic discourse for white audiences to tackle, even in their pursuit to embrace it.

Performance as a Technology of Forgetting in West German and Austrian Opera Houses

When asked in 1967 what might be a solution to some of opera's contemporary ailments, the conductor Pierre Boulez scandalized the classical music world by replying, "Blow up the opera houses."[2] Boulez's now-infamous quip might seem glib, but it resonated with a new generation of opera composers, conductors, and directors seeking to rehabilitate, revitalize, revolutionize, or even eradicate opera, depending on their perspectives and beliefs. Much like writers and intellectuals wrestling with Theodor Adorno's statement that it was barbaric to write poetry after Auschwitz, opera producers and enthusiasts also struggled with how to compose, stage, and perform operas after WWII and the Holocaust. In an interview shortly before his death, Wieland Wagner said:

> It would be unjust to condemn us, the so-called skeptical generation, as simply destructive. We have seen and experienced things that our fathers and grandfathers were powerless to prevent: acts of destruction which go far beyond human imagining. *If one wants to build a new house, one must first dig up the ground in which the foundations are to be laid.*[3]

New opera houses required new ground and fresh starts. Avoiding frivolity and sentiment, opera directors sought to transform—if not to destroy outright—opera houses and their legacies of bourgeois comfort.[4] To do so, opera administrators sought to change audiences' relationship to the operatic canon itself through their stagings of it. How an opera was staged—the directions, lighting, costumes, set design, acting, and musicianship that produce the performance—became an increasingly important method of speaking to a larger public, because by changing the opera's settings and characters opera directors rethought the work itself. In the postwar era, opera stagings became a powerful way in which opera directors offered social and political commentary. In radically altering the perception of an opera such as Mozart's *Don Giovanni*, opera stagings could become provocateurs of political and national transformation by scrutinizing and challenging contemporary claims and norms.[5]

One way that opera houses chose to speak to their contemporary moment was by hiring Black singers to fill the main roles, something that had been previously been either unwelcome or, by the late 1930s, unfathomable. In fact, for the first time in German history, Black musicians signed lengthy, competitive, and expensive contracts with German-speaking opera houses. Beginning in 1954, when Camilla Williams became the first Black opera singer to perform with the Vienna State Opera, Black opera singers appeared in major operatic venues throughout German-speaking Europe and they also sang in major festivals. Prior to 1945, the majority of Black musicians had performed lieder in concert halls or instrumental music in orchestra halls or conservatories. But in the postwar period, Austrian and West German opera houses emerged as the most powerful institutions backing Black performers. Some earned annual contracts, such as Lawrence Winters, who was a fixed member of the ensemble of the Hamburg State Opera in the 1950s, or Annabelle Bernard, who became the first Black woman to become part of an ensemble cast when the Deutsche Oper Berlin hired her in 1962. Others took on administrative roles, such as Muriel Rahn, who became the first African American musician to run a German musical institution in 1959.[6] For seven years, the legendary Sylvia Lee, the wife of the conductor Everett Lee, worked as a staff accompanist and opera coach for two opera houses in Munich and across West Germany in the 1950s.[7]

African Americans were not only successful as American opera singers internationally but they were also some of the only successful American opera singers at the time, and disproportionally so.[8] There were more African American opera singers at the Vienna State Opera House in the 1950s than there were white American singers, for example, and they dominated regional opera houses and won international competitions hosted in Germany as well. African American mezzo-soprano Shirley Verrett reflected on Germany's special role in the opera world, asserting that American opera houses "are not like Europe, let's face it. And let's not even say Europe. It's still not like Germany."[9]

It is quite striking that Black women in particular were at the center of opera stagings in West Germany and Austria. Many of our narratives of postwar West Germany and Austria examine the relationship between African Americans and white Germans through a gendered lens that skews masculine.[10] Understandably, secondary scholarship discussing African American encounters with Germans and Austrians in the postwar period focuses on the presence of Black men in the American military stationed in occupied West Germany and Austria.[11] Yet a glance at cultural production in German-speaking Europe reveals arenas where Black women were the primary agents of transnational conversation, a gendered distinction that may reflect the nature of their travel and work in Europe. Whereas African American men arrived with tanks, guns, and the power of the military, when Black women arrived in German-speaking Europe, they often came to perform in films, on stages, or in opera halls. In other words, white encounters with Black women in German-speaking Europe came primarily through cultural productions.

In the context of opera, Black women outnumbered Black men for one important reason: romantic entanglements between a Black man and a white woman remained taboo in the operatic world on both sides of the Atlantic—including after 1945, when white German and Austrian women became romantically involved with African American soldiers. Black male opera singers were well aware of this discrepancy. Before the baritone Simon Estes became the first Black male singer to perform at Bayreuth in 1974, for example, Leontyne Price warned him that he would have difficulties finding acceptance in the opera world as a Black man. "Simon," she told him, "it's going to be even more difficult for you. Because you are a Black male, the discrimination will be greater. You have a beautiful voice, you are musical, intelligent, independent, and handsome. With all of those ingredients, you are a threat. It will be more difficult for you than it was for me."[12] The tenor George Shirley recalled in an interview the difficulties that he and other Black men experienced in German opera houses specifically. "I think of Jim Wagner, a fine tenor, who for years tried to find a place for himself in Germany," Shirley recalled, continuing, "He finally did. There were many refusals, however: 'Thank you very much.' 'We like your voice, but we don't have a position for you now.' Jim says that finally someone just came out and told him point-blank, 'I like your voice, but I won't hire you because you're

Black.'[13] Because of their gender, Black men were not part of the new wave of hires that brought African American opera singers to German-speaking Europe. The majority of racial barriers broken at opera houses in the postwar era were at the hands (or voices) of Black women.

Although opera directors and conductors frequently argued that they were hiring Black women solely because of their talent, their statements must be treated with a strong degree of skepticism. After all, classically trained Black singers had performed in German-speaking Europe before WWII, including Luranah Aldridge, Sissieretta Jones, and Marian Anderson. Their voices were no less exceptional and well-trained than the dozens of Black singers who sang in West Germany and Austria after 1945. Rather, the practice of hiring and staging Black singers after 1945 was always a political decision as much as an aesthetic choice. Black opera singers, by virtue of their performances, challenged audiences to ask themselves what roles were acceptable for Black singers to perform on stage, what opera meant, and how operas could speak to a postwar audience. Hiring a Black singer such as Price to perform in *Don Giovanni*, then, became a method of confronting audiences' notions about race and identity on the German opera stage and in the German public sphere.

There was, however, a fundamental problem with opera houses' use of racial hiring and typecasting to overcome their Nazi pasts. Practices of confronting the past frequently demanded the presence of people of color in order for white audiences to enact their guilt and emotional catharsis. White producers and listeners thus imbricated people of color into their processes of historical remembering. Having excised the word "race" from public vocabulary and unable to mention their recent genocide against Jews, white Germans and Austrians rendered Black people symbols of rehabilitation and repentance in order to process their past. Opera houses were no less guilty of this practice, for they, too, depended on Black bodies to transform their image of themselves.

In postwar Austria, the newly emergent status of Austrians as the victims of Nazism became an essential tool they wielded to sever any ties to Germany and to deny the complicity of Austrians in WWII and the Holocaust. They clung to the label "Hitler's First Victim," a term that Allied forces had ascribed to Austria in the Moscow Declaration of 1943 in the hopes of turning Austria against Nazi Germany during the war.[14] The label stuck after 1945, when it became clear that Austria's geopolitical position along the Iron Curtain made it an invaluable and necessary ally. Austrians embraced their newly anointed Cold War–inflected status as victims of Nazi aggression to absolve themselves of having to confront their roles during the Third Reich.

Moreover, they not only participated in narratives of selective victimization but also valorized Austrian soldiers of the Wehrmacht. By memorializing Austrian soldiers as fallen heroes of WWII, Heidemarie Uhl argues, Austrians became "not victims of Nazism, but rather victims of the war against Nazism."[15]

Austria's new postwar project of nationalization, built on the myth of victimization, excluded Jews and people of color. A stoic silence surrounded white Austrian resistance fighters against Nazism, for example, and an even greater silence clouded Jewish survivors, who so easily threatened white Austrians' claims of victimization. After 1945, Matti Bunzl writes, "Jews had no space in the Austrian state's ritualized narrations of Self."[16] For these reasons, Jews were absent from public discourse, or appeared marginally at best. At the reopening of the Vienna State Opera House in 1955, the conductor Karl Böhm—who had led concerts celebrating Hitler's annexation of Austria in 1938—lent his musical direction to Vienna's new moment of memorialization and celebration. No Jewish survivors were invited to participate.[17]

Anti-Blackness also ran through Austrian modes of victimization and memorialization during American occupation and the early years of the Cold War. Decrying their downgraded status under American military occupation, many Austrians called themselves "Austrian Negroes."[18] Just like how African Americans were second class citizens in the United States, one Austrian said in an interview, "us Austrians are also [second class] because we lost the war."[19] Similarly, Austrians also compared their situation to colonized peoples in Africa, using images and rhetoric to call attention to what they perceived to be their downgraded status in geopolitical affairs.

These kinds of comparisons, however, showed little sympathy for actual Black people in Africa or in the United States. Rather, white Austrians perpetuated long-standing anti-Black biases, reproducing the very logics of racism that had existed under the Nazis.[20] They called soldiers of color sleeping with white Austrian women "Jonnys," for example, a derogatory term taken from Krenek's 1920s opera *Jonny spielt auf* that coded Black men as sexually promiscuous, and they compared Black troops to orangutans who had "just hopped down from the tree."[21] Following an incident in 1952 involving two African American GIs who had become involved in an altercation with Swedish tourists in Salzburg, the city's residents campaigned against "these Negro-troops" and their "Congo mentality."[22] White Austrians also reinforced the long-standing idea that Black people were antithetical to Europe. Austrian organizations sent Black Austrian children born of African American soldiers and white German-speaking women to the United States on the grounds that "there is no chance for the child in Europe."[23]

White Austrian silence, denial, and practices of victimization meant that performances featuring Black women on stage were both celebrated and contested in a whole host of complicated and contradictory ways. Eager to disassociate from Nazi Germany, opera houses hired Black opera singers early and quickly, even if their administrators had actively participated and even celebrated in the annexation of Austria by Nazi Germany. Unlike Austrian Jews, African American opera singers could be comfortably exotic, foreign, and different enough to be welcome on stage even while these productions, as we will see, fetishized them and caused outcry.

In postwar West Germany, on the other hand, a different kind of deafening silence surrounded the Nazi past, imposed by the challenge of answering for a litany of horrifying crimes.[24] Katrin Sieg argues that because of the terror and shame that wracked West German society, the Nazi past "required a sophisticated orchestration of 'forgetting.'" Yet the act of forgetting, she writes, created an even greater conundrum: "how to forget something you cannot acknowledge knowing, since that acknowledgment would consign matter to memory rather than oblivion?"[25] The solution was to develop a pattern of silence and denial that formed a near continuous loop.

In that silence a particular triangulation between white Germans, Jews, and other racial minorities emerged. Indeed, one of the primary methods for breaking from the past was through an encounter with another racial or ethnic minority. Leslie Adelson has dubbed interracial engagements such as these a "riddle of referentiality," which describes how racial and ethnic minorities such as Turks become stand-ins for Jews.[26] African American soldiers and Afro-German children born during the occupation years also often functioned as litmus tests of changing race relations after WWII. They, too, were supposed to be proof that Germans had overcome their Nazi past.[27]

Performances in postwar West Germany could be messy sites of negotiation and identity formation precisely because they offered temporary moments of collective catharsis. One example of this metonymical mixing in German musical culture concerns the production and reception of Schoenberg's Holocaust cantata, *A Survivor from Warsaw*, at the now-famous avant-garde Darmstadt International Summer Courses for New Music in 1950. Many members of the orchestra simply did not want to perform Schoenberg's cantata—in fact, the decision to play it won by a slim margin. Rather, an orchestra member stated in an interview with the musicologist Anne Shreffler, "The Amis [Americans] should play it themselves." When Shreffler prodded a little bit more by asking if "'the Amis' were stand-ins for 'the Jews,'" the interview subject confirmed that was indeed what he had meant.[28]

Metonyms, equivalences, and references shaped and occluded postwar West German cultural formation.

Black bodies and "Black music" also participated in a complicated triangulation where West Germans worked out the Nazi past without often directly alluding to it or to the matter of race. Examining Günter Grass's 1959 novel, *The Tin Drum*, Priscilla Layne argues that the protagonist, a jazz musician, "plays music not for money but to help white Germans deal with their fascist past."[29] The jazz band that plays music in the Onion Cellar, a place where Germans peel onions so they can finally cry, was necessary for white Germans to experience collective catharsis, Layne argues. After the band gets fired, it is replaced by a violinist "who, if you squinted a little, might have been taken for a gypsy." Foreign music, "Black music," was necessary to induce white German mourning. Angelica Fenner finds a similar emotional process underway in the 1952 film *Toxi*, a story about an Afro-German girl who is temporarily adopted by a white, middle class German family. She attributes the film's overwhelming popularity in West Germany to its ability to permit white Germans to indulge in feelings of a collective catharsis. Through the character of Toxi, they satisfactorily mourned their own perceived rejections or displacements in society, "misrecognizing in their plight their own sense of dislocation," she writes.[30] Through the medium of performance, Blackness frequently functioned as an initiator of mourning and catharsis.

There are many problems with this process of using people of color to work out the Nazi past. First, it is not clear, Adelson writes, what this triangulation is meant to accomplish.[31] What, exactly, is being worked out in these moments? What is actually achievable in these performances? Indeed, many historians argue that the problem with employing people of color as a solution to dealing with the past was the very notion that the past could be overcome at all.[32] Moreover, trying to perform racial reconciliation through musical performances featuring Black bodies allowed West Germans to seek comfort in symbolic gestures and to avoid the more difficult work of material reparation.[33]

Such was the case for many opera houses, which operated under the assumption that breaking with the past required hiring non-white musicians. When protest erupted over Wieland Wagner's decision to cast the African American soprano Grace Bumbry in the role of Venus at the Bayreuth Festival, for example, Wieland argued vociferously that it did not matter to him "which nation, religion, or race a soloist belongs to."[34] He accused protesters of not understanding Richard Wagner's music, and he proclaimed to the international press that he would "take black, yellow, or brown artists if the production needs them." He argued, somewhat disingenuously, that "my grandfather did not write for skin color, but for voice color."[35] As we will see below, however, it had always been Wieland's plan to hire a Black woman to sing the role of Venus for his 1961 production of *Tannhäuser*. While preaching a color-blind mythology, Wieland himself practiced a race-based approach to operatic stagings, even if it was in the service of moving West German audiences into what Wieland deemed to be a more progressive and open democratic society.

Similarly, Herbert von Karajan was insistent upon hiring Price to perform in *Don Giovanni* at the Salzburg Festival in 1961 in part to rebuke what he thought was a small-minded provincialism that had clung to the Salzburg Festival in the postwar years.[36] Yet Price paid the cost of von Karajan's decision when someone threw a stone in her hotel window out of spite.[37] In both cases, a German conductor or director insisted on his right to employ a Black woman as he saw fit. And in both cases, the leaders had hired the singer all along as a means of dragging the audience into their definition of a more open and progressive German musical culture.

Black opera singers, then, fulfilled a variety of goals for opera houses invested in pursuing new audiences and in cultivating new legacies for themselves. First, they became a symbol by which cultural institutions could

FIGURE 26. The African American opera singer Leontyne Price meets with the conductor Herbert von Karajan in a recording studio in Vienna, 1962. Photo: FO600048/21, The Austrian National Library, Bildarchiv, Vienna, Austria.

demonstrate their readiness and eagerness to break from their Nazi past, regardless of their motives for doing so. Second, hosting Black opera singers became a means through which German and Austrian opera houses could then educate the public on becoming better members of civil society. Regardless of the reasoning behind their respective silences—Austrian or West German—showcasing Black musicians was a complex and often hidden process of (mis)recognizing their own recent pasts.

Racial Typecasting and the Production of Race on the Opera Stage

Yet *how* opera houses presented Black singers on the opera stage in front of thousands of listeners often demonstrated that one step forward could mean two steps back. The majority of Black women were cast in exotic operas, for example, either because administrators believed that it was a "natural fit" for them to play non-white characters or because their Blackness was expected to lend itself to the performance somehow. Opera directors, dramaturges, and conductors repeatedly chose to showcase Black musicians' racial difference, even while maintaining their own professions of color-blindness.

Casting African American women to sing in exotic operas had a precedent in European history, one from which postwar opera directors chose not to depart. Lillian Evanti, for example, was the first Black singer to perform in a European opera house in 1925 at the Casino Theater in Nice, France. She sang the title role in Léo Delibes's exotic opera *Lakmé*, set in faraway India and featuring a Hindu princess who commits suicide when she learns that her lover, a British officer named Gerald, has ended the affair. Florence Cole Talbert followed suit, becoming the first Black singer to land a major recurring role with an opera company in Europe. She performed in March of 1927 at the Teatro Comunale in Cosenza, Italy, in the title role of Verdi's exotic opera, *Aida*. Likewise, the soprano Caterina Jarboro also sang *Aida* throughout Europe, followed by Giacomo Meyerbeer's *L'Africaine* and Karl Goldmark's *The Queen of Sheba*, which she sang throughout Central and Eastern Europe.[38] Tellingly, for Jarboro's performance of *Aida* in Riga, Latvia, the Italian conductor, "afraid of a vendetta because of Mussolini's assault on Ethiopia, refused to start *Aida* until he had assurances that the soprano wasn't a real Ethiopian."[39] In other words, the conductor conflated the singer with the role she had been hired to perform.

It is no wonder then that the first Black woman to perform in a major opera house in German-speaking Europe appeared in an exotic role. The soprano Camilla Williams was the first Black woman to perform at the Vienna

State Opera House in 1956, where she sang the title role in Puccini's opera, *Madame Butterfly*. Her debut offers a striking example of racial hiring and typecasting. Born and raised in Virginia, Williams studied at Virginia State College for Negroes before moving to Philadelphia on a scholarship to study with Marion Freschl, a contralto who had been an attendee at Anderson's Salzburg recital in 1935.[40] After performing in New York City in the 1940s and 1950s, Williams traveled to Vienna where, under Erich von Wymetal's direction, she made her debut in *Madame Butterfly*. Virtually all Viennese newspapers reported this stunning news, noting, "It was the first time that a Negro singer graced the stage of the [Vienna] State Opera."[41]

A few factors may explain why Williams's debut went so smoothly. First, Williams had already sung the title role in *Madame Butterfly*, having received accolades for her debut performance at the City Center Opera Company in New York City in 1946. This opera was clearly one Williams could sing, and sing well. Second, Viennese audiences already knew Williams and liked her. A critic for the *Wiener Journal* proudly pointed out that Williams had given a Liederabend in Vienna before her turn as the "Black butterfly," and claimed her Liederabend in Vienna had prepared her for the Vienna State Opera.[42] What had brought Williams to the musical capital, actually, was the encouragement of Roland Hayes. "It's time for you to go to Europe," Hayes purportedly told Williams, "and I want you to see how *you* will be accepted."[43] And like Hayes, Williams eventually returned to the United States with glowing words of praise from Viennese critics.

But most important for this chapter, a primary reason why Williams as Butterfly might not have caused any headshaking is because audiences were willing to make the racial leap and believe that a Black singer could play an Asian role. A critic for *Neues Österreich* wrote, "The dark-skinned artist fulfilled all demands (including the optical ones)."[44] Naomi André argues that these kinds of remarks are not incidental. When Marian Anderson debuted at the Metropolitan Opera House just a year earlier than Williams in Vienna, she also played an "exotic" character, that of Ulrica in Verdi's opera *Un Ballo in Maschera*. "For the first Black voice featured on the Met opera stage," André writes, "Anderson fulfilled and mirrored the role of a foreign character, invited as a featured presence to peer into an alternate plane of reality and predict a new future."[45] Only in a foreign role could a Black woman like Anderson or Williams have made their debuts.

Following Williams's turn as Madame Butterfly, other Black women also took on title roles in operas—above all, Verdi's opera, *Aida*. While *Madame Butterfly* is an opera that rests on the premise of Asian women's sexual innocence, operas such as *Aida* with Black female characters produced stagings built on German fantasies of Black female sexuality. Indeed, whereas relationships between Black men and white women were considered taboo, West German culture produced images and representations of Black women that were often voyeuristic and directed at white male desire. West German magazine articles, for example, portrayed Black women as "pretty exotic bird[s]" whose dark skin inspired male fantasies.[46]

More specifically, Black women in Germany were often told that they were only desirable because they were deemed exotic. In the groundbreaking book *Showing Our Colors*, for example, an Afro-German woman named Laura Baum shared an encounter that reflected how her desirability could only be understood in these fetishized terms. After she was accosted by two drunk white German men, one of them said "Hey, she's good looking!" to which the other replied, "But she's not European." Baum concluded from that experience, "As a colored woman you're mostly viewed as exotic, it fits the usual stereotype found everywhere."[47]

Elfie Fiegert, the Afro-German child actress who starred in the film *Toxi*, also faced similar German attitudes toward Blackness, beauty, and exoticism in the early 1960s when she began trying to find jobs as a teen actress. Her agent told her that "dark types are harder to sell than blondes"—unless, of course, she could be cast in an exotic role. In the case of the Afro-German actress Marie Nejar, who had performed both in Nazi and postwar West Germany and Austria, her manager lied to the press and changed Nejar's name without her consent to Leila Negra to make her appear foreign and exotic.[48] Black women existed in the German imagination as exotic sex objects. Nuns charged with the task of raising Afro-German girls in orphanages frequently castigated them for their supposed innate sexual deviance. In a memoir detailing her Black girlhood in postwar West Germany, for example, Ika Hügel-Marshall recalls a nun telling her that she "would need to choose between a future as a Christian missionary or a prostitute."[49] The nuns believed that because Hügel-Marshall was a Black girl, it was in her nature to behave inappropriately and sexually with boys.[50]

West German assumptions of Black sexuality informed opera productions as well. In the Deutsche Oper Berlin's 1961 production of *Aida*, for example, Wieland Wagner set the opera deep in the heart of "primitive" Congo instead of ancient Egypt, calling Verdi's *Aida* "an African mystery." Wagner's decision to "Africanize" *Aida* deserves more analysis. In his production, enslaved Ethiopians dragged totemic poles and African sculptures across the stage for heathen rituals and indigenous worship.[51] Audiences, in turn, wielded an ethnographic and anthropological gaze at the spectacle, being drawn into what was not actually any real or meaningful African religious practice so much as a fictitious imagining of African peoples.[52] Wagner sought to make *Aida* a primitivist story about earthly love between doomed lovers. Everything from the masks and costumes to animal worship and, according to one critic, a "dabbling in fetishisms" led one German music critic to observe, "There was definitely an Africa to see [tonight]."[53] Wagner's production of *Aida* was also deeply erotic. Wagner thought of *Aida* as Verdi's *Tristan and Isolde* (although critics jokingly called his production "Wieland Wagner's *L'Africaine*"), a dramatic tale where the lovers could only be united in death. Wagner placed a large phallus in the bedroom of Amneris, the Egyptian princess, stating, "This gigantic phallus is Amneris' constant dream."[54]

If staging Black women in exotic operas often reproduced racial hierarchies and desires, hiring Black singers for "white" roles posed its own set of problems. Above all opera directors worried that the singer might appear (to them) inauthentic or out of place on stage. One approach that some directors took was to cast Black singers in strange and aesthetically provocative productions, so as to not "distract" the listener with the singer's Blackness. In that regard, the Salzburg Festival presented a bombed-out, post-apocalyptic Seville for their staging of *Don Giovanni* in 1961, rendering Price's performance as Donna Anna uncontroversial. Instead, critics found Price to be well suited for the "weirdly baroque night scene."[55] In these kinds of productions, the singer's Blackness did not detract from the production, which was already considered strange.

Yet even an abstract or avant-garde staging could not stave off cries of outrage when Black women were cast in "white" roles, which the Bayreuth Festival Opera House discovered in 1961 when they cast Bumbry as Venus in *Tannhäuser*. Bumbry, a soprano from St. Louis, Missouri, had recently performed in Basel, and when she auditioned privately for Wolfgang Sawallisch, conductor of the Bayreuth Festival, she had never sung any German opera in her life.[56] Nonetheless, the conductor recommended her to Wagner, who had been searching for a Venus, and he excitedly accepted her.

Why did Wagner hire Bumbry, especially if she was unfamiliar with the German operatic repertoire? "What I was looking for," he said to the German press in July 1961, "was the best Venus in voice and appearance."[57] In fact, that statement is misleading, because Bumbry's appearance most likely mattered more than her voice, regardless of whether Wagner would admit this fact publicly. Bumbry was not the first Black woman to audition for the role of Venus. A letter dated October 1960 from Friedelind Wagner to Walter Felsenstein, the director of the Komische Oper in East Berlin, discussed the possibility of the African American soprano Ella Lee performing Venus for the Bayreuth Festival. In it, Friedelind tells Felsenstein in passing,

"[Ella] arrived with me last night in Bayreuth, where she first wants to sleep, and then work on Venus for Wieland."[58] Although it remains unclear why Bumbry debuted at Bayreuth in 1961 instead of Lee, Wieland's documented interest in finding a Black singer to perform at Bayreuth goes against his misleading statements to the German public. He specifically looked for an "elemental erotic quality" in his new Venus that only a Black woman such as Lee or Bumbry was supposedly capable of possessing.

Like the Salzburg production of *Don Giovanni*, Bayreuth's new *Tannhäuser* production in 1961 sought out a different interpretation of the opera and an entirely different concept of Venus, one that showcased a new erotic goddess. In Wagner's production, Venus reigned on a throne from a dark cavern, where naked young men and women climbed down from the ceiling or lurked in the shadows miming sex acts.[59] Many opera critics applauded Wagner's exploitation of the Black Venus to subvert portrayals of a Western goddess and instead present a "powerful goddess, a bronze, archaic idol, an Asiatic Astarte rather than the usual Hellenic Venus."[60] Looking back on the 1961 production of *Tannhäuser*, the historian Geoffrey Skelton concluded, "The Black Venus did no more than show that, *once one frees oneself from realism*, such matters of outward appearance become almost irrelevant."[61] To Skelton and others, Wagner appropriately used Bumbry's race to liberate the audience from realist and "authentic" depictions of medieval Germany.

By depicting Venus as an erotic, otherworldly beauty, however, Wagner—intentionally or not—reinforced modern German notions of the primeval Otherness of Black female sexuality. In the process of subverting the audience's expectations of Venus away from a beautiful blonde toward a Black goddess, Wagner also instructed his crew to "present eroticism in a repulsive way."[62] The nature and the role of Venus shifted for the first time at Bayreuth to reflect a racial undercurrent, and because of Bumbry's race, Venus became, in the words of *Die Kölnische Rundschau*, an "Ethiopian-heathenish Venus."[63] Wagner acknowledged that his portrayal of Venus was different from any other production that had ever been staged, yet he never articulated how intimately race, gender, and sexuality were intertwined in his aesthetic vision. "Venus must convey eroticism without resorting to the clichés of the Hollywood sex bomb, yet she cannot personify the passive ideal," he explained in an article for *Opera News* in 1961. "Venus must find the middle ground between two extremes, and no European singer I know has thus far succeeded."[64] Only a non-white singer could embody Wagner's vision for an exotic, primitive, powerful, and highly erotic Venus.

Wieland Wagner's concoction of a Black Venus for Bayreuth opened a Pandora's box. The term "Black Venus" had earlier historical roots, explaining why Bumbry came to symbolize a savage femme fatale to German audiences. During the early nineteenth century, an African woman named Sara Baartman, nicknamed the Hottentot Venus or Black Venus, was exhibited throughout Europe and forced to display her body to onlookers in various exhibitions, museums, and venues. The term Black Venus signifies a historic fascination with Black female bodies, a history of white male voyeurism, and a history of colonial exhibitionism that became inextricably linked to sexual fantasies.[65]

Europeans in the nineteenth century found Baartman's body fascinating and believed that she represented a physical example of sexual and racial difference. Widespread in their discourse on the Black Venus was a belief that underneath Black female sexuality lurked something deviant and repulsive. Sander Gilman has argued that Germans believed that Black women had a primitive and "animal-like sexual appetite." "Black females," Gilman writes, "do not merely represent the sexualized female, they also represent the female as the source of corruption and disease."[66] The Hottentot or Black Venus ultimately became the symbol of Black female sexuality during the nineteenth century, one that embodied sexual lasciviousness and primitive sexual desires. Its resuscitation in postwar West Germany was not some abstract aberration or departure from racist norms but rather a confirmation of them.

One incident in particular stands out in the swirling Bumbry debates of 1961 and illuminates Germans' and the Bayreuth administration's struggle to come to terms with her race. During a press conference, spokespeople for the Bayreuth Festival told the reporters that although they had hired an "exotic Black goddess," they wanted to reassure German audiences that "the new production presents Venus as a symbolic figure, draped in gold cloth and wearing gold make-up. *Her skin color will not be recognizable.*"[67] This statement runs counter to Wagner's demand for a Black goddess. Moreover, by minimizing Bumbry's physical appearance to the press while simultaneously trying to disguise her skin color on the stage with gold paint, the Bayreuth staff eased the fears of those who found dark skin abhorrent. Both views of her—exotic Black goddess or racially altered singer—reflected an attitude of cultural superiority found in Germans' intrinsic whiteness.[68]

Bumbry was not the first or last Black singer whose skin would be covered up for the sake of making the audience more comfortable. The practice was so widespread that African American singers gossiped about it behind stage. When Jessye Norman debuted at the Deutsche Oper Berlin in 1969, Sylvia Lee remembers speaking to her about how she would present herself to the public. "Jessye Norman made a beautiful Elisabeth. They had been in the

FIGURE 27. Grace Bumbry as the "Black Venus" at the Bayreuth Festival, July 1961. Photo by Keystone/Hulton Archive/Getty Images.

habit of chalking up the faces of Blacks when they were doing white parts. 'Jessye,' I said, 'I hope they're not putting that ugly clown makeup on you.' 'No,' she said. 'I got that straight. I make myself up.'"[69] Although Williams became known internationally as a singer of Puccini's *Madame Butterfly*, she confessed in a 1995 interview, "I would have loved to sing the Countess and Susanna in *Le Nozze di Figaro*. Mozart was so right for my voice. But [opera companies] were afraid to put me in a white wig and whiter makeup."[70] Rarely, it seems, were the practices of staging Black performers in white roles as simple or as color-blind as opera houses may have presented to the public.

Whether staging exotic operas or canonical works by Mozart or Wagner, opera directors relied on Black female opera singers to provide a new direction for their aesthetic and political agendas. Their casting decisions, informed by the new postwar era in which they were producing musical works, frequently tried to upend audiences' expectations and understandings of an opera and its meanings and ramifications after WWII. Yet opera directors' assumptions of Black opera singers' capabilities and their presentations of Black womanhood as sexually deviant or wild were often tied to longer histories of race and gender, even while they strove to move their institutions away from any associations with racism.

Seeing and Hearing Blackness in Opera

It was one thing for opera directors to stage Black women. How audiences responded to these stagings was another matter. Frequently, operatic stagings featuring Black performers that aspired to something akin to color-blindness provoked public outcry.[71] By its very nature, opera cannot uphold mythologies of color-blindness because, André writes, "people do not *not* see race and gender."[72] German and Austrian listeners certainly connected Black singers' race and gender to the operas they were attending. Above all, they expected Black opera singers to perform on stage in a way that recalled their Blackness. They assumed, in other words, that a singer's supposedly inherent Blackness would somehow be funneled through her performance. While white singers were always free to dabble in performing other ethnicities, German-speaking listeners considered the most egregious acts of racial transgression to have occurred when Black singers took on white roles.

African American opera singers faced a set of expectations and stereotypes surrounding their sexuality that attracted operagoers while simultaneously limiting what roles they could play and how they could perform them. As I discussed in the previous chapter, white audiences conflated singers of color with the roles that they play in opera productions. After hearing a recording of Florence Cole Talbert in *Aida* from the 1920s, George Shirley concluded, "This was not an *Aida* voice. She had high notes, but certainly not the heft that *Aida* requires. Nevertheless, she was Black; her debut had to be as *Aida*."[73] Expectations of a singer's Blackness informed listeners' reception of her musical performance.

This conflation between the singer and the role shaped opera reception in postwar German-speaking Europe, where audiences were unwilling to ignore or even forget the racial identity of the opera singer in order to suspend their disbelief.[74] Rather, the opposite usually occurred. Blackness informed their operatic experiences, either positively or negatively, depending on whether the audience believed the singer's perceived Blackness was a convincing component of the opera.

In the postwar era, no opera demonstrated audiences' dependencies on Black authenticity like Verdi's *Aida*. In a 1961 newspaper article with the headline "An Ethiopian from America in the [Vienna] State Opera House," for example, a music critic from *Neues Österreich* praised Martina Arroyo for bringing authenticity to Verdi's Italian opera. "The audience didn't feel 'among equals,' when watching all those people in brown and black makeup," he stated.[75] Arroyo, the critic believed, was simultaneously saving (white) German singers from having to suffer the indignity of using blackface and rescuing the audience from participating in an unrealistic and ethnologically inaccurate experience. No one, however, embodied the role of Aida quite like famous soprano and diva Leontyne Price. Praised as the "optically ideal interpreter" of this Ethiopian princess who sang "with the warm musicality of the colored people," Price was admired for her "naturalness" and lauded for her "noble primitiveness."[76] To many Germans, Price's Blackness granted her an authenticity that few other singers possessed. Newspapers also praised Gloria Davy's performance in Wieland Wagner's erotically charged production of *Aida* at the Deutsche Oper Berlin in a way that highlights her race and gender. *Der Kurier* believed that Davy "brought with her everything from nature" to become a convincing Ethiopian princess.[77] Her "animalistic" and "naturalistic" performance enhanced what was already a dark, Africanized, and highly sexualized production of *Aida*.

Surprisingly, performances of *Madame Butterfly* by Camilla Williams and Price also encouraged critics to link the opera to Black authenticity. One Viennese critic praised Williams for bringing to the performance "the grace of a race that is eloquent down to the fingertips of her long, slender hands."[78] Moreover, Price chose to play Butterfly, they declared, less as a girl and more as a soulful woman.[79] Indeed, one critic explained that Price's African American heritage was precisely what had made her performance so convincing. "This story reminds one of so many Black women who bore children by white men during slavery," he writes. "These men had no intention of loving that woman or caring for that woman. So Miss Price not only brings her magnificent voice to the role of Butterfly, but she also brings her history, the history of her people, and the African musical practices of coloring, intonation, and a deep, deep level of understanding to the role of Madame Butterfly."[80] Through the historical traumas endured by African Americans, Price, the critic claimed, could understand and sympathize with Cio-Cio San in *Madame Butterfly*.

Other Black women received similar praise for bringing their African American heritage to the operatic stage. After hearing Bumbry sing as the "Black Venus," one critic noted, "Most Black singers are blessed with an apparently innate performing temperament that enables them to enact their roles with far more ease [than their white counterparts]."[81] Bumbry's supposed inborn musicality as a Black performer—a racial logic at work since the nineteenth century—meant that she could perform better in Wagner's opera. In a promotional interview with Vera Little before her debut in Bizet's *Carmen*, the *Berliner Morgenpost* interviewer depicted Little as a singer with "big black eyes," a passionate gaze, and a look of childish joy on her face as she described singing in church as a child in her hometown, Memphis.[82] Many articles spoke, as the *Tagesspiegel* did, about "the American Vera Little, who brought with her to the role of the gypsy child the naturalness of her dark race."[83] Such comments would not have been out of place in 1920s Weimar criticism.

Similarly, critics racialized Black singers' voices in a manner similar to music criticism in the 1920s and 1930s. Critics continued to describe singers' voices in visual terms, calling them smoky, dark, or colorful, regardless of vocal range. Much like descriptions of Marian Anderson's voice from the 1930s, which critics called "dark" like her skin color and "brownish-black," a description of Gloria Davy's voice in *Aida* attributed to it a "dark undertone" that matched her skin color.[84] *Die Welt* praised Little for being a proper Carmen because of her exotic background. "She is a real mezzo with an opalescent bronze toning," the critic praised.[85] It is unclear if the critic was describing Little's voice or skin tone. *Der Kurier* also praised Vera Little for bringing color to the role of Carmen and called her the "ideal representative of the title role. Her soprano has that Gypsy-brown Carmen timbre. It's not big but feline in its sleekness . . . and in the Habanera and the Seguidilla, it endears itself to our ears with beguiling tenderness."[86] The voice, the body, and the role of the singer all blended into one.

When Black singers performed in white roles, however, the tables turned viciously. Two particular criticisms stood out when Black singers performed in so-called white roles. The first was that their Blackness destroyed the illusion of race in the opera. This common refrain affected Leontyne Price's debut as Pamina in Mozart's *The Magic Flute* at the Vienna State Opera House in 1959, when she stepped in to perform at the last minute. Critics cried foul. What was a Black singer doing in what was obviously a white role? Price's performance was upsetting to them because that particular staging of *The Magic Flute* was traditional, relying on costumes and set designs that depicted an eighteenth-century magical kingdom. This production first premiered on the Vienna opera stage in 1958 under the direction of Günther Rennert and Georges Wakhévitch and had been performed multiple times with various singers.[87] The only aspect of the opera that was different in 1959 was the addition of Price. Audiences certainly had their own expectations of what *The Magic Flute* meant, and some had perhaps even seen this production before Price joined the cast.

In one article titled "Well-Sung but Makes No Sense," the local music critic explained why Price should not sing in a white role, and his argument reveals how he and others viewed Black women and their place on the German stage. Price, the critic began, "has a wonderful voice, and behind the tenderness [in her voice] is a dramatic timbre that finely glimmers." However, he continued, "Intensity of feeling (a typical womanly characteristic of Negroes!) is a contradiction for this Mozart opera."[88] Here, the critic relied on established tropes of Black performance and Black womanhood to argue against Price's debut. The dark passion that critics perceived and desired from Price in *Aida* and *Porgy and Bess* was now thought to be out of place in this allegorical opera. The critic for the *Österreichische Neue Tageszeitung* shared similar sentiments. Although he admired the "dark timbre and exotic beauty" in Price's voice, and he freely admitted that she had a good grasp of the German text—"often more so than what her white sisters can claim"— he still argued that having a "dark-skinned Pamina" went against Mozart's wishes.[89]

Not only was Price's voice and personality out of place in the opera, critics claimed, but her skin color destroyed a much beloved scene by altering its plot. In act 2, scene 7 of the opera, the Black slave of Sarastro named Monostatos (usually played by a white man in blackface) discovers Pamina sleeping on a bed of flowers and sings about how ugly he is in contrast to her. To many audiences, the scene was highly comedic because it played on the racial contrast between the characters. However, Price's skin color destroyed this moment of surprise and discovery, and critics called foul on this production of *The Magic Flute*, arguing that a white Pamina was necessary to display this sense of racial difference, since "the opposite of a white Pamina is a Black Monostatos."[90] How strange it was, the *Österreichische Neue Tageszeitung* commented, that Price should be the "dark daughter of the Sun King," and that "Monostatos should meet a fellow member of his race on

[Pamina's] bed."[91] *Das Kleine Volksblatt* also thought Price as Pamina ruined what was intended to be a funny scene: "The text expressly states that Monostatos requires a white Pamina." The punch line of the joke had fallen flat, and the moment of contrast between Monostatos's Black ugliness and Pamina's white beauty was gone. Postwar Viennese audiences, it seems, enjoyed racial difference, but only when it supported their preconceived notions of race and place on the German stage. "A dark-skinned Aida," the critic for *Das Kleine Volksblatt* concluded, "would actually be the ideal occupation [for a woman of color]."[92]

Funnily enough, critics had hurled the same critique decades earlier against Roland Hayes when he sang Tamino's "Dies Bildnis ist bezaubernd schön" from *The Magic Flute* in Vienna in 1923. Heinrich Kralik at the *Neues Wiener Tagblatt* writes, "It is a perverse world, and miracles and wonders happen: Tamino a Black man! There will be nothing left but for the white race to be represented by Monostatos."[93] The constant concern about role reversal suggested that listeners thought of Black and white performers as diametric opposites from each other, as opposed to the equals some listeners frequently proclaimed them to be.

Similarly, Bumbry received the same complaints that her race was a distraction at best or had destroyed the illusion of opera at worst. The *Stuttgarter Zeitung* critic Hans Habe called Bumbry's presence at Bayreuth an enormous distraction because of her race. And a critic for *Die Tat* agreed: "Hans Habe said it right," the critic writes. "Wagner would have protested against a Black Venus, not because she was of another race, but rather because she would have destroyed the illusion, without which no theater—and also opera—can exist."[94] Black performers—not white ones, who for centuries could apparently perform in exotic operas with aplomb—were capable of destroying the illusion of theater.

Ultimately, *Deutscher Anzeiger*'s music critic suggested, Black women should sing only Black parts. In an article called "The Black Venus of Bayreuth: *Tannhäuser* is not *Porgy and Bess*," he condemned Wagner for hiring Bumbry on these grounds. "Of course Venus should have the right to represent the arts of temptation that nature has given her," he writes, "but when she is embodied by a Black woman, then her color holds an accent, [one] that is simply not 'in' the work." He states, "A beautiful voice is not enough to be Madame Venus." Most tellingly, he suggests that Bumbry should continue instead to play exotic characters in exotic operas, namely Cleopatra, the Queen of Sheba, Aida, or Meyerbeer's *L'Africaine*, roles in which "one is—without reservation—entitled to have a brown to coffee-brown skin color." He continues, "But this Black Venus is a contradiction, one diametrically opposite to what the idea of the work stands for. That is, unless one casts the entire opera with Negroes, as was done in Gershwin's 'Porgy and Bess.'"[95]

The second criticism that Black opera singers faced for singing white roles was that they were taking away jobs from white German singers. Boos and whistles accompanied the debut of Vera Little in Bizet's *Carmen* at the Deutsche Oper Berlin in 1958 for this reason.[96] Although Carmen became over time a role associated with Black singers, in 1958 German listeners apparently did not see the role as something within Black performers' repertoire. The upper balcony of the opera house became so rowdy at Little's debut that the incident made international news. Local Berliners wrote numerous letters to newspapers stating that the problem they had with Little's performance was that she had taken a German singer's job. Hildegard Kuhn, a resident of Wilmersdorf, wrote a letter to *Der Tagesspiegel*, arguing, "The rejection of Vera Little did not mean racial resentment, but rather that people were annoyed that especially in the premiere, a singer like Sieglinde Wagner was not used, who both vocally and theatrically was an ideal embodiment of Carmen in the earlier years."[97] Brigitte Werr, a resident of Tempelhof, was more overt in her protest. She protested because she was upset that "more and more good German singers are being laid off. Instead, foreigners are engaged who are not better, but at best just as good. I would be interested to hear how the intendant of the City Opera justifies this fact."[98] Tellingly, in Werr's remarks, she defines Blackness and Germanness in opposing terms. The sight of Little as Carmen could only remind Werr of the growing presence of foreigners in opera.

In a letter to *Der Kurier*, an operagoer from Charlottenburg also argued that too many foreign singers were dominating German stages:

> There are only five soloists in the ensemble of the State Opera who have world class status and who are beloved by opera visitors: Ms. Grümmer, Ms. Trötschel, Mr. Greindl, Mr. Fischer-Dieskau, Mr. Suthaus. But how much longer before these last great talents will also leave? None of these soloists were engaged by Intendant Ebert, but rather underused. Who does he engage? Names like Parabas, Lane, Pilarczyk, Konya, Heater, Roth-Ehrang, and Neralic.[99]

The names she mentioned, of course, are all foreign. For Berlin audiences, Little was emblematic of a growing problem in Berlin's opera scene: the hiring of non-German artists. Sure enough, a year later when Price performed as Pamina, the same comments emerged. Although Price was talented, many wrote, she was no better or worse than Vienna and Berlin's "homegrown" singers. So why hire her at all? In fact, after witnessing Price sing as Pamina in

Vienna in 1959, one critic issued an omen: "The inclusion of colored singers in the ensemble will definitely become polemicized [in the future]."[100]

And it did. Three years later, Bumbry's performance as Venus brought up the same complaints. "If [Wagner] should come to us with the excuse that he did not find one equally capable performer of the role of Venus among female German singers, then he will hardly be able to convince us of his argument," the critic for Die Tat complained. "We could count singers for him on both hands with no hesitation. Why this sad theater that does nothing other than symbolize the betrayal of Bayreuth?!"[101] Over and over again, listeners decried the presence of Black singers on German opera stages in nationalistic terms, lamenting their perceived loss of German talent.

What is so striking about the majority of white German criticisms against Black singers is the same rhetorical gesture that they all make: all of the critics make sure to mention in their comments that they are not racists. Indeed, the remarks usually began by insisting that race had nothing to do with the critic's discontent. This statement of disassociation reveals both how necessary it had become to illustrate that white Germans no longer had any associations with Nazism and also how little the Nazi past had actually been worked out in spite of protestations otherwise. Letters to the editor protesting Little's performance as Carmen in 1958 began by distancing themselves from any potential accusation of racism. For example, Werr's letter to the editor of Der Tagesspiegel begins by stating, "In reference to your Carmen critique, I would like to say that the booing did not refer to the singer Vera Little herself, to her achievements, or to her being a Negress."[102] It had become unacceptable to protest on racial grounds, but nonetheless the purpose of the letter was to question why a white German singer had not been given a role as the lead in an exotic opera. Similarly, the Deutscher Anzeiger's critic insisted that "this has nothing, absolutely nothing to do with the race question. Due to the fate of our people we have survived such intolerance."[103] Declaring that West Germans had survived—and overcome—racial atrocities reveals that the critic understood that to speak of Bumbry's performance within the context of race meant acknowledging West Germany's most recent past.

In the case of Bumbry's debut, there was a political dimension to her reception caused by the nature of the institution in which she sang and its previous ties to Nazism. Because her performance was supposed to illustrate that even Bayreuth could break away from its Nazi past, anyone who stood in Bayreuth's way represented the last remaining vestiges of Nazism in West German society. Those who defended Wagner's decision to cast Bumbry as Venus dismissed any aesthetic objections and instead launched attacks that painted anti-Bumbry critics as racist Nazi sympathizers who longed for a return to the "thousand-year Reich."[104] In one letter to the editor, a local

Hamburg resident asked if Germans had really forgotten what Bayreuth had stood for prior to 1945 and the ugly and indelible stamp it bore because of its relationship to the Nazi party.[105] Several articles and letters to the editor snidely referred to anti-Bumbry protesters as the "not-so-anonymous defenders of our white 'noble race,'" and an op-ed in the *Kölnische Rundschau* stated that one could hardly believe such racist ideas and ugly debates were still possible in Germany.[106]

An editorial in *Die Welt* was the most explicit about tying Bumbry's debut to the most recent Nazi past. Placing Bumbry's debut within the context of the ongoing Adolf Eichmann trial in Israel, the author implores West Germans to be more vigorous in recognizing and fighting against racism. The author writes, "They are going to have to learn, whether they want to or not, that in the practice of art other colors exist aside from white ones, among which is also black."[107]

Operatic performances featuring Black women symbolized something greater than the music itself—even if or when listeners pretended otherwise. Audience reactions to Black women on West German and Austrian stages confirmed the pessimistic assumptions of opera directors and conductors that German-speaking Europe was not as racially accepting as its citizens claimed it to be. Music critics, rowdy fans, and bourgeois listeners alike reacted strongly to the presence of Black opera singers in both exotic and non-exotic operas, judging their performances along racial and nationalistic lines. A singer's Blackness could only be embraced or understood if it fit into the audience's preconceived notion of just what, exactly, Blackness was. Much of the audience's formulations of Black authenticity still relied on notions that predated WWII, ones that depicted Black musicians as somehow more naturally gifted to emote suffering than white Europeans on the one hand, or possessing an intoxicating and exotic sexuality on the other. Their judgments, often masked in aesthetic criticisms, informed how they listened to the music of Mozart, Verdi, or Wagner.

Singing Against the Grain: Black Opera Singers Speak Out

In 1959, Shirley Verrett was living in Cologne and performing with some regularity in local opera houses. Although she was enjoying her stay in West Germany, she soon became aware that the topic of race remained complex and often hidden. She writes in her memoir:

> After I got my bearings, I was stunned to realize how American I was and how much I loved my country. During one rehearsal break, a

group of cast members and I sat in the canteen, speaking in German (with some broken English). Someone was going on about how terribly America treated its Black citizens. My stomach turned, even though the conversation was clearly intended to be sympathetic to me. Finally, I had to respond.

"What you say is true. It is absolutely correct, but we are trying to do something about it. But what about you and the six million Jews? What about your history? What about your Hitler?" The others shut up. An ex-soldier in the group said, "You are right." I thought to myself, People think the Nazis are out of Germany even today? That's a big joke.[108]

Verrett's conversation with her fellow musicians illustrates how Black musicians occasionally found themselves at the heart of a discussion on race in a place that was still coming to terms with its own recent racist history.

Black opera singers' place within this shifting German-speaking landscape is contradictory. In cities such as Vienna and Berlin, African American opera singers had more opportunities to perform in major opera houses than they did in the United States. Yet the problems of racial typecasting stymied the careers of Black opera singers in West Germany and Austria. Reflecting on his long career in German-speaking Europe, George Shirley indicates how vexing this problem was for Black musicians. "Given the fact that I had gained cachet as a desirable racial token due to the groundswell of social change that was beginning to erupt across the Continent when I set out upon my career path," he writes, "it was subsequently impossible to discern the role my artistic virtues played upon my successes and failures." Where, in other words, did his successes or failures stem from? "Were critics being especially kind in writing good reviews of my performances?" he asks. "Were they incapable of subduing their racial biases when their reviews were harsh?"[109] The nature of Shirley's popularity, cast against the light of West Germany and Austria's recent Nazi past, made it difficult for him to parse out when he was being evaluated on musical terms and not political ones.

The reality for Black opera singers was that they were always evaluated on both terms, whether they wished to be or not. By taking on any role—exotic or otherwise—they immediately partook in a greater conversation on race in opera. They either fulfilled the requirements placed upon them as a Black singer or they drew ire for singing outside their exotic frame. The problems of racial typecasting on German-speaking opera stages never went away. When asked in 1996 about her experience with race and typecasting in Europe, the retired opera coach Sylvia Lee observed, "If [an opera company] put on *Aida* and they have a blue-eyed blonde in the title role they'll darken the complexion [and] the eyes. But then nobody cares because the singer is one of them. But with Blacks [they say], 'Oh, you're not Nordic!' "[110] In 1990, George Shirley made similar observations:

> I remember a young Black woman who was successful in getting employment in Europe. She wrote me a number of times about her frustration at being denied roles that she knew she could do: roles that in the eyes of the Germans were roles that she couldn't possibly do because she didn't really look the part. They would give her Mimì [in *La Bohème*] because after all Mimì is French; but they wouldn't give her an Ännchen in [Weber's] *Der Freischütz*, for instance, which she knew that she could do, or Blonde in [Mozart's] *The Abduction from the Seraglio*. They would look at her and think she couldn't possibly be blonde, but Mimì just might be Black. I'm sure that's the way they thought of it, and they were right. Blonde and Ännchen were out of the question! So even though she was accepted on one level, and was able to perform . . . she was still limited.[111]

The roles of Blonde or Ännchen, Shirley observed, "for Germans were considered to be, how can I say, the paragon of whiteness."[112]

But what, ultimately, were Black opera singers to do when faced with the choice of having a career in Europe or the United States? Annabelle Bernard's response sums up the position for many Black singers. In 1962, Bernard became the first Black woman to win a contract to become part of an ensemble cast in Germany, and in 1970 she earned the German honorific *Kammersängerin*. In an interview with the American military newspaper *Stars and Stripes*, she reflected, "I would eventually like to return to the States, but there's so little opportunity there if you want to sing opera. And if it means staying in Europe to sing—I stay."[113]

CHAPTER 9

Singing in the Promised Land

Black Musicians in the German Democratic Republic

The crowds were ecstatic, near hysterical, when the African American entertainer and socialist activist Paul Robeson stepped onto the podium at Humboldt University in East Berlin to receive his peace prize and honorary doctorate. Plans to bring Robeson to the German Democratic Republic (GDR) had begun in earnest in 1958, and finally in October 1960 Robeson and the East Germans who had supported him were able to celebrate the fruits of their labor. After being serenaded by university professors in full regalia with an arrangement of the nineteenth-century abolitionist song "John Brown's Body," Robeson gave the Berlin crowd exactly what they wanted: his booming voice echoed through the loudspeakers, and beautiful melodies washed over the adoring crowd.[1]

Robeson's visit to East Germany in 1960 symbolized an exchange between a version of the United States that the US State Department was uncomfortable representing and a new nation-state (the GDR) whose existence most nations refused to recognize. The GDR praised Robeson as a "son of a former slave" and civil rights hero, and music lovers and party officials alike found in him a cultural ambassador who testified to the virtues of international socialism. Yet their admiration for Robeson also reveals a distinctly East German ideology that promoted a certain kind of Black authenticity over others. Robeson characterized the kind of African American musician that was acceptable to his East German audience: a jovial, anticapitalist folk-singing giant who was unswervingly loyal to the GDR.

Performances by African American musicians in the communist East German state provide us with a window into GDR views on music and race in an officially antiracist state.[2] East Germans preached and practiced solidarity with African Americans because they viewed them as victims of colonialism, capitalism, and institutionalized racism. The GDR eagerly welcomed African American musicians behind the Iron Curtain because their backgrounds and credentials legitimized East Germans' musical endeavors. Black musicians such as Robeson, Aubrey Pankey, George Byrd, and Ella Lee supported East Germans' visions of the United States and strengthened the GDR's international status as a cosmopolitan state that was welcoming to others.

The East German state, I argue, composed its own ideology of racial harmony and universalism in classical music. Music critics, cultural leaders, and some Black musicians developed the following position: that East Germany was the most suitable state for Black musicians to achieve their full potential. Released from the strictures of capitalism and imbued with the ideals of universalism and international solidarity, only in communist East Germany could Western art music truly reach people of all races. Here, in their antiracist state, they avowed that Black musicians could finally fulfill their destiny as artists of high culture and join an international brotherhood of musicians.

But what East German audiences practiced was different from what musical and political elites preached. East German reception of Black musicians reveals the limitations of their claims to international solidarity. However much GDR officials identified Black musicians as part of the global struggle for communism, they also created racial interpretations of their music-making. East German attitudes toward Black Americans came to the fore especially when Black musicians performed German music. However sincerely members of the German Socialist Unity Party (SED) may have supported the freedom of African American musicians to perform German music, East German listeners and music critics expressed the opposite just as sincerely: they were either uninterested in or confused by these musicians' performances of Bach, Beethoven, and Brahms. In fact, music critics were often skeptical or even resentful of Black performances of German music in cities such as Rostock, Halle, Leipzig, and Berlin. In reviews, personal letters, and interviews, East German critics, musicians, and producers opined that they would much rather have a Black musician sing spirituals for them, play an exotic character in an opera, or perform "Black music" with other Black international residents of the state (such as Ghanaians and Kenyans) than perform

German music. Local responses to Black performers of German music reveal the limitations of East Germany's public discourse of international solidarity and of music-making as a form of community building. The musicians in this chapter whose performances listeners applauded the most enthusiastically either fit preexisting Marxist paradigms of oppression and struggle or evoked romantic and inaccurate depictions of African American culture.

Racism and Antiracism in the GDR

Much like in the Federal Republic of Germany, the myth of zero hour (*Stunde null*) after the collapse of the Nazi racial state prevented historians for decades from seeing how race functioned in the postwar period. Although public discourse asserted for a long time that racism died alongside Hitler, race thinking in both East and West Germany did not disappear. In the case of East Germany, it was the state's vows and public declarations of antiracism, rooted in anti-imperialism and anticapitalism, that masked its own racial history.[3] In other words, fascism, not racism, was the root cause of pain or suffering around the world. From the state's beginnings until the fall of the Berlin Wall, the horrors of racism in East Germany took a rhetorical backseat to the evils of fascism, capitalism, and imperialism that the SED claimed it was fighting. GDR constructs of racism were complicated by the frequent declaration that East Germans had eliminated the existence of racism in their society. They were the good guys, protesting the racist practice of segregation in the United States, supporting the quests of African nations for political and economic independence from their European oppressors, and calling for an international brotherhood of racial equals in the name of communism. After having vanquished the evils of racism through their antifascist measures at home, East Germans were now eager to join the fight to liberate others abroad.

Unfortunately, the SED's stated commitment to fighting fascism and its proclamations that racism posed little threat to the state meant that the party was often ill equipped to deal with acts of racism when they occurred on East German soil.[4] Moreover, its handling of minorities and outsiders often betrayed its public sentiments of goodwill. Although the GDR banned racism in its 1949 constitution, the persecution of Jews and other ethnic minorities nonetheless continued.[5] Racial and ethnic minority groups faced a double-edged sword, hearing one thing in public but experiencing another in their daily lives. The GDR publicly embraced foreign nationals who had immigrated to East Germany (by the time the Berlin Wall fell, there were almost 200,000) but had trouble acknowledging that foreigners were frequent targets of violence in their state.⁶ As late as 1989, the SED celebrated its own panoptic rainbow of ethnic minorities from Angola, Algeria, Cuba, and Mozambique while continually barring marriages between foreign workers and East German citizens. And although the rise of neo-Nazi and other racist hate groups was undeniable, their activities remained shrouded in silence as people proclaimed loudly in public that their state had conquered racism.

Strikingly, amid the silence shrouding racism in East Germany, praise for African Americans rang very loud, from the Palace of the Republic in the capital city of Berlin to local elementary schools in the countryside. East German definitions of African American identity demonstrate how essential constructs of race were to the GDR (even if state officials and party dignitaries were unwilling to admit this fact). African Americans became important to the state's legitimation, and, according to Sara Lennox, were regularly "appropriated into political narratives that promoted East German visions of society." African Americans became part of "a broader, undifferentiated vision of humanity," and the SED argued that "unlike imperialist powers, the GDR considered Black people as human beings destined for the happy socialist future already achieved in the GDR."⁷

The GDR published volumes of African American poetry and literature by writers such as Richard Wright and Langston Hughes as well as memoirs by Robeson and tracts by W.E.B. Du Bois. They invited African American intellectuals, entertainers, activists, and artists to their state and awarded many of them medals of freedom or peace. A ninety-year-old Du Bois—who had lost much of his intellectual credibility in the United States as a result of his communist sympathies—received the East German Peace Medal in 1958, and Robeson received the honor in 1960.⁸ The East German–Black American relationship was symbiotic, for African Americans also needed East Germans. African Americans enjoyed traveling to East Germany because the state provided them a forum where their viewpoints, many of which flew directly in the face of American Cold War propaganda, found a receptive audience. Angela Davis, Martin Luther King, Jr., and other Black Americans gained new audiences in East Germany. People were eager to accept their messages and shame the West for its current social conditions that kept Black people under the oppressive thumbs of colonialism and Jim Crow.

Yet GDR discussions of musicians such as Robeson and Pankey illuminate how much they believed in romanticized notions of African Americans that bore little resemblance to the realities African Americans experienced in the latter half of the twentieth century. East Germans painted a Weberian image of African American laborers toiling away on the Mississippi. Their depictions preserved them in the late nineteenth century, as if Black Americans were trapped in a music box that continually played "Swing Low, Sweet Chariot." As Lennox has argued, East Germans saw African Americans as useful exercises to educate their citizens on the history of Marxism. Schoolteachers informed their students about the history of American slavery to teach them of the evils of capitalism and the struggles Black Americans still faced to overcome institutionalized racism. By framing African American history and identity in nineteenth- and early-twentieth-century language, East Germans often relied on much older historical depictions of African Americans to praise them. These antiracist sentiments also made it difficult for East Germans to relate to African Americans who did not correlate to their depictions.

Robeson's own trip to East Berlin in 1960 illustrates exactly what the GDR portrayal of the ideal African American looked like. A committed socialist who had experienced an awakening of his political consciousness in the 1930s, Robeson firmly believed that the African American struggle against racism, discrimination, and economic oppression could be overcome by throwing off the chains of capitalism and racist Western imperialism.[9] Robeson's first visit to the USSR in 1934 proved to be a life-altering event; during his visit, he said, "Here, I am not a Negro but a human being for the first time in my life . . . I walk in full human dignity."[10]

Robeson's views went against the United States' cultural and political agenda in the Cold War. Although the US State Department had been sending African American musicians to Europe frequently to combat international concerns about the country's institutionalized racism, they attempted to control the message of racial (in)equality in the United States by controlling who could travel abroad on behalf of the United States. Musicians such as the pianist Natalie Hinderas were ideal musical ambassadors because they fostered an image of Black respectability and American patriotism. A prim and proper Marian Anderson singing a Schubert lied in Austria was one thing, but an outspoken Robeson promoting the political worldview of the enemy and proclaiming that the United States was being held hostage by Jim Crow was quite another. To prevent him from touring, the US government stripped Robeson of his passport from 1950 until 1958. After successfully suing the United States to regain permission to travel abroad, Robeson toured Europe between 1958 and 1961 under an international campaign called "Let Paul Robeson Sing."[11]

When Robeson traveled to the promised land of East Germany in October 1960, he met an audience eager to confirm that the legends surrounding the Black activist and performer were true. GDR newspaper articles as far back as 1949 had consistently portrayed the concert singer as a Black giant who soulfully sang the "songs of his people." His musical performances were both profound and simple, rooted in the earthiness of the American South and the struggles of enslaved people. Calling Robeson the "Black [St.] Francis" in one headline, the East German writer Stephan Hermlin reported in hagiographic language on an encounter he had with Robeson at a restaurant in Warsaw in 1949, for example. He marveled at Robeson's "dark face, one of the most animated, sage faces that I know." According to Hermlin, Robeson had near supernatural abilities to soothe the audience: "[Robeson] looked ahead, laid his knife and fork on the table, and scrutinized everyone in our circle. He began to sing with some restraint, with an unforgettable dark, melting voice that distinguishes his voice from all others."[12] Much of this language echoed earlier decades of music criticism, fixating on the perceived darkness of both the Black singer's skin color and his voice.

Moreover, the account also assigns an almost supernatural quality to Robeson's singing abilities. According to Hermlin, when Robeson sang "Water Boy" and "Moorsoldaten," everyone, including the waiter, stopped what they were doing to hear him. The image that Hermlin depicts next is one of a Black prophet singing children to sleep as mothers laid themselves at his feet: "In the monstrous heat sat a mother at Robeson's feet, her children—with shoulders that drooped with exhaustion—at her bosom, their eyes big and dreaming in the evening light." When Robeson sang "Curly Headed Baby" for the group of weary travelers, Hermlin writes, "in this moment, I saw, I saw it quite clear, that one of the children [gently fell asleep] in its mother's lap . . . Robeson continued to sing under the evening sky, with the children at his feet, a dark St. Christopher, a Black St. Francis."[13] This early portrayal of Robeson turns him into saint capable of calming stormy waters with his voice.

During Robeson's visit to East Germany, both the cultural ministry in charge of his tour and the East German press presented Robeson as a kind, soulful, musical giant, thereby making him an acceptable socialist commodity to musical audiences. They rolled out the red carpet for their "Black brother," built him a special big bed for the duration of his stay, and assigned him a private doctor and bodyguard (who was shorter than Robeson but who jokingly said he could still leap in front of Robeson's heart).[14] The East German press and the culture ministry arranged a photograph depicting Robeson with a small (white) eight-year-old girl named Anka who asks him to stay in the GDR. The composition of the image highlights the contrast between the large Black "Negro singer" and the innocent child. The caption that the *Berliner Zeitung am Abend* utilized under the image simply reads, "Paul Robeson, Your Big Black Friend."[15] Such verbal gestures, Layne argues, often functioned as mechanisms to contain "the fear of the Other."[16] It was necessary to present Robeson as friendly, admirable, and, above all, harmless.

Robeson's visit allowed East Germans to indulge in nineteenth-century Romantic portrayals of African Americans in particular and Blackness more generally. On the evening of Robeson's arrival into East Germany, for example, a Berliner ensemble offered a concert program featuring "Negro music" to their audience at the Volksbühne Berlin. Music critics placed the music of the evening within the political narrative of slavery and oppression. "Black music," according to the *Berliner Zeitung am Abend*, sounded like "melancholy, sadness, and restrained rage against the white robber."[17] Located "deep in the American South," and emitted out of the "body and tragedy of Negro slaves," the "Negro music" performed that evening expressed adversity and redemption. Much of their vocabulary was similar to nineteenth-century portrayals of the Fisk Jubilee Singers.

For Robeson's Liederabend in East Berlin, he sang works by Bach, Béla Bartók, Zoltán Kodály, Modest Mussorgsky, and Hanns Eisler; a Chinese folk song; a fighting song of the Warsaw Ghetto; and Jerome Kern and Oscar Hammerstein II's "Ol' Man River" (his most popular song) to a packed house. Robeson's art, many declared, was the "real thing," a musical expression

FIGURE 28.   Paul Robeson meets with an eight-year-old East German girl and her Black baby doll. Before meeting Robeson, she had written him a letter pleading with him to stay in the GDR, writing, "When you're in America, I'm always afraid for you." Newspapers such as the *Berliner Zeitung am Abend* disseminated this image with the caption, "Paul Robeson, Your Big Black friend." Bundesarchiv, Bild 183–76870–0001 / photo: Ulrich Kohls.

of freedom from the capitalist and imperialist oppression of the American South. Through his soulful performance, Robeson successfully brought to East Germany the song of the Negro, the *Neue Zeit* gushed, whose music "reaches not only aesthetes and friends of music but speaks to the hearts of men [as well]."[18] In other words, Robeson's musicianship—like Anderson's in the 1930s—had universal appeal. East Germans praised Robeson and other Black musicians for singing to them the unique and separate story of African Americans, one that was altogether comfortably un-German and foreign. African American music, Robeson's tour confirmed, was based on slavery and Black labor, evoking a solemnity and ethnic melancholy. East Germans celebrated his music for its perceived inherent socialist message while also praising it for its differences separating it from the German music of Bach and Schumann. Robeson embodied everything the GDR needed from Black musicians: an exotic spectacle who could be explained by Marxist depictions of the American South and who promoted international socialism.

Composing a Universal Brotherhood: German Music in the GDR

In his memoir on growing up as an American in the GDR, the white American émigré Joel Agee could still recall his experience watching Aubrey Pankey perform German music in Rostock:

> When Aubrey Pankey, a Black American singer of German lieder and Negro spirituals, a refugee from McCarthyism and a close friend of our family, came to sing for us during the lunch hour, I stood among my peers, the workers of the Warnow Werft [dockyards], incognito at last, not to them but to Aubrey, the classy and exotic guest from Berlin, whose artful interpretations of Schubert, amplified by loudspeakers, sounded so alien in the temporarily silenced shipyard.[19]

Pankey's performance of German lieder for shipyard workers in Rostock illuminates how much German music was at the foundation of the East German state.[20] After 1945 and in the wake of Nazism, music became an important tool for refashioning German identity. Broadcasting music by Beethoven and Mendelssohn, East Berlin's culture ministry believed in the 1940s and 1950s that musical performance was a powerful way to destroy fascism and encourage socialism. Moreover, Pankey's performance speaks to the GDR's commitment to disseminate high culture and art music to the masses.[21] The state intentionally promoted a variety of musical concerts and programs to create the kind of socialist musical life from which they believed their citizens could benefit.[22] To that end, farmers, workers, youth groups, and other members of the socialist state were encouraged to create choirs, sing mass songs, and participate in East German musical culture. They held on to a belief first vocalized in the late nineteenth century that all classes of society should have equal access to the music of Germany's great composers.[23] In so doing, GDR musicians and dignitaries often promoted an image of their nation of music-makers as more community oriented than the decadent West. People in the countryside and in the city, they posited, should equally celebrate the music of Beethoven and be able to hear the music of Bach.[24]

The music of Bach, Beethoven, and, in the case of Pankey's performance, Schubert, mattered greatly to the East German state's legitimation efforts and attempts to foster national pride. Lacking the political legitimacy and strength of its western neighbor, the SED relied on culture to bolster its claims that the GDR was the "real" Germany. The GDR's past became essential to the culture ministry's definitions of the present. As they turned to historical narratives to locate their present, GDR officials used historical composers to cultivate, in Laura Silverberg's words, "an image of the GDR as the exclusive heir to German musical heritage."[25] Writers such as Frank Schneider, an East German who published in the journal *Musik und Gesellschaft*, penned maudlin sentiments that tied Beethoven's musical legacy and perceived political activism directly to the goals of the East German state. Beethoven, according to Schneider, was not worthy of praise simply because he had been a masterful composer; rather, he had entered the realms of greatness because he had been "one of the early fighters for the principles and ideals that we have made reality in the conditions of the socialist society."[26]

In the process of fortifying their Germanness, the SED reimagined the German masters as national heroes whose fiery music foreshadowed the creation of their glorious East German state.[27] Members of the SED worked tirelessly to create a cultural heritage that reflected a teleological arc of progressive humanism from the Enlightenment to the origins of the GDR by way of the 1848 revolutions.[28] Bach became a proto-revolutionary, Beethoven a fighter against the aristocracy, and Wagner stood as a champion of socialist revolutionary ideals.

What they created, in other words, and what Black musicians such as Pankey performed, was their own national canon of music. Rehabilitating German composers such as Wagner, Handel, and others, musicologists and music critics in the GDR such as Ernst Hermann Meyer insisted that their revisionist histories of music were more accurate than those of the recent past.[29] What made these figures great was their connection to the people, their strong, individual commitments to Enlightenment humanism, and their music, which functioned as a mirror of the German people.[30] To that end, the culture ministry dictated in 1964 that the purpose of missions of cultural diplomacy should be to "spread the truth abroad that the GDR is the true protector and champion of the great cultural heritage of the German nation."[31]

This new narrative of German musical universalism thrived in the small but active world of East German musicology and music criticism. In the case of music, the GDR was the true heir. The Nazi past represented a horrifying betrayal of German musical values, and the decadent West across the Iron Curtain had departed from them, instead becoming a musical snake pit of formalism and Americanism. East German musical culture, released from the bonds of capitalism and fascism, maintained a civic duty to uphold the great musical masters of Central Europe and share their music with the world.

The GDR as a Promised Land to Black Musicians?

The GDR's discourses of antiracism and German musical universalism syncretized into an ideological position unique to the East German state: only in the GDR were Black classical musicians fully able to perform the music they loved dearly for an audience who appreciated their worth. The reasons for this were twofold: first, East Germany offered the same historical tradition of musical excellence that traced back to the times of Bach; and second, East Germany offered Black musicians political freedom from racial persecution.

The case of the African American conductor George Byrd captures East German formulations of Black success and German musical uplift in the GDR. Byrd was a successful guest conductor in East Germany between 1950 and 1990 who led orchestras in Berlin, Halle, Magdeburg, Eisenach, Jena, Schwerin, Leipzig, and Dresden. A Juilliard-trained musician, he rose to prominence in 1955 after attending a workshop led by Herbert von Karajan. Byrd made frequent public declarations of his love and admiration for the Austro-German musical canon (German Romantic composers were his favorites), which the *Sächsische Neueste Nachrichten* highlighted in their 1961 interview. "You are coming to Dresden," the interviewer begins, "with an emphatically classical German program. May we ask where your musical bond to German classical music traces back to?" After Byrd responds that he first fell in love with German music at Juilliard and then later under Herbert von Karajan (who in particular expanded his love of Schubert and Schumann), the reporter circles back again to Byrd's insistence on performing German music. "We are delighted," he told Byrd, "about how highly you regard and how well you know our composers."[32] The reporter's use of the possessive ("our composers") suggests that music and German national belonging were intertwined—and out of Byrd's natural musical range.

Wherever Byrd went, his performances inspired conversations about his commitment to performing classical (and mostly German) music. Following a performance of works by Handel, Debussy, and Brahms in Magdeburg in December 1959, music critics praised Byrd's handling of the orchestra, reporting that Byrd "is very familiar with the German-speaking world."[33] The Dresden newspaper *Die Union* remarked that "as a master apprentice of Herbert von Karajan, [Byrd] has shown a remarkable intimacy with German music. Above all he honors Bach, Beethoven, Schubert, Schumann, and Brahms, his special 'favorite.'"[34] Some figured that Byrd's uncanny familiarity with German music and German culture could be related to his remarkable language capabilities, implying in the process that Black people speaking German was unusual: "Byrd speaks a very good German; his language skills are there not just grammatically, but rather [he has acquired] everything from the basis of sound."[35] Upon attending a performance of Byrd's in which he conducted music by Haydn, Schumann, and Hector Berlioz in Leipzig, the critic for *Der Morgen* remarked that the conducting of this "dark-skinned, slender, spirited artist" was not "any more foreign than concepts of performances under German conductors." Byrd was an ideal interpreter of German music because of his cultural immersion in the German-speaking world.

But Byrd was more than an authentic interloper of German music. He was proof that the possibility for cultural authenticity and musical mastery lay within the Black diaspora's grasp—but only in East Germany. Musicians like Byrd, critics argued, had opportunities to perform in the GDR that were unavailable to them in the United States. Following a performance that Byrd conducted on the 216th anniversary of the Leipzig Gewandhausorchester, the music critic for the popular and arts-heavy daily newspaper *Leipziger Volkszeitung* praised Byrd. "Just twenty years ago," the critic writes, "something like this would have been inconceivable. People filled with racial hatred would have made such a guest performance impossible, just as when they chased Gewandhaus Kapellmeister Bruno Walter away because he was a Jew."[36] Unlike West Germany, East Germany had overcome its history of racial hatred.

Byrd's performance in Leipzig, the critic believed, also had to be placed within the context of Black people's struggles against capitalism and colonialism. Using the same line of thinking as Adorno and other German critics in the 1920s, the critic writes, "when people in capitalistic countries acknowledge—by sheer necessity—the musicality of Negroes to some extent, do not forget that the Negroes (with a few exceptions) still have the dubious privilege of playing in jazz bands as exploited and showcased objects. Only very few Negroes succeeded in obtaining a solid music education and an opportunity for development of their respective capabilities."[37] Black people in the capitalist West, in other words, were limited to playing jazz instead of the more "elevated" music that the Leipzig Gewandhausorchester offered its listeners.[38]

To this critic, Black concertizing in East Germany was evidence that Black people could finally achieve their full potential—but only under socialism. "At the 16th Gewandhaus concert [of the season]," the author writes, "George Byrd proved what high musicality the Negro possesses in the interpreting of classical music from European nations. This [high musicality] can only let us guess what other achievements we can expect from the Negroes, once their full equality exists not just on paper in the USA, and once the still oppressed countries of Africa have ultimately freed themselves from colonial slavery."[39] This common belief in Black people's eventual-but-never-realized progress confirms Elaine Kelly's argument that, "in the context of solidarity art, Black and Asian heroes could be imagined as preterm incarnations of the fully developed socialist being. There was little scope, however, for more complex or embodied realizations of the other."[40] At the same time, however, the author tapped into a historical discourse of Black potentiality that stretched all the way back to the Fisk Jubilee Singers' arrival into Germany in 1877. Since at least the nineteenth century critics have suggested that Black people were capable of great musical achievement; yet that moment of arrival never seems to come.

Byrd's reception is no different from this established mode of thought. Although the decks had been stacked against Byrd as an African American growing up under racist Jim Crow, he had remarkably overcome the limitations imposed on Black musical achievements. Thankfully, the writer implied, East Germany was different from the capitalist West, because only in the GDR could Black people break away from the constraints of capitalism, fight against the culture industry, and achieve new musical heights. Only in antifascist and antiracist nations such as the GDR could Black people finally accept the gift of German music and all of the promises of racial uplift that came with it.

In these formulations, East Germany was the most suitable place for Black classical musicians to do what they wished. And perhaps sometimes it was. Take, for instance, the premiere of Ella Lee in the title role of Tosca at the Komische Oper Berlin in East Berlin in November 1961. Only a few short months after Grace Bumbry sang as the exotic "Black Venus" in Bayreuth,

Lee's debut on the other side of the Berlin Wall broke new ground in the opera world, albeit quietly and lacking international fanfare.

Puccini's opera *Tosca* tells the tale of a young woman named Floria Tosca caught between love and politics in Napoleonic-era Italy. Desperate to save her beloved from a vengeful and obsessed Baron Scarpia, Tosca strikes a deal with Scarpia to ensure her lover's freedom in exchange for submitting to Scarpia's sexual advances. Tosca falls victim to Scarpia's ploy to kill her lover anyway. Unable to rescue the man she loves from political execution, she takes her own life rather than let Scarpia's evil schemes succeed.

Ella Lee's performance differed considerably from Grace Bumbry's premiere for three reasons. First, Lee's performance as Tosca was a much bigger role than Bumbry's Venus. Unlike Venus in Bayreuth, which required Bumbry to be on stage for approximately thirty minutes, the majority of the opera rested on Lee's shoulders. The part of Tosca is, as operagoers call it, a diva role. Singing one of the most popular numbers in opera, "Vissi d'arte," Tosca showcases a soprano's musical talents and emotional depth.

Second, whereas Bumbry's portrayal of Venus in Bayreuth tapped into preexisting orientalist notions of hypersexualized Black women, Lee's time on stage as Tosca was a noticeable departure from this kind of typecasting because the opera *Tosca* was not a musical work featuring exotic or otherworldly characters—nor did the Komische Oper Berlin choose to portray Lee as such. The character of Tosca is, as Puccini and his librettists Luigi Illica and Giuseppe Giacosa made her, a romanticized heroine in love with a man of noble heart.[41] Julian Budden writes, "Puccini's Tosca is a credible woman of the theater, lacking neither intelligence nor humor, and capable of genuine dignity."[42]

Third, the character of Tosca is at the center of a romantic love triangle as the object of two men's attention. Beautiful, pious, and steadfastly loyal to the man she loves, Tosca is a popular figure among opera's women.[43] Her beauty and grace are so great that they cause Scarpia to utter, "Tosca, you make me forget God!"[44] On stage, the two white male singers vied for Lee's affections for reasons other than her perceived exoticism.

The GDR was eager to tout Lee's performance as proof that their state was the most suitable to host Black classical musicians—not West Germany. Because the GDR had eliminated racism, Black opera singers such as Lee could finally pursue their musical calling. East Germany was especially keen to point out how frequently West German opera stages had improperly handled Black singers in their productions. Witnessing the scandal of Bumbry's performance unfold in West Germany, the *Berliner Zeitung* reported that racist, vitriolic attacks did not happen in East Germany. Unlike West Germany, which harassed Vera Little at the Deutsche Oper Berlin in *Carmen* in 1952 and booed Schoenberg's *Moses und Aron* at the same house, East Germans, the reporter scoffed, do not discriminate against "Negroes and Jews." Such terrible acts of discrimination do not "exist [in the GDR], as is evidenced by the enthusiastic applause for the American Negro singer[s] Ella Lee and William Ray in the Komische Oper or [our] accommodations for Negro students."[45] As I discussed in chapter 7, West German critics made the same rhetorical gesture: holding up African American musicians as evidence of their political progress. Both West and East Germany were eager to condemn the other, and used Black musicians as evidence of the other side's failings.

East German critics articulated their denunciations of West Germany within the framework of both the civil rights movement and the Holocaust. One critic referenced Nazism and the Holocaust in his estimation of the Bayreuth Festival Opera House and its treatment of Bumbry. He writes that only "where the mentality is still brown [fascist] could such terrible demonstrations of German master-race thinking [*Herrenmenschentums*] arise."[46] For Vera Little's debut as Carmen in 1958, East German newspapers compared the West German audience's treatment of her to "the discrimination [against] colored students at West Berlin high schools."[47] They also tied her performance to American attempts at desegregation in Little Rock, Arkansas, arguing that West Germany was heading down the path to Jim Crow. After recounting a Ghanaian student's experience being barred from West German establishments and comparing it to the "*Carmen* scandal" at the Berlin City Opera (the precursor to today's Deutsche Oper Berlin), one op-ed piece asked "if people in West Berlin also wanted to [have] a Little Rock."[48] East German newspapers declared that West German actions against Black opera singers were "race baiting," plain and simple.[49] Which stages, a *Neue Zeit* editorial asked, are willing to celebrate Black women instead of marginalizing them?[50]

Black musicians also argued that East Germany was a better environment for their musicianship. Although the conductor George Byrd never overtly expressed his political views, choosing instead to see himself as a great arbiter of German Romantic music, one of his performances nonetheless invites a political reading. In April 1961, Byrd conducted the Rundfunk-Sinfonieorchester Berlin (or RSB, East Berlin's answer to the Berlin Philharmonic) in a concert program of pieces by Dmitri Shostakovich. Featuring the Soviet violinist Leonid Kogan as soloist, the RSB performed Shostakovich's *Violin Concerto in A Minor* with Byrd on the podium. Performing for a sold-out crowd, the evening's artists included an American, a Soviet Russian, and many East Germans. These performers exuded a different kind of international solidarity than the capitalist West, critics gloated. Newspapers such as the *Berliner Zeitung*, for example, called the event "A Concert as a Sign of the Fraternity of Peoples" (Konzert im Zeichen der Völkerfreundschaft), and they saw the evening's festivities as a musical collaboration between several Cold War nations.[51]

In an interview with the *Sächsische Neueste Nachrichten* in 1961, a reporter asked Byrd why he was willing to risk traveling to the other side of the Iron Curtain to perform in spite of pressure from West Germany and the United States to pull out of his engagements. His answers are interesting although perhaps misleading. "Those kinds of bans don't interest me," Byrd replied. "I'm coming as a guest conductor to the orchestras willing to have me as a human being and as an artist. I am happy that, through the general political situation, we Negroes can breathe a bit more freely, and I see it as my great task to work for the universal art and for my oppressed brothers. Advocating for world peace is a matter dear to my heart."[52]

Of course this is a bit glib. Byrd, like many Black conductors during the 1950s, '60s, and '70s, was frustrated by the difficulties Black conductors encountered finding permanent positions as music directors of orchestral ensembles.[53] Indeed, his own career was an emblem of these frustrations: Byrd never managed to secure a permanent position as the head of an orchestra. Instead, he guest-conducted orchestras throughout Europe until his retirement. Byrd's frequent trips to East Germany, then, serve as a reminder that the GDR offered Black Americans paid opportunities to perform regardless of their ideological commitments or political views.

When confronted about her decision to perform *Tosca* in the GDR, Lee also minimized the political ramifications. In an interview in 1961, Lee argued, "Art has nothing to do with politics." Defending herself on the telephone from her West Berlin apartment, she said, "[Walter] Felsenstein offered me the first major role of my life . . . Anyway, I have no idea what is going on here in Berlin—I'm not interested in politics. If you wish to speak with me about art: anytime! But politics: never! Politics does not have anything to do with art!" An editor from the *Berliner Zeitung* disagreed: "She has no idea what she is doing. She is ready to betray not only West Berlin but also her American countrymen for her career. But she has no idea what she is doing."[54]

It seems highly doubtful that Lee had not considered the political implications of her decision to perform with the Komische Oper Berlin only one month after the erection of the Berlin Wall. It is more likely, however, that she, like Byrd, refused to be entirely forthcoming in her reasons for taking on this musical work. As an African American opera singer, would she have been able to sing the role of Tosca in the United States? Although it had become somewhat easier for African Americans to land principal roles in operas in the United States since Marian Anderson broke the racial barrier at the Metropolitan Opera House in 1954, it was still difficult to find work.

What the GDR offered, what it claimed it could give that other nation states could not or would not, was freedom from typecasting and racial pigeonholing. Positioning themselves as a musical promised land for Black talent, opera houses, symphony orchestras, and other musical institutions sometimes made radical choices in the hiring and promoting of Black musicians to show the West that there were better ways to support marginalized peoples in the world of classical music.

Performing Race on East German Stages

Nevertheless racism continued to exist and persist in East Germany. As Robeson's own stay in East Berlin has already illustrated, the conflict between promoting antiracist ideologies within East Germany's music scene and desiring Blackness to function and form in familiar patterns shaped German musical culture. Holding both aims and wishes at the same time was not a contradiction to audiences attending Black performances across the Iron Curtain.

The Komische Oper Berlin's use of Black singers provides a striking example of how a musical institution and its audience could be capable of performing racism and antiracism. Led by Felsenstein, the Komische Oper Berlin was the premiere opera house in East Germany. It had won international acclaim for its commitment to creating believable music theater. "To astonish with honesty is Felsenstein's artistic purpose," the critic Ronald Mitchell marveled.[55] Crucial to the Komische Oper Berlin's success was its international cast of singers. Felsenstein was relentless about hiring international guests to sing, even when it became increasingly difficult to do so.

It was the Komische Oper Berlin that showcased Lee as Tosca, and it was also the opera house that hired Lee and William Ray, an African American baritone, to perform as the fairy Queen Titania and King Oberon in Benjamin Britten's opera, *A Midsummer Night's Dream*. Paired together as a Black couple, the actors embodied the supernatural world of the fairy kingdom, one visibly different from the "real" Athenian one. Always implicit but never fully articulated, their shared Blackness performed a dramaturgical function in the opera and in GDR high culture of the 1960s.

Reviews of the opera, which appeared on the front page of East German newspapers, including *Der Morgen* and *Berliner Zeitung*, also emphasized the unique pairing in the Komische Oper Berlin's casting. Ilse Schütt, the music critic at the *Berliner Zeitung am Abend*, commended Felsenstein's casting as an appropriate choice, saying that the hiring of the African American singers "fulfilled a part of the director's concept."[56] Heinrich Lüdicke, the critic at *Neue Zeit*, writes, "The elven pair Titania/Oberon were embodied by Ella Lee and William Ray, two American singers with dark skin, who in their appearance ideally match the exotic sovereign dynasty of the elf kingdom."[57]

Most important, the singers' exotic appearance convinced listeners of the magic realism Felsenstein strove to create in the opera. The critic Ronald Mitchell, an attendee, also applauded Felsenstein for "using the Negro singers William Ray and Ella Lee as Oberon and Titania" to project the otherworldliness of the play in an outer-space atmosphere of exploding atoms, satellites, and spacecraft.[58] A Berliner critic also insisted that the Black singers' unique voices were elemental in contributing to the fantasy-like setting of the opera. "Oberon and Titania were embodied by Negro singers William Ray and Ella Lee, and *the natural tone of their voices*, [especially] the first-rate, light, brilliant soprano of the female singer, lifted the two figures out of the world of men."[59] Praising the supposedly natural tone of Black voices traces back to the time of the Fisk Jubilee Singers.

Although listeners loved Lee, whom they called "a dark-skinned artist from the USA" with a "sensual" and "dark-glowing" voice, they were not in love with Ray as Oberon.[60] Ray was a convincing Oberon on stage—until he opened his mouth to sing. Britten's original libretto and musical score called for a countertenor in the role of Oberon, but Ray was a baritone singing a transposed version of the role. Most critics argued that the change of range obscured the musical effect Britten had intended. One critic complained that in this new production, "Oberon, the light elf king, was not a high falsetto tenor like Britten wants, but rather a grave, earthy baritone; the acoustic shade of the spheres were therewith blurred."[61] Even outright praise of Ray's abilities still couched his performance within the framework of Britten's original score. It was possible, one critic said, that Britten's scoring for countertenor "hindered the [musical effect]" when transposed down to the baritone range.[62]

If Ray made for a terrible Oberon, why, then, had Felsenstein hired him for the role? Implicit in Felsenstein's staging, whether Felsenstein wished to admit it or not, was an assumption that placing two Black singers together was a natural pairing. Although Felsenstein rarely described the physical appearance of Ray and Lee, their race and gender nonetheless mattered to his production. Evidence suggests that Felsenstein's gendered interpretation of the countertenor role overwhelmingly informed his reading of Britten's opera. In short: Felsenstein did not find a countertenor role for this opera believable. In an internal memo written to the staff of the Komische Oper Berlin long before Felsenstein began working on this production, he disparaged the idea of Oberon as a countertenor. "Assigning Oberon to a countertenor is for all of us as inconceivable as casting an alto, because the love conflict of OBERON-TITANIA is the central starting point for the whole piece and its poetry; and therefore demands in every way a *manly* OBERON embodiment."[63] Because countertenors have historically been understood as gender subversive, being tied to histories of castration and emasculation, Felsenstein could find nothing supposedly masculine in Oberon singing in a high falsetto voice.[64]

Expressing again his core value that opera must convince audience members to suspend their disbelief, Felsenstein demonstrated in this internal document that he was entirely comfortable altering Britten's work to deliver on what he thought to be a more believable portrayal of the tumultuous love affair between Titania and Oberon in their magical elf kingdom. Felsenstein desired a performance of heteromasculinity that he thought only a deep-voiced baritone could provide. Ray could be, then, the ideal singer for Felsenstein's staging of the opera in terms of Felsenstein's understanding of gender roles for this work.

The detail-oriented Felsenstein sent Ray a letter before the premiere asking him to make changes to his acting and singing that emphasized Felsenstein's wish for Ray to play an assertive, hetero-masculine character in contrast to Lee's feminine Titania. His suggestions ranged from smaller details ("Can you please pick up the flowers off the floor with your right hand? It will make it more direct and passionate.") to ruminating on central themes in the opera. For example, Felsenstein encouraged Ray not to restrain himself during his first fight with Titania on the stage, since the fight established Oberon's motivation for tricking Titania into falling in love with a donkey.[65] Felsenstein's stage directions and hiring of Ray reflect his belief that it was necessary to find a more traditionally heteromasculine baritone for the role of Oberon to provide balance and symmetry to the feminine and spirited Titania.

Because Felsenstein had long discarded Britten's request for a countertenor as the fairy king, it was easy for him to envision instead a Black baritone to pair with a Black soprano. Race remained the silent yet visible agent that sparked Felsenstein's imagining and created public conversations on magic realism in musical theater. Further proof of Felsenstein and the Komische Oper Berlin's belief that racial difference was essential to their production of *A Midsummer Night's Dream*: as they continued to stage the opera throughout the 1960s, they continually sought out African American opera singers to play the roles of Titania and Oberon.[66]

The Komische Oper Berlin's practice of Black casting to visibly authenticate a production did not dissipate. In the 1970s, they again turned to hiring two Black American singers to constantly perform the roles of Porgy and Bess in Gershwin's opera of the same name. Prior to the Komische Oper Berlin's premiere of the work in January 1970, all productions of *Porgy and Bess* in Europe had been tours sponsored by the US State Department. But the Komische Oper Berlin's production was entirely German-led in its initiative and in its production, staffing, and staging. And the Komische Oper Berlin stated that they wanted to produce this opera to express solidarity musically with those suffering from oppression, seeing African American victimization as a result of capitalism. So the Komische Oper Berlin—now led by Götz Friedrich—took on a controversial opera that even some American opera houses still wouldn't touch.

But they forgot about race's power. They misunderstood or underestimated how central race and Black American culture were to the performance and reception of this work. However much they wanted race to disappear or for it to not matter, race ended up coloring the politicized production they wanted to stage. After agreeing to take on Gershwin's "Negro opera" and deciding to translate the work into vernacular Saxon German (the song "It Ain't Necessarily So" became "Wer's glaubt, der ist selber dran schuld"), one of the first questions that emerged among the production staff was how to portray the characters. Although the production team stated they were against using blackface, they nevertheless smeared a coppery brownish tint on the cast. But that still was not satisfactory. Throughout the many months that the show went on, the opera house hired several different African Americans to perform the two lead roles of Porgy and Bess.[67] Implicit in hiring them was the assumption that the musicians' Black bodies and Black voices provided in their estimation a racial authenticity to this musical performance.

The show was one of the most popular productions in East Berlin that year and was sold out for its entire run. And although critics praised Friedrich for not distracting his viewers with the question of race (which they called "of secondary importance") and instead keeping their gaze on what really mattered (capitalist oppression), nearly all reviews focused on the perceived authentic Blackness of the opera and its performers. Race was an inescapable, unshakable element of this production and its reception. Both racially progressive and conservative in its casting, the Komische Oper Berlin was never able to escape the problems of race-based casting throughout its tenure.

Fighting Back: Aubrey Pankey Speaks Out

No figure encapsulates the tensions and contradictions of racism and musical universalism quite like the African American baritone Aubrey Pankey. Outspoken, unapologetic, and firm in his convictions that communist East Germany should be working harder to support its communities of color, Pankey led a life in East Germany battling against the racism he witnessed in East German cultural productions and in representations of African Americans. Utilizing the same rhetoric of freedom from adversity that the East German state espoused, he consistently threw their turns of phrase back in their faces. As a Black classical musician in East Germany, he argued that he should be able to pursue his musical ambitions. Yet it was the racist imagination of the East Germans that was stymieing his progress.

Pankey's career in East Germany is an important case study because he had not only performed in German-speaking Europe prior to WWII but also lived in Germany after the war, pleading asylum in East Germany in the 1950s. He had tried for a while to find a home beyond the Iron Curtain before landing in East Berlin in 1955. After having been denied residency in France following his protestation of the execution of Julius and Ethel Rosenberg (convicted of spying for the USSR), Pankey had spent several years concertizing in Hungary, Czechoslovakia, Poland, Bulgaria, and Romania, pleading asylum in several of those countries without much success.[68]

During his concert tour to Czechoslovakia in February and March of 1955, for example, Pankey pled asylum, and his asylum letter to the minister of foreign affairs in Czechoslovakia, dated February 23, 1955, reveals Pankey's deep commitment to minority rights and socialism. As "an American citizen and especially a Black American that has continuously identified himself with the cause of peace, the rights of minorities, and most of all the oppression of Black Americans," Pankey argued that he was especially exposed to persecution, which led to his expulsion from France in 1953. His passport, which he argued the US government had been trying to take from him since 1951, was to expire in June 1955, four months after he wrote his asylum letter. He wrote that there were several reasons why the West, and the French especially, were persecuting him and his wife, first and foremost: "Because I am a member of the American Communist Party." He noted that he had befriended cultural representatives in various countries across the Iron Curtain and had participated in trade unions, organizations that supported communist principles, and other "peace organizations and organizations fighting against discrimination." Because of all this involvement, he argued, the French and American communist presses were continuously reporting on his activities.[69]

The Czech Communist Party inquired in Budapest on March 4 why Hungary had denied Pankey asylum and learned that "he was not granted political asylum because the relevant Hungarian authorities were not convinced that the named indeed faced discrimination or political persecution from the authorities of the United States of America." Czech officials' hesitancy to grant Pankey asylum concerned "whether Pankey who is a singer, and his wife, who does not speak Czech, would be able to earn a living wage. In connection with this it is also necessary to decide if Pankey would be allowed to go on concert tours to democratic countries."[70]

In the same month that Pankey applied for asylum in Czechoslovakia, members of the SED in East Germany also picked up his case. Jan Koplowitz, a German-Jewish author and member of the SED, brought Pankey's situation to the attention of the German intellectual Karl Tümmler, who wrote an official letter to Professor Hans Pischner, musicologist and head of the department of music at the Ministry of Culture. Noting that Pankey, "a Negro with American citizenship," was touring East Germany before embarking on a tour to Denmark, Tümmler wrote to Pischner to see if Pankey could settle in the GDR. "Above all," Tümmler opined, "we need to examine what his life would look like after such a step. Is he the kind of artist who, for example, can live on his concerts for a longer period of time, or is he suitable to be a teacher at a music conservatory, as Koplowitz said? Politically, there will hardly be any difficulties in granting him political asylum; he isn't a member of a party."[71] After these deliberations, Pankey's petition was approved, and he officially became a refugee in the GDR. Following his successful appeal for asylum, Pankey settled in East Berlin with his wife and concertized throughout East Germany.

Pankey had a successful career in the 1950s and 1960s as a concert artist. But he also faced conflicts because of his decisions to perform classical music. His interactions with Germans are so fascinating because, unlike other musicians featured in this book, Pankey seemed to have had no qualms about accusing German musicians and music lovers of racism, no misgivings about documenting his experiences with race and racism in the German public. For example, in April 1959, Pankey contacted Erich Went, Albert Norden, Hanns Eisler, and Gerhart Eisler regarding his decision to boycott a concert of American music in which he had been asked to perform. His letter of complaint, which found its way to Alfred Kurella, the head of the culture ministry, accused members of the German State Opera in East Berlin of typecasting him for the role of a stereotypical Black preacher against his will. The German State Opera had planned a musical program of American works by composers with communist leanings, such as Earl

FIGURE 29.   Paul Robeson and Aubrey Pankey in East Berlin, 1960. Photo: Herbert Görzing ©
Akademie der Künste, Berlin, Paul Robeson Archive, no. 516.014.

Robinson, for a performance in May 1959. They invited Pankey, a trained
classical singer, to perform in the composer's cantata, *The Lonesome Train*,
and Pankey initially believed that the invitation had been offered because of
the merits of his musicianship. Pankey later refused to perform in this musical work because, "as it turns out, the invitation was extended to me not
because I am a singer, or an American, but strictly because I am a Negro."[72]

In asking Pankey to play the African American preacher, the German State
Opera administration illuminated its own ideas of what constituted African
American identity. They believed, rightly or wrongly, that Pankey could lend
an element of authenticity to the role that an East German performer could
not. Whereas other musicians in the cantata would have singing roles, the
role offered to Pankey required no singing. Pankey's race and the perceived
cultural traits associated with it superseded his nationality and his training.
Writing to Gerhart Eisler, Pankey stated:

> I can only regard this as an unfortunate instance of Jim Crow. It must
> be understood that the preacher's role is not music, Negro or any other
> kind; but it is Negro atmosphere—it is recitative peculiar to a race, a
> section, and an activity, namely, a revivalist meeting in a Negro Baptist

Church in the Deep South of the United States. I appreciate the fact that as a Negro I understand the feeling that prompts this type of recitative. There still remains the fact that no Negro can view with dignity the proposition that he be relegated to supplying Negro atmosphere to a performance.[73]

The SED's responses, all documented internally, reveal a sincere attempt to address the problems of race, authenticity, and stereotyping in which Pankey and the German State Opera were embroiled. A few days after receiving Pankey's letter, Norden contacted Kurella to inquire if the SED could take action against the German State Opera and the state broadcasting committee (StKfR or SRK) in charge of this performance. Kurella replied, "It appears to me that we should have also commented on behalf of the culture department of the party against this discrimination." He continued, "The letter by the Negro singer Aubrey Pankey that you sent me gives us cause to finally take a stand against . . . the sadly still widespread form of racial discrimination against Negroes. When certain people hide behind their very loud working propaganda for the 'poor Negroes' . . . what they show as their culture is actually backhanded racial hatred."[74] Kurella recognized that Pankey had been assigned a role that fit well-known stereotypes in East German culture about African Americans.

Following this exchange, Kurella wrote immediately to Pankey to thank him for making the SED aware of this discriminatory act. Although Kurella seemed unsure how to proceed, he invited Pankey to discuss the matter with him further and made clear his own opinions on race under socialism:

This gives us the opportunity to appear publicly against the pseudo-sympathy for "Negroes" which actually conceals a racist attitude. I especially agree with your protest against the intention to have you perform the role of the preacher in this cantata. Generally, I find that the same condescending and belittling attitudes toward "Negroes" exist also in the uncritical cult certain people even here show toward spirituals.[75]

Pankey replied to Kurella, thanking him for understanding his situation. The concert went on as scheduled on May 22, 1959, without him. Headlines called it "Music of the True America" and "Earl Robinson—The Voice of America."[76] The concert, officially called "New American Music," offered a series of pieces on the theme of social justice. Pieces included "Schwarz und Weiß," "Blues der Freiheit und Gleichheit," a few compositions by Hanns Eisler (Robinson studied with Eisler when Eisler was in the United States), and "Casey Jones," an American left-wing parody about railway workers.[77] The evening concluded with Robinson's cantata *About Lincoln, The Lonesome Train*.[78]

No music reviews mentioned Pankey, so we must assume that he did indeed follow through with his decision to boycott the performance. Hanns Eisler appeared at the beginning of the performance, however, to talk about the cantata, and critics framed it in terms of the fight for justice and racial equality between Black and white people.[79] "Blacks and whites who fight for freedom and peace," a music critic for the *Berliner Zeitung* explained, "are prevented in America from having their works performed."[80] No article mentioned Pankey's conflict with the German State Opera; rather, they all emphatically emphasized how this performance supported the cause of African American civil rights.

This was not the only time Pankey contacted officials in the SED to protest his treatment. In February 1961, Pankey wrote again to the SED, asking that his letter be published in the *Norddeutsche Zeitung*. The situation closely resembled his first protest to state officials. Pankey had just given a Liederabend in Rostock, and the music critic from the *Norddeutsche Zeitung* criticized Pankey's performance, arguing that Pankey should have taken on the "thankless role of prophet in the fatherland" and performed more African American spirituals, especially in the Volkstheater Rostock, a stage on which he felt at home. As a result of his poor repertoire selection, Pankey did not live up to his international reputation. "This time there were three English Baroque arias, (including Handel), five international pieces, and ten German art songs," the critic complained. Worse, the critic argued, Pankey had only performed six spirituals for the audience. Considering that was the one genre the audience had expected him to perform, why, the critic asked, had Pankey neglected his duties?[81]

In many ways, this critic's review illustrated the gulf between Pankey's reasons for singing German music and East German listeners' desires for an exotic, African American musical performance. "How many beautiful possibilities could there have been if Pankey had performed Negro art first and foremost and not oriented his [concert program] around the supposed wishes of a traditional concert public?" the critic asked. He was also displeased with Pankey's performance because he believed that he fundamentally lacked the language skills, the intonation, and the expressive potential to carry the weight and significance of these German lieder, especially lieder like Schubert's "Der Doppelgänger," which the critic called "a central piece of German music literature."[82] Pankey's only real appeal came when he performed Argentinean songs by Carlos Guastavino and French pieces by Fauré and Debussy. Moreover, the critic argued, Pankey's performance of spirituals was his best and perhaps only real contribution to the evening's festivities. In other words, Pankey was the most convincing, sincere, earnest, and authentic when he was not performing German music.

On February 28, 1961, Pankey responded to the critic in a letter he hoped would be published in the *Norddeutsche Zeitung* and circulated in the culture ministry. He noted that throughout all his travels across the globe, concertizing in London, Paris, Prague, Budapest, Beijing, Berlin, Dresden, and Vienna, he had never before responded to a music critic's review. "Had [the critic] constricted his criticisms to my voice, my interpretation, and technique, there would be no reason for this letter," Pankey wrote. But, he continued, "Your reporter has assigned himself the task of politically analyzing my [concert] program. His ideas regarding my political and cultural obligations towards my people are actually and effectively racist." Pankey continued, "I consider it a serious political problem when a music critic of the GDR sings the same tune as white chauvinists. They are the ones who ask Negro singers to limit themselves to singing spirituals. This is the attitude your commentator takes. He might have other reasons for it, but the effect is the same."[83]

What Pankey wanted was the right to sing German music. Much as in 1932 when he faced criticism for singing German lieder in Salzburg, he defended his decision to do so. He lamented, "Any progress by a Negro artist was solely achieved through struggle—nothing was handed to him. What he has achieved encompasses the same rights that non-Negro artists are granted: when he is a singer, to have the freedom to choose what he will sing, and even to specialize in German lieder as I have done." "Negro actors," he continued, "were limited to the roles of servant, rapist, clown, or church singer, and Negro musicians were only allowed to play jazz. Yet even under capitalism, there was some progress, even though the fight continues, because Negro artists are still discriminated against."[84] African Americans had fought for years, Pankey fumed, to destroy the barriers imposed on them that limited their musical opportunities. Yet in the GDR, East Germans perpetuated the same stereotypes that Pankey had faced on the other side of the Atlantic.

In response to the critic's expression of disappointment that Pankey did not live up to his expectations of what a concert by an African American artist was supposed to entail, Pankey mentioned Roland Hayes, Marian Anderson, Todd Duncan, and Ellabelle Davis as examples of African American concert musicians who had successfully performed a variety of repertoire. His concert program was no different from these internationally acclaimed musicians, he argued, who also sang music by Handel, Schubert, and Richard Strauss in addition to performing African American spirituals. As for the reporter's claim that Pankey had an accent when he sang German, Pankey argued that the reporter's sentiments revealed yet another form of anti-Black racism, one rooted in nationalism:

> Millions of people around the world have welcomed the performance of foreign artists. The fact that an artist has sung in a foreign language has never diminished his value as an artist. We do not expect anything less from international artists. Let's take a typical example, an artist who Germans are very familiar with—Richard Tauber. His German accent has never prevented him from singing English songs. If one were to follow your reporter's logic, then a Jew must solely sing Jewish songs, a Frenchman only French, a Chinese solely Chinese, and a Russian only Russian songs. . . . I know of no concert program in the world where an artist would be forced to perform only one style of music.[85]

In this regard, Pankey's comments echo Laura Tunbridge's argument that by the 1920s, the Liederabend was understood as an international concert program.[86] If the goal was for the singer to offer a wide selection of musical works in multiple languages and styles, Pankey had indeed accomplished that task. Pankey finds the critic's remarks about his accent hypocritical considering how willing listeners are to hear German singers perform English folk music. His accusations confirm that when it came to German art music, East German audiences desired a uniform musical identity.

Pankey also found grave offense in the critic's assertion that he had somehow betrayed the African American people with his Liederabend. "In my position as an artist I have always represented my people," he argued. "When I sing, this is a part of the struggle that is happening in our world today—the struggle for the rights of every American Negro, for the rights of the African people in his home country, for the right of the oppressed to freedom and dignity. My professional and personal life is closely linked to the struggle of my people for equal rights, freedom, and peace."[87] Pankey was a political exile and refugee in East Germany who believed in the cause of African American civil rights. How dare this critic believe otherwise?

"I am of the conviction," Pankey concluded, "that an artist serves his people through art. I have been punished for that conviction by the authorities in my native country. That's why I live in the German Democratic Republic, where I have found a new home."[88] East Germany was supposed to be different from the West, Pankey implied. The citizens of the GDR were supposed to be involved in the fight against racism and its effects on people of African descent because of the ideology the GDR had been founded on and promoted. Yet in this instance, a prominent voice in GDR culture had disappointed the performer, disseminating instead the messages Pankey had been fighting against since his departure from the United States.

Pankey's letters of protest against the German State Opera and the *Norddeutsche Zeitung* illustrate the types of miscommunications, misunderstandings, and misconceptions that occurred between Black people living, working, or traveling in East Germany and the white Germans who observed them. From the GDR's foundation until the fall of the Berlin Wall, some East

FIGURE 30.   Aubrey Pankey holding a copy of Matthew Josephson's biography of the nineteenth-century French writer Stendhal. Photographer unknown © Akademie der Künste, Berlin, Jan Koplowitz Archive, no. 86.

Germans continued to disseminate beliefs and perspectives of authentic African American music and culture that differed from the actual experiences of African Americans performing music in their country. Pankey, a singer who had survived Nazism, expulsion from France, and a few years wandering through Eastern Europe as a nomad, was aware of these tropes and he was steadfast in his refusal to accept their promulgation.

Pankey's experiences and outspoken criticism of his treatment highlight in a way that Robeson and others could not the conflict between abstract notions of African American identity and the local encounters that threatened to undo these constructs and dispel them as myths. Pankey's performance of German lieder illuminate two different levels of thinking at work: the socialist antiracism that the state promoted and the ongoing depictions of African American identity rooted in the pre-1945 era. He makes it possible for us to see how difficult it was for *Musikfreunde* who thought that they were being racially welcoming to see outside their own worldview. Pankey, a musician committed to building socialism and fighting against racism, used the language of the East German state (language he believed in) to encourage the people he encountered to rethink their own racial and musical understandings.

Race and German Music After 1989

A few months before the Berlin Wall fell in 1989, George Byrd conducted the RSB at the Palace of the Republic and the Dresden Philharmonic at the Dresden Kulturpalast in what would be his last performances in the soon-to-be extinct German Democratic Republic. Byrd had been a conductor of the Dresden Philharmonic off and on for more than twenty-five years.[89] Unlike past concerts that were German-centered, this concert featured the music of Gershwin (both *An American in Paris* and *Rhapsody in Blue*), Leonard Bernstein, Heitor Villa-Lobos, and Camargo Guarnieri. The evening's activities provided the audience with much joy and excitement, according to the presses: "Everywhere the dancing demeanor dominated [the concert hall] with a distinct African American impact."[90] Byrd and the Berlin and Dresden orchestras had given East German listeners fun, exciting evenings of American music. "Due to his vitality, his spontaneity, his special 'feelings' for the music of his homeland," one critic concluded, "he guaranteed [his audience] an authentic rendition of these works."[91] Here, Byrd offered East German audiences a concert of American music that would have been right at home in New York's Lincoln Center.

But here, Byrd also fulfills the role of the African American musical entertainer bringing an authentic interpretation of American music to the East.

African American music—deemed melancholic and an expression of oppressive systems of capitalism and imperialism—fit the bill, and East Germans applauded performances that offered them the "real thing": authentic Black experiences that could speak to their particular musical, political, and social worldview. Reporters wrote that they eagerly anticipated Byrd's next guest appearances with both ensembles for the next season, but those performances never took place. The East German state disappeared, and its history of hosting African American musicians was quickly forgotten.

A month after Byrd's last performances in the GDR, protestors at one of the increasingly well-attended Monday demonstrations held up a sign that said, "Germany for Germans, Blacks out of the GDR."[92] The two events—Byrd's last performance and the Monday demonstration—should not be divorced from each other. Rather, they offer another illustration of how German nationalism functioned to keep Black people out of it. Black musicianship was to be celebrated in the GDR—so long as it stayed comfortably outside the bounds of German culture. Contrary to contemporary discourses that have expressed surprise at the resurgence of German nationalism after 1989, German nationalism was not a new phenomenon after all but rather an ideological continuity that remained in the region even after the end of the East German dictatorship.[93]

East German approaches to Black classical musicians were dualistic in nature. Cultural figures and state leaders were committed to upholding a longstanding German musical tradition on the one hand and expressing a vocal commitment to antiracism and anticolonialism on the other, perhaps not recognizing just how antagonistic to each other the two ideals had become in German history. The GDR claimed that it was the nation most suited to fostering Black musicianship because of its anticapitalist, anti-imperialist, and antiracist stances. Linking their musical culture to the tradition of musical universalism grounded in the nineteenth century, GDR leaders argued that their musical canon belonged to everyone, including Black people. Their musical past was a beautiful and harmonious one, stretching back to the music of Bach and Handel and reaching to the present day through the practices of musical ensembles such as the Leipzig Gewandhausorchester. Yet the GDR's antiracist, anticolonialist self-image starkly differed from the musical and cultural identity that the state and its listeners had constructed.[94] East German reception of African American musicians reveals how it was possible for audiences to hold multiple and even competing notions of musicianship and belonging in their minds. And East German praise and condemnation of Black musicians also reveal how the desire for Black authenticity could undo their own public commitment to musical and racial egalitarianism.

Conclusion

> "If I would have had white skin and blonde braids
> then everybody would have seen, yup, that's a
> German singing."
>
> —Afro-German singer Marie Nejar

In the 1968 film *Gottes zweite Garnitur* (God's second string), a white German family invites an American GI over for dinner—only to have the evening go terribly awry. Made for West German public television, the film functions as a German-speaking version of the 1967 classic *Guess Who's Coming to Dinner*, which depicted a white upper-class family torn over their daughter's romance with an African American doctor. Premiering only a year after *Guess Who's Coming to Dinner*, *Gottes zweite Garnitur* tells the story of a young white German woman who falls in love with an African American soldier to the great concern of her white fiancé and his family.

The film begins by depicting the Fehringer family and Claire Heggelbacher, their future daughter-in-law, waiting anxiously for an unknown American soldier to arrive at their front door. The family had invited the soldier over for Christmas dinner as part of a local initiative to take in American troops separated from their loved ones over the holidays. In preparation for the occasion, the father purchased a Beethoven recording to give to the American as a form of cultural exchange because it was "sophisticated" and "above all else, German!" But upon discovering that their guest was Black, the family bickers over whether to give the gift at all. In a heated conversation in the kitchen about what to do with their now-inappropriate present, someone exclaims, "What would a Negro do with Beethoven?!"[1] It had been perfectly acceptable for the family to give their gift of Beethoven to the American soldier when they had believed him to be white. Yet the soldier's Blackness, to their eyes, rendered their gift useless. Blackness and Beethoven had nothing to do with each other.

Their assumption was not uncommon. Since at least the nineteenth century, white Germans have questioned Black people's relationship to German music. The purpose of my book has been not only to showcase the number of Black performances of canonical German composers over time but also to uncover the hidden racial logics that then erased their presence on German stages. The story of Black classical musicians in Central Europe is a story of both Black musicians performing Beethoven and white Germans who forgot them. The white family in *Gottes zweite Garnitur* could claim ignorance about the history of Black classical musicians because West German racial thinking made it possible for them to do so—even after Rudolph Dunbar had conducted the Berliner Philharmonic in 1945, even after Grace Bumbry sang in Bayreuth in 1961, even after countless Black musicians had landed prominent contracts with opera houses or orchestras across Germany and Austria.

Yet in nearly every way imaginable the white German family's neat bifurcation of Beethoven and Blackness was wrong. In fact, a Black classical musician was part of Beethoven's musical circle during the composer's lifetime: the Afro-European violinist George Bridgetower. Born in Biała, Poland, to a Polish mother and an Afro-Caribbean father who was personal page to Nikolaus I, Prince Esterházy (1714–90), at his estate in Eisenstadt (now in Austria), Bridgetower most likely spent his childhood in Eisenstadt taking lessons from the legendary composer Joseph Haydn.[2] As an adult, he began his musical career in the cities of Dresden and Vienna before settling in England in 1811. Beethoven dedicated his fiery and technically demanding Violin Sonata no. 9, op. 47, to Bridgetower after befriending him in 1803. Indeed, its name, "Sonata Mulattica," leaves no question. After an altercation over a mutual love interest, the two stopped speaking and Beethoven chose to rename it "Kreutzer Sonata" for the violinist Rudolph Kreutzer instead—without Kreutzer's knowledge. Beethoven's notoriously difficult violin sonata, part of the Austro-German canon, symbolizes Austria and Germany's lasting musical dominance in European history. But Beethoven's initial dedication of the musical work to Bridgetower tells us that, contrary to the family's skepticism in *Gottes zweite Garnitur*, Western art music was never divorced from Black people.[3]

It is important to note that the cultural token the family wished to share with the visiting soldier is a musical one. German music's supposed universality, established in the eighteenth and early nineteenth centuries, lasted well through the twentieth, becoming part of both Germanies' strategies of rehabilitation and renewal after 1945. For example, Friedrich Meinecke's 1946 rumination on the disasters of Nazism and WWII, *The German Catastrophe*, turns to the power of German music as a restorative force in German society. Meinecke asks, "What is more individual and German than the great German music from Bach to Brahms?" To Meinecke, German music could rehabilitate German honor, for it alone could express the German spirit while also still possessing a "universal Occidental effect."[4] Unfortunately, by the time Meinecke penned his book, German public discourse had made anything deemed Black an exception from German music's "universal Occidental effect," whether that was African or African American. German music's universality often rested on listeners' assumptions of its whiteness.

Indeed, in the same year that Meinecke wrote his book, German-speaking listeners were already weaponizing German music's universality against any racial undesirables. A young housewife in postwar West Germany, for example, spoke out against a Duke Ellington film screened by the American military's US Information Control Division in the most vicious and racist terms. "It fills me with disgust to look at these bestial faces and to listen to this horrible music," she stated. "It is depressing for us white people to attend such a session. Give each race its own. Let the Negro listen to his own music; he might like it better. We Germans delight in the creations of the great German masters of German music."[5] Her demarcation of Black and white, bestial and civilized, un-German and German could not be drawn in sharper relief.

What is imperative to hear in this woman's remarks is not her derision of jazz but rather her praise of German music. As we continue to have conversations in musicology and history about the creation of the canon and of German cultural works, it is important to consider that what we know about Western art music comes from this particularly German framework—one that considers Black people to be outside of it. Musicological scholarship on the whiteness of classical music is growing, but it has yet to consider how German musical culture itself might have contributed to the problem of musical gatekeeping that transatlantic racism created.[6]

Black performances of German music, however, have routinely exposed the music's political, national, and racial affiliations, in spite of its universalist claims. Indeed, the reasons why Black musical performances have posed such significant threats to the racial and national order were precisely because they were performances of cultural citizenship. African American classical musicians in particular were powerful in this regard. Deemed outsiders to Germany, they nonetheless became cultural chameleons who could perform

German cultural identity and linguistic fluency in such an effective manner that white listeners were forced to contend with the question of just what, exactly, Germanness was and to whom it belonged. If, for example, an African American concert singer could sound like a German on the concert stage then, in theory, anyone could. Black performances of Bach, Beethoven, and Brahms suggested that German identity was not contingent upon whiteness but rather could be learned through study and musical mastery. For these reasons, intentionally or not, Black musicians constantly challenged the Black-white binary that shaped German history in the nineteenth and twentieth centuries.

For these very same reasons, however, German-speaking listeners responded to Black classical musicians by reestablishing racial orders and listening regimes, even in new and radically different political circumstances. Listeners consistently drew upon older models and forms of recognition to make sense of the sounds that they heard, even reaching decades back to earlier modes of racial listening to explain their acceptance or rejection of a Black musician's interpretation of the most canonical composer. Across decades, white listeners racially marked Black voices as different through language that described them as guttural or negroid. In 1972, for example, a critic for *DIE ZEIT* noted that the African American soprano Jessye Norman possessed a Mozart-like subtlety to her musicianship without the "corpulent, guttural timbre of her other colored female colleagues from [Leontyne] Price to Bumbry."[7] As we saw in chapter 5, this practice also existed in earlier decades. In the 1930s, Marian Anderson's concert manager and accompanist also praised Anderson for lacking the guttural quality they believed that they heard in most Black voices. Such praise illuminates different kinds of racial logic. In each example—both before and after the Nazi racial state—the white listener rendered Black voices biologically different and even deviant. Simultaneously, praising Black women's musicianship by distancing it from other Black artists meant rescuing those musicians from any associations with Blackness itself. Elevating Black musicians, in short, often meant whitening them.

In addition to racializing Black voices, white listeners often insisted on understanding Black musicianship only through a particular lens of Black authenticity—located outside of Germany—and in so doing reduced Black musicality to well-worn, reliable stereotypes of American Blackness, thus denying the full and rich spectrum of Black talent and creativity. Black classical musicians' successes or failures in performing Schubert or Brahms could, at times, only be explained through well-established tropes of sorrowful plantation slavery or wild, primeval jazz. Oftentimes, Black classical musicians only made sense to white listeners when they sang African American spirituals, even if the Black performer was German born or, like Norman, simply uninterested in gospel. "Some people ask me why I don't sing Jazz or spirituals," she stated in an interview for the *New York Times* in 1973. "I can't sing them, that's why."[8] Unfortunately, the stereotype of the Black entertainer and the assumption that African American musicians were pious Christian worshippers or cultural degenerates had real effects on Black people living and working in West Germany and Austria. In 1964, the African American jazz musician Eric Dolphy, Jr. collapsed onstage during a performance in Berlin. Because doctors assumed that he had taken ill due to a drug overdose, they left him untreated, not realizing that he was actually suffering from diabetic shock. He died shortly thereafter.[9]

Black Germans have historically borne the brunt of this violent process of aural bifurcation between Blackness and whiteness in German history. Their performances of German identity have long been challenged, questioned, or rejected—rarely understood as German outright. Their biographies indicate that far too often, how German listeners determined the legitimacy or validity of a Black person's performance—musical or otherwise—had little to do with questions of cultural immersion or fluency but rather what Rosina Lippi-Green calls "the social identity of the messenger."[10] In other words: public conversations on the accuracy, veracity, and validity of a performance by a person of color have historically functioned as barriers to cultural citizenship.

The experiences of the Afro-German singer and dancer Marie Nejar offer striking examples of everyday racism (*Alltagsrassismus*) and how white listeners rejected Black Germans' daily performances of Germanness. Born and raised in Hamburg in the 1930s and 1940s, Nejar recalls in her memoir her experience trying to make a cash transfer at a local post office. Before she could even fully articulate her request, the white German clerk stopped her from speaking further: the woman claimed that she could not understand Nejar and stated that she refused to work with foreigners since they did not understand the German language.[11] Nejar's native German language sounded inscrutable to the white German woman's ears. Another example is equally illuminating. Once, while Nejar was purchasing items in a grocery store, a white German cashier asked her "how [she] could speak such perfect German." Nejar replied that German was her mother tongue, to which the white German woman behind her in line replied, "But that can't be. You're not of our stock."[12] Nejar's Blackness prevented her from being understood as German to white ears. Black performances of German identities—whether an African American soprano or a Black German woman at the store—have been subject to "willful mishearings" because the performers' appearances (Black) did not match how they sounded (European, ergo white).[13]

Similarly, in a contemporary context, the demand for Black authenticity has meant that Black Germans still find themselves being tasked with performing modes of Blackness that have nothing to do with their own biographies or family histories. Kevin John Edusei, a Black German musician and the conductor of the Munich Symphony Orchestra, notes that he occasionally receives requests to conduct orchestral works associated with African American music, such as Gershwin's *Rhapsody in Blue*. "I mean those [musical pieces] are all well and nice but I'm not an American," Edusei joked in a 2016 interview. "I actually have a stronger connection to Mendelssohn, Schumann, and Brahms."[14] Edusei's story is part of a larger history of Black German music-making tied to white German expectations created by the transatlantic musical marketplace. His story is reminiscent of Black German musicians in the 1920s and 1930s, for example, who had taken up performing jazz—not because they felt an affinity for the music but rather because it offered guaranteed work. It was irrelevant, Robbie Aitken observes, "whether Africans played African Americans or vice versa, what counted was the performer's skin color and the authenticity or at least the illusion of authenticity of their supposed otherness that this brought."[15] Black authenticity, however artificially understood, drove white listeners' demands for Black musicianship—sometimes over Black musicians' own desires, interests, training, or capabilities.

But Black people claimed Germanness sonically and musically anyway, and in so doing constantly undermined what appeared to be both German and universal at the same time. From the moment Jessye Norman debuted as Elisabeth in Wagner's opera *Tannhäuser* at the Deutsche Oper Berlin in 1969—a year after the film *Gottes zweite Garnitur* appeared on West German televisions—she rejected white expectations of her.[16] Even though Norman preferred to sing the music of Wagner and Strauss, she observed, "People look at me and say 'Aida.' "[17] Norman spent a lifetime rejecting roles in operas that Black women were hired to sing—*Aida*, *Porgy and Bess*, or Italian operas such as Verdi's *Don Carlos*. Instead, she chose to make her mark in the opera world as a Wagnerian soprano. As a lieder singer, Norman became known for her renditions of works by Brahms, Hugo Wolf, and Strauss and later gravitated toward Wagner's Wesendonck Lieder and Mahler's Rückert Lieder. Most remarkable, early in her career Norman also began to program music that even most opera singers hesitated to touch. She sang not only Wagner but also Schoenberg, Alban Berg, Leoš Janáček, and Olivier Messiaen. Moreover, she demonstrated her mastery over German music by offering her own German translations of the pieces she sang and by giving interviews in German on German radio.[18] Comparing her to the white German soprano Elisabeth Schwarzkopf and the white German baritone Dietrich Fischer-Dieskau, German critics declared her diction perfect and every note that she sang imbued with meaning.

Throughout her career in Germany and in the United States, Norman was absolutely unapologetic about being Black and a singer of German repertoire. When asked about being Black in the world of Western art music, Norman was quick to shut down any needling questions about her success. "I don't feel guilty about making it in a largely white or European world—not at all," she stated.[19] "She gave me this look," the African American dancer Bill T. Jones once recalled, following a rehearsal on a collaborative performance project on civil rights history and the anti-apartheid struggle. "I think, that as African American artists working in very Eurocentric environments, it was her way of saying, 'I am in touch with who I am.'"[20]

Moreover, Norman attributed the successes of her Germanic career to her time as a student at Howard, an HBCU, as well as to other Black musicians—not to European teachers. Repeatedly in her career, she stated in interviews that Black women such as Anderson, Price, Dorothy Maynor, and Mattiwilda Dobbs "made it possible for me to say, 'I will sing French opera' or 'I will sing German opera,' instead of being told, 'You will sing 'Porgy and Bess.'"[21] She acknowledged, in other words, that her career as a singer of Wagner, Mahler, and Schoenberg had been able to flourish because of Black classical musicians who had come before her in Europe and in the United States. Norman's insistence on crediting other Black musicians and institutions for her education also suggests that learning German music was no longer dependent on white German teachers. Musical Germanness did not belong to the purview of white Germans alone. Norman's experience suggests that constructing Germanness is, indeed, a global project, formed by contributors both in- and outside of German-speaking Europe.[22]

In a contemporary context, people of African descent continue to push back against white definitions of German national identity through musical performance. The Berlin-based Nigerian sound and installation artist Emeka Ogboh's 2015 piece *The Song of the Germans* effectively demonstrates what it means for Black artists to join and thus to change a conversation to which they have, historically, not been invited. First appearing at the 2015 Venice Art Biennale, the sound installation features a choir of African refugees singing the German national anthem in unison in ten different African languages (Igbo, Yoruba, Bamoun, More, Twi, Ewondo, Sango, Douala, Kikongo, and Lingala). The sound installation thus dismantles long-standing ideas of just what the German national anthem sounds like and for whom it resonates.

Ogboh's choice to have different African refugees sing the German national anthem works on multiple levels because of the melody's complex history. The tune for the anthem itself has historically been vulnerable to different national interpretations. Taken from the second movement of Haydn's
String Quartet in C Major, op. 76, the melody is part of the Austro-German
canon and its shared tradition in both countries reflects the importance of
classical music to national identity formation in German-speaking Europe.
Most important, the words assigned to the melody have changed repeatedly
over time. Perhaps for these reasons the melody has been the basis for two
Austrian national anthems in addition to the German national anthem. First
assigned to Francis II, Holy Roman Emperor in 1797 ("Gott erhalte Franz
den Kaiser"), the tune later functioned as the anthem for the newly-created
Austrian republic in the 1920s. In the case of modern German history, the
poet August Heinrich Hoffmann von Fallersleben first set the melody to
words ("Das Lied der Deutschen") in 1841, and it became the national anthem of Germany under the Weimar Republic in 1922.

In other words: the "nationality" of Germany's national anthem has always been contested. In Vienna in 1938, for example, shortly before Hitler's annexation of Austria into Nazi Germany, rowdy crowds in the capital
city attending the Austrian Chancellor Kurt Schuschnigg's defiant speech
sang three completely different political anthems at the same time, all of
them using the same "German" melody by Haydn: one group sang the old
Habsburg anthem, another the new Austrian national anthem created in
1929 that represented the Austrian republic, and the last group sang the German nationalist one. All three versions relied on Haydn's tune as the basis for
their visions of an Austrian, German, or Austro-German future. Since 1945
and the collapse of the Third Reich, it has been hard to shake the German
national anthem's Nazi connotations. In postwar West Germany, the state
commissioned a new anthem in 1950, only for it to fail in popularity and for
the government to return to Haydn's melody. To eradicate any further ties
to Nazism, however, West Germany declared that only the third verse of the
song—and not its more contentious first verse ("Deutschland, Deutschland
über alles")—could be sung.

Ogboh's sound installation reclaims the "Song of the Germans." For the
version at the 2015 Venice Art Biennale, the chorus of African voices sings
in E-flat major, the key most commonly performed today. Yet the unrecog-
nizability (to most German speakers) of the words the African refugees are
using to sing the anthem unsettles its textual meaning. To further complicate
matters, each singer's voice projects through an individual stereo speaker,
and the only information telling visitors about the language employed is a

label underneath the stereo. No textual translation is provided, forcing visitors to trust the African translation of the German anthem. Yet the melody still sounds German, even if the words are not. Linguistic fluency in German is not, in this case, a requirement in order for the German national anthem to be sung—or recognized as such. Even if Ogboh's anthem sounds unrecognizable to German speakers, it is recognizable to the African refugees singing it. Their knowledge, in this case, matters more than that of German speakers. Ogboh's installation thus blows up the question of whether fluency is necessary for Black people to perform Germanness. Rather than waste his time trying to answer it, Ogboh's work chooses to ignore the question altogether.

Because the visitor encounters the African singer only through a stereo speaker, Ogboh's artwork rejects the (usually white) audience's desire to see Black people sing. Across the nineteenth and twentieth centuries, white German audiences had become conditioned to see a Black man or woman and anticipate a kind of sonic authentic Blackness. For example, in the 1920s, the Jewish-German critic Rudolf Arnheim said upon hearing a choir of African American singers perform spirituals, "One must *see* these Negroes when they sing." They sing, he writes, "exactly like they look, and they each look a little forbidden, if one takes our cosmetic ideal of beauty as a basis."[23] The relationship between sight and sound was intertwined in German culture, as German listeners became accustomed to both seeing and hearing Blackness as part of the same synesthetic experience. Yet Ogboh's sound art challenges the viewer to sever the ties between sight and sound that transatlantic racism had bound. Moreover, Ogboh's work calls into question the relationship of the racialized body to German national identity. Who could sing the German national anthem? By divorcing the body of the performer from the music itself, Ogboh's installation lays bare the long-standing assumptions of just whose music this was and to whom it belonged.

Part of Ogboh's motivation to create this sonic piece was his frustration with German assimilationist narratives. As a Nigerian artist living in Berlin, Ogboh is well aware of white German demands of him in relation to his perceived African identity and he has repeatedly questioned contemporary rhetoric encouraging integration and assimilation. In June 2018, for example, the art curator Okwui Enwezor, another Nigerian involved in Germany's contemporary art scene, stepped down from his position as director of Munich's Haus der Kunst. Among Enwezor's complaints at his former position was white German treatment of him as an African in the Bavarian capital. "Some people do not even bother to pronounce my name correctly," he told *Der Spiegel*, "but they demand that I speak German."[24] Ogboh, who had worked with Enwezor at the Venice Art Biennale, understood his colleague's complaint. "This is what migration is all about, it's not one-sided," he said. "You give and you take. If someone has to speak German, good—but also make an attempt to understand where they're from."[25] The politics of German language and German identity, in Ogboh's case, might have little to do with who speaks it. Singing the German anthem in any language could, perhaps, free the singer and the listener to imagine German national identity as a global, mutually-shared process.

In both Norman and Ogboh's cases, German music takes on different, deeper meanings because of the musicians performing it. If white German audiences demanded that Black musicians shed their Blackness in order to perform "universal" German art music, Norman and Ogboh's artistic practices—based on their own African or African American histories—argue just the opposite. Rather, Black musicianship opens up the potential for developing and pushing the concept of musical Germanness to richer and more riveting places and provides a better and more meaningful representation of Western art music in all its diversity and multiplicity.

The story of Black musicians in German-speaking Europe reveals the Austro-German canon's globality all along, even while audiences in Austria and Germany constantly found ways to undermine or erase any traces of Blackness from their histories. Austro-German musical life was a revolving door, accepting Black musicians onto German and Austrian stages in greater number than the United States and elsewhere while also rejecting the very premise that Black musicianship could exist outside of an exotic racial frame. But Black musicians from the Americas, the Caribbean, and from within Europe studied and performed anyway. Their stories are ones of resilience, true, but also of musical mastery.

In 1952, years before *Gottes zweite Garnitur* made its premiere, the African American music critic Nora Holt expressed the same sentiment: "It is becoming a bit out-of-date, and we might add, discriminative, to label American Negro singers of professional stature as unqualified to interpret the works of such masters as Bach, Beethoven, Brahms, German lieder, or operatic roles in which they have proved their capabilities."[26] Indeed, as we have seen, Black performances of the Austro-German canon have been subject to scrutiny since at least the nineteenth century. But instead of marginalizing their musicianship by framing it within the language of exceptionalism and exoticism, this book places Black music-making—and Black lives—at the center of our musical and historical narratives. In doing so, a richer and more resonant story has emerged, one of a global musical past and Black diasporic present in Germany and Austria. Black people have been part of German-speaking Europe's musical history all along. We simply had to listen.

Notes

Introduction

1. See Celia Applegate and Pamela Potter, eds., *Music and German National Identity* (Chicago: University of Chicago Press, 2006).

2. Black musical contributions to German music date back to at least the twelfth century under the Hohenstaufen dynasty. Black musicians such as the seventeenth-century trumpeters Christian Real and Christian Gottlieb or the nineteenth-century violinist and composer George Bridgetower concertized in different German and Austrian courts. See Arne Spohr, " 'Mohr und Trompeter': Blackness and Social Status in Early Modern Germany," *Journal of the American Musicological Society* 72, no. 3 (2019): 613–63

3. For more information on this topic, see Alex Ross's book *Wagnerism*, which offers the most authoritative account of Luranah Aldridge's time with the Wagner family. Alex Ross, *Wagnerism: Art and Politics in the Shadow of Music* (New York: Farrar, Strauss, and Giroux, 2020).

4. Nearing more than one million in Germany and Austria, Afro-Germans represent about one percent of the total population of these two countries combined. Marion Kraft's *Coming In from the Cold* provides a brief introductory overview of the history of Black Germans. See Marion Kraft, *Coming In from the Cold: The Black German Experience, Past and Present* (New York: Rosa Luxemburg Stiftung, 2014). For more information on Afro-German history, see the groundbreaking book by May Opitz, Katharina Oguntoye, and Dagmar Schultz, eds., *Showing Our Colors: Afro-German Women Speak Out* (Amherst: University of Massachusetts Press, 1992); Sara Lennox, ed., *Remapping Black Germany: New Perspectives on Afro-German History, Politics, and Culture* (Amherst: University of Massachusetts Press, 2016); Patricia Mazón and Reinhild Steingröver, eds., *Not So Plain as Black and White: Afro-German Culture and History, 1890–2000* (Rochester, NY: University of Rochester Press, 2005); Tiffany Florvil, *Mobilizing Black Germany: Afro-German Women and the Making of a Transnational Movement* (Urbana, IL: University of Illinois Press, 2020); and Tiffany N. Florvil and Vanessa Plumly, eds., *Rethinking Black German Studies: Approaches, Interventions, and Histories* (New York: Peter Lang, 2018). We do not know the exact number of Afro-Germans because Germany and Austria refuse to identify citizens by race.

5. As Ann Laura Stoler, George Frederickson, and others have argued, an increasingly rigid Black-white binary came into existence in the modern era across the Black Atlantic, and this binary functioned like two sides of the same coin. European whiteness, historical scholarship has demonstrated, was dependent on the racialization of non-European peoples. In creating this racial bifurcation, white Europeans ensured that people of African descent would be outsiders to Europe. See Frederickson, *Racism: A Short History* (Princeton, NJ: Princeton University Press, 2002); Stoler, *Race*

and the Education of Desire: Foucault's History of Sexuality and the Colonial Order of Things (Durham, NC: Duke University Press, 1995). For more information on how white Europeans have consistently denied Black Europeans' claims to citizenship and on the history of European anti-Black racism more generally, see Rita Chin, Atina Grossmann, Heide Fehrenbach, and Geoff Eley, After the Nazi Racial State: Difference and Democracy in Germany and Europe (Ann Arbor: University of Michigan Press, 2009); Darlene Clark Hine, Trica Danielle Keaton, and Stephen Small, eds., Black Europe and the African Diaspora (Urbana: University of Illinois Press, 2009); and Neil MacMaster, Racism in Europe, 1870–2000 (New York: Palgrave MacMillan, 2001).

6. See Robbie Aitken and Eve Rosenhaft, Black Germany: The Making and Unmaking of a Diaspora Community, 1884–1960 (Cambridge: Cambridge University Press, 2013).

7. Minneapolis Journal, January 14, 1897.

8. Clarence Cameron White, "The Negro in Musical Europe," New York Age, December 24, 1908, 13.

9. See, for example, Wallace Cheatham, Dialogues on Opera and the African-American Experience (Lanham, MD: Scarecrow Press, 1997); Elizabeth Nash, Autobiographical Reminiscences of African American Classical Singers, 1853—Present: Introducing Their Spiritual Heritage into the Concert Repertoire (Lewiston: Edwin Mellen Press, 2007); Rosalyn Story, And So I Sing: African-American Divas of Opera and Concert (New York: Warner Books, 1990); Naomi André, Black Opera: History, Power, Engagement (Urbana: University of Illinois Press, 2018); and Darryl Glenn Nettles, African American Concert Singers Before 1950 (Jefferson: McFarland, 2003).

10. "Final Audition to Be in Town Hall August 7," New York Amsterdam News, July 29, 1925, 1.

11. See Robin D. G. Kelley, Freedom Dreams: The Black Radical Imagination (Boston: Beacon Press, 2002); and Kendahl Radcliffe, Jennifer Scott, and Anja Werner, eds., Anywhere but Here: Black Intellectuals in the Atlantic World and Beyond (Jackson: University of Mississippi Press, 2015).

12. Richard Taruskin, Oxford History of Western Music (Oxford: Oxford University Press, 2005), 346.

13. Marc Matera, Black London: The Imperial Metropolis and Decolonization in the Twentieth Century (Berkeley: University of California Press, 2015); Kennetta Hammond Perry, London Is the Place for Me: Black Britons, Citizenship and the Politics of Race (New York: Oxford University Press, 2016); and Susan Pennybacker, From Scottsboro to Munich: Race and Political Culture in 1930s Britain (Princeton, NJ: Princeton University Press, 2013).

14. Sue Peabody and Tyler Stovall, eds., The Color of Liberty: Histories of Race in France (Durham, NC: Duke University Press, 2003); and Tyler Stovall, Paris Noir: African Americans in the City of Light (Boston: Houghton Mifflin, 1996).

15. Meredith Roman, Opposing Jim Crow: African Americans and the Soviet Indictment of Racism, 1928–1937 (Lincoln: University of Nebraska, 2012); Kate Baldwin, Beyond the Color Line and the Iron Curtain: Reading Encounters Between Black and Red, 1922–1963 (Durham, NC: Duke University Press, 2002).

16. Christopher Small, Musicking: The Meanings of Performing and Listening (Hanover, NH: University of New England Press, 1998), 10.

17. By "musical Germanness," I mean the discourse that developed in the late eighteenth century by which Germans were described as the "people of music" and

a particularly German essence was attributed to musical composition and/or expression. As scholars such as Applegate and Potter have argued, no one could define what musical Germanness actually was. But by the mid-nineteenth century many believed that Germans "understood the deeper sources of music more fully and intuitively than others." Applegate, "Saving Music: Enduring Experiences of Culture," *History and Memory* 17, nos. 1–2 (2005): 217–37. In the 1930s, Potter writes, "many studies simply accept[ed] musical Germanness as a given without defining it." See Potter, *Most German of the Arts: Musicology and Society from the Weimar Republic to the End of Hitler's Reich* (New Haven: Yale University Press, 1998), 211.

18. Hoi-eun Kim, "Made in Meiji Japan: German Expatriates, German-Educated Japanese Elites, and the Construction of Germanness," *Geschichte und Gesellschaft* 41, no. 2 (April–June 2015): 291–92.

19. Ibid.

20. Inga Clendinnen, *Dancing with Strangers: Europeans and Australians at First Contact* (Cambridge: Cambridge University Press, 2005), 11.

21. James H. Johnson, *Listening in Paris: A Cultural History* (Berkeley: University of California Press, 1995).

22. See Christian Thorau and Hansjakob Ziemer, *The Oxford Handbook of Music Listening in the 19th and 20th Centuries* (New York: Oxford University Press, 2019), accessed online November 11, 2019, https://www.oxfordhandbooks.com/view/10.1093/oxfordhb/9780190466961.001.0001/oxfordhb-9780190466961-e-1; Daniel Morat, ed., *Sounds of Modern History: Auditory Cultures in 19th and 20th Century Europe*, (New York: Berghahn, 2014); Jan-Friedrich Missfelder, "Period Ear: Perspektiven einer Klanggeschichte der Neuzeit," *Geschichte und Gesellschaft* 38, no. 1, (January–March 2012): 21–47.

23. See Nina Sun Eidsheim, *The Race of Sound: Listening, Timbre, and Vocality in African American Music* (Durham, NC: Duke University Press, 2019); Grace Wang, *Soundtracks of Asian America: Navigating Race Through Musical Performance* (Durham, NC: Duke University Press, 2015).

24. Jennifer Lynn Stoever, *The Sonic Color Line: Race and the Cultural Politics of Listening* (New York: New York University Press, 2016).

25. Mark Burford, "Sam Cooke as Pop Album Artist—A Reinvention in Three Songs," *Journal of the American Musicological Society* 65, no. 1 (Spring 2012): 169.

26. For information on how bodies racialized as non-white have challenged the notion of classical music's universality, see Minna Yang, "East Meets West in the Concert Hall: Asians and Classical Music in the Century of Imperialism, Post-Colonialism, and Multiculturalism," *Asian Music* 38, no. 1 (Winter–Spring 2007): 1–30; Mari Yoshihara, *Musicians from a Different Shore: Asians and Asian Americans in Classical Music* (Philadelphia: Temple University Press, 2007); and Wang, *Soundtracks*. Since the 1990s, the field of critical whiteness studies has produced a dynamic body of scholarship examining how whiteness functions in global contexts. Richard Dyer argued that "as long as race is something only applied to non-white peoples, as long as white people are not racially seen and named, they/we function as a human norm. Other people are raced, we are just people." See Dyer, *White: Essays on Race and Culture* (New York: Routledge, 1997), 1. Whiteness's invisibility is in fact one of its central characteristics, Dyer argues. For a Black German critique of whiteness, see Maureen Maisha Eggers, Grada Kilomba, Peggy Piesche, and Susan Arndt, eds., *Mythen,*

Masken, und Subjekte: Kritische Weißseinforschung in Deutschland (Münster: Unrast, 2005). See also Wulf Hund, *Wie die Deutschen weiß wurden: Kleine (Heimat)Geschichte des Rassismus* (Stuttgart: Metzler, 2017). Fatima El-Tayeb provides us with a contemporary German context for un/marking in her book, *Undeutsch: Die Konstruktion des Anderen in der postmigrantischen Gesellschaft* (Bielefeld: Transcript, 2016), 134. "The unmarked Germans have the run of the place, of course. Unmarked again necessarily means white and (socialized) Christian. If the 'Germans' weren't that, they would be mixed German-something or from Arab or Turkish families. The unmarked status of Christian (-socialized) whites is only possible then if all others remain marked and don't become normal 'Germans'—since otherwise there wouldn't be anything to tell a person what the deal is with Germans and perhaps one with non-German roots would be foisted upon them." See El-Tayeb, *Undeutsch*, 134.

27. Leo Frobenius, *Und Afrika Sprach . . .: Bericht über den Verlauf der dritten Reise-Periode der D.I.A.F.E. in den Jahren 1910 bis 1912* (Berlin: Vita, 1912), G.

28. Heide Fehrenbach, "Of German Mothers and 'Negermischlingskinder': Race, Sex, and the Postwar Nation," in *The Miracle Years: A Cultural History of West Germany, 1949–1968*, ed. Hanna Schissler (Princeton, NJ: Princeton University Press, 2001), 171.

29. Fatima El-Tayeb, "Dangerous Liaisons: Race, Nation, and German Identity," in *Not So Plain*, ed. Mazón and Steingröver 29.

30. The historian Lara Putnam cautions scholars against our growing reliance on digitized materials, arguing that digitization efforts have the power to obscure as much as illuminate. "[The] digitized revolution is not inherently egalitarian, open, or cost-free," she argues; rather, the corpus of digitized documents has thus far privileged Western materials and researchers over others. See Putnam, "The Transnational and the Text-Searchable: Digitized Sources and the Shadows They Cast," *American Historical Review* 121, no. 2 (April 2016): 377–402.

31. "Music: Rhythm in Berlin," *Time*, September 10, 1945.

32. Neil Gregor, "Bruckner, Munich, and the Longue Durée of Musical Listening between the Imperial and Postwar Eras," in *Dreams of Germany: Musical Imaginaries from the Concert Hall to the Dance Floor*, ed. Neil Gregor and Thomas Irvine (New York: Berghahn, 2018), 114.

33. Kennell Jackson, "Traveling While Black," in *Black Cultural Traffic: Crossroads in Global Performance and Popular Culture*, ed. Harry J. Elam and Kennell Jackson (Ann Arbor: University of Michigan Press, 2005), 4.

34. Chin, Grossman, Fehrenbach, and Eley, *After the Nazi Racial State*, 6.

35. Katrin Sieg, *Ethnic Drag: Performing Race, Nation, and Sexuality in West Germany* (Ann Arbor: University of Michigan Press, 2002), 84.

36. *Jet Magazine*, September 10, 1959.

37. Celia Applegate, "Mendelssohn on the Road," in *The Necessity of Music: Variations on a German Theme* (Toronto: University of Toronto Press, 2017), 119–34. Pieter Judson, for example, calls for historians to "broaden their understanding of the term *German* beyond a nation state-centered concept that for too long has privileged the German state founded in 1871 as the social, cultural, and political embodiment of a German nation." Judson, "When Is a Diaspora Not a Diaspora? Rethinking Nation-Centered Narratives about Germans in Eastern Europe," in *The Heimat Abroad: The Boundaries of Germanness*, eds. Krista O'Donnell, Renate Bridenthal, and Nancy Reagin (Ann Arbor: University of Michigan Press, 2005), 219.

38. Scholars of Austrian history have also pushed back against an earlier genera-tion of Cold War historical scholarship that sought to carve out an Austrian identity distinct from the two Germanies after WWII. Instead, historians such as Erin Hoch-man, Michael Steinberg, and David Luft have pointed out that it is possible to speak of a shared Austro-German culture between 1900 and 1938. Even Austrian conser-vatives who were against the German annexation of Austria nonetheless expressed their position as one of "German—Austro-German—cultural superiority," Steinberg argues. Despite constant political change in Central Europe in the 1930s, many lis-teners in Germany and Austria continued to assume that German music was their rightful heritage. See Steinberg, *The Meaning of the Salzburg Festival: Austria as Theater and Ideology, 1890–1938* (Ithaca, NY: Cornell University Press, 1990), 117. See also Luft, "Austria as a Region of German Culture: 1900–1938," *Austrian History Yearbook* 23 (1992): 135–48.

39. Erin Hochman, *Imagining a Greater Germany: Republican Nationalism and the Idea of Anschluss* (Ithaca, NY: Cornell University Press, 2016), 9.

40. See Walter Sauer, *Von Soliman zu Omofuma: Afrikanische Diaspora in Österreich 17. bis 20. Jahrhundert* (Innsbruck: Studienverlag, 2006); Nancy Nenno, "Here to Stay: Black Austrian Studies," in *Rethinking*, ed. Florvil and Plumly; Claudia Unterweger, *Talking Back: Strategien Schwarzer österreichischer Geschichtsschreibung* (Vienna: Zaglos-sus, 2016); Niko Wahl, Tal Adler, and Philipp Rohrbach, *Schwarz Österreich: Die Kinder afroamerikanischer Besatzungssoldaten* (Vienna: Löcker Verlag, 2016).

41. Priscilla Layne, *White Rebels in Black: German Appropriation of Black Popular Cul-ture* (Ann Arbor: University of Michigan Press, 2018), 2.

42. Scholars are of course trying to change this. See André, *Black Opera*.

43. Ingrid Monson, "Introduction," in *The African Diaspora: A Musical Perspective*, ed. Ingrid Monson (New York: Garland, 2003), 13–14.

44. See Fatima El-Tayeb, *European Others: Queering Ethnicity in Postnational Europe* (Minneapolis: University of Minnesota Press, 2011).

45. Story, *And So I Sing*, 181.

46. Ibid.

1. How Beethoven Came to Black America

1. For an overview on *Hausmusik* in the nineteenth and twentieth centuries, see Celia Applegate, "Hausmusik in the Third Reich," in *The Necessity of Music: Variations on a German Theme* (Toronto: University of Toronto Press, 2017).

2. Tuskegee University Course Catalog, 1890–91. Tuskegee University Archives Repository.

3. Lynn Abbot and Doug Seroff, eds., *Out of Sight: The Rise of African American Popular Music, 1889–95* (Jackson: University of Mississippi Press, 2002).

4. Khalil Gibran Muhammad, *The Condemnation of Blackness: Race, Crime, and the Making of Modern Urban America* (Cambridge: Harvard University Press, 2010).

5. "From Bell Stand to Throne Room: A Remarkable Autobiographical Interview with the Eminently Successful American Negro Composer R. Nathaniel Dett," *Black Perspective in Music* 1, no. 1 (1973): 74. First appeared in *Etude* (1934): 79–80.

6. Jessica Gienow-Hecht, *Sound Diplomacy: Music and Emotions in Transatlantic Relations, 1850–1920* (Chicago: University of Chicago Press, 2012), 12.

7. Berndt Ostendorf, "The Diluted Second Generation: German-Americans in Music 1870–1920," in *German Worker's Culture in the US: 1850–1920*, ed. Hartmut Keil (Washington, DC: Smithsonian Institution, 1988), 266. For information on German-Americans and music, see Barbara Lorenzkowski, *Sounds of Ethnicity: Listening to German North America, 1850–1914* (Winnipeg: University of Manitoba Press, 2010); and Philip Bohlman and Otto Holzapfel, eds., *Land without Nightingales: Music in the Making of German-America* (Madison: University of Wisconsin Press, 2002).

8. James Monroe Trotter, *Music and Some Highly Musical People* (Boston: Lee and Shepherd, 1878), 9.

9. Ibid., 59. Emphasis added.

10. "Greatest Musical Nation," *Chicago Defender*, September 26, 1914.

11. *Negro Music Journal* 1, no. 6 (February 1903): 113.

12. Vanessa Agnew, *Enlightenment Orpheus: The Power of Music in Other Worlds* (Oxford: Oxford University Press, 2008); Mary Sue Morrow, *German Music Criticism in the Late Eighteenth Century: Aesthetic Issues in Instrumental Music* (Cambridge: Cambridge University Press, 1997).

13. David Gramit, *Cultivating Music: The Aspirations, Interests, and Limits of German Musical Culture, 1770–1848* (Berkeley: University of California Press, 2007), 7.

14. Ibid., 21.

15. Wang, *Soundtracks*, 11.

16. Lawrence Schenbeck, *Racial Uplift and American Music, 1878–1943* (Jackson: University of Mississippi Press, 2012), 7.

17. Douglas Shadle, *Orchestrating the Nation: The Nineteenth-Century American Symphonic Enterprise* (New York: Oxford University Press, 2016), 136. See also William Weber, *The Great Transformation of Musical Taste: Concert Programming from Haydn to Brahms* (Cambridge: Cambridge University Press, 2008).

18. Kevin Gaines, *Uplifting the Race: Black Leadership, Politics, and Culture in the Twentieth Century* (Chapel Hill: University of North Carolina Press, 1996), 2. See also Douglas Egerton, *The Wars of Reconstruction: The Brief, Violent History of America's Most Progressive Era* (New York: Bloomsbury Press, 2015).

19. Caroline Gebhard and Barbara McCaskill, "Introduction," in *Post-Bellum, Pre-Harlem: African American Literature and Culture, 1877–1919*, ed. McCaskill and Gebhard (New York: New York University Press, 2006), 8.

20. Clarence Cameron White, "The American Negro in Music," *Negro Music Journal* 1, no. 5 (1903): 78. See also Doris E. McGinty, "The Washington Conservatory of Music and School of Expression," *Black Perspective in Music* 7, no. 1 (Spring 1979): 59–74.

21. *Crisis* 4, no. 2 (June 1912): 68.

22. Theodore Albrecht, "Julius Weiss: Scott Joplin's First Piano Teacher," *College Music Symposium* 19, no. 2 (Fall 1979): 89–105.

23. Ibid.

24. *St. Louis Dispatch*, February 28, 1901. Cited in Albrecht, "Julius Weiss."

25. "Musical Matters," *Cleveland Plain Dealer*, April 22, 1900.

26. *Cleveland Plain Dealer*, March 17, 1900, Cleveland Public Library, Johann Heinrich Beck Collection, box 11.

27. Columbia University, Lawrence Freeman Collection, box 36, folder 6, series IX.

28. David Gutkin, "The Modernities of H. Lawrence Freeman," *Journal of the American Musicological Society* 72, no. 3 (Fall 2019): 719–79.

29. The Bohemian impresario Max Strakosch wrote a letter endorsing Marie Selika Williams, a New York opera singer, in 1877. "Signor Farini's Concert," *Folio* 20, no. 12 (December 1881): 454. Ignaz Moscheles also endorsed the pianist Thomas "Blind Tom" Wiggins in 1866. See *The Marvelous Musical Prodigy, Blind Tom* (New York: French and Wheat, 1868), 11.

30. Andrea Olmstead, *Juilliard: A History* (Urbana: University of Illinois Press, 1999), 17.

31. Loren Kajikawa, "The Possessive Investment in Classical Music: Confronting Legacies of White Supremacy in U.S. Schools and Departments of Music," in *Seeing Race Again: Countering Colorblindness Across the Disciplines*, ed. Kimberlé Williams Crenshaw (Berkeley: University of California Press, 2019), 158.

32. Bruce McPherson, *Measure by Measure: A History of New England Conservatory from 1867* (Boston: The Trustees of the New England Conservatory of Music, 1995), 137.

33. Ibid., 119.

34. David Levering Lewis, *W. E. B. Du Bois: Biography of a Race, 1868–1919* (New York: Holt Books, 1994), 105–6.

35. McPherson, *Measure by Measure*, 119.

36. When interviewed about which music institutions were most likely to accept Black students, Still replied immediately, "Oberlin." See McPherson, *Measure by Measure*, 119. Cook said the same thing in his unpublished memoir: "The place for a Negro to study was Oberlin." See Marva Carter, "The Life and Career of Will Marion Cook" (PhD diss., University of Illinois, 1988), 401.

37. Ronald M. Baumann, *Constructing Black Education at Oberlin College: A Documentary History* (Athens: University of Ohio Press, 2010), 6.

38. Ibid., 7.

39. Oberlin Conservatory of Music Course Catalogs, 1908, 1913, 1916, and 1929, Oberlin College Archives, Conservatory of Music Records, 1841–present, RG/10.

40. Oberlin Conservatory of Music Course Catalog, 1901, Oberlin College Archives, Conservatory of Music Records, 1841–present, RG/10.

41. Oberlin Conservatory of Music Course Catalogs, 1908, 1913, 1916, and 1929, Oberlin College Archives, Conservatory of Music Records, 1841–present, RG/10.

42. Baumann, *Constructing Black Education*, 6.

43. Oberlin Conservatory of Music Course Catalog, 1908. Oberlin College Archives, Conservatory of Music Records, 1841—present, RG/10.

44. Oberlin Conservatory of Music Course Catalog, 1916; William Terry, "The Consummate Collaborator: Conversation with William Duncan Allen," *Black Perspective in Music* 15, no. 2 (Autumn 1987): 182–218; Oberlin Conservatory of Music Course Catalog, 1928.

45. Oberlin College Archives, Alumni Development Records, Edith Baker file.

46. Baumann, *Constructing Black Education*, 73.

47. Spelman Course Catalog 1890–91, Spelman College Archives.

48. Oberlin College Archives, Alumni Development Records, Edith Baker file. Emphasis added. An expert in music theory, Baker also became a delegate of the interracial Youth Movement Conference on the Problems of Colonialism that took place at the castle of Freusburg, Germany. "A week of plain living and high thinking in a miniature of this world of many peoples and tongues!" she writes. "We wished that the world from which we had come could have been like that one at Freusburg."

49. Fisk University Course Catalog 1915–16, 47, Fisk University Special Collections and Archive.

50. Joe M. Richardson, *A History of Fisk University, 1865–1946* (Tuscaloosa: University of Alabama Press, 1980), 152.

51. Fisk University Course Catalog 1925–26, 79, Fisk University Special Collections and Archive.

52. *Fisk Herald* 1, no. 1 (1883): 1; *Fisk Herald*, January 1884: 6.

53. Lewis, *W. E. B. Du Bois*, 74.

54. W. E. B. Du Bois, "Editorial," *Fisk Herald*, April 1888. Located in Herbert Aptheker, *Annotated Bibliography of the Published Writings of W. E. B. Du Bois* (Milwood: Kraus-Thompson Organization, 1973), 8. Quoted in Lewis, *W. E. B. Du Bois*, 74. Lewis mistakenly writes that the article is on page 8 of Aptheker rather than page 7.

55. Fisk University Course Catalogs, 1896–1945, Fisk University Special Collections and Archive.

56. Connecticut Historical Society, Raymond Augustus Lawson Papers, box 2, folder 16.

57. *Scroll* (March 1902): 63.

58. Raymond Augustus Lawson, "Real Joys from the Land of Art," *Fisk Herald*, May 1915.

59. "The Value of Fisk's Music Recitals," *Fisk Herald*, May 1915, 34.

60. "The Artistic Genius of the Afro-Americans," *Scroll* (November 1899): 10.

61. Grove Music Online, s.v. "Ragtime," by Edward A. Berlin, accessed on February 12, 2018. https://www.oxfordmusiconline.com/grovemusic/view/10.1093/gmo/9781561592630.001.0001/omo-9781561592630-e-1002252241

62. *Negro Music Journal* 1, no. 7 (March 1903): 138.

63. "From Bell Stand," 74.

64. Ibid., 75.

65. Jean E. Cazort, *Born to Play: The Life and Career of Hazel Harrison* (Westport, CT: Greenwood Press, 1983), 5.

66. Ibid., 7.

67. Ibid., 8.

68. Undated letter of Raymond Augustus Lawson, Connecticut Historical Society, Raymond Augustus Lawson Collection, box 2, folder 16.

2. African American Intellectual and Musical Migration to the Kaiserreich

1. Carter, "Life and Career," 413.

2. Marva Carter, *Swing Along: The Musical Life of Will Marion Cook* (Oxford: Oxford University Press, 2008), 16–17.

3. Carter, "Life and Career," 413.

4. Nadia Ellis, *Territories of the Soul: Queered Belonging in the Black Diaspora* (Durham, NC: Duke University Press, 2015), 6.

5. Radcliffe, Scott, and Werner, eds., *Anywhere But Here*, 8.

6. Kelley, *Freedom Dreams*, 17.

7. Brent Hayes Edwards, *The Practice of Diaspora: Literature, Translation, and the Rise of Black Internationalism* (Cambridge: Harvard University Press, 2003), 4.

8. Corey D. B. Walker, "'Of the Coming of John [and Jane]': African American Intellectuals in Europe, 1888–1938," *Amerikastudien / American Studies* 47, no.1 (2002): 9.

9. Ethel Newcomb, *Leschetizky as I Knew Him* (New York: Appleton Company, 1921), 243.

10. Gienow-Hecht, *Sound Diplomacy*, 55.

11. Ibid. See also Anja Werner, *The Transatlantic World of Higher Education: Americans at German Universities, 1776–1914* (New York: Berghahn, 2013).

12. *Crisis* 4, no. 2 (June 1912): 68.

13. "James C. Thomas to Tour Europe," *Colored American Magazine* 9, no. 2 (August 1905): 457–58.

14. Schülerverzeichnis, Leota Henson (3923), December 10, 1866. University of Music and Theater "Felix Mendelssohn Bartholdy" (HMT) Leipzig Archives, A.I. 2. Nora Holt, "Musicians Here and There," *New York Amsterdam News*, July 5, 1947, 4.

15. *Colored American Magazine* 6, no. 7 (July 1903): 523.

16. *Freeman*, May 2, 1896. Quoted in Abbot and Seroff, eds., *Out of Sight*, 100.

17. Ronald High, "Three African-American Tenors of the Nineteenth Century: Thomas J. Bowers, Wallace King, Sidney Woodward," *Journal of Singing—The Official Journal of the National Association of Teachers of Singing* 54, no. 5, (May 1998): 20. See also Lindsay Patterson, *The Negro in Music and Art* (New York: Publishers Co., 1967), 184.

18. "From Bell Stand," 78.

19. Roy L. Hill, *Booker T.'s Child: The Life and Times of Portia Marshall Washington Pittman* (Washington, DC: Three Continents Press, 1993), 44; Ruth Ann Stewart, *Portia: The Life of Portia Washington Pittman, the Daughter of Booker T. Washington* (Garden City: Doubleday, 1977), 66. For more on the story of German colonialism and Booker T. Washington, see Andrew Zimmerman, *Alabama in Africa: Booker T. Washington, the German Empire, and the Globalization of the New South* (Princeton, NJ: Princeton University Press, 2010).

20. *Washington Post*, February 27, 1978.

21. Connecticut Historical Society, Raymond Augustus Lawson Papers, box 1, folder 10.

22. Years later, when Gabrilowitsch visited the United States and toured in 1917, he invited Lawson to attend one of his concerts in New York City and provided him with two spare tickets. See: Connecticut Historical Society, Raymond Augustus Lawson Papers, box 1, folder 10, The Stratford Hotel, May 3, 1917.

23. Music department of the Berlin State Library (SBB-PK) Historical Research Library Unter den Linden: MUS LS Tbu 7027. The original letter is in English.

24. Carter, *Swing Along*, 17.

25. Ibid., 18.

26. Stewart, *Portia*, 62. Hill, *Booker T.'s Child*, 45.

27. *New York Times*, October 12, 1905. Washington later recalled meeting the German Crown Prince while out on the town. After discovering that she was an American piano student studying music in Berlin, he asked her to play some music for him and applauded her performance of African American spirituals in equal measure to her performances of classical music. Stewart, *Portia*, 65.

28. Carter, "Life and Career," 419.

29. *Chicago Defender*, "Carl R. Diton Coming May 28," May 15, 1915, 6.

30. Gerald L. Smith, Karen Cotton McDaniel, and John A. Hardin, eds., *The Kentucky African American Encyclopedia* (Lexington: University of Kentucky Press, 2015), 320.

31. Mary Church Terrell, *A Colored Woman in a White World* (New York: Humanity Books, 2005), 104, 106.

32. Ibid., 109.

33. W. E. B. Du Bois, *The Autobiography of W. E. B. Du Bois: A Soliloquy on Viewing My Life from the Last Decade of Its First Century* (New York: International Publishers, 1968), 159.

34. Terrell, *Colored Woman*, 107.

35. "Jahresbericht der Hochschule für Musik, 1888–89," 9–10, Berlin University of the Arts (UdK) Archives.

36. University of Music and Theater "Felix Mendelssohn Bartholdy" (HMT) Leipzig Archives. Document provided by Joshua Navon.

37. Jeffrey Stewart, *The New Negro: The Life of Alain Locke* (Oxford: Oxford University Press, 2018), 256.

38. Hill, *Booker T.'s Child*, 47.

39. Stewart, *Portia*, 71.

40. Terrell, *Colored Woman*, 110.

41. Carter, "Life and Career," 420–21, 414.

42. Du Bois, *Autobiography*, 157.

43. Kwame Anthony Appiah, *Lines of Descent: W. E. B. DuBois and the Emergence of Identity* (Cambridge: Harvard University Press, 2014), 43.

44. See Michael Largey, *Voudou Nation: Haitian Art Music and Cultural Nationalism* (Chicago: University of Chicago Press, 2006).

45. See Robert Fikes, Jr., and Douglas A. Cargille, "The Bittersweet Career of José Manuel Jiménez, the 'Ebony Liszt,'" *Afro-Hispanic Review* 7, nos. 1–3 (1988), 23–26. In 1902, Lico had a daughter, Andrea Jiménez-Berroa, who later had a son she named José Manuel. She was first married to Alexander Douala Manga Bell, from the German colony of Cameroon. In August 1929 she met and fell in love with Joseph Roth and fled with him to France in 1933 when the Nazis came to power. See Aitken and Rosenhaft, *Black Germany*, 114–15. See also David Bronsen, *Joseph Roth: Eine Biographie* (Cologne: Kiepenheuer & Witsch, 1974).

46. Lewis, *W. E. B. Du Bois*, 148.

47. Cazort, *Born to Play*, 35. Harreld and his wife were expecting Josephine. They intended to stay in Germany and raise their daughter bilingually, but the war scratched those plans. Undated journal entry, Josephine Harreld Love Collection, Spelman College Archives, group 1, box 13.

48. Carter, "Life and Career," 408.

49. Douglas Hales, *A Southern Family in Black and White: The Cuneys of Texas* (College Station: Texas A&M Press, 2002), 12.

50. Terrell, *Colored Woman*, 112.

51. Ella Sheppard, Diary of Ella Sheppard, transcr. Andrew Ward, Fisk University Franklin Library Special Collections, November 23, 1877, 17–18.

52. Appiah, *Lines of Descent*, 41.

53. Clarence Cameron White, "The Negro in Musical Europe," in *New York Age*, December 24, 1908, 13.

54. Ibid.

55. Jacqueline Brown, "Black Liverpool, Black America, and the Gendering of Diasporic Space," *Cultural Anthropology* 13 (1998): 291-325; Edwards, *Practice of Diaspora*.

56. Tina Campt, *Other Germans: Black Germans and the Politics of Race, Gender, and Memory in the Third Reich* (Ann Arbor: University of Michigan Press, 2004), 178.

57. Maria Diedrich, "Black 'Others'?: African Americans and Black Germans in the Third Reich," in *Remapping Black Germany: New Perspectives on Afro-German History, Politics, and Culture*, ed. Sara Lennox (Amherst: University of Massachusetts Press, 2017), 142.

3. The Sonic Color Line Belts the World

1. Schüler Verzeichnis, University of Music and Theater "Felix Mendelssohn Bartholdy" (HMT) Leipzig Archives, A.I.2.

2. Ibid. He landed in Bremerhaven on Friday, July 21, 1854.

3. See Daphne Brooks, *Bodies in Dissent: Spectacular Performances of Race and Freedom, 1850-1910* (Durham, NC: Duke University Press, 2006); Harry J. Elam, Jr., and Kennell Jackson, eds., *Black Cultural Traffic: Crossroads in Global Performance and Popular Culture* (Ann Arbor: University of Michigan Press, 2005); Bernth Lindfors, *Early African Entertainments Abroad: From the Hottentot Venus to Africa's First Olympians* (Madison: University of Wisconsin Press, 2014); and Rainer Lotz, *Black People: Entertainers of African Descent in Europe and Germany* (Bonn: Birgit Lotz, 1997).

4. Catherine Hall, *Civilizing Subjects: The Metropole and the Colony* (Oxford: Polity, 2002), 440.

5. See Michael Perraudin and Jürgen Zimmerer, eds., *German Colonialism and National Identity* (New York: Routledge, 2011).

6. Sara Friedrichsmeyer, Sara Lennox, and Suzanne Zantop, eds., *The Imperialist Imagination: German Colonialism and Its Legacy* (Ann Arbor: University of Michigan, 1998), 23. See also Lora Wildenthal, *German Women for Empire, 1884-1945* (Durham: Duke University Press, 2001).

7. "Richard Wagners sechzigster Geburtstag," *Neue Zeitschrift für Musik*, June 20, 1873, 273. The Jiménez Trio performed at Wagner's birthday party. Likewise, Nicasio performed at Villa Wahnfried. Later, Luranah Aldridge was a guest at the Wagner family home while she prepared to sing as a Valkyrie in Bayreuth.

8. See Ulrich van der Heyden, *Unbekannte Biographien: Afrikaner im deutschsprachigen Raum vom 18. Jahrhundert bis zum Ende des Zweiten Weltkrieges* (Berlin: Homilius, 2008).

9. Stoever, *Sonic Color Line*, 80.

10. Sheppard, Diary, 9.

11. MacMaster, *Racism in Europe*, 85.

12. Mischa Honeck, Martin Klimke, and Anne Kuhlmann, "Introduction," in *Germany and the Black Diaspora: Points of Contact, 1250-1914* (New York: Berghahn, 2013), 3.

13. Jeff Bowersox, *Raising Germans in the Age of Empire: Youth and Colonial Culture, 1871-1914* (Oxford: Oxford University Press, 2013), 34.

14. David Ciarlo, *Advertising Empire: Race and Visual Culture in Imperial Germany* (Cambridge: Harvard University Press, 2011), 225.

15. Kira Thurman, "Singing the Civilizing Mission," *Journal of World History* 27, no. 3 (2016): 443–71.

16. Sieglinde Lemke, *Primitivist Modernism: Black Culture and the Origins of Transatlantic Modernism* (Oxford: Oxford University Press, 1998), 4.

17. Kira Thurman, "'Africa in European Evening Attire': Defining African American Spirituals and Western Art Music in Central Europe, 1870s–1930s," in *Rethinking Black German Studies: Approaches, Interventions, and Histories*, eds. Tiffany N. Florvil and Vanessa Plumly (New York: Peter Lang, 2018), 199–234.

18. Andrew Zimmerman, *Anthropology and Anti-Humanism in Imperial Germany* (Chicago: University of Chicago Press, 2001), 3.

19. Jonathan Wipplinger, "The Racial Ruse: On Blackness and Blackface Comedy in *fin-de-siècle* Germany," *German Quarterly* 84, no. 3 (Fall 2011): 471.

20. See James Deaville, "African American Entertainers in *Jahrhundertwende* Vienna: Austrian Identity, Viennese Modernism, and Black Success," *Nineteenth-Century Music Review* 3, no. 1 (June 2006): 89–112; Lotz, *Black People*; and Astrid Kusser, *Körper in Schieflage: Tanzen im Strudel des Black Atlantic um 1900* (Bielefeld: Transcript, 2013).

21. Eric Ames, *Carl Hagenbeck's Empire of Entertainments* (Seattle: University of Washington Press, 2008).

22. *"Der beste Neger-Komik der Welt"* poster, Columbia College Chicago, Center for Black Music Research, box 29.

23. Ella Sheppard, "Historical Sketch of the Jubilee Singers," *Fisk University News*, October 1911. Quoted in Andrew Ward, *Dark Midnight When I Rise: The Story of the Jubilee Singers Who Introduced the World to the Music of Black America* (New York: Farrar, Straus, and Giroux, 2000), 349.

24. T. J. Tallie, "Sartorial Settlement: The Mission Field and Transformation in Colonial Natal, 1850–1897," *Journal of World History* 27, no. 3 (2016): 389–410.

25. "Die Jubiläumssänger," *Neue Berliner Musikzeitung*, November 15, 1877, 362.

26. *Die Post*, November 11, 1877, 3.

27. *Christian Recorder*, January 3, 1878.

28. Unidentified German newspaper, trans. Frazelia Campbell, rep. in *Christian Recorder*, January 17, 1878. Campbell was a student at Philadelphia's Institute for Colored Youth.

29. *Christian Recorder*, January 3, 1878.

30. Unidentified Berlin newspaper, trans. and rep. in *Christian Recorder*, January 17, 1878. Sentiments such as these reflect Ronald Radano's argument that white listeners "cast Black music as a primordial cure for the ills of a civilized and increasingly mechanized modern society." Radano, "Hot Fantasies: American Modernism and the Idea of Black Rhythm," in *Music and the Racial Imagination*, ed. Radano and Philip V. Bohlman (Chicago: University of Chicago Press, 2000), 460.

31. *Neue Berliner Musikzeitung*, November 15, 1877, 362.

32. Jonathan Bellman, *The Style Hongrois in the Music of Western Europe* (Boston: Northeastern University Press, 1993).

33. *Musikalisches Wochenblatt*, September 24, 1885, 489.

34. Quoted in Nettles, *African American Concert Singers*, 153.

35. *Neue Zeitschrift für Musik*, no. 20, May 20, 1891, 283.

36. Abbot and Seroff, eds., *Out of Sight*, 146.

37. Maureen D. Lee, *Sissieretta Jones: The "Greatest Singer of Her Race,"* 1868–1933 (Columbia: University of South Carolina Press, 2012), 87.

38. Josephine Wright, "Black Women and Classical Music," *Women's Studies Quarterly* 12, no. 3 (Fall 1984): 18–21; Eileen Southern, "In Retrospect: Black Prima Donnas of the Nineteenth Century," *The Black Perspective of Music* 7, no. 1 (Spring 1979): 95–106; Sonya Gable-Wilson, "Let Freedom Sing! Four African American Concert Singers in Nineteenth-Century America" (PhD diss., University of Florida, 2005).

39. An 1894 *Chicago Daily Tribune* article claimed Marie Selika went to Europe in 1888, but we know she was definitely in Germany in 1891. In the early 1880s, she traveled to Europe to perform, and she visited Germany, Austria, Denmark, Sweden, Belgium, England, Russia, and Scotland between 1882 and 1886.

40. *Chicago Daily Tribune*, January 21, 1894.

41. Quoted in Minnie Brown, "Among Noted Negro Musicians: Madame Selika," *New York Amsterdam News*, August 23, 1927. See also Maud Cuney Hare, *Negro Musicians and Their Music* (Washington, DC: The Associated Publishers, 1936), 223.

42. *Schweinfurter Anzeiger*, February 26, 1884. Quoted in Pauline Hopkins, "Famous Women of the Negro Race," *Colored American Magazine* II, no. 2 (December 1900): 52.

43. *Dresdner Nachrichten*, date unknown. Quoted in Hopkins, "Famous Women," 52.

44. Quoted in Nora Holt, "Scotching the Myth that Negro Singers Are Unqualified for Opera or Top Concerts," *New York Amsterdam News*, May 31, 1952.

45. Ibid.

46. Willia Daughtry, "Sissieretta Jones: A Study of the Negro's Contribution to Nineteenth-Century American Concert and Theatrical Life" (PhD diss., Syracuse University, 1968), 198.

47. *Detroit Plaindealer*, December 30, 1892. Quoted in Abbot and Seroff, eds., *Out of Sight*, 290.

48. *Berliner Lokal-Anzeiger*, February 16, 1895, 3; *Nationalzeitung*, February 17, 1895, 9.

49. *Beilage des Berliner Börsen-Couriers*, no. 79, February 16, 1895, 1.

50. Ibid.

51. *Berliner Intelligenzblatt-Berliner Anzeiger*, February 21, 1895, 2.

52. *Berliner Börsen-Courier*, February 17, 1895.

53. Ibid.

54. Nina Sun Eidsheim, "Marian Anderson and 'Sonic Blackness' in American Opera," in *American Quarterly* 63, no. 3 (2011): 644.

55. *Berliner Morgen-Zeitung und Tägliches Familienblatt*, February 20, 1895, 3.

56. Southern, "In Retrospect," 100.

57. See Jon Cruz, *Culture on the Margins: The Black Spiritual and the Rise of American Cultural Interpretation* (Princeton, NJ: Princeton University Press, 1999); Schenbeck, *Racial Uplift*.

58. *Das Kleine Journal* (date and page not listed). Quoted in Southern, "In Retrospect," 102.

59. *Die Post* (date and page not listed). Quoted in Southern, "In Retrospect," 101.

60. Ibid.

61. *Berliner Börsen-Courier* (date and page not listed). Quoted in Southern, "In Retrospect," 101.

62. Nana Badenberg, "Mohrenwäschen, Völkerschauen: Der Konsum des Schwarzen um 1900," in *Colors 1800/1900/2000: Signs of Ethnic Difference*, ed. Birgit Tautz, (New York: Brill, 2004), 164.

63. *Die Post* (date and page not listed). Quoted in Southern, "In Retrospect," 101.

64. *Berliner Börsen-Courier* (date and page not listed). Quoted in Southern, "In Retrospect," 101.

65. For a recent scholarly work discussing European evaluations of skull size as a method of racial science and anthropology, see Fenneke Sysling, *Racial Science and Human Diversity in Colonial Indonesia* (Singapore: National University of Singapore Press, 2016).

66. Kristin Moriah, "On the Record: Sissieretta Jones and Black Performance Praxes," *Performance Matters* 6, no. 2 (2020): 32

67. *Berliner Fremdenblatt*, February 20, 1895, 5; *Berliner Morgen-Zeitung und Tägliches Familienblatt*, February 20, 1895, 3.

68. *Nationalzeitung*, February 17, 1895, 9.

69. *Beilage des Berliner Börsen-Couriers*, no. 79, February 16, 1895, 1.

70. Silke Hackenesch, *Chocolate and Blackness: A Cultural History* (Frankfurt: Campus Verlag, 2018), 48.

71. Trans. and rep. in *Indianapolis Freeman*, May 4, 1895. Quoted in Southern, "In Retrospect," 100.

72. *Das Kleine Journal* (date and page not listed). Quoted in Southern, "In Retrospect," 102.

73. *Minneapolis Journal*, January 14, 1897.

74. Max Paddison, "Music as Ideal: The Aesthetics of Autonomy," *Cambridge Companion to Nineteenth-Century Music*, ed. Jim Samson (Cambridge: Cambridge University Press, 2001), 318–42.

75. Of course, Elizabeth Taylor Greenfield had been in Europe—but not in Central Europe—to perform in 1852. See Julia Chybowski, "Becoming the 'Black Swan' in Mid-Nineteenth-Century America: Elizabeth Taylor Greenfield's Early Life and Debut Concert Tour," *Journal of the American Musicological Society* 67, no. 1 (Spring 2014): 125–65.

76. Fikes, Jr., and Cargille, "Bittersweet Career." Faculty also reviewed their exams. Schüler Verzeichnis, University of Music and Theater "Felix Mendelssohn Bartholdy" (HMT) Leipzig Archives, A.I.2.

77. *Neue Zeitschrift für Musik*, May 27, 1870, 211.

78. Later reviews of Nicasio's student recitals brought similar praise: his "sonorous tone, sensitive handling of the Cantilene [sic], and brilliant technique brought the highest honors to his teacher Hegar [sic]." *Neue Zeitschrift für Musik*, May 12, 1871, 191.

79. See Fikes, Jr., and Cargille, "Bittersweet Career"; Daniel Jütte, "Schwarze, Juden und die Anfänge des Diskurses über Rasse und Musik im 19. Jahrhundert. Überlegungen anhand von Claudio José Domingo Brindis de Salas' Reise durch Württemberg und Baden im Jahre 1882," *Archiv für Kulturgeschichte* 88 (2006), 117–40.

80. *Neue Zeitschrift für Musik*, November 5, 1875, 447.

81. *Musikalisches Wochenblatt*, March 28, 1873.

82. This rationality that one can be educated out of one's ignorant and primitive state into a more cultivated one follows the lines of sociological racism, a concept which Zimmerman discusses at length in *Alabama in Africa*, 66–100.

83. *Musikalisches Wochenblatt*, January 20, 1871.

84. Jean Schutt, *Neue Zeitschrift für Musik*, October 13, 1871. Quoted in Josephine Wright, "'Das Negertrio' Jiménez in Europe," *Black Perspective in Music* 9, no. 2 (Autumn 1981): 165.

85. *Musikalisches Wochenblatt*, March 13, 1874, 138.

86. Ibid.

87. Fatima El-Tayeb, "'We Are Germans, We Are Whites, and We Want to Stay White!' African Germans and Citizenship in the Early 20th Century," in *Colors 1800/1900/2000*, 192.

88. *Musikalisches Wochenblatt*, June 3, 1870, 362.

89. Jütte, "Schwarze."

90. *Neue Zeitschrift für Musik*, September 14, 1882, 405.

91. Ibid.

92. Ovide Musin, *My Memories* (New York: Musin Publishing Company, 1920), 65.

93. See Mark Rowe, *Heinrich Wilhelm Ernst: Virtuoso Violinist* (Burlington: Ashgate, 2008).

94. "Music in Darmstadt," *Musical Times*, April 1885, 220.

95. On virtuosity in nineteenth-century German musical culture, see Alexander Stefaniak, *Schumann's Virtuosity: Criticism, Composition, and Performance in Nineteenth-Century Germany* (Bloomington: Indiana University Press, 2016).

96. *Allgemeine Musikalische Zeitung*, December 6, 1882, 780.

97. Ibid.

98. *Musikalisches Wochenblatt*, February 8, 1883, 83.

99. *Musikalisches Wochenblatt*, September 13, 1883, 466.

100. Jütte, "Schwarze," 123. My translation.

101. *Musikalisches Wochenblatt*, February 8, 1883, 83.

102. *Stuttgarter Neues Tagblatt*, October 20, 1882, 4. Quoted in Jütte, "Schwarze," 119.

103. *Freiburger Zeitung*, November 12, 1882; *Stuttgarter Neues Tagblatt*, October 20, 1882, 4, quoted in Jütte, "Schwarze," 119.

104. *Ulmer Tagblatt*, October 31, 1882, 1438. Quoted in Jütte, "Schwarze," 127.

105. *Stuttgarter Neues Tagblatt*, October 20, 1882, 4. Quoted in Jütte, "Schwarze," 119.

106. "Allerlei," *Deutsche Militärmusiker-Zeitung*, March 13, 1908, 129. The original letter slandering Gustav Chabac el Cher appeared in the *Deutsche Zeitung* on October 18, 1907.

107. Musin, *My Memories*, 65.

108. *Stuttgarter Neues Tagblatt*, October 20, 1882, 4. Quoted in Jütte, "Schwarze," 119.

109. *LaPorte Daily Herald*, May 24, 1904.

110. Katherine Ellis, "Female Pianists and Their Male Critics in Nineteenth-Century Paris," *Journal of the American Musicological Society* 50, no. 2/3 (Summer-Autumn 1997): 361.

111. Alexander Stefaniak, "Clara Schumann and the Imagined Revelation of Musical Works," *Music and Letters* 99, no. 2 (2018), 205.

112. *Berliner Tageblatt*, October 26, 1904, 2.

113. Anonymous Berlin review (trans. anonymous), October 23, 1904, Howard University, Moorland-Spingarn Research Center, box 139–2.

114. *Berliner Tageblatt*, October 26, 1904, 2.

115. Walther Pauli, "Hazel Harrison," *Allgemeine Deutsche Musik-Zeitung*, October 28, 1904, 718.

116. Anonymous Berlin review (trans. anonymous), October 23, 1904, Howard University, Moorland-Spingarn Research Center, box 139–2.

117. Ibid.

118. Ibid.

119. Michelle Wright, *Becoming Black: Creating Identity in the African Diaspora* (Durham, NC: Duke University Press, 2008), 8.

120. Ibid.

121. Krista Molly O'Donnell, "The First Besatzungskinder: Afro-German Children, Colonial Childrearing Practices, and Racial Policy in German South West Africa, 1890–1914" in *Not So Plain as Black and White: Afro-German Culture and History, 1890–2000*, ed. Patricia Mazón and Reinhild Steingröver (Rochester, NY: University of Rochester Press, 2005), 62.

122. El-Tayeb, "'We Are Germans,'" 192.

123. Eduard von Liebert, "Speech," in Verhandlungen des Deutschen Reichstags, Protokolle 1907/1909, 2225, Sitzung March 16, 1909: 7509–14. Quoted in Martin Rempe, "Cultural Brokers in Uniform: The Global Rise of Military Musicians and Their Music," *Itinerario* 41, no. 2 (2017): 327–52.

124. Ibid. Rempe's translation.

125. Ibid. Rempe's translation.

126. Ibid. My translation.

127. "Allerlei," *Deutsche Militärmusiker-Zeitung*, March 13, 1908, 129.

128. Even contemporary writings on Sabac el Cher do not recognize him as German, as headlines such as DIE ZEIT's "The Moor from Berlin" ["Der Mohr von Berlin"] (2007), *Die Welt*'s "How an African Came to Wear a Prussian Uniform" ["Wie ein Afrikaner zu einem Preußischem Uniform kam"] (2007), or the *Tagesspiegel*'s "Gustav Sabac el Cher, an African in Berlin" ["Gustav Sabac el Cher, ein Afrikaner in Berlin"] (2015) indicate.

129. Nicholas Cook, "Seeing Sounds, Hearing Images: Listening Outside the Modernist Box," *Musical Listening in the Age of Technological Reproduction*, ed. Gianmario Borio (New York: Routledge, 2015), 186.

4. Blackness and Classical Music in the Age of the Black Horror on the Rhine Campaign

1. For information on the "Black Horror on the Rhine" propaganda campaign, see Iris Wigger, *The "Black Horror on the Rhine": Intersections of Race, Nation, Gender, and Class in 1920s Germany* (London: Palgrave Macmillan, 2017).

2. Christopher A. Brooks and Robert Sims, *Roland Hayes: The Legacy of an American Tenor* (Bloomington: Indiana University Press, 2015), 120–21.

3. Moritz Föllmer, "Which Crisis? Which Modernity? New Perspectives on Weimar Germany," in *Beyond Glitter and Doom: The Contingency of the Weimar Republic*, eds. Jochen Hung, Godela Weiss-Sussex, and Geoff Wilkes (Munich: Ludicum, 2012), 27.

4. Peter Fritzsche, "Did Weimar Fail?" *Journal of Modern History* 68, no. 3 (1996): 633. The picture of Weimar Germany as existing on a fine line between renewal and

collapse has been an especially dominant theme in scholarship since Friedrich Meinecke first called the Weimar Republic an emergency construction (*Notbau*) in 1947. As the title of Stephen Brockmann and Thomas Kniesche's book, *Dancing on the Volcano*, suggests, historians often describe Weimar Germany as a society teetering on the edge of joy and despair, of economic ruin or social triumph. See Stephen Brockmann and Thomas W. Kniesche, *Dancing on the Volcano: Essays on the Culture of the Weimar Republic* (Columbia, SC: Camden House, 1994).

5. Kathleen Canning, Kerstin Barndt, and Kristin McGuire, eds., *Weimar Publics / Weimar Subjects: Rethinking The Political Culture of Germany in the 1920s* (New York: Berghahn, 2010).

6. Karl Christian Führer, "German Cultural Life and the Crisis of National Identity During the Depression, 1929–33," *German Studies Review* 24, no. 3 (2001): 468. For example, the *Neues Wiener Journal* reported on November 21, 1935, that Anderson's upcoming performance that same evening was already sold out, leaving only one opportunity to see her perform. "Heute Marian Anderson Ausverkauft," *Neues Wiener Journal*, November 21, 1935, 11.

7. Much of historians' formulation of Weimar Germany as a site of avant-garde modernism came from Peter Gay, *Weimar Culture: The Outsider as Insider* (New York: Harper and Row, 1968); and Detlev Peukert, *The Weimar Republic: The Crisis of Classical Modernity*, trans. Richard Deveson (New York: Hill and Wang, 1992). Since then, historians have challenged this perception of Weimar Germany. Similarly, scholarship on Austria in the interwar era has also reevaluated the relationship between culture and politics. See Judith Beniston and Robert Vilain, eds., *Culture and Politics in Red Vienna* (Leeds: Maney, 2006).

8. Karl Christian Führer, "High-Brow and Low-Brow Culture," in *Weimar Germany*, ed. Anthony McElligott (Oxford: Oxford University Press, 2009), 260. See also Brendan Fay, *Classical Music in Weimar Germany: Culture and Politics before the Third Reich* (New York: Bloomsbury Press, 2019).

9. Alex Ross, *The Rest Is Noise: Listening to the Twentieth Century* (New York: Picador, 2007), 346.

10. Jochen Hung, "'Bad' Politics and 'Good' Culture: New Approaches to the History of the Weimar Republic," *Central European History* 49, no. 3–4 (2016): 451.

11. Fritz Trümpi, *The Political Orchestra: The Vienna and Berlin Philharmonics During the Third Reich*, trans. Kenneth Kronenberg (Chicago: University of Chicago Press, 2016).

12. Elizabeth Harvey, "Culture and Society in Weimar Germany: The Impact of Modernism and Mass Culture," in *German History since 1800*, ed. Mary Fulbrook, (London: Arnold, 1997), 279–97.

13. Ivan Goll, "The Negroes Are Conquering Europe," in *The Weimar Republic Sourcebook*, eds. Anthony Kaes, Martin Jay, and Edward Dimendberg (Berkeley: University of California Press, 1994), 559–60.

14. Moritz Ege and Andrew Wright Hurley, "Periodizing and Historicizing German Afro-Americanophilia: From Antebellum to Postwar (1850–1967)," *Portal: Journal of Multidisciplinary International Studies* 12, no. 2 (2015): 12.

15. Christine Naumann, "African American Performers and Culture in Weimar Germany," *Crosscurrents: African Americans, Africa, and Germany in the Modern World*, eds. David McBride, Leroy Hopkins, and Carol Aisha Blackshire-Belay (Columbia, SC: Camden House, 1998), 96. I have been unable to locate a figure for Austria.

16. Jonathan Wipplinger, *The Jazz Republic: Music, Race, and American Culture in Weimar Germany* (Ann Arbor: University of Michigan Press, 2017), 34.

17. Julia Roos, "Women's Rights, National Anxiety, and the 'Moral' Agenda in the Early Weimar Republic," *Central European History* 42, no. 3 (September 2009): 473–508; Raffael Scheck, *Hitler's African Victims: The German Army Massacres of Black French Soldiers in 1940* (Cambridge: Cambridge University Press, 2006).

18. Christian Koller, "Enemy Images: Race and Gender Stereotypes in the Discussion on Colonial Troops: A Franco-German Comparison, 1914–23," in *Home/Front: The Military, War, and Gender in Twentieth-Century Germany*, eds. Karen Hagemann and Stefanie Schüler-Springorum (Oxford: Berg, 2002), 139–57; Campt, *Other Germans*, 31–62.

19. Fatima El-Tayeb, "'Blood Is a Very Special Juice': Racialized Bodies and Citizenship in Twentieth-Century Germany," *International Review of Social History* 44, no. S7 (1999): 149–69.

20. Tina Campt, "Converging Spectres of an Other Within: Race and Gender in Prewar Afro-German History," *Callaloo* 26, no. 2 (2003): 338.

21. Ibid., 323.

22. *Grenzland Korrespondent*, April 24, 1922. Translated and cited in Tina Campt, Pascal Grosse, and Yara-Colette Lemke-Muniz de Faria, "Blacks, Germans, and the Politics of Imperial Imagination, 1920–1960," in *The Imperialist Imagination: German Colonialism and Its Legacy*, eds. Sara Lennox, Sara Friedrichsmeyer, and Susanne Zantop (Ann Arbor: University of Michigan Press, 1998), 211.

23. Wigger, *"Black Horror,"* 9.

24. Paul Bang, *Die farbige Gefahr* (Göttingen: Vanderhoeck & Ruprecht, 1938).

25. Julia Roos, "Nationalism, Racism and Propaganda in Early Weimar Germany: Contradictions in the Campaign against the 'Black Horror on the Rhine,'" *German History* 30, no. 1, (March 2012): 45–74.

26. Goll, "Negroes."

27. Jonathan Wipplinger, "Performing Race in Ernst Krenek's *Jonny spielt auf*," in *Blackness in Opera*, ed. Naomi André, Karen Bryan, and Eric Saylor (Champaign: University of Illinois Press, 2012), 237.

28. Alan Lareau, "Jonny's Jazz: From Kabarett to Krenek," in *Jazz and the Germans: Essays on the Influence of "Hot" Americans Idioms on 20th-Century German Music*, ed. Michael Budds (Hillsdale, NY: Pendragon Press, 2002), 28.

29. See Sander Gilman, *Difference and Pathology: Stereotypes of Sexuality, Race, and Madness* (Ithaca, NY: Cornell University Press, 1985), 37–128.

30. Edward Timms and Karl Kraus, *Apocalyptic Satirist: Culture and Catastrophe in Habsburg Vienna* (New Haven: Yale University Press, 1986).

31. The now iconic image of a Black jazz saxophonist with the Jewish Star of David on his lapel first appeared on the title page of the exhibition guide for the "Degenerate Music" exhibit sponsored by the Reich Music Examination Office and the Reich Propaganda Ministry. The exhibit opened in Düsseldorf on May 24, 1938.

32. Nancy Nenno, "Femininity, the Primitive, and Modern Urban Space: Josephine Baker in Berlin," in *Women in the Metropolis: Gender and Modernity in Weimar Culture*, ed. Katharina von Ankum (Berkeley: University of California Press, 1997), 146.

33. Wipplinger, *Jazz Republic*, 125.

34. Nenno, "Femininity," 155.

35. Samir Dayal, "Blackness as Symptom: Josephine Baker and European Identity," in *Blackening Europe: The African American Presence*, ed. Heike Raphael-Hernandez (New York: Routledge, 2004), 41; Nenno, "Femininity," 148.

36. Ottomar Starke, "Revue," *Der Querschnitt*, February 1926. Translated and quoted in Paul Edwards, "Louis Douglas and *Jonny spielt auf*: Performing Blackness in Interwar Germany," (PhD diss., Boston University, 2018), 204.

37. *Neues Wiener Tagblatt*, February 2, 1928, 7.

38. Bruce F. Pauley, *From Prejudice to Persecution: A History of Austrian Anti-Semitism* (Chapel Hill: University of North Carolina Press, 1992), 71, 82, 84–85, 182–83.

39. "'La Baker' in Vienna," *Atlanta Constitution*, March 17, 1928, 6.

40. See, for example, the news coverage in *Illustrierte Kronen-Zeitung*. The Catholic Church held a special mass to atone for the sins she had committed in the city.

41. "Für und gegen die Baker," *Illustrierte Kronen-Zeitung*, February 8, 1928, 10.

42. Lynn Haney, *Naked at the Feast: A Biography of Josephine Baker* (New York: Dodd, Mead, 1981), 149.

43. "Die schwarze Tänzerin," *Illustriertes Wiener Extrablatt*, March 1, 1928, 1.

44. "Patti Highly Praised," *Chicago Defender*, April 2, 1921, 5.

45. It is quite telling that Wilberforce's comments appear a few years after Ossian Sweet, an African American doctor who had studied in Vienna in the early 1920s, had tried to move into a white neighborhood in Detroit, causing a riot.

46. Dr. A. Wilberforce Williams, "Why Go to Europe?" *Chicago Defender*, April 14, 1928, 4.

47. Letter from Palace Hotel, Prague, April 10, 1924, Detroit Public Library, Roland Hayes Collection, series I, box I, folder 22.

48. Letter from Prague, May 5, 1924, Detroit Public Library, Roland Hayes Collection, series I, subsection B, box 10, file 58.

49. Lara Putnam, *Radical Moves* (Chapel Hill: University of North Carolina Press, 2013), 195.

50. Baldwin, *Beyond the Color Line*.

51. George Lipsitz, *Dangerous Crossroads: Popular Music, Postmodernism, and the Poetics of Place* (New York: Verso, 1994), 31.

52. Marc Matera, *Black London* (Berkeley: University of California Press, 2015), 203.

53. Robbie Aitken, "Surviving in the Metropole: The Struggle for Work and Belonging Amongst African Colonial Migrants in Weimar Germany," *Immigrants & Minorities* 28, no. 2–3 (2010): 203–23.

54. Ibid., 213.

55. Allan Keiler, *Marian Anderson: A Singer's Journey* (New York: Scribner, 2000), 94.

56. Letter from Dr. Eduard Coumont to Hayes, September 24, 1925, Detroit Public Library, Roland Hayes Collection, series 1, box 1, file 39.

57. Letter from Internationale Konzertdirektion "Symphonia" Wien, October 22, year unknown, Detroit Public Library, Roland Hayes Collection, series I, subsection B, box 10, folder 57.

58. Brooks and Sims, *Roland Hayes*, 130.

59. Roland Hayes, with F. W. Woolsey, "Roland Hayes," *The Black Perspective in Music* 2, no. 2 (Autumn 1974): 184.

60. Marian Anderson, *My Lord What a Morning: An Autobiography* (New York: Viking Press, 1956), 146.

61. "Paul Robeson, der Negerbaß," *Neues Wiener Journal*, April 11, 1929, 14.

62. Letter to Mr. Zid from London, England, March 29, 1924, Detroit Public Library, Roland Hayes Collection, series I, subsection B, box 10, file 58.

63. "Young Harpist to Study in Austria," *Pittsburgh Courier*, June 30, 1928, A2.

64. Tibbs had previously been married to Lillian Evanti, who performed in Germany and Austria in the 1920s and 1930s. "Prof. Tibbs Will Study in Vienna," *Pittsburgh Courier* (1911–50), City Edition, October 13, 1934, A6.

65. "In Retrospect: W. Rudolph Dunbar; Pioneering Orchestra," *Black Perspective in Music* 9, no. 2 (Autumn 1981): 193–225.

66. MacKinley Helm, *Angel Mo' and Her Son, Roland Hayes* (Boston: Little Brown and Co., 1942), 145.

67. *Musical Courier* 25, no. 1238 (December 16, 1903): 11.

68. William Armstrong, "Dr. Theodor Lierhammer on the German Lied," *Etude* 22, no. 6 (June 1904).

69. *Musical Courier* 25, no. 1238 (December 16, 1903): 11.

70. Roland Hayes, *My Favorite Spirituals: 30 Songs for Piano and Voice* (Mineola: Dover Publications, 2001), 12.

71. Letter to Hayes from Lierhammer, July 14, 1925, Detroit Public Library, Roland Hayes Collection, series I, box 1, file 37.

72. Howard Rye, "Southern Syncopated Orchestra: The Roster," *Black Music Research Journal* 29, no. 2 (Fall 2009): 28. See also Helm, *Angel Mo'*. See also "Aubrey Pankey, American Baritone, Tours Europe," *Chicago Defender*, January 2, 1937, 21; and Raoul Abdul, "Up, Up and Away: Three Weeks of Study at Vienna's Wiener Musikseminar," *New York Amsterdam News*, July 31, 1982, 26.

73. "Ithma-Abende," *Neue Freie Presse*, November 15, 1931, 14.

74. Spelman College Archives, Josephine Harreld Love Collection.

75. Private letters written to her parents during her stay, Spelman College Archives, Josephine Harreld Love Collection.

76. Wipplinger, *Jazz Republic*, 167–68.

77. Letter from Anni Schnitzler to Hayes in Vienna, February 25, 1926, Detroit Public Library, Roland Hayes Collection, series 1, box 2, file 2.

78. Letter from Edyth Walker, October 16, 1926, Detroit Public Library, Roland Hayes Collection, series II, box 1, file 7.

79. Letter from Anni Schnitzler to Hayes in Vienna, February 25, 1926, Detroit Public Library, Roland Hayes Collection, series 1, box 2, file 2.

80. Letter from A. Vilma Jurenkova, Karlsgasse 9, September 28, 1925, Detroit Public Library, Roland Hayes Collection, series 1, box 1, file 39.

81. Brooks and Sims, *Roland Hayes*, 105.

82. Hans Massaquoi, *Destined to Witness: Growing up Black in Nazi Germany* (New York: William Morrow, 2001), 9.

83. Letter dated May 1924, Detroit Public Library, Roland Hayes Collection, series I, box 1, file 23.

84. Detroit Public Library, Roland Hayes Collection, series I, box 1, file 23, May 9, 1924.

85. Anderson, *My Lord*, 158, 144, 157. Anderson's autobiography was translated into German and published in 1960.

86. Josephine Harreld letter, September 1, 1935, Spelman College Archives, Josephine Harreld Love Collection. See also Keiler, *Marian Anderson*, 156. It is possible that Moulton was the cousin of the US undersecretary of state, Sumner Welles. "Unable to Return to US: Americans Marooned on Riviera by Ship's Withdrawal," *New York Times*, June 19, 1941.

87. Helm, *Angel Mo'*, 202.

88. Ibid., 149.

89. Ibid., 143.

90. Meredith Roman, *Opposing Jim Crow: African Americans and the Soviet Indictment of US Racism, 1928–37* (Lincoln: University of Nebraska Press, 2012), 1.

91. James A. Miller, Susan D. Pennybacker, and Eve Rosenhaft, "Mother Ada Wright and the International Campaign to Free the Scottsboro Boys, 1931–34," *American Historical Review* 106, no. 2 (April 2001): 389.

92. From Paris to the States, August 12, 1924, Detroit Public Library, Roland Hayes Collection, series I, box 1, file 25.

93. Letter from Anni Schnitzler to Hayes in Vienna, February 25, 1926, Detroit Public Library, Roland Hayes Collection, series 1, box 2, file 2.

94. Letter from Anni Schnitzler to Hayes in Vienna, March 22, 1926, Detroit Public Library, Roland Hayes Collection, series II, box 1, file 3.

95. Letter from Dr. Pieta, sent via Dr. Eduard Coumont, Rechtsanwalt, Wien 1, Walfischgasse 4, January 31, 1927, Detroit Public Library, Roland Hayes Collection, series II, box 1, file 14.

96. Alain Locke, "Roland Hayes: An Appreciation," *Opportunity* (December 1923): 356.

97. Naumann, "African American Performers," 98.

98. Susann Lewerenz, *Geteilte Welten: Exotisierte Unterhaltung und Artist*innen of Color in Deutschland 1920–1960* (Cologne: Böhlau, 2017), 70.

99. Helm, *Angel Mo'*, 208.

100. Lewerenz, *Geteilte Welten*, 85.

101. Helm, *Angel Mo'*, 210–11.

102. *Time Magazine*, September 15, 1924, 13.

103. Lareau, "Jonny's Jazz," 23.

104. "Der Negertenor, der böse ist, weil der Saal nicht ausverkauft ist," *Die Stunde*, October 7, 1925, 7.

105. "Der Negertenor," *Wiener Morgenzeitung*, October 6, 1925, 7.

106. Helm, *Angel Mo'*, 214; "Der Negertenor, der böse ist, weil der Saal nicht ausverkauft ist," *Die Stunde*, October 7, 1925, 7.

107. "Protests Against Our Negroes Appearing on the Berlin Stage," *New York Times*, March 9, 1926, 1.

108. From the Jewish newspaper, *Forward*, translated from Yiddish into English and reported by the *Philadelphia Tribune*, December 5, 1926, 1.

109. Ibid.

110. Helm, *Angel Mo'*, 235.

111. He was indeed having an affair with a Czech countess. They had a daughter. See Brooks and Sims, *Roland Hayes*, 127–45.

112. "Afrika Singt . . . Paul Robeson im Mittleren Konzerthaussaal," *Die Stunde*, April 11, 1929, 7.

113. Campt, *Other Germans*, 139.

114. Spelman College Archives, Josephine Harreld Love Collection, August 27, 1935.

115. Anna Nussbaum, "Die afro-amerikanische Frau," *Der Tag*, February 12, 1928. For the English translation, see Anna Nussbaum, *The Afro-American Woman* [fragment], ca. 1928, University of Massachusetts Amherst Libraries, Special Collections and University Archives, W.E.B. Du Bois Papers (MS 312).

116. Letter, August 29, 1935, Spelman College Archives, Josephine Harreld Love Collection.

117. Spelman College Archives, Josephine Harreld Love Collection.

118. *Wiener Zeitung*, March 4, 1928, 2.

119. Keiler, *Marian Anderson*, 67.

120. Hayes, with Woolsey, "Roland Hayes," 184.

121. Peter Martin and Christine Alonzo, *Zwischen Charleston und Stechschritt: Schwarze im Nationalsozialismus* (Hamburg: Dölling & Galitz, 2004). Quoted in Wigger, "*Black Horror*," 142.

122. Ernest Rice McKinney, "Views and Reviews," *Pittsburgh Courier*, March 19, 1932, A1.

5. Singing Lieder, Hearing Race

1. Grove Music Online, s.v. "Lied," by Norbert Böker-Heil et al., accessed November 28, 2012, http://www.oxfordmusiconline.com/subscriber/article/grove/music/16611.

2. Richard Taruskin, "Chapter 3 Volkstümlichkeit," in *Oxford History of Western Music Online. Music in the Nineteenth Century*, Oxford University Press, accessed August 12, 2013, http://www.oxfordwesternmusic.com/view/Volume3/actrade-9780195384833-chapter-003.xml.

3. Ibid.

4. Roland Hayes Collection, Detroit Public Library, series IV, box 1, file 67, undated.

5. See Führer, "A Medium of Modernity?."

6. Laura Tunbridge, *Singing in the Age of Anxiety: Lieder Performances in New York and London between the World Wars* (Chicago: University of Chicago Press, 2018), 35.

7. "Musical Notes from Abroad," *Musical Times*, January 3, 1932, 77.

8. Stewart, *New Negro*, 369.

9. Roland Hayes, "Lieder Is of the People," *Musical Courier*, December 1954, 11, Detroit Public Library, Roland Hayes Collection, series IV, box 1, file 73.

10. Helm, *Angel Mo'*, 171.

11. Ibid., 172.

12. Ibid., 168–69.

13. Ibid., 168.

14. William Armstrong, "Dr. Theodor Lierhammer on the German Lied," *The Etude* (1904): 227.

15. Ibid.

16. Helm, *Angel Mo'*, 169.

17. *Wiener Mittags-Zeitung*, April 1923 (original German text not provided). Quoted in Helm, *Angel Mo'*, 170.

18. *Wiener Allgemeine Zeitung* (original German text not provided). Quoted in Helm, *Angel Mo'*, 171.

19. Dyer, *White*, 3.

20. Helm, *Angel Mo'*, 198.

21. Brooks and Sims, *Roland Hayes*, 127.

22. "Konzerte," *Deutsche Tageszeitung*, May 15, 1924. Many music critics in daily newspapers, entertainment magazines, or gossip tabloids published anonymously,

thus making it occasionally difficult to attribute a political leaning or ideology to the writer. For references on German and Austrian newspapers including political affiliations, dissemination records, and editorial staff, see Gabriele Melischek and Josef Seethaler, eds., *Die Wiener Tageszeitungen: Eine Dokumentation. Vol. 3, 1918–38* (Frankfurt am Main: Peter Lang, 1992); and Rudolf Stöber, *Deutsche Pressegeschichte: Von den Anfängen bis zur Gegenwart*, 2nd ed. (Constance: UVK, 2005).

23. "Der Schwarze Tenor," *Deutsche Allgemeine Zeitung*, May 16, 1924.

24. "Konzerte," *Deutsche Tageszeitung*, May 15, 1924.

25. "Konzerte," *Der Tag*, May 17, 1924, 2

26. *Berliner Tageblatt und Handels-Zeitung*, May 17, 1924, 4.

27. "Der Schwarze Tenor," *Deutsche Allgemeine Zeitung*, May 16, 1924.

28. "Konzertchronik," *Berliner Börsen-Zeitung*, May 14, 1924, 4. The newspaper supported the German National People's Party (DNVP). See Bernhard Fulda, *Press and Politics in the Weimar Republic* (Oxford: Oxford University Press, 2009).

29. "Konzertchronik," 4.

30. Arne Spohr, "Mohr und Trompeter: Blackness and Social Status in Early Modern Germany," *Journal of the American Musicological Society* 72, no. 3 (2019): 615.

31. "Konzerte," *Der Tag*, May 17, 1924, 2.

32. *Berliner Tageblatt und Handels-Zeitung*, May 17, 1924, 4.

33. O.T., *Berliner Börsen-Courier*, May 13, 1924, 3.

34. Helm, *Angel Mo'*, 212.

35. Letter dated October 10, 1925, from Dr. Alfred Lederer to Roland Hayes, Detroit Public Library, Roland Hayes Collection, series 1, box, 1, file 40.

36. "Konzerte," *Neue Freie Presse*, October 11, 1925, 17.

37. Kosti Vehanen, *Marian Anderson: A Portrait* (New York: Whittlesey House, 1941), 153.

38. Keiler, *Marian Anderson*, 156.

39. Anderson, *My Lord*, 127.

40. Ibid., 119.

41. Ibid., 125.

42. Ibid., 26.

43. Vehanen, *Marian Anderson*, 150.

44. Concert program, University of Pennsylvania, Annenberg Rare Book and Manuscript Collection, MS Coll 200, box 178, 08532. Anderson provided the text for every lied appearing in her concert programs.

45. Anderson, *My Lord*, 138.

46. German reviewers described Sissieretta Jones and Hazel Harrison in such a manner in the 1890s and early 1900s.

47. "Konzert Marian Anderson," *Salzburger Volksblatt*, August 29, 1935, 6.

48. *Berliner Morgenpost*, October 12, 1930, 9–10.

49. "Die Negersängerin Anderson in Wien," *Neue Freie Presse*, November 21, 1935, 6.

50. "Die Neger-Altistin Anderson," *Deutsche Allgemeine Zeitung*, October 17, 1930, 8.

51. "Konzert Marian Anderson," *Salzburger Volksblatt*, August 29, 1935, 6, University of Pennsylvania, Annenberg Rare Book and Manuscript Collection, MS Coll 200, box 225, 09574.

52. M.F., "Die Negersängerin," *Das Echo*, November 22, 1935, 5.

53. "Marian Anderson als Konzertsolistin," *Neues Wiener Journal*, June 17, 1936, 11.

54. "Die Negersängerin Anderson in Wien," *Neue Freie Presse*, November 21, 1935, 6.

55. Patrick Johnson, *Appropriating Blackness: Performance and the Politics of Authenticity* (Durham, NC: Duke University Press, 2003), 7.

56. *New York Times*, July 19, 1936. Quoted in Keiler, *Marian Anderson*, 172–73.

57. "Der Schwarze Tenor auf der Probe," *Neues Wiener Journal*, October 8, 1925, 9.

58. "Die Negersängerin mit der weißen Seele," unnamed newspaper, University of Pennsylvania, Annenberg Rare Book and Manuscript Collection, University of Pennsylvania, MS Coll 200, box 225, 09577.

59. Quoted in Helm, *Angel Mo'*, 215.

60. *Kleine Volks-Zeitung*, April 27, 1923, 7.

61. H.E.H., "Konzert," *Wiener Zeitung*, November 23, 1935, 8.

62. Locke, "Roland Hayes," 356. Original German text not provided.

63. "Konzert Marian Anderson," *Neues Wiener Tagblatt*, November 23, 1937, 10.

64. "Die Negersängerin mit der weißen Seele."

65. "Konzerte," *Neue Freie Presse*, October 11, 1925, 17.

66. "Der Neger-Tenor Roland Hayes," *Berliner Allgemeine Zeitung*, May 13, 1924, 2.

67. *Wiener Allgemeine Zeitung*, November 26, 1931. Quoted in Nettles, *African American Concert Singers*, 126.

68. Helm, *Angel Mo'*, 171.

69. Locke, "Roland Hayes," 357. Original German text not provided.

70. *Neues Wiener Journal*, April 26, 1923.

71. Eidsheim, "Sonic Blackness," 643.

72. Ibid., 644.

73. Ibid.

74. *Phonogram*, January 1891, 23. Quoted in Tim Brooks, *Lost Sounds: Blacks and the Birth of the Recording Industry, 1890–1919* (Urbana: University of Illinois Press, 2004), 30.

75. *Vossische Zeitung*, anonymously translated into English, University of Pennsylvania, Annenberg Rare Book and Manuscript Collection, MS Coll 200, box 178, 08532.

76. *Berliner Morgenpost*, October 12, 1930, 9–10.

77. Dr. Joseph Marr, "Konzert der Negersängerin Marian Anderson," *Neues Wiener Journal*, November 22, 1935, 7.

78. "Konzert Marian Anderson," *Salzburger Volksblatt*, August 29, 1935, 6.

79. "Konzerte," *Neue Freie Presse*, November 26, 1935, 5; "Maryan Anderson" [sic], *Das Echo*, November 22, 1935, 5.

80. "Konzert Marian Anderson," *Salzburger Volksblatt*, August 29, 1935, 6.

81. *Signale für die musikalische Welt* 91, no. 10 (1933): 163–64.

82. "Theater und Kunst: Konzert Cahier," *[Linzer] Tagblatt*, May 7, 1920, 6.

83. "Sophie Braslau," *Signale für die musikalische Welt* 23 (June 10, 1925): 62.

84. "Brahms Abend Bruno Walters," *Wiener Zeitung*, June 19, 1936, 8.

85. Dr. Joseph Marr, "Konzert der Negersängerin Marian Anderson," *Neues Wiener Journal*, November 22, 1935, 7.

86. Balduin Bricht, "Der Negersänger Roland Hayes," *Kleine Volks-Zeitung*, April 27, 1923, 7.

87. "Negergesang unter Polizeibegleitung," *Salzburger Volksblatt*, May 10, 1932, 10.

88. I.S., "Ein Negerbariton," *Berliner Tageblatt*, May 17, 1924, 4.

89. Vehanen, *Marian Anderson*, 19.

90. "Konzert," *Die Stunde*, November 19, 1931, 7.

91. *Berliner Tageblatt und Handels-Zeitung*, May 17, 1924, 4.

92. "Konzert Marian Anderson," *Neues Wiener Tageblatt*, November 23, 1937, 10.

93. See Paul Allen Anderson, *Deep River: Music and Memory in Harlem Renaissance Thought* (Durham, NC: Duke University Press, 2001); Cruz, *Culture on the Margins*; Sandra Graham, *Spirituals and the Birth of a Black Entertainment Industry* (Urbana: University of Illinois Press, 2018); Schenbeck, *Racial Uplift*; Eileen Southern, *The Music of Black Americans: A History*, 3rd ed. (New York: W. W. Norton, 1997); Jon Michael Spencer, *The New Negroes and Their Music: The Success of the Harlem Renaissance* (Knoxville: University of Tennessee Press, 1997).

94. *Berliner Börsen-Courier*, September 15, 1925. Stewart, *New Negro*, 372–73.

95. *Das Echo*, November 22, 1937, 5–6.

96. "Marian Anderson," *Die Stunde*, November 23, 1937, 4.

6. "A Negro Who Sings German Lieder Jeopardizes German Culture"

1. Vehanen, *Marian Anderson*, 129.

2. Prussian Parliament, 244th Session, May 14, 1923, col. 17407, Geheimes Staatsarchiv Preußicher Kulturbesitz. Quoted and translated by Dörte Schmidt, "The Most American City in Europe: America and Images of America in Berlin Between the Wars," in *Crosscurrents: American and European Music in Interaction, 1900–2000*, eds. Felix Meyer, Carol J. Oja, Wolfgang Rathert, and Anne C. Shreffler (Woodbridge: Boydell Press, 2014), 74.

3. Föllmer, "Which Crisis?," 23.

4. Ibid., 28. Tina Campt and Omer Bartov make similar arguments. See Campt, "Converging Spectres," 322–41; Bartov, "Defining Enemies, Making Victims: Germans, Jews, and the Holocaust," *American Historical Review* 103, no. 3 (1998): 771–816.

5. Föllmer, "Which Crisis?," 28.

6. Hung, "'Bad' Politics," 453.

7. Recent scholarship argues against thinking of 1933 as a "vanishing point" in German history. See Tim B. Müller, *Nach dem Ersten Weltkrieg: Lebensversuche moderner Demokratien* (Hamburg: HIS, 2014); Helmut Walser Smith, *The Continuities of German History: Nation, Religion, and Race Across the Long Nineteenth Century* (Cambridge: Cambridge University Press, 2008). Moreover, cultural historians such as Sabine Hake and Irene Gunther suggest that more cultural overlap existed between the 1920s and 1930s than historians have assumed. See Sabine Hake, *Popular Cinema in the Third Reich* (Austin: University of Texas Press, 2001) and Irene Guenther, *Nazi Chic? Fashioning Women in the Third Reich* (Oxford: Berg, 2004).

8. Pamela Potter, *The Art of Suppression: Confronting the Nazi Past in Histories of the Visual and Performing Arts* (Berkeley: University of California Press, 2016), 4.

9. Ibid., 18.

10. Lewerenz, *Geteilte Welten*.

11. Anderson, *My Lord*, 140.

12. "Sails to Vienna June 5," *Atlanta Daily World*, May 26, 1936; Marvel Cooke, *New York Amsterdam News*, March 30, 1940, 13.

13. Steinberg, *Meaning*, 117.

14. *Pittsburgh Courier*, May 3, 1924.

15. "Austrian Nazis Riot at Recital of US Negro," *Chicago Daily Tribune*, May 11, 1932, 10.

16. Nettles, *African American Concert Singers*, 125.

17. *Neues Wiener Journal*, November 17, 1931, 11.

18. "Demonstration gegen ein Negerbariton," *Neues Wiener Journal*, May 11, 1932, 9.

19. "Negergesang unter Polizeibegleitung," *Salzburger Volksblatt*, May 10, 1932, 6.

20. Ibid., 5.

21. Ibid.

22. Ibid.

23. Ibid.

24. Ibid.

25. "Die Demonstration," *Salzburger Volksblatt*, May 11, 1932, 5.

26. Ibid.

27. Ibid.

28. "Austrian Nazis," 10.

29. "Beaten in Georgia, Says Roland Hayes," *New York Times*, July 17, 1942, 9.

30. Robbie Aitken, "Embracing Germany: Interwar German Society and Black Germans through the Eyes of African American Reporters," *Journal of American Studies* 52, no. 2 (2018): 449.

31. Dr. Frank G. Smith, "Doctor Ends Trip Abroad in Austria: Swim in Famous Blue Danube River," *Chicago Defender*, October 22, 1927, A1.

32. J. A. Rogers, "Vienna Today," *New York Amsterdam News*, January 9, 1929, 16.

33. "Forum of Fact and Opinion," *Pittsburgh Courier*, October 17, 1936, 124.

34. Ibid., 125. My use of religious or spiritual imagery here is deliberate, for Du Bois described Wagner and Bayreuth in such terms.

35. Ibid., 126.

36. Diedrich, "Black 'Others'?," 139.

37. Letter from Josephine Harreld to William Kemper Harreld, August 21, 1935, Spelman College Archives, Josephine Harreld Love Collection, group 1, box 32, folder 2.

38. Ibid.

39. Ibid.

40. J. A. Rogers, "Germany as 1927 Closes: Berlin—Most Modern of European Cities," *New York Amsterdam News*, December 14, 1927, 14.

41. Ibid. Emphasis added.

42. Carter G. Woodson, "Has Jazz Been a Help or a Hindrance to Racial Progress?" *Afro-American*, October 14, 1933, 18.

43. Martin Duberman, *Paul Robeson* (New York: Knopf, 1989), 185.

44. *New York Amsterdam News*, April 2, 1938.

45. Ibid. "A couple of years ago," a reporter for the *New York Amsterdam News* wrote, "Mr. Tatten said there were a few native African, West Indian, and American Negroes in Vienna's medical schools."

46. "Fisk Pianist Who Escaped Nazis Performs at Tuskegee," *Atlanta Daily World*, August 30, 1943, 2.

47. "Jarboro Back in the States," *New York Amsterdam News*, October 21, 1939.

48. *New York Amsterdam News*, April 9, 1938.

49. Roi Ottley, *No Green Pastures* (New York: Scribner, 1951), 147.

50. Ibid., 154–55.

51. Lewerenz, *Geteilte Welten*.

52. Clarence Lusane, *Hitler's Black Victims: The Historical Experiences of Afro-Germans, European Blacks, Africans, and African Americans in the Nazi Era* (New York: Routledge, 2002); Scheck, *Hitler's African Victims*; Campt, *Other Germans*; Aitken and Rosenhaft, *Black Germany*.

53. Anderson, *My Lord*, 156.

54. Ibid.

55. *New York Times*, July 9, 1935.

56. Helmer Enwall to Wilhelm Stein, May 21, 1935. Quoted in Keiler, *Marian Anderson*, 155.

57. "Die 'exotische Nachtigall' in Salzburg," unnamed newspaper (most likely *Salzburger Volksblatt*), August 28, 1935, University of Pennsylvania, Annenberg Rare Book and Manuscript Library, MS Coll 200, box 225, 09574.

58. Vehanen, *Marian Anderson*, 128.

59. Vincent Sheean, *Between the Thunder and the Sun* (New York: Random House, 1943), 25.

60. Marian Anderson, recital program notes, August 18, 1935, University of Pennsylvania, Annenberg Rare Book and Manuscript Library, MS Coll 200, box 195, 08801.

61. Sheean, *Between the Thunder*, 25.

62. Vehanen, *Marian Anderson*, 130.

63. Concert program, Vienna Philharmonic Orchestra, June 1936, University of Pennsylvania, Annenberg Rare Book and Manuscript Library, MS Coll 200, box 174, 08547.

64. Bruno Walter, *Theme and Variations: An Autobiography*, trans. James. A. Galson (New York: Knopf, 1946), 294.

65. Erik Ryding and Rebecca Pechefsky, *Bruno Walter: A World Elsewhere* (New Haven: Yale University Press, 2001), 171–72.

66. Brooks and Sims, *Roland Hayes*, 134.

67. Letter from Josephine Harreld to William Kemper Harreld, May 15, 1935, Spelman College Archives, Josephine Harreld Collection, group 1, box 32, folder 2.

68. Walter, *Theme and Variations*, 301–2.

69. Ibid., 320.

70. "Walter und Marian Anderson," *Die Stunde*, June 19, 1936, 3.

71. "Brahms-Abend Bruno Walter," *Neues Wiener Journal*, June 19, 1936, 11.

72. "Jubel um eine schwarze Sängerin," *Neues Wiener Journal*, November 23, 1937, 10.

73. Ibid.

74. Ibid.

75. "Maryan [sic] Anderson," *Das Echo*, November 22, 1937, 5–6. Emphasis added.

76. "Marian Anderson," *Die Stunde*, November 23, 1937, 4. Emphasis added.

77. George Kugel, "Letter to the Editor," *New York Times*, February 22, 1942, 6. The Jewish German conductor Ignatz Waghalter, who fled Nazi Germany and later founded one of the first all-Black symphony orchestras, apparently promoted Black talent to the outrage of white Germans. James Nathan Jones, Franklin F. Johnson, and Robert B. Cochrane, "Alfred Jack Thomas: Performer, Composer, Educator," *Black Perspective in Music* 11, no. 1 (1983): 67.

78. "Stage Star Is Held in Camp By Germans," *Chicago Defender*, December 25, 1945, 12.

79. Alfred Duckett, "Life in Nazi Prison Camp," *Afro-American*, April 23, 1943, 1. See also William Shack, *Harlem in Montmartre: A Paris Jazz Story Between the Great Wars* (Berkeley: University of California Press, 2001).

80. Rudolph Dunbar, "Four Years in Nazi Prison Camp: Arthur Briggs, Famous Trumpet Player, Recounts Experiences," *Philadelphia Tribune*, September 23, 1944, 15.

7. "And I Thought They Were a Decadent Race"

1. William Kemper Harreld journal entry, Spelman College Archives, Josephine Harreld Love Collection, box 27, folder 31, June 18–August 1953.

2. Ibid.

3. Maria Höhn and Martin Klimke, *A Breath of Freedom: The Civil Rights Struggle, African American GIs, and Germany* (New York: Berghahn, 2010), 43.

4. Ibid.

5. Frank P. Model, "Elmer Spyglass, Salesman for Democracy: A Courier Profile," *Pittsburgh Courier*, March 26, 1955, A8.

6. Chin, Grossmann, Fehrenbach, and Eley, *After the Nazi Racial State*, 5.

7. Applegate, "Saving Music," 221–22.

8. Ruth Andreas-Friedrich, *Schauplatz Berlin: Tagebuchaufzeichnungen 1945 bis 1948* (Frankfurt: Suhrkamp, 1985), 374. Many thanks to Abby Anderton for providing this document. The Ahasuerus reference could be Wagnerian or might also allude to Achim von Arnim's play, "Halle und Jerusalem."

9. Höhn and Klimke, *Breath of Freedom*, 46.

10. Ibid., 47.

11. "Rudolph Dunbar," *Musical Times* 129, no. 1749 (November 1988): 619.

12. "In Retrospect: W. Rudolph Dunbar: Pioneering Orchestra Conductor," *Black Perspective in Music* 9, no. 2 (Autumn 1981): 193–225.

13. Rudolph Dunbar, "Trumpet Player Briggs Freed after Four Years in Nazi Camp near Paris," *Chicago Defender*, September 23, 1944, 3.

14. W. Randy Dixon, *Pittsburgh Courier*, March 6, 1943, 21. George Padmore, *Chicago Defender*, January 9, 1943, 9.

15. "Music: Debut in the Bowl," *Time*, September 2, 1946.

16. Amy C. Beal, *New Music, New Allies: American Experimental Music in West Germany from the Zero Hour to Reunification* (Berkeley: University of California Press, 2006), 15–16.

17. John Bitter, interview by Brewster Chamberlain and Jürgen Wetzel, November 6, 1981, Landesarchiv Berlin, B Rep. 037, nr. 79–82. Cited in Abby Anderton, "'It Was Never a Nazi Orchestra': The American Reeducation of the Berlin Philharmonic," *Music and Politics* 7, no. 1 (2013): 12.

18. TNA/PRO/FO 1049/71, Van Cutsem, Research Branch, Political Division, German Military and Nazi Music, March 3, 1945. Quoted in Toby Thacker, *Music after Hitler, 1945–55* (Burlington: Ashgate, 2007), 21.

19. David Monod, *Settling Scores: German Music, Denazification, and the Americans* (Chapel Hill: University of North Carolina Press, 2005), 3.

20. Potter, *Art of Suppression*, 111.

21. Abby Anderton, *Rubble Music: Occupying the Ruins of Postwar Berlin, 1945–1950* (Bloomington: Indiana University Press, 2019).

22. Matthias Sträßner's biography, *Der Dirigent Leo Borchard: eine unvollendete Karriere* (Berlin: Transit, 1999), is the most authoritative account of the conductor's life and work and he, too, was unable to discern the development of Borchard's relationship to Dunbar.

23. Anderton, "'It Was Never a Nazi Orchestra,'" 9.

24. Abby Anderton, "Hearing Democracy in the Ruins of Hitler's Reich: American Musicians in Postwar Germany," *Comparative Critical Studies* 13, no. 2 (June 2016): 216.

25. Michael Kater, *Different Drummers: Jazz in the Culture of Nazi Germany* (New York: Oxford University Press, 1992), 30.

26. No primary source for this quotation is given. Quoted in Timothy Schroer, *Recasting Race after World War II: Germans and African Americans in American-Occupied Germany* (Boulder: University of Colorado Press, 2007), 157.

27. Thacker, *Music after Hitler*, 96.

28. "Berlin Ovation Given to Marian Anderson," *New York Times*, June 5, 1950.

29. Ibid.

30. IfZ/OMGUS 5/348–3/4, Report of Meeting on February 15, 1947. Quoted in Thacker, *Music after Hitler*, 96.

31. Schroer, *Recasting Race*, 157.

32. "Negro Wins Plaudits Conducting Berlin Phil," *New York Times*, September 3, 1945, 25.

33. "Music: Rhythm in Berlin," *Time*, September 10, 1945.

34. "Germans Meet a Non-Aryan: Berlin Gets Hep to Classics via Negro Conductor," *Chicago Defender*, September 8, 1945, 1.

35. Höhn and Klimke, *Breath of Freedom*, 41.

36. "Drew Line on Marian Anderson," *Daily Boston Globe*, June 18, 1950, C14.

37. Monod, *Settling Scores*, 4.

38. Thacker, *Music after Hitler*, 226.

39. Joy Calico, *Arnold Schoenberg's "A Survivor from Warsaw" in Postwar Europe* (Berkeley: University of California Press, 2014), 40.

40. Potter, *Art of Suppression*, 90.

41. Deborah Barton argues something similar: Women journalists like Andreas-Friedrich and Ursula von Kardorff "distorted the degree of assistance ordinary Germans provided to those who had been persecuted, downplayed the population's support of Nazism, and highlighted Germany's own suffering during the Third Reich. In so doing, they contributed to, legitimized, and reflected West Germany's own self-perception as a victim of Nazism and the postwar occupation." Barton, "Rewriting the Reich: German Women Journalists as Transnational Mediators for Germany's Rehabilitation," *Central European History* 51, no. 4 (December 2018): 584.

42. Thacker, *Music after Hitler*, 18.

43. "Music: Rhythm in Berlin," *Time*, September 10, 1945. Newspapers reported on Dunbar's magnanimity and generosity in ways that immediately echo African American soldiers passing out goods to German civilians. The orchestra also appreciated Dunbar's investment in the ensemble. Dunbar brought a contrabassoon with him from Paris after hearing that the orchestra had lost all of theirs in the bombings some months prior.

44. Carol Oja, "'New Music' and the 'New Negro': The Background of William Grant Still's *Afro-American Symphony*," *Black Music Research Journal* 22 (2002): 107–30.

45. "Negro Given Big Ovation as Conductor," *Washington Post*, September 3, 1945, 10.

46. "Dirigent und Musik aus Amerika," *Der Morgen*, September 6, 1945.

47. "Rudolph Dunbar dirigiert," *Allgemeine Zeitung*, August 31, 1945.

48. "Berliner Philharmoniker von einem Neger dirigiert," *Tägliche Rundschau*, September 6, 1945.

49. *Berliner Zeitung*, September 4, 1945. In September 1945, only a handful of national newspapers were running.

50. "Dirigent und Musik aus Amerika," *Der Morgen*, September 6, 1945.

51. "Ein Amerikanischer Gastdirigent," *Die Neue Zeit*, September 5, 1945.

52. "Berliner Philharmoniker von einem Neger dirigiert," *Tägliche Rundschau*, September 5, 1945.

53. Moritz Ege, *Schwarz werden: 'Afroamerikanophilie' in den 1960er und 1970er Jahren* (Bielefeld: Transcript, 2007), 163. Translated and quoted in Layne, *White Rebels*, 4. Ege's italics.

54. "Rudolph Dunbar dirigiert," *Allgemeine Zeitung*, September 5, 1945.

55. Ibid.

56. John Canarina, *"Uncle Sam's Orchestra": Memories of the Seventh Army Symphony* (Rochester: University of Rochester Press, 1998).

57. Ibid.

58. Josef Häusler, *Badisches Tageblatt*. Translated in Paul Moor, "Military Orchestra: Seventh Army Symphony Wins Europe's Respect," *New York Times*, February 6, 1956, 119.

59. "Symphony 'Sells' US Culture Abroad," *Washington Post and Times Herald*, December 21, 1958.

60. Carol Oja, "Everett Lee and the Racial Politics of Orchestral Conducting," *American Music Review* 43, no. 1 (Fall 2013): 1–8.

61. See "For Black Conductors, a Future? Or Frustration?," *New York Times*, March 15, 1970.

62. *New York Amsterdam News*, August 11, 1951, 32. At one of his concerts in Paris, Dixon was greeted backstage by the African American classical musicians Byrd, Muriel Smith, Leonora Lafayette, and Mattiwilda Dobbs.

63. *Chicago Defender*, April 11, 1970, 36.

64. "From the Mail Pouch," *New York Times*, November 15, 1959, X8.

65. *New York Amsterdam News*, September 5, 1959, 19.

66. "Schwarzer Dirigent für die Berliner Philharmoniker," *Neues Österreich*, August 22, 1959, 6.

67. *Der Kurier*, August 21, 1959.

68. Press report. Private collection of Sonja Ibrahim.

69. Fehrenbach, "Of German Mothers," 164.

70. Danielle Fosler-Lussier, *Music in America's Cold War Diplomacy* (Berkeley: University of California Press, 2015), 12.

71. Emily Abrams Ansari, *The Sound of a Superpower: Musical Americanism and the Cold War* (New York: Oxford University Press, 2017), 17.

72. Fosler-Lussier, *Music in America's Cold War Diplomacy*, 16.

73. Ibid., 17.

74. Beal, *New Music*, 6.

75. Fosler-Lussier, *Music in America's Cold War Diplomacy*, 18.

76. André, *Black Opera*, 91.

77. Howard Pollack, *George Gershwin: His Life and Work* (Berkeley: University of California Press, 2006), 704. Christopher Reynolds, *"Porgy and Bess*: An American *Wozzeck," Journal of the Society for American Music* 1, no. 1 (February 2007): 1, 28.

78. "Gershwin Gets His Music Cues for 'Porgy' on Carolina Beach," *New York Herald Tribune*, July 8, 1934. Quoted in Owen Lee, *A Season of Opera: From Orpheus to Ariadne* (Toronto: University of Toronto Press, 1998), 188.

79. André, *Black Opera*, 91.

80. Richard Crawford, "It Ain't Necessarily Soul: Gershwin's *Porgy and Bess* as a Symbol," *Anuario Interamericano De Investigacion Musical* 8 (1972): 27.

81. Richard Middleton, "Musical Belongings: Western Music and Its Low-Other," in *Western Music and Its Others: Difference, Representation, and Appropriation in Music*, eds. Georgina Born and David Hesmondhalgh (Berkeley: University of California Press, 2000), 67, 69.

82. Richard L. Coe, "Critics Miss Whole Point," *Washington Post*, August 26, 1952, 10.

83. Langston Hughes, *"Porgy and Bess* Goes to Europe to Show that 'The Negroes Have a Chance,'" *Chicago Defender*, September 13, 1952, 10.

84. Ansari, *Sound of a Superpower*, 6.

85. Ellen Noonan, *The Strange Career of "Porgy and Bess": Race, Culture, and America's Most Famous Opera* (Chapel Hill: University of North Carolina Press, 2012).

86. Minutes of meeting of US delegation to UN, November 10, 1950, *FRUS, 1950*, 2: 564–69; "United States Policy Toward Dependent Territories" *FRUS, 1952–54*, 3: 1097. Quoted in Thomas Borstelmann, *The Cold War and the Color Line: American Race Relations in the Global Arena* (Cambridge: Harvard University Press, 2001), 76.

87. Roman, *Opposing Jim Crow*.

88. Borstelmann, *Cold War*, 75.

89. *Cleveland Call and Post*, November 30, 1957.

90. *Chicago Defender*, September 13, 1958, 19. Apparently Phillips slapped a USSR officer on a train in Vienna after he had made repeated unwelcomed advances toward her. "Soprano Stuns 'Fresh' Russian with Slap in Face," *Afro-American*, April 26, 1952, 7. Other singers performed quickly after the war. Anne Brown sang in Vienna in September 1946, according to the *Wiener Kurier*, for example, as did Ellabelle Davis, Theresa Greene, Georgia Laster, and Frederick Wilkerson.

91. Penny von Eschen, *Satchmo Blows up the World: Jazz Ambassadors Play the Cold War* (Cambridge: Harvard University Press, 2004); Fosler-Lussier, *Music*, 14.

92. "'Porgy and Bess' Stars Announce They Will Wed," *Afro-American*, July 12, 1952, 6.

93. Ellen Noonan, *"Porgy and Bess* and the American Racial Imaginary, 1925–85" (PhD diss., New York University, 2002), 224.

94. Ibid.

95. Ibid., 190.

96. Noonan, *Strange Career*, 188.

97. Ibid., 208.

98. *Die Welt*, September 16, 1952, 8.

99. Walter Felsenstein to Mr. Munsing, September 23, 1952, Akademie der Künste Archives, Felsenstein 4053.

100. John Harper Taylor, "Ambassadors of the Arts: An Analysis of the Eisenhower Administration's Incorporation of *Porgy and Bess* into Its Cold War Foreign Policy" (PhD diss., Ohio State University, 1994), 89.

101. Telegram from Robert Breen to Rose Tobias, December 22, 1954, Ohio State University, Jerome Lawrence and Robert Lee Theatre Research Institute, Robert Breen Archives, box F27, 3 of 3, folder P&B "Public Relations Near East Publicity." Quoted in Noonan, "*Porgy and Bess*," 211.

102. *Wiener Kurier*, September 4, 1952, 3.

103. Mari Yoshihara, "The Flight of the Japanese Butterfly: Orientalism, Nationalism, and Performances of Japanese Womanhood," *American Quarterly* 56, no. 4 (2004): 981.

104. "Berlin Loves 'Bess' as Much as 'Porgy,'" *New York Times*, September 18, 1952, 36.

105. Ibid.

106. *Süddeutsche Zeitung*, September 23, 1952, 2.

107. *Die Presse*, September 10, 1952, 6.

108. Noonan, *Strange Career*, 188.

109. "Berlin Loves 'Bess,'" 36.

110. Naima Prevots, *Dance for Export: Cultural Diplomacy and the Cold War* (Hanover, NH: Wesleyan University Press, 1998), 21.

111. Dale O. Smith, "Letter to Robert Breen," April 30, 1955, Ohio State University, Jerome Lawrence and Robert Lee Theatre Research Institute, Robert Breen Archives, box 22. Quoted in Taylor, "Ambassadors of the Arts," 98.

112. Dwight D. Eisenhower, "Supplemental Appropriation—Funds Appropriated to the President: Communication From the President of the United States," microfiche, *Miscellaneous Senate Documents*, Senate Documents, vol. 9, 83rd Congress, 2nd session (Washington, DC: GPO, 1954), 2. Quoted in Taylor, "Ambassadors of the Arts," 99.

113. "*Porgy and Bess* Helps Spread Supremacy Myth," *Norfolk Journal and Guide*, December 18, 1954, Ohio State University, Jerome Lawrence and Robert Lee Theatre Research Institute, Robert Breen Archives, box F106 (1 of 4), scrapbook "P&B International 1954–55." Quoted in Noonan, "*Porgy and Bess*," 238.

114. Moritz Ege and Andrew Wright Hurley, "Introduction: Special Issue on Afro-Americanophilia in Germany," *Portal* 12, no. 2 (2015): 1–14.

115. Thacker, *Music after Hitler*, 96.

116. Story, *And So I Sing*, 181.

117. *General-Anzeiger Wuppertal*, February 10, 1958.

118. Unnamed newspaper, February 17, 1958, Akademie der Künste Archives, Ebert 103.

119. Fosler-Lussier, *Music in America's Cold War Diplomacy*, 121.

120. Gregor, "Bruckner," 114.

8. Breaking with the Past

1. Spelman College Archives, Josephine Harreld Love Collection, box 27, folder 31, June 18–August 1953.

2. *Der Spiegel*, September 29, 1967. Quoted in Emily Richmond Pollock, "'To Do Justice to Opera's "Monstrosity"': Bernd Alois Zimmermann's *Die Soldaten*," *Opera Quarterly* 30, no. 1 (2014): 89.

3. Wieland Wagner, *The Ring at Bayreuth: Some Thoughts on Operatic Production* (London: Gollancz, 1966), 110. Emphasis added. For a longer history of Wagner reception in Germany, see Sven Oliver Müller, *Richard Wagner und die Deutschen: Eine Geschichte von Hass und Hingabe* (Munich: C.H. Beck, 2013).

4. Emily Richmond Pollock, *Opera after the Zero Hour: The Problem of Tradition and the Possibility of Renewal in Postwar West Germany* (Oxford: Oxford University Press, 2019).

5. David Levin, *Unsettling Opera: Staging Mozart, Verdi, Wagner, and Zemlinsky* (Chicago: University of Chicago Press, 2007), 1

6. "Muriel Rahn Named German Music Head," *Afro-American*, October 31, 1959, 15.

7. Wallace Cheatham and Sylvia Lee, "Lady Sylvia Speaks," *Black Music Research Journal* 16, no. 1 (Spring 1996): 206.

8. Andreas Lang, ed., *Chronik der Wiener Staatsoper, 1945 bis 2005: Aufführungen, Besetzungen und Künstlerverzeichnis* (Vienna: Löcker, 2006). Additionally, Black singers such as Anne Brown, Theresa Greene, and Georgia Laster also had careers in Austria in the 1940s and 1950s. Brown sang in Vienna in 1946.

9. Nash, *Autobiographical Reminiscences*, 257.

10. Damani Partridge, "We Were Dancing in the Club, Not on the Berlin Wall: Black Bodies, Street Bureaucrats, and Exclusionary Incorporation into the New Europe," *Cultural Anthropology* 23, no. 4 (November 2008): 660–87; Uta Poiger, *Jazz, Rock, and Rebels: Cold War Politics and American Culture in a Divided Germany* (Berkeley: University of California Press, 2000).

11. See Maria Höhn, *GIs and Fräuleins: The German-American Encounter in 1950s West Germany* (Chapel Hill: University of North Carolina Press, 2002); Höhn and Klimke, *Breath of Freedom*; Schroer, *Recasting Race*; Petra Goedde, *GIs and Germans: Culture, Gender, and Foreign Relations, 1945–49* (New Haven: Yale University Press, 2003).

12. Nash, *Autobiographical Reminiscences*, 287.

13. Wallace Cheatham and George Shirley, "A Renowned Divo Speaks," *The Black Perspective in Music* 18, no. 1/2 (1990): 131.

14. Hella Pick, *Guilty Victim: Austria from the Holocaust to Haider* (London: I.B. Tauris Publishers, 2000); Günter Bischof and Anton Pelinka, eds., *Austrian Historical Memory & National Identity* (New Brunswick: Transaction Publishers, 1997); Peter Thaler, *The Ambivalence of Identity: The Austrian Experience of Nation-Building in a Modern Society* (West Lafayette: Purdue University Press, 2001).

15. Heidemarie Uhl, "Of Heroes and Victims: World War II in Austrian Memory" in *Austrian History Yearbook* 42 (April 2011): 186.

16. Matti Bunzl, *Symptoms of Modernity: Jews and Queers in Late-Twentieth-Century Vienna* (Berkeley: University of California Press, 2004), 36.

17. Pick, *Guilty Victim*, 96. Quoted in Hilary Hope Herzog, *Vienna is Different: Jewish Writers in Austria from the Fin de Siècle to the Present* (New York: Berghahn, 2011).

18. Ingrid Bauer, "'Die Amis, die Ausländer und wir': Zur Erfahrung und Produktion von Eigenem und Fremdem im Jahrzent nach dem Zweiten Weltkrieg," in *Walz—Migration—Besatzung: Historische Szenarien des Eigenen und des Fremden*, edited by Ingrid Bauer, Josef Ehmer, and Sylvia Hahn (Klagenfurt: Drama, 2004), 234.

19. Ibid., 235.

20. Bunzl, *Symptoms of Modernity*, 23.

21. Ingrid Bauer, "'Leiblicher Vater: Amerikaner (Neger)': Besatzungskinder österreichisch-afroamerikanischer Herkunft" in *Früchte der Zeit: Afrika, Diaspora,*

Literatur und Migration, ed. Helmuth A. Niederle (Vienna: WUV Universitätsverlag, 2001), 59.

22. Bauer, "Die Amis," 255.

23. Historisches Archiv der Stadt Salzburg, Aktenbestand Jugendamt/Fürsorge F4, Ordner 70, R.A. Mündelbericht 1953 and Aktennotiz 1955. Quoted in Bauer, "Leiblicher Vater," 60.

24. Konrad Jarausch, *After Hitler: Recivilizing Germans, 1945–95* (Oxford: Oxford University Press, 2006), 14.

25. Sieg, *Ethnic Drag*, 84–85.

26. Leslie Adelson, "Touching Tales of Turks, Germans, and Jews: Cultural Alterity, Historical Narrative, and Literary Riddles for the 1990s," *New German Critique* 80, (Spring/Summer 2000): 100.

27. In a contemporary context, that means that those who can remember the Nazi past directly or have family who can are given the full weight of citizenship and status, as opposed to so-called immigrants and outsiders, who still function as referents to the Holocaust, objects that function as stand-ins, substitutions, or metonyms for a violent past that white Germans must atone for and never forget, but never as subjects in this process of nationalizing memory themselves. Writing about the paradox of German memory culture, Michael Rothberg and Yasemin Yildiz explain, "It has seemed necessary to preserve an ethnically homogenous notion of German identity in order to ensure Germans' responsibility for the crimes of the recent past, even though that very notion of ethnicity was one of the sources of those crimes." Rothberg and Yildiz, "Memory Citizenship: Migrant Archives of Holocaust Remembrance in Contemporary Germany," *Parallax* 17, no. 4 (2011): 35.

28. Calico, *Arnold Schoenberg's "A Survivor from Warsaw,"* 28.

29. Layne, *White Rebels*, 35.

30. Fenner, *Race Under Reconstruction*, 158.

31. Adelson, "Touching Tales," 99.

32. Damani Partridge, "Holocaust Mahnmal (Memorial): Monumental Memory amidst Contemporary Race," *Comparative Studies in Society and History* 52, no. 4 (2010): 835.

33. Sieg, *Ethnic Drag*, 10.

34. *Frankfurter Rundschau*, July 26, 1961, 14.

35. *Chicago Daily Tribune*, July 23, 1961, 22.

36. Robert Jacobson, "Collard Greens and Caviar," *Opera News*, August 1985. Quoted in Nash, *Autobiographical Reminiscences*, 230.

37. Richard Osborne, *Herbert von Karajan: A Life in Music* (London: Chatto & Windus, 1998), 454. Also, this strategy is dangerous and puts Black people at risk. A few years earlier, the Black soprano Theresa Greene had been denied a hotel room in Salzburg because she was Black.

38. *New York Amsterdam News*, November 9, 1935. She supposedly performed with the Vienna State Opera but no record of her performances exists in Lang's *Chronik der Wiener Staatsoper*.

39. George Shirley, "The Black Performer: It's Been a Long, Hard Road from the Minstrels to the Met," *Opera News*, January 30, 1971. Quoted in Nash, *Autobiographical Reminiscences*, 148.

40. Cheatham, *Dialogues*, xi.

41. "Madame Butterfly in Schwarz," *Wiener Journal*, April 20, 1955, 5.

42. Ibid.

43. Nash, *Autobiographical Reminiscences*, 175.

44. "Grossartige Butterfly," *Neues Österreich*, April 20, 1955.

45. André, *Black Opera*, 16

46. Heide Fehrenbach, *Race after Hitler: Black Occupation Children in Postwar Germany and America* (Princeton: Princeton University Press, 2005), 176.

47. Laura Baum, Katharina Oguntoye, and May Opitz, "Three Afro-German Women in Conversation with Dagmar Schultz: The First Exchange for This Book," in *Showing Our Colors: Afro-German Women Speak Out* (Amherst: University of Massachusetts Press, 1992), 145.

48. Priscilla Layne, " 'Don't Look So Sad Because You're a Little Negro': Marie Nejar, Afro-German Stardom, and Negotiations with Black Subjectivity," *Palimpsest: A Journal on Women, Gender, and the Black International* 4, no. 2 (2015): 182.

49. Fehrenbach, *Race after Hitler*, 179–80.

50. Ika Hügel-Marshall, *Invisible Woman: Growing up Black in Germany*, trans. Elizabeth Gaffney (New York: Peter Lang, 2008), 8–9; 21; 42–45.

51. A. M. Nagler, *Misdirection: Opera Production in the Twentieth Century* (Hamden: Archon Books, 1981), 89.

52. André, *Black Opera*, 5.

53. *DIE ZEIT*, October 6, 1961, 14.

54. Nagler, *Misdirection*, 89.

55. Osborne, *Herbert von Karajan*, 456.

56. Story, *And So I Sing*, 149. In fact, having no German pieces in her repertoire, she auditioned with the Italian aria "O don fatale" from Verdi's *Don Carlo*.

57. *Chicago Daily Tribune*, July 22, 1961, 22.

58. Friedelind Wagner to Walter Felsenstein, October 1960, Akademie der Künste Archives, Felsenstein 4322.

59. Geoffrey Skelton, *Wagner at Bayreuth: Experiment and Tradition* (London: White Lion, 1976), 173.

60. Oswald Georg Bauer, *Richard Wagner: The Stage Designs and Productions from the Premieres to the Present* (New York: Rizzoli, 1983), 97.

61. Skelton, *Wagner at Bayreuth*, 174. Emphasis added.

62. Geoffrey Skelton, *Wieland Wagner: The Positive Sceptic* (New York: St. Martin's Press, 1971), 157.

63. *Die Kölnische Rundschau*, July 25, 1961.

64. Martin Bernheimer, "Die Schwarze Venus," *Opera News*, October 28, 1961.

65. T. Denean Sharpley-Whiting, *Black Venus: Sexualized Savages, Primal Fears, and Primitive Narratives in French* (Durham, NC: Duke University Press, 1999), 3.

66. Gilman, *Difference and Pathology*, 83, 101.

67. *New York Times*, July 22, 1961, 12. Emphasis added.

68. Fehrenbach, *Race after Hitler*, 181.

69. Cheatham and Lee, "Lady Sylvia Speaks," 207. Similarly, on June 4, 1961, Bumbry's teacher Lotte Lehmann wrote to the *Chicago Daily Tribune*'s music critic Claudia Cassidy to notify her that Bumbry would be singing at Bayreuth but not

in white makeup. "She wanted to know if I will be at the opening of Bayreuth [on] July 23 when Grace Bumbry—and you can be quite sure not in whitened makeup—sings Venus in Wieland Wagner's new production of *Tannhäuser*."

70. Margalit Fox, "Camilla Williams, Barrier-Breaking Opera Star, Dies at 92," *New York Times*, February 2, 2012.

71. *DIE ZEIT*'s music critic aptly called Wieland Wagner's agenda the "De-Wagnering of Wagner." "Die Entwagnerung Wagners," *DIE ZEIT*, August 4, 1961.

72. André, *Black Opera*, 14.

73. Cheatham, *Dialogues*, 104.

74. André, *Black Opera*, 15.

75. "Äthioperin aus Amerika in der Staatsoper," *Neues Österreich*, September 15, 1961.

76. "Staatsoper: Aida im Dunkeln," *Heute*, June 7, 1958.

77. *Der Kurier*, September 30, 1961, 9.

78. "Dunkle Butterfly: Negersängerin Camilla Williams begeistert in der Volksoper," *Österreichische Neue Tageszeitung*, April 20, 1955, 5.

79. "Leontine Price als Butterfly," *Das Kleine Volksblatt*, September 27, 1960.

80. Private interview between Wallace and Frierson in the chapter, "Andrew Frierson: A Singer Speaks Out on Racism and Other Issues," in Cheatham, *Dialogues*, 13.

81. *Bayreuther Stadtzeitung*, February 14, 1961.

82. *Berliner Morgenpost*, January 26, 1958.

83. *Der Tagesspiegel*, February 8, 1958.

84. *Der Kurier*, September 30, 1961, 9.

85. *Die Welt*, February 18, 1958.

86. *Der Kurier*, February 7, 1958.

87. Lang, *Chronik der Wiener Staatsoper*, 672.

88. *Wiener Journal*, April 28, 1959.

89. *Österreichische Neue Tageszeitung*, September 16, 1959.

90. *Wiener Journal*, April 28, 1959.

91. *Österreichische Neue Tageszeitung*, September 16, 1959.

92. *Das Kleine Volksblatt*, April 28,1959.

93. Heinrich Kralik, *Neues Wiener Tagblatt*, April 30, 1923, 3.

94. *Die Tat*, Zurich, September 2, 1961.

95. *Deutscher Anzeiger*, February 15, 1961.

96. "Zwiespältige 'Carmen' mit turbulentem Echo," *Der Tagesspiegel*, February 8, 1958.

97. "*Carmen* in der Städtische Oper," *Der Tagesspiegel*, February 23, 1958. Sieglinde Wagner (no relation to Richard, Wieland, or Wolfgang Wagner) had performed in *Carmen* in 1953.

98. Ibid.

99. *Der Kurier*, February 13, 1958.

100. Peter Ebert, *In This Theatre of Man's Life: The Biography of Carl Ebert*, 214.

101. *Die Tat* [Zurich], September 2, 1961.

102. "*Carmen* in der Städtische Oper," *Der Tagesspiegel*, February 23, 1958.

103. *Deutscher Anzeiger*, February 15, 1961.

104. "Nochmals, Schwarze Venus von Bayreuth," *Deutscher Anzeiger*, March 1, 1961.

105. Ibid.

106. *Kölnische Rundschau*, July 25, 1961.

107. Ibid.

108. Shirley Verrett and Christopher Brooks, *I Never Walked Alone: The Autobiography of an American Singer* (Hoboken: John Wiley & Sons, 2003), 62–63.

109. George Shirley, "Il Rodolfo Nero, or The Masque of Blackness" in *Blackness in Opera*, 261.

110. Cheatham and Lee, "Lady Sylvia Speaks," 206.

111. Cheatham and Shirley, "A Renowned Divo Speaks," 43.

112. Jason Oby, *Equity in Operatic Casting as Perceived by African American Male Singers* (Lewiston: Edwin Mellen Press, 1998), 43.

113. Annabelle Bernard papers, 1956–2001, Tulane University, Amistad Research Center, accessed November 17, 2019, https://www.amistadresearchcenter.org/single-post/2018/06/11/A-Shining-Star-Soprano-Annabelle-Bernard.

9. Singing in the Promised Land

1. "DDR ehrt den Sänger der Völkerfreundschaft," *Neues Deutschland*, October 6, 1960, 1.

2. Ned Richardson Little, *The Human Rights Dictatorship: Socialism, Global Solidarity and Revolution in East Germany* (Cambridge: Cambridge University Press, 2019).

3. Quinn Slobodian, *Comrades of Color: East Germany in the Cold War World* (New York: Berghahn, 2015); Jan C. Behrends, Thomas Lindenberger, Patrice G. Poutrus, eds., *Fremde und Fremd-Sein in der DDR: zu historischen Ursachen der Fremdenfeindlichkeit in Ostdeutschland* (Berlin: Metropol, 2003); Peggy Piesche, "Black and German? East German Adolescents Before 1989: A Retrospective View of a 'Non-Existent Issue' in the GDR," in *The Cultural After-Life of East Germany: New Transnational Perspectives*, ed. Leslie A. Adelson (Washington, DC: American Institute of Contemporary Studies, 2002), 37–59.

4. Mike Dennis and Norman LaPorte, *State and Minorities in Communist East Germany* (New York: Berghahn, 2011), 1–27.

5. Jeffrey Herf, *Divided Memory: The Nazi Past in the Two Germanys* (Cambridge, MA: Harvard University Press, 1997), 106–61; Thomas C. Fox, *Stated Memory: East Germany and the Holocaust* (Rochester, NY: Camden House, 1998), 69–96.

6. Dennis and LaPorte, *State and Minorities*, 112.

7. Sara Lennox, "Reading Transnationally: The GDR and Black American Writers" in *Art Outside The Lines: New Perspectives on GDR Art Culture*, eds. Elaine Kelly and Amy Wlodarski (New York: Rodopi, 2011), 112, 113–14.

8. Hamilton Beck, "Censoring Your Ally: W.E.B. Du Bois in the German Democratic Republic," in *Crosscurrents: African Americans, Africa, and Germany in the Modern World*, eds. David McBride, Leroy Hopkins, and Carol Aisha Blackshire-Belay (Columbia, SC: Camden House, 1998), 197–232.

9. Duberman, *Paul Robeson*, 227–28.

10. Mead Dodd, ed., *Paul Robeson: The Great Forerunner* (New York: International Publishers, 1985), 76.

11. Duberman, *Paul Robeson*, 389–432.

12. Unidentified East German newspaper, July 12, 1949, Bundesarchiv Berlin-Lichterfelde, SgY 30/1021/2 (3 of 5).

13. Ibid.

14. "Hohe Ehrungen für Robeson," *Der Morgen*, October 6, 1960, 1.

15. "Paul Robeson, ihr grosser schwarzer Freund," *Berliner Zeitung am Abend*, October 10, 1960, 4.

16. Layne, *White Rebels*, 18. In a poll conducted in West Germany in the 1960s, Layne writes, "87% of white German men polled expressed interest in having a Black friend."

17. "Paul Robeson in Berlin," *Berliner Zeitung am Abend*, October 5, 1960, 3.

18. *Neue Zeit*, October 8, 1960.

19. Joel Agee, *Twelve Years: An American Boyhood in East Germany* (New York: Farrar Straus Giroux, 1981), 313–14.

20. See Elaine Kelly, *Composing the Canon in the German Democratic Republic* (Oxford: Oxford University Press, 2014); Joy Calico, "'Für eine neue deutsche Nationaloper': Opera in the Discourses of Unification and Legitimation in the German Democratic Republic," in *Music and German National Identity*, eds. Celia Applegate and Pamela Potter (Chicago: University of Chicago Press, 2002); David Tompkins, "Sound and Socialist Identity: Negotiating the Musical Soundscape in the Stalinist GDR," in *Germany in the Loud Twentieth Century: An Introduction*, eds. Florence Feiereisen and Alexandra Merley (New York: Oxford University Press, 2012).

21. Margarete Myers Feinstein, *State Symbols: The Quest for Legitimacy in the Federal Republic of Germany and the German Democratic Republic, 1949–59* (Boston: Brill Academic Publishers, 2001); Heiner Stahl, "Mediascape and Soundscape: Two Landscapes of Modernity in Cold War Berlin," in *Berlin: Divided City, 1945–89*, eds. Philip Broadbent and Sabine Hake (New York: Berghahn, 2010); Tompkins, "Sound and Socialist Identity," 111.

22. Tompkins, 111.

23. See Margaret Notley, *Lateness and Brahms: Music and Culture in the Twilight of Viennese Liberalism* (Oxford: Oxford University Press, 2007); Helmut Gruber, *Red Vienna: Experiment in Working-Class Culture, 1919–34* (New York: Oxford University Press, 1991).

24. Elizabeth Janik, *Recomposing German Music: Politics and Tradition in Cold War Berlin* (Boston: Brill, 2005), 221–28.

25. Laura Silverberg, "(Re)defining the Musical Heritage: Confrontations with Tradition in East German New Music," in *Contested Legacies: Constructions of Cultural Heritage in the GDR*, ed. Matthew Philpotts and Sabine Rolle (Rochester, NY: Camden House, 2009), 125.

26. Frank Schneider, "Beethoven-Konferenz des deutschen Kulturbundes in Potsdam," *Musik und Gesellschaft*, 20, no. 1 (1970): 7. Quoted in David Dennis, *Beethoven in German Politics, 1870–1989* (New Haven: Yale University Press, 1996), 181.

27. Dennis, *Beethoven in German Politics*, 179.

28. Matthew Philpotts and Sabine Rolle, "Introduction," in *Contested Legacies: Constructions of Cultural Heritage in the GDR*, ed. Matthew Philpotts and Sabine Rolle (Rochester, NY: Camden House, 2009), 1.

29. Toby Thacker, "'Renovating' Bach and Handel: New Musical Biographies in the German Democratic Republic," in *Musical Biography: Towards New Paradigms*, ed. Jolanta T. Pekacz (Burlington: Ashgate, 2006).

30. Elaine Kelly, "Imagining Richard Wagner: The Janus Head of a Divided Nation," *Kritika: Explorations in Russian and Eurasian History* 9, no. 4 (Fall 2008): 826.

31. Elaine Kelly, "Performing Diplomatic Relations: Music and East German Foreign Policy in the Middle East during the Late 1960s," *Journal of the American Musicological Society* 72, no. 2 (2019): 496–97.

32. *Sächsische Neueste Nachrichten*, September 21, 1989.

33. *Der Neue Weg* [Magdeburg], December 22, 1959; unnamed newspaper [Halle], November 1959. Private collection of Sonja Ibrahim.

34. *Die Union*, September 29, 1961.

35. *Leipziger Volkszeitung*, March 15, 1959. Private collection of Sonja Ibrahim.

36. Ibid.

37. Ibid.

38. See Wipplinger, *Jazz Republic.*

39. *Leipziger Volkszeitung*, March 15, 1959.

40. Elaine Kelly, "Music for International Solidarity: Performances of Race and Otherness in the German Democratic Republic," *Twentieth Century Music* 16, no. 1 (2019): 137.

41. Deborah Burton, Susan Vandiver Nicassio, and Agostino Ziino, eds., *Tosca's Prism: Three Moments of Western Cultural History* (Boston: Northeastern University Press, 2004); Alexandra Wilson, *The Puccini Problem: Opera, Nationalism, and Modernity* (Cambridge: Cambridge University Press, 2007).

42. Grove Music Online, s.v. "Tosca," by Julian Budden, accessed November 18, 2019. https://www.oxfordmusiconline.com/grovemusic/view/10.1093/gmo/9781 561592630.001.0001/omo-9781561592630-e-5000005948

43. Catherine Clement, *Opera, or, The Undoing of Women*, trans. Betsy Wing (Minneapolis: University of Minnesota Press, 1998); Susan McClary, *Feminine Endings: Music, Gender, and Sexuality*, 2nd ed. (Minneapolis: University of Minnesota Press, 2002).

44. Grove Music Online, s.v. "Tosca."

45. *Berliner Zeitung*, "Der Geist von Bonn," July 23, 1961, 6.

46. Ibid.

47. *Die Welt*, February 7, 1958.

48. *Berliner Zeitung* (Ostsektor), February 8, 1958. "Ob solche Leute aus Westberlin auch ein Little Rock machen wollten?"

49. *Berliner Morgenpost*, February 9, 1958.

50. "Die dunkelhäutige Venus," *Neue Zeit*, July 26, 1961, 4.

51. "Schostakowitsch-Kogan-Byrd: Konzert im Zeichen der Völkerfreundschaft," *Berliner Zeitung*, April 10, 1961. "Fraternity of peoples" (*Völkerfreundschaft*) was a popular Stalinist-era term.

52. *Sächsische Neueste Nachrichten*, September 16, 1961.

53. "For Black Conductors, A Future? Or Frustration?" *New York Times*, March 15, 1970.

54. *Berliner Zeitung*, September 8, 1961.

55. Ronald E. Mitchell, *Opera—Dead or Alive: Production, Performance, and Enjoyment of Musical Theater* (Madison: University of Wisconsin Press, 1970), 34.

56. "Ein Sommernachtstraum: Zu Walter Felsensteins Inszenierung in der Komischen Oper," *Berliner Zeitung am Abend*, July 10, 1961, 3.

57. *Die Neue Zeit*, July 8, 1961.

58. Mitchell, *Opera—Dead or Alive*, 285.

59. My italics. "Mittsommernachtszauber der Opernbühne: Benjamin Britten-Erstaufführung bei Felsenstein," unnamed newspaper, Akademie der Künste Archives, Felsenstein 1015.

60. In order: *Berliner Zeitung*, July 8, 1961; unnamed newspaper, Akademie der Künste Archives, Felsenstein 1015; *Der Morgen*, July 8, 1961; "Im Zauberwald der Töne: Brittens 'Sommernachtstraum' in der Komischen Oper," unnamed newspaper, Akademie der Künste Archives, Felsenstein 1015.

61. "Mittsommernachtszauber der Opernbühne: Benjamin Britten-Erstaufführung bei Felsenstein," Akademie der Künste Archives, Felsenstein 1015.

62. "Wenn Phantasie im Spiel ist: 'Ein Sommernachtstraum,' Oper von Britten und Pears, inszeniert von Walter Felsenstein," unnamed newspaper, Akademie der Künste Archives, Felsenstein 1015.

63. Internal document of Komische Oper Berlin, Akademie der Künste Archives, Felsenstein 999. Emphasis added.

64. Roger Freitas, *Portrait of a Castrato: Politics, Patronage, and Music in the Life of Atto Melani* (Cambridge: Cambridge University Press, 2009).

65. Walter Felsenstein to William Ray, July 4, 1961, Akademie der Künste Archives, Felsenstein 324.

66. Peter Paul Fuchs, ed. and trans., *The Music Theater of Walter Felsenstein: Collected Articles, Speeches, and Interviews* (New York: Norton, 1975).

67. The African American leads were Carolyn Smith-Meyer and Cullen Maiden, as reported in the *Christian Science Monitor*, February 20, 1970.

68. Letter from Václav David, Czechoslovak minister of foreign affairs, to Anna Baramova, head of the international department of the Central Committee of the Communist Party of Czechoslovakia, trans. Kathleen Geaney, National Archives of the Czech Republic, Prague, KSC–UV–100/3, sv. 178, aj. 603: 42–47. The letter was marked "Secret!" and "Urgent!" Many thanks to Geaney for procuring this document.

69. Ibid.

70. Ibid.

71. Letter from Karl Tümmler to Hans Pischner, March 31, 1955. Bundesarchiv Berlin-Lichterfelde, DR/1/8285.

72. Letter from Aubrey Pankey to Gerhart Eisler, April 19, 1959. Bundesarchiv Berlin-Lichterfelde, DY 30/IV/2/2.026/105. The letter was written in English.

73. Ibid.

74. Letter from Alfred Kurella to Albert Norden, May 2, 1959. Bundesarchiv Berlin-Lichterfelde, DY 30/IV/2/2.026/105.

75. Ibid.

76. "Musik des wahren Amerika," *Berliner Zeitung am Abend*, May 26, 1959, 3; "Earl Robinson—Die Stimme Amerikas," *Neues Deutschland*, May 30, 1959, 5.

77. "Musik des wahren Amerika," 3.

78. "Neue amerikanische Musik," *Berliner Zeitung*, May 24, 1959, 6. The German title was *Lincolns letzte Reise*.

79. *Berliner Zeitung am Abend*, May 23, 1959, 1.

80. Ibid.

81. *Norddeutsche Zeitung*, February 15, 1961, Bundesarchiv Berlin-Lichterfelde, DY 30/IV 2/2.028/94. Many thanks to Natalia Rasmussen for locating this document.

82. Ibid.

83. Letter from Aubrey Pankey to Albert Norden, February 28, 1961, Bundesarchiv Berlin-Lichterfelde, DY 30/IV 2/2.028/94.

84. Ibid.

85. Ibid.

86. Tunbridge, *Singing in the Age of Anxiety*.

87. Letter from Aubrey Pankey to Albert Norden, February 15, 1961, Bundesarchiv Berlin-Lichterfelde, DY 30/IV/2/2.2028/94.

88. Ibid.

89. *Sächsische Neueste Nachrichten*, September 21, 1989.

90. *Die Union*, September 8, 1989.

91. Ibid.

92. Behrends et al., eds., *Fremde und Fremd-Sein*, 15.

93. Ibid., 10.

94. Kelly, "Music for International Solidarity," 125.

Conclusion

1. Marie Nejar interview, Schwarz Rot Gold TV, YouTube video, 12:13, posted May 1, 2015 https://www.youtube.com/watch?v=X3oCfXQNfbc.

Michelle René Eley, "Anti-Black Racism in West German Living Rooms: The ZDF Television Film Adaptation of Willi Heinrich's *Gottes zweite Garnitur*," *German Studies Review* 39, no. 2 (2016): 319.

2. Clifford D. Panton Jr., *George Augustus Polgreen Bridgetower, Violin Virtuoso and Composer of Color in Late Eighteenth-Century Europe* (Lewiston: Mellen Press, 2005); Josephine Wright, "George Polgreen Bridgetower: An African Prodigy in England, 1789–99," *Musical Quarterly* 66, no. 1 (January 1980): 65–82.

3. See Spohr, "Mohr und Trompeter," 613–63.

4. Friedrich Meinecke, *The German Catastrophe: Reflections and Recollections*, translated by Sidney B. Fay (Boston: Beacon Press, 1963), 117–18. Quoted in Schroer, *Recasting Race*, 178.

5. Reactions of German Civilians to a Program of Short Films (program no. 2), August 6, 1945, Film, Test Screenings (Audience Reactions, Etc.) File, Records Relating to Motion Picture Production and Distribution, 1945–49, Records of the Motion Picture Branch, ICD, Headquarters, USFET, RG 260, NACP. Quoted in Schroer, *Recasting Race*, 163–64.

6. Observing how the notion of musical Germanness traveled to Great Britain, Thomas Irvine writes, "Our sense of musical Germanness could, in other words, rest on white supremacist foundations." Irvine, "Hubert Parry, Germany, and the 'North,'" in *Dreams of Germany: Musical Imaginaries from the Concert Hall to the Dance Floor*, edited by Neil Gregor and Thomas Irvine (New York: Berghahn, 2018), 210.

7. "'Aida' in der Deutschen Oper Berlin: Prunkende Repräsentation," *DIE ZEIT*, February 4, 1972.

8. Donal Henahan, "Jessye Norman—'People Look at Me and Say Aida,'" *New York Times*, January 21, 1973, A15.

9. Richard Brody, "How Eric Dolphy Sparked My Love of Jazz," *New Yorker*, January 25, 2019.

10. Rosina Lippi-Green, *English with an Accent: Language, Ideology, and Discrimination in the United States* (New York: Routledge, 1997), 17.

11. Marie Nejar, *Mach nicht so traurige Augen, weil du ein Negerlein bist: Meine Jugend im Dritten Reich* (Hamburg: Rowohlt, 2007). Memoirs by other Afro-Germans such as Hans Massaquoi or Theodor Wonja Michael, both of whom also reached adolescence in the interwar era, share similar stories of everyday racism. See Massaquoi, *Destined to Witness: Growing Up Black in Nazi Germany* (New York: W. Orro, 1999); and Michael, *Black German: An Afro-German Life in the Twentieth Century*, trans. Eve Rosenhaft (Liverpool: Liverpool University Press, 2017).

12. Nejar, *Mach nicht so traurige Augen*, 234.

13. Stoever, *Sonic Color Line*, 1. Indeed, in the European Union's first-ever survey on the status of Black people in Europe, the European Agency for Fundamental Rights (FRA) noted that after skin color, accents were the primary reason why Black respondents felt discriminated against when seeking employment. European Agency for Fundamental Rights (FRA), "Being Black in the EU—Second European Union Minorities and Discrimination Survey," Luxembourg, Publications Office of the European Union, 54.

14. Interview with Kevin John Edusei, Schwarz Rot Gold TV, YouTube video, 7:25, posted March 1, 2016, https://www.youtube.com/watch?v=3nkVJgNUm30.

15. Aitken, "Surviving in the Metropole," 214.

16. "Black artists, performing in a culture of surveillance, always anticipate a white audience." Jayna Brown, *Babylon Girls: Black Women Performers and the Shaping of the Modern* (Durham, NC: Duke University Press, 2008), 6.

17. Henahan, "People Look at Me," A15.

18. Leslie Kandell, "Music: A Soprano Does It (Precisely) Her Way," *New York Times*, June 7, 1998.

19. Felicia R. Lee, "Breaking Out of Old Categories; Jessye Norman and Bill T. Jones Create a Performance," *New York Times*, May 20, 1999.

20. Ibid.

21. John Gruen, "An American Soprano Adds the Met to Her Roster," *New York Times*, September 18, 1983.

22. Kim, "Made in Meiji Japan," 288–320.

23. Arnheim, *Stimme von der Galerie*, 15. Emphasis added.

24. Ulrike Knöfel, "Es ist eine Beleidigung, ja," *Spiegel Online*, August 17, 2018, https://www.spiegel.de/kultur/okwui-enwezor-ueber-seinen-schmaehlichen-abschied-aus-muenchen-a-00000000-0002-0001-0000-000158955211.

25. Kate Brown, "How Artist Emeka Ogboh Became One of Europe's Fastest-Rising Stars—Without a Gallery, a Dealer, or Even Self-Promotion," Artnet News, November 2, 2018, https://news.artnet.com/art-world/emekah-ogboh-hkw-1385746.

26. Nora Holt, "Scotching the Myth that Negro Singers Are Unqualified for Opera or Top Concerts," *New York Amsterdam News*, May 31, 1952.

Bibliography

Abbot, Lynn, and Doug Seroff, eds. *Out of Sight: The Rise of African American Popular Music, 1889–95.* Jackson: University of Mississippi Press, 2002.

Adelson, Leslie. "Touching Tales of Turks, Germans, and Jews: Cultural Alterity, Historical Narrative, and Literary Riddles for the 1990s." *New German Critique* 80 (Spring/Summer 2000): 93–124.

Agee, Joel. *Twelve Years: An American Boyhood in East Germany.* New York: Farrar Straus Giroux, 1981.

Agnew, Vanessa. *Enlightenment Orpheus: The Power of Music in Other Worlds.* Oxford: Oxford University Press, 2008.

Aitken, Robbie. "Embracing Germany: Interwar German Society and Black Germans through the Eyes of African American Reporters." *Journal of American Studies* 52, no. 2 (2018): 447–73.

——. "Surviving in the Metropole: The Struggle for Work and Belonging Amongst African Colonial Migrants in Weimar Germany." *Immigrants & Minorities* 28, no. 2–3 (2010): 203–23.

Aitken, Robbie, and Eve Rosenhaft. *Black Germany: The Making and Unmaking of a Diaspora Community, 1884–1960.* Cambridge: Cambridge University Press, 2013.

Albrecht, Theodore. "Julius Weiss: Scott Joplin's First Piano Teacher." *College Music Symposium* 19, no. 2 (1979): 89–105.

Ames, Eric. *Carl Hagenbeck's Empire of Entertainments.* Seattle: University of Washington Press, 2008.

Anderson, Marian. *My Lord What a Morning: An Autobiography.* New York: Viking Press, 1956.

Anderson, Paul Allen. *Deep River: Music and Memory in Harlem Renaissance Thought.* Durham, NC: Duke University Press, 2001.

Anderton, Abby. "Hearing Democracy in the Ruins of Hitler's Reich: American Musicians in Postwar Germany." *Comparative Critical Studies* 13, no. 2 (June 2016): 215–31.

——. "'It Was Never a Nazi Orchestra': The American Reeducation of the Berlin Philharmonic." *Music and Politics* 7, no. 1 (2013): 1–16.

——. *Rubble Music: Occupying the Ruins of Postwar Berlin, 1945–1950.* Bloomington: Indiana University Press, 2019.

André, Naomi. *Black Opera: History, Power, Engagement.* Urbana: University of Illinois Press, 2018.

Andreas-Friedrich, Ruth. *Schauplatz Berlin: Tagebuchaufzeichnungen 1945 bis 1948.* Frankfurt: Suhrkamp, 1985.

Ansari, Emily Abrams. *The Sound of a Superpower: Musical Americanism and the Cold War.* New York: Oxford University Press, 2017.

Appiah, Kwame Anthony. *Lines of Descent: W. E. B. Du Bois and the Emergence of Identity*. Cambridge: Harvard University Press, 2014.

Applegate, Celia. "Hausmusik in the Third Reich." In *The Necessity of Music: Variations on a German Theme*, 260–74. Toronto: University of Toronto Press, 2017.

———. "Mendelssohn on the Road." In *The Necessity of Music: Variations on a German Theme*, 119–34. Toronto: University of Toronto Press, 2017.

———. "Saving Music: Enduring Experiences of Culture." *History & Memory* 17, nos. 1–2 (2005): 217–37.

Applegate, Celia, and Pamela Potter, eds. *Music and German National Identity*. Chicago: University of Chicago Press, 2006.

Badenberg, Nana. "Mohrenwäschen, Völkerschauen: Der Konsum des Schwarzen um 1900." In *Colors 1800/1900/2000: Signs of Ethnic Difference*, edited by Birgit Tautz, 163–84. New York: Brill, 2004.

Baldwin, Kate. *Beyond the Color Line and the Iron Curtain: Reading Encounters Between Black and Red, 1922–1963*. Durham, NC: Duke University Press, 2002.

Bang, Paul. *Die farbige Gefahr*. Göttingen: Vanderhoeck & Ruprecht, 1938.

Barton, Deborah. "Rewriting the Reich: German Women Journalists as Transnational Mediators for Germany's Rehabilitation." *Central European History* 51, no. 4 (December 2018): 563–84.

Bartov, Omer. "Defining Enemies, Making Victims: Germans, Jews, and the Holocaust." *American Historical Review* 103, no. 3 (1998): 771–816.

Bauer, Ingrid. "'Die Amis, die Ausländer und wir': Zur Erfahrung und Produktion von Eigenem und Fremdem im Jahrzent nach dem Zweiten Weltkrieg," In *Walz—Migration—Besatzung: Historische Szenarien des Eigenen und des Fremden*, edited by Ingrid Bauer, Josef Ehmer, and Sylvia Hahn, 197–276. Klagenfurt: Drama, 2004.

———. "'Leiblicher Vater: Amerikaner (Neger)': Besatzungskinder österreichisch-afroamerikanischer Herkunft." In *Früchte der Zeit: Afrika, Diaspora, Literatur und Migration*, edited by Helmuth A. Niederle, 49–67. Vienna: WUV Universitätsverlag, 2001.

Bauer, Oswald Georg. *Richard Wagner: The Stage Designs and Productions from the Premieres to the Present*. New York: Rizzoli, 1983.

Baum, Laura, Katharina Oguntoye, and May Opitz. "Three Afro-German Women in Conversation with Dagmar Schultz: The First Exchange for This Book." In *Showing Our Colors: Afro-German Women Speak Out*, 145–64. Amherst: University of Massachusetts Press, 1992.

Baumann, Ronald M. *Constructing Black Education at Oberlin College: A Documentary History*. Athens: University of Ohio Press, 2010.

Beal, Amy C. *New Music, New Allies: American Experimental Music in West Germany from the Zero Hour to Reunification*. Berkeley: University of California Press, 2006.

Beck, Hamilton. "Censoring Your Ally: W. E. B. Du Bois in the German Democratic Republic." In *Crosscurrents: African Americans, Africa, and Germany in the Modern World*, edited by David McBride, Leroy Hopkins, and Carol Aisha Blackshire-Belay, 197–232. Columbia, SC: Camden House, 1998.

Behrends, Jan C., Thomas Lindenberger, and Patrice G. Poutrus, eds. *Fremde und Fremd-Sein in der DDR: zu historischen Ursachen der Fremdenfeindlichkeit in Ostdeutschland*. Berlin: Metropol, 2003.

Bellman, Jonathan. *The Style Hongrois in the Music of Western Europe*. Boston: Northeastern University Press, 1993.

Beniston, Judith, and Robert Vilain, eds. *Culture and Politics in Red Vienna*. Leeds: Maney, 2006.

Bischof, Günter, and Anton Pelinka, eds. *Austrian Historical Memory & National Identity*. New Brunswick: Transaction Publishers, 1997.

Bohlman, Philip, and Otto Holzapfel, eds. *Land without Nightingales: Music in the Making of German-America*. Madison: University of Wisconsin Press, 2002.

Borstelmann, Thomas. *The Cold War and the Color Line: American Race Relations in the Global Arena*. Cambridge: Harvard University Press, 2001.

Bowersox, Jeff. *Raising Germans in the Age of Empire: Youth and Colonial Culture, 1871–1914*. Oxford: Oxford University Press, 2013.

Brockmann, Stephen and Thomas W. Kniesche. *Dancing on the Volcano: Essays on the Culture of the Weimar Republic*. Columbia, SC: Camden House, 1994.

Bronsen, David. *Joseph Roth: Eine Biographie*. Cologne: Kiepenheuer & Witsch, 1974.

Brooks, Christopher A., and Robert Sims. *Roland Hayes: The Legacy of an American Tenor*. Bloomington: Indiana University Press, 2015.

Brooks, Daphne. *Bodies in Dissent: Spectacular Performances of Race and Freedom, 1850–1910*. Durham, NC: Duke University Press, 2006.

Brooks, Tim. *Lost Sounds: Blacks and the Birth of the Recording Industry, 1890–1919*. Urbana: University of Illinois Press, 2004.

Brown, Jacqueline. "Black Liverpool, Black America, and the Gendering of Diasporic Space." *Cultural Anthropology* 13 (1998): 291–325.

Brown, Jayna. *Babylon Girls: Black Women Performers and the Shaping of the Modern*. Durham, NC: Duke University Press, 2008.

Bunzl, Matti. *Symptoms of Modernity: Jews and Queers in Late-Twentieth-Century Vienna*. Berkeley: University of California Press, 2004.

Burford, Mark. "Sam Cooke as Pop Album Artist—A Reinvention in Three Songs." *Journal of the American Musicological Society* 65, no. 1 (2012): 113–78.

Burton, Deborah, Susan Vandiver Nicassio, and Agostino Ziino, eds. *Tosca's Prism: Three Moments of Western Cultural History*. Boston: Northeastern University Press, 2004.

Calico, Joy. *Arnold Schoenberg's "A Survivor from Warsaw" in Postwar Europe*. Berkeley: University of California Press, 2014.

——. "'Für Eine Neue Deutsche Nationaloper': Opera in the Discourses of Unification and Legitimation in the German Democratic Republic." In *Music and German National Identity*, edited by Celia Applegate and Pamela Potter, 190–204. Chicago: University of Chicago Press, 2002.

Campt, Tina. "Converging Spectres of an Other Within: Race and Gender in Prewar Afro-German History." *Callaloo* 26, no. 2 (2003): 322–41.

——. *Other Germans: Black Germans and the Politics of Race, Gender, and Memory in the Third Reich*. Ann Arbor: University of Michigan Press, 2004.

Campt, Tina, Pascal Grosse, and Yara-Colette Lemke-Muniz Faria. "Blacks, Germans, and the Politics of Imperial Imagination, 1920–1960." In *The Imperialist Imagination: German Colonialism and Its Legacy*, edited by Sara Lennox, Sara Friedrichsmeyer, and Susanne Zantop, 205–32. Ann Arbor: University of Michigan Press, 1998.

Canarina, John. *"Uncle Sam's Orchestra": Memories of the Seventh Army Symphony.* Rochester: University of Rochester Press, 1998.

Canning, Kathleen, Kerstin Barndt, and Kristin McGuire, eds. *Weimar Publics/Weimar Subjects: Rethinking The Political Culture of Germany in the 1920s.* New York: Berghahn, 2010.

Carter, Marva. *Swing Along: The Musical Life of Will Marion Cook.* Oxford: Oxford University Press, 2008.

——. "The Life and Career of Will Marion Cook." PhD diss., University of Illinois, 1988.

Cazort, Jean E. *Born to Play: The Life and Career of Hazel Harrison.* Westport, CT: Greenwood Press, 1983.

Cheatham, Wallace. *Dialogues on Opera and the African-American Experience.* Lanham, MD: Scarecrow Press, 1997.

Cheatham, Wallace, and Sylvia Lee. "Lady Sylvia Speaks." *Black Music Research Journal* 16, no. 1 (1996): 183–213.

Cheatham, Wallace, and George Shirley. "A Renowned Divo Speaks." *Black Perspective in Music* 18, no. 1/2 (1990): 141–78.

Chin, Rita, Atina Grossmann, Heide Fehrenbach, and Geoff Eley. *After the Nazi Racial State: Difference and Democracy in Germany and Europe.* Ann Arbor: University of Michigan Press, 2009.

Chybowski, Julia. "Becoming the 'Black Swan' in Mid-Nineteenth-Century America: Elizabeth Taylor Greenfield's Early Life and Debut Concert Tour." *Journal of the American Musicological Society* 67, no. 1 (2014): 125–65.

Ciarlo, David. *Advertising Empire: Race and Visual Culture in Imperial Germany.* Cambridge: Harvard University Press, 2011.

Clement, Catherine. *Opera, or the Undoing of Women.* Translated by Betsy Wing. Minneapolis: University of Minnesota Press, 1998.

Clendinnen, Inga. *Dancing with Strangers: Europeans and Australians at First Contact.* Cambridge: Cambridge University Press, 2005.

Cook, Nicholas. "Seeing Sounds, Hearing Images: Listening Outside the Modernist Box." In *Musical Listening in the Age of Technological Reproduction*, edited by Gianmario Borio, 185–202. New York: Routledge, 2015.

Crawford, Richard. "It Ain't Necessarily Soul: Gershwin's Porgy and Bess as a Symbol." *Anuario Interamericano de Investigacion Musical* 8 (1972): 27.

Cruz, Jon. *Culture on the Margins: The Black Spiritual and the Rise of American Cultural Interpretation.* Princeton, NJ: Princeton University Press, 1999.

Daughtry, Willia. "Sissieretta Jones: A Study of the Negro's Contribution to Nineteenth-Century American Concert and Theatrical Life." PhD diss., Syracuse University, 1968.

Dayal, Samir. "Blackness as Symptom: Josephine Baker and European Identity." In *Blackening Europe: The African American Presence*, edited by Heike Raphael-Hernandez, 35–52. New York: Routledge, 2004.

Deaville, James. "African American Entertainers in Jahrhundertwende Vienna: Austrian Identity, Viennese Modernism, and Black Success." *Nineteenth-Century Music Review* 3, no. 1 (June 2006): 89–112.

Dennis, David. *Beethoven in German Politics, 1870–1989.* New Haven: Yale University Press, 1996.

Dennis, Mike, and Norman LaPorte. *State and Minorities in Communist East Germany*. New York: Berghahn, 2011.

Diedrich, Maria. "Black 'Others'?: African Americans and Black Germans in the Third Reich." In *Remapping Black Germany: New Perspectives on Afro-German History, Politics, and Culture*, edited by Sara Lennox, 135–48. Amherst: University of Massachusetts Press, 2017.

Dodd, Mead, ed. *Paul Robeson: The Great Forerunner*. New York: International Publishers, 1985.

Du Bois, W. E. B. *The Autobiography of W. E. B. Du Bois: A Soliloquy on Viewing My Life from the Last Decade of Its First Century*. New York: International Publishers, 1968.

Duberman, Martin. *Paul Robeson*. New York: Knopf, 1989.

Dyer, Richard. *White: Essays on Race and Culture*. New York: Routledge, 1997.

Ebert, Peter. *In This Theatre of Man's Life: The Biography of Carl Ebert*. Lewes: Book Guild, 1999.

Edwards, Brent Hayes. *The Practice of Diaspora: Literature, Translation, and the Rise of Black Internationalism*. Cambridge: Harvard University Press, 2003.

Edwards, Paul. "Louis Douglas and *Jonny spielt auf*: Performing Blackness in Interwar Germany." PhD diss., Boston University, 2018.

Ege, Moritz. *Schwarz werden: 'Afroamerikanophilie' in den 1960er und 1970er Jahren*. Bielefeld: Transcript, 2007.

Ege, Moritz, and Andrew Wright Hurley. "Introduction: Special Issue on Afro-Americanophilia in Germany." *Portal* 12, no. 2 (2015): 1–14.

——. "Periodizing and Historicizing German Afro-Americanophilia: From Antebellum to Postwar (1850–1967)." *Portal: Journal of Multidisciplinary International Studies* 12, no. 2 (2015): 1–37.

Egerton, Douglas. *The Wars of Reconstruction: The Brief, Violent History of America's Most Progressive Era*. New York: Bloomsbury Press, 2015.

Eggers, Maureen Maisha, Grada Kilomba, Peggy Piesche, and Susan Arndt, eds. *Mythen, Masken, und Subjekte: Kritische Weißseinforschung in Deutschland*. Münster: Unrast, 2005.

Eidsheim, Nina Sun. "Marian Anderson and 'Sonic Blackness' in American Opera." *American Quarterly* 63, no. 3 (2011).

——. *The Race of Sound: Listening, Timbre, and Vocality in African American Music*. Durham, NC: Duke University Press, 2019.

Elam, Jr., Harry J., and Kennell Jackson, eds. *Black Cultural Traffic: Crossroads in Global Performance and Popular Culture*. Ann Arbor: University of Michigan Press, 2005.

Eley, Michelle René. "Anti-Black Racism in West German Living Rooms: The ZDF Television Film Adaptation of Willi Heinrich's Gottes Zweite Garnitur." *German Studies Review* 39, no. 2 (2016): 315–34.

Ellis, Katherine. "Female Pianists and Their Male Critics in Nineteenth-Century Paris." *Journal of the American Musicological Society* 50, no. 2/3 (1997): 353–85.

Ellis, Nadia. *Territories of the Soul: Queered Belonging in the Black Diaspora*. Durham, NC: Duke University Press, 2015.

El-Tayeb, Fatima. "'Blood Is a Very Special Juice': Racialized Bodies and Citizenship in Twentieth-Century Germany." *International Review of Social History* 44, no. S7 (1999): 149–69.

——. "Dangerous Liaisons: Race, Nation, and German Identity." In *Not So Plain as Black and White: Afro-German Culture and History, 1890–2000*, edited by Patricia Mazón and Reinhild Steingröver, 27–60. Rochester, NY: University of Rochester Press, 2005.

——. *European Others: Queering Ethnicity in Postnational Europe*. Minneapolis: University of Minnesota Press, 2011.

——. *Undeutsch: Die Konstruktion des Anderen in der postmigrantischen Gesellschaft*. Bielefeld: Transcript, 2016.

——. "'We Are Germans, We Are Whites, and We Want to Stay White!' African Germans and Citizenship in the Early 20th Century." In *Colors 1800/1900/2000: Signs of Ethnic Difference*, edited by Birgit Tautz, 185–205. New York: Brill, 2004.

Eschen, Penny von. *Satchmo Blows up the World: Jazz Ambassadors Play the Cold War*. Cambridge: Harvard University Press, 2004.

European Agency for Fundamental Rights (FRA). "Being Black in the EU—Second European Union Minorities and Discrimination Survey." Luxembourg: Publications Office of the European Union, n.d.

Fay, Brendan. *Classical Music in Weimar Germany: Culture and Politics before the Third Reich*. New York: Bloomsbury Press, 2019.

Fehrenbach, Heide. "Of German Mothers and 'Negermischlingskinder': Race, Sex, and the Postwar Nation." In *The Miracle Years: A Cultural History of West Germany, 1949–1968*, edited by Hanna Schissler, 164–86. Princeton, NJ: Princeton University Press, 2001.

——. *Race after Hitler: Black Occupation Children in Postwar Germany and America*. Princeton: Princeton University Press, 2005

Feinstein, Margarete Myers. *State Symbols: The Quest for Legitimacy in the Federal Republic of Germany and the German Democratic Republic, 1949–59*. Boston: Brill Academic Publishers, 2001.

Fenner, Angelica. *Race under Reconstruction in German Cinema: Robert Stemmle's Toxi*. Toronto: University of Toronto Press, 2011.

Fikes, Jr., Robert, and Douglas A. Cargille. "The Bittersweet Career of José Manuel Jiménez, the 'Ebony Liszt.'" *Afro-Hispanic Review* 7, nos. 1–3 (1988): 23–26.

Florvil, Tiffany N., and Vanessa Plumly, eds. *Rethinking Black German Studies: Approaches, Interventions, and Histories*. New York: Peter Lang, 2018.

Föllmer, Moritz. "Which Crisis? Which Modernity? New Perspectives on Weimar Germany." In *Beyond Glitter and Doom: The Contingency of the Weimar Republic*, edited by Jochen Hung, Godela Weiss-Sussex, and Geoff Wilkes, 19–31. Munich: Ludicum, 2012.

Fosler-Lussier, Danielle. *Music in America's Cold War Diplomacy*. Berkeley: University of California Press, 2015.

Fox, Thomas C. *Stated Memory: East Germany and the Holocaust*. Rochester, NY: Camden House, 1998.

Frederickson, George. *Racism: A Short History*. Princeton, NJ: Princeton University Press, 2002.

Freitas, Roger. *Portrait of a Castrato: Politics, Patronage, and Music in the Life of Atto Melani*. Cambridge: Cambridge University Press, 2009.

Friedrichsmeyer, Sara, Sara Lennox, and Suzanne Zantop, eds. *The Imperialist Imagination: German Colonialism and Its Legacy*. Ann Arbor: University of Michigan, 1998.

Fritzsche, Peter. "Did Weimar Fail?" *Journal of Modern History* 68, no. 3 (n.d.): 629–56.

Frobenius, Leo. *Und Afrika Sprach . . .: Bericht über den Verlauf der dritten Reise-Periode der D.I.A.F.E. in den Jahren 1910 bis 1912.* Berlin: Vita, 1912.

"From Bell Stand to Throne Room: A Remarkable Autobiographical Interview with the Eminently Successful American Negro Composer R. Nathaniel Dett." *Black Perspective in Music* 1, no. 1 (1973): 74.

Fuchs, Peter Paul, ed. *The Music Theater of Walter Felsenstein: Collected Articles, Speeches, and Interviews.* Translated by Peter Paul Fuchs. New York: Norton, 1975.

Führer, Karl Christian. "A Medium of Modernity? Broadcasting in Weimar Germany, 1923–32." *Journal of Modern History* 69 (1997): 722–53.

———. "German Cultural Life and the Crisis of National Identity During the Depression, 1929–33." *German Studies Review* 24, no. 3 (2001): 461–86.

———. "High-Brow and Low-Brow Culture." In *Weimar Germany*, edited by Anthony McElligott, 260–81. Oxford: Oxford University Press, 2009.

Fulda, Bernhard. *Press and Politics in the Weimar Republic.* Oxford: Oxford University Press, 2009.

Gable-Wilson, Sonya. "Let Freedom Sing! Four African American Concert Singers in Nineteenth-Century America." PhD diss., University of Florida, 2005.

Gaines, Kevin. *Uplifting the Race: Black Leadership, Politics, and Culture in the Twentieth Century.* Chapel Hill: University of North Carolina Press, 1996.

Gay, Peter. *Weimar Culture: The Outsider as Insider.* New York: Harper and Row, 1968.

Gebhard, Caroline, and Barbara McCaskill. "Introduction." In *Post-Bellum, Pre-Harlem: African American Literature and Culture, 1877–1919*, edited by McCaskill and Gebhard, 1–16. New York: New York University Press, 2006.

Gienow-Hecht, Jessica. *Sound Diplomacy: Music and Emotions in Transatlantic Relations, 1850–1920.* Chicago: University of Chicago Press, 2012.

Gilman, Sander. *Difference and Pathology: Stereotypes of Sexuality, Race, and Madness.* Ithaca, NY: Cornell University Press, 1985.

Goedde, Petra. *GIs and Germans: Culture, Gender, and Foreign Relations, 1945–49.* New Haven: Yale University Press, 2003.

Goll, Ivan. "The Negroes Are Conquering Europe." In *The Weimar Republic Sourcebook*, edited by Anthony Kaes, Martin Jay, and Edward Dimendberg, 559–60. Berkeley: University of California Press, 1994.

Graham, Sandra. *Spirituals and the Birth of a Black Entertainment Industry.* Urbana: University of Illinois Press, 2018.

Gramit, David. *Cultivating Music: The Aspirations, Interests, and Limits of German Musical Culture, 1770–1848.* Berkeley: University of California Press, 2007.

Gregor, Neil. "Bruckner, Munich, and the Longue Durée of Musical Listening between the Imperial and Postwar Eras." In *Dreams of Germany: Musical Imaginaries from the Concert Hall to the Dance Floor*, edited by Neil Gregor and Thomas Irvine, 97–122. New York: Berghahn, 2018.

Gruber, Helmut. *Red Vienna: Experiment in Working-Class Culture, 1919–34.* New York: Oxford University Press, 1991.

Guenther, Irene. *Nazi Chic? Fashioning Women in the Third Reich.* Oxford: Berg, 2004.

Gutkin, David. "The Modernities of H. Lawrence Freeman." *Journal of the American Musicological Society* 72, no. 3 (2019): 719–79.

Hackenesch, Silke. *Chocolate and Blackness: A Cultural History.* Frankfurt: Campus Verlag, 2018.

Hake, Sabine. *Popular Cinema in the Third Reich*. Austin: University of Texas Press, 2001.

Hales, Douglas. *A Southern Family in Black and White: The Cuneys of Texas*. College Station: Texas A&M Press, 2002.

Hall, Catherine. *Civilizing Subjects: The Metropole and the Colony*. Oxford: Polity, 2002.

Haney, Lynn. *Naked at the Feast: A Biography of Josephine Baker*. New York: Dodd, Mead, 1981.

Hare, Maud Cuney. *Negro Musicians and Their Music*. Washington, DC: The Associated Publishers, 1936.

Harvey, Elizabeth. "Culture and Society in Weimar Germany: The Impact of Modernism and Mass Culture." In *German History since 1800*, edited by Mary Fulbrook, 279–97. London: Arnold, 1997.

Hayes, Roland. *My Favorite Spirituals: 30 Songs for Piano and Voice*. Mineola: Dover Publications, 2001.

Hayes, Roland, with F. W. Woolsey. "Roland Hayes." *Black Perspective in Music* 2, no. 2 (1974): 179–85.

Helm, MacKinley. *Angel Mo' and Her Son, Roland Hayes*. Boston: Little, Brown, and Co., 1942.

Herf, Jeffrey. *Divided Memory: The Nazi Past in the Two Germanys*. Cambridge, MA: Harvard University Press, 1997.

Herzog, Hilary Hope. *Vienna Is Different: Jewish Writers in Austria from the Fin de Siècle to the Present*. New York: Berghahn, 2011.

Heyden, Ulrich van der. *Unbekannte Biographien: Afrikaner im deutschsprachigen Raum vom 18. Jahrhundert bis zum Ende des Zweiten Weltkrieges*. Berlin: Homilius, 2008.

High, Ronald. "Three African-American Tenors of the Nineteenth Century: Thomas J. Bowers, Wallace King, Sidney Woodward." *Journal of Singing — The Official Journal of the National Association of Teachers of Singing* 54, no. 5 (May 1998): 19–25.

Hill, Roy L. *Booker T.'s Child: The Life and Times of Portia Marshall Washington Pittman*. Washington, DC: Three Continents Press, 1993.

Hine, Darlene Clark, Trica Danielle Keaton, and Stephen Small, eds. *Black Europe and the African Diaspora*. Urbana: University of Illinois Press, 2009.

Hochman, Erin. *Imagining a Greater Germany: Republican Nationalism and the Idea of Anschluss*. Ithaca, NY: Cornell University Press, 2016.

Höhn, Maria. *GIs and Fräuleins: The German-American Encounter in 1950s West Germany*. Chapel Hill: University of North Carolina Press, 2002.

Höhn, Maria, and Martin Klimke. *A Breath of Freedom: The Civil Rights Struggle, African American GIs, and Germany*. New York: Berghahn, 2010.

Honeck, Mischa, Martin Klimke, and Anne Kuhlmann. "Introduction." In *Germany and the Black Diaspora: Points of Contact, 1250–1914*, 1–20. New York: Berghahn, 2013.

Hügel-Marshall, Ika. *Invisible Woman: Growing Up Black in Germany*. Translated by Elizabeth Gaffney. Vol. 21. New York: Peter Lang, 2008.

Hund, Wulf. *Wie die Deutschen weiß wurden: Kleine (Heimat)Geschichte des Rassismus*. Stuttgart: Metzler, 2017.

Hung, Jochen. "'Bad' Politics and 'Good' Culture: New Approaches to the History of the Weimar Republic." *Central European History* 49, no. 3–4 (2016): 441–53.

"In Retrospect: W. Rudolph Dunbar; Pioneering Orchestra." *Black Perspective in Music* 9, no. 2 (1981): 193–225.

Irvine, Thomas. "Hubert Parry, Germany, and the 'North.'" In *Dreams of Germany: Musical Imaginaries from the Concert Hall to the Dance Floor*, edited by Neil Gregor and Thomas Irvine, 194–220. New York: Berghahn, 2018.

Jackson, Kennell. "Traveling While Black." In *Black Cultural Traffic: Crossroads in Global Performance and Popular Culture*, edited by Harry J. Elam, Jr. and Kennell Jackson, 1-39. Ann Arbor: University of Michigan Press, 2005.

Janik, Elizabeth. *Recomposing German Music: Politics and Tradition in Cold War Berlin*. Boston: Brill, 2005.

Jarausch, Konrad. *After Hitler: Recivilizing Germans, 1945–95*. Oxford: Oxford University Press, 2006.

Johnson, James H. *Listening in Paris: A Cultural History*. Berkeley: University of California Press, 1995.

Johnson, Patrick. *Appropriating Blackness: Performance and the Politics of Authenticity*. Durham, NC: Duke University Press, 2003.

Jones, James Nathan, Franklin F. Johnson, and Robert B. Cochrane. "Alfred Jack Thomas: Performer, Composer, Educator." *Black Perspective in Music* 11, no. 1 (1983): 64–75.

Judson, Pieter. "When Is a Diaspora Not a Diaspora? Rethinking Nation-Centered Narratives about Germans in Eastern Europe." In *The Heimat Abroad: The Boundaries of Germanness*, edited by Krista O'Donnell, Renate Bridenthal, and Nancy Reagin, 219–47. Ann Arbor: University of Michigan Press, 2005.

Jütte, Daniel. "Schwarze, Juden und die Anfänge des Diskurses über Rasse und Musik im 19. Jahrhundert. Überlegungen anhand von Claudio José Domingo Brindis de Salas' Reise durch Württemberg und Baden im Jahre 1882." *Archiv für Kulturgeschichte* 88 (2006): 117–40.

Kajikawa, Loren. "The Possessive Investment in Classical Music: Confronting Legacies of White Supremacy in U.S. Schools and Departments of Music." In *Seeing Race Again: Countering Colorblindness Across the Disciplines*, edited by Kimberlé Williams Crenshaw, 155–74. Berkeley: University of California Press, 2019.

Kater, Michael. *Different Drummers: Jazz in the Culture of Nazi Germany*. New York: Oxford University Press, 1992.

Keiler, Allan. *Marian Anderson: A Singer's Journey*. New York: Scribner, 2000.

Kelley, Robin D.G. *Freedom Dreams: The Black Radical Imagination*. Boston: Beacon Press, 2002.

Kelly, Elaine. *Composing the Canon in the German Democratic Republic*. Oxford: Oxford University Press, 2014.

——. "Imagining Richard Wagner: The Janus Head of a Divided Nation." *Kritika: Explorations in Russian and Eurasian History* 9, no. 4 (2008): 799–829.

——. "Music for International Solidarity: Performances of Race and Otherness in the German Democratic Republic." *Twentieth Century Music* 16, no. 1 (2019): 123–39.

——. "Performing Diplomatic Relations: Music and East German Foreign Policy in the Middle East during the Late 1960s." *Journal of the American Musicological Society* 72, no. 2 (2019): 493–540.

Kim, Hoi-eun. "Made in Meiji Japan: German Expatriates, German-Educated Japanese Elites, and the Construction of Germanness." *Geschichte und Gesellschaft* 41, no. 2 (April 2015): 288–320.

Koller, Christian. "Enemy Images: Race and Gender Stereotypes in the Discussion on Colonial Troops: A Franco-German Comparison, 1914–23." In *Home/Front: The Military, War, and Gender in Twentieth-Century Germany*, edited by Karen Hagemann and Stefanie Schüler-Springorum, 139–57. Oxford: Berg, 2002.

Kraft, Marion. *Coming In from the Cold: The Black German Experience, Past and Present.* New York: Rosa Luxemburg Stiftung, 2014.

Kusser, Astrid. *Körper in Schieflage: Tanzen im Strudel des Black Atlantic um 1900.* Bielefeld: Transcript, 2013.

Lang, Andreas, ed. *Chronik der Wiener Staatsoper, 1945 bis 2005: Aufführungen, Besetzungen und Künstlerverzeichnis.* Vienna: Löcker, 2006.

Lareau, Alan. "Jonny's Jazz: From Kabarett to Krenek." In *Jazz and the Germans: Essays on the Influence of "Hot" American Idioms on 20th-Century German Music*, edited by Michael Budds, 19–60. Hillsdale, NY: Pendragon Press, 2002.

Largey, Michael. *Voudou Nation: Haitian Art Music and Cultural Nationalism.* Chicago: University of Chicago Press, 2006.

Layne, Priscilla. "'Don't Look So Sad Because You're a Little Negro': Marie Nejar, Afro-German Stardom, and Negotiations with Black Subjectivity." *Palimpsest: A Journal on Women, Gender, and the Black International* 4, no. 2 (2015): 171–87.

———. *White Rebels in Black: German Appropriation of Black Popular Culture.* Ann Arbor: University of Michigan Press, 2018.

Lee, Maureen D. *Sissieretta Jones: The "Greatest Singer of Her Race," 1868–1933.* Columbia: University of South Carolina Press, 2012.

Lee, Owen. *A Season of Opera: From Orpheus to Ariadne.* Toronto: University of Toronto Press, 1998.

Lemke, Sieglinde. *Primitivist Modernism: Black Culture and the Origins of Transatlantic Modernism.* Oxford: Oxford University Press, 1998.

Lennox, Sara. "Reading Transnationally: The GDR and Black American Writers." In *Art Outside The Lines: New Perspectives on GDR Art Culture*, edited by Elaine Kelly and Amy Wlodarski, 111–30. New York: Rodopi, 2011.

———, ed. *Remapping Black Germany: New Perspectives on Afro-German History, Politics, and Culture.* Amherst: University of Massachusetts Press, 2016.

Levin, David. *Unsettling Opera: Staging Mozart, Verdi, Wagner, and Zemlinsky.* Chicago: University of Chicago Press, 2007.

Lewerenz, Susann. *Geteilte Welten: Exotisierte Unterhaltung und Artist*innen of Color in Deutschland 1920–1960.* Cologne: Böhlau, 2017.

Lewis, David Levering. *W. E. B. Du Bois: Biography of a Race, 1868–1919.* New York: Holt Books, 1994.

Lindfors, Bernth. *Early African Entertainments Abroad: From the Hottentot Venus to Africa's First Olympians.* Madison: University of Wisconsin Press, 2014.

Lippi-Green, Rosina. *English with an Accent: Language, Ideology, and Discrimination in the United States.* New York: Routledge, 1997.

Lipsitz, George. *Dangerous Crossroads: Popular Music, Postmodernism, and the Poetics of Place.* New York: Verso, 1994.

Little, Ned Richardson. *The Human Rights Dictatorship: Socialism, Global Solidarity and Revolution in East Germany.* Cambridge: Cambridge University Press, 2019.

Lorenzkowski, Barbara. *Sounds of Ethnicity: Listening to German North America, 1850–1914.* Winnipeg: University of Manitoba Press, 2010.

Lotz, Rainer. *Black People: Entertainers of African Descent in Europe and Germany.* Bonn: Birgit Lotz, 1997.

Luft, David. "Austria as a Region of German Culture: 1900–1938." *Austrian History Yearbook* 23 (1992): 135–48.

Lusane, Clarence. *Hitler's Black Victims: The Historical Experiences of Afro-Germans, European Blacks, Africans, and African Americans in the Nazi Era.* New York: Routledge, 2002.

MacMaster, Neil. *Racism in Europe, 1870–2000.* New York: Palgrave MacMillan, 2001.

Martin, Peter, and Christine Alonzo. *Zwischen Charleston und Stechschritt: Schwarze im Nationalsozialismus.* Hamburg: Dölling & Galitz, 2004.

Massaquoi, Hans. *Destined to Witness: Growing Up Black in Nazi Germany.* New York: William Morrow, 2001.

Matera, Marc. *Black London: The Imperial Metropolis and Decolonization in the Twentieth Century.* Berkeley: University of California Press, 2015.

Mazón, Patricia, and Reinhild Steingröver, eds. *Not So Plain as Black and White: Afro-German Culture and History, 1890–2000.* Rochester, NY: University of Rochester Press, 2005.

McClary, Susan. *Feminine Endings: Music, Gender, and Sexuality.* 2nd ed. Minneapolis: University of Minnesota Press, 2002.

McGinty, Doris E. "The Washington Conservatory of Music and School of Expression." *Black Perspective in Music* 7, no. 1 (1979): 59–74.

McPherson, Bruce. *Measure by Measure: A History of New England Conservatory from 1867.* Boston: The Trustees of the New England Conservatory of Music, 1995.

Meinecke, Friedrich. *The German Catastrophe: Reflections and Recollections.* Translated by Sidney B. Fay. Boston: Beacon Press, 1963.

Melischek, Gabriele, and Josef Seethaler, eds. *Die Wiener Tageszeitungen: Eine Dokumentation, 1918–38.* Vol. 3. Frankfurt am Main: Peter Lang, 1992.

Michael, Theodor Wonja. *Black German: An Afro-German Life in the Twentieth Century.* Translated by Eve Rosenhaft. Liverpool: Liverpool University Press, 2017.

Middleton, Richard. "Musical Belongings: Western Music and Its Low-Other." In *Western Music and Its Others: Difference, Representation, and Appropriation in Music,* edited by Georgina Born and David Hesmondhalgh, 59–85. Berkeley: University of California Press, 2000.

Miller, James A., Susan D. Pennybacker, and Eve Rosenhaft. "Mother Ada Wright and the International Campaign to Free the Scottsboro Boys, 1931–34." *American Historical Review* 106, no. 2 (April 2001): 387–430.

Missfelder, Jan-Friedrich. "Period Ear: Perspektiven einer Klanggeschichte der Neuzeit." *Geschichte und Gesellschaft* 38, no. 1 (January 2012): 21–47.

Mitchell, Ronald E. *Opera — Dead or Alive: Production, Performance, and Enjoyment of Musical Theater.* Madison: University of Wisconsin Press, 1970.

Monod, David. *Settling Scores: German Music, Denazification, and the Americans.* Chapel Hill: University of North Carolina Press, 2005.

Monson, Ingrid. "Introduction." In *The African Diaspora: A Musical Perspective*, edited by Ingrid Monson, 1–20. New York: Garland, 2003.

Morat, Daniel, ed. *Sounds of Modern History: Auditory Cultures in 19th- and 20th-Century Europe*. New York: Berghahn, 2014.

Moriah, Kristin. "On the Record: Sissieretta Jones and Black Performance Praxes." *Performance Matters* 6, no. 2 (2020): 26–42.

Morrow, Mary Sue. *German Music Criticism in the Late Eighteenth Century: Aesthetic Issues in Instrumental Music*. Cambridge: Cambridge University Press, 1997.

Muhammad, Khalil Gibran. *The Condemnation of Blackness: Race, Crime, and the Making of Modern Urban America*. Cambridge: Harvard University Press, 2010.

Müller, Sven Oliver. *Wagner und die Deutschen. Eine Geschichte von Hass und Hingabe*. Munich: C. H. Beck, 2013.

Müller, Tim B. *Nach dem Ersten Weltkrieg: Lebensversuche moderner Demokratien*. Hamburg: HIS, 2014.

Musin, Ovide. *My Memories*. New York: Musin Publishing Company, 1920.

Nagler, A. M. *Misdirection: Opera Production in the Twentieth Century*. Hamden: Archon Books, 1981.

Nash, Elizabeth. *Autobiographical Reminiscences of African American Classical Singers, 1853–Present: Introducing Their Spiritual Heritage into the Concert Repertoire*. Lewiston: Edwin Mellen Press, 2007.

Naumann, Christine. "African American Performers and Culture in Weimar Germany." In *Crosscurrents: African Americans, Africa, and Germany in the Modern World*, edited by David McBride, Leroy Hopkins, and Carol Aisha Blackshire-Belay. Columbia, SC: Camden House, 1998.

Nejar, Marie. *Mach nicht so traurige Augen, weil du ein Negerlein bist: Meine Jugend im Dritten Reich*. Hamburg: Rowohlt, 2007.

Nenno, Nancy. "Femininity, the Primitive, and Modern Urban Space: Josephine Baker in Berlin." In *Women in the Metropolis: Gender and Modernity in Weimar Culture*, edited by Katharina von Ankum, 145–61. Berkeley: University of California Press, 1997.

———. "Here to Stay: Black Austrian Studies." In *Rethinking Black German Studies: Approaches, Interventions, and Histories*, edited by Tiffany N. Florvil and Vanessa Plumly, 71–104. New York: Peter Lang, 2018.

Nettles, Darryl Glenn. *African American Concert Singers Before 1950*. Jefferson: McFarland, 2003.

Newcomb, Ethel. *Leschetizky as I Knew Him*. New York: Appleton Company, 1921.

Noonan, Ellen. "*Porgy and Bess* and the American Racial Imaginary, 1925–85." PhD diss., New York University, 2002.

———. *The Strange Career of "Porgy and Bess": Race, Culture, and America's Most Famous Opera*. Chapel Hill: University of North Carolina Press, 2012.

Notley, Margaret. *Lateness and Brahms: Music and Culture in the Twilight of Viennese Liberalism*. Oxford: Oxford University Press, 2007.

Oby, Jason. *Equity in Operatic Casting as Perceived by African American Male Singers*. Lewiston: Edwin Mellen Press, 1998.

O'Donnell, Krista Molly. "The First Besatzungskinder: Afro-German Children, Colonial Childrearing Practices, and Racial Policy in German South West Africa, 1890–1914." In *Not So Plain as Black and White: Afro-German Culture and History,*

1890–2000, edited by Patricia Mazón and Reinhild Steingröver, 61–81. Rochester, NY: University of Rochester Press, 2005.

Oja, Carol. "Everett Lee and the Racial Politics of Orchestral Conducting." *American Music Review* 43, no. 1 (2013): 1–8.

———. "'New Music' and the 'New Negro': The Background of William Grant Still's Afro-American Symphony." *Black Music Research Journal* 22 (2002): 107–30.

Olmstead, Andrea. *Juilliard: A History*. Urbana: University of Illinois Press, 1999.

Opitz, May, Katharina Oguntoye, and Dagmar Schultz, eds. *Showing Our Colors: Afro-German Women Speak Out*. Amherst: University of Massachusetts Press, 1992.

Osborne, Richard. *Herbert von Karajan: A Life in Music*. London: Chatto & Windus, 1998.

Ostendorf, Berndt. "The Diluted Second Generation: German-Americans in Music 1870–1920." In *German Worker's Culture in the US: 1850–1920*, edited by Hartmut Keil, 261–87. Washington, DC: Smithsonian Institution, 1988.

Ottley, Roi. *No Green Pastures*. New York: Scribner, 1951.

Paddison, Max. "Music as Ideal: The Aesthetics of Autonomy." In *Cambridge Companion to Nineteenth-Century Music*, edited by Jim Samson, 318–42. Cambridge: Cambridge University Press, 2001.

Panton, Clifford D., Jr. *George Augustus Polgreen Bridgetower, Violin Virtuoso and Composer of Color in Late Eighteenth-Century Europe*. Lewiston: Mellen Press, 2005.

Partridge, Damani. "Holocaust Mahnmal (Memorial): Monumental Memory amidst Contemporary Race." *Comparative Studies in Society and History* 52, no. 4 (2010): 820–50.

———. "We Were Dancing in the Club, Not on the Berlin Wall: Black Bodies, Street Bureaucrats, and Exclusionary Incorporation into the New Europe." *Cultural Anthropology* 23, no. 4 (November 2008): 660–87.

Patterson, Lindsay. *The Negro in Music and Art*. New York: Publishers Co, 1967.

Pauley, Bruce F. *From Prejudice to Persecution: A History of Austrian Anti-Semitism*. Chapel Hill: University of North Carolina Press, 1992.

Peabody, Sue, and Tyler Stovall, eds. *The Color of Liberty: Histories of Race in France*. Durham, NC: Duke University Press, 2003.

Pennybacker, Susan. *From Scottsboro to Munich: Race and Political Culture in 1930s Britain*. Princeton, NJ: Princeton University Press, 2013.

Perraudin, Michael, and Jürgen Zimmerer, eds. *German Colonialism and National Identity*. New York: Routledge, 2011.

Perry, Kennetta Hammond. *London Is the Place for Me: Black Britons, Citizenship and the Politics of Race*. New York: Oxford University Press, 2016.

Peukert, Detlev. *The Weimar Republic: The Crisis of Classical Modernity*. Translated by Richard Deveson. New York: Hill and Wang, 1992.

Philpotts, Matthew, and Sabine Rolle. "Introduction." In *Contested Legacies: Constructions of Cultural Heritage in the GDR*, edited by Matthew Philpotts and Sabine Rolle, 1–6. Rochester, NY: Camden House, 2009.

Pick, Hella. *Guilty Victim: Austria from the Holocaust to Haider*. London: I.B. Tauris Publishers, 2000.

Piesche, Peggy. "Black and German? East German Adolescents Before 1989: A Retrospective View of a 'Non-Existent Issue' in the GDR." In *The Cultural After-Life of East Germany: New Transnational Perspectives*, edited by Leslie A. Adelson, 37–59. Washington, DC: American Institute of Contemporary Studies, 2002.

Poiger, Uta. *Jazz, Rock, and Rebels: Cold War Politics and American Culture in a Divided Germany*. Berkeley: University of California Press, 2000.

Pollack, Howard. *George Gershwin: His Life and Work*. Berkeley: University of California Press, 2006.

Pollock, Emily Richmond. *Opera After the Zero Hour: The Problem of Tradition and the Possibility of Renewal in Postwar West Germany*. Oxford: Oxford University Press, 2019.

——. "'To Do Justice to Opera's "Monstrosity"': Bernd Alois Zimmermann's Die Soldaten." *Opera Quarterly* 30, no. 1 (2014): 69–82.

Potter, Pamela. *The Art of Suppression: Confronting the Nazi Past in Histories of the Visual and Performing Arts*. Berkeley: University of California Press, 2016.

——. *Most German of the Arts: Musicology and Society from the Weimar Republic to the End of Hitler's Reich*. New Haven: Yale University Press, 1998.

Prevots, Naima. *Dance for Export: Cultural Diplomacy and the Cold War*. Hanover, NH: Wesleyan University Press, 1998.

Putnam, Lara. *Radical Moves*. Chapel Hill: University of North Carolina Press, 2013.

——. "The Transnational and the Text-Searchable: Digitized Sources and the Shadows They Cast." *American Historical Review* 121, no. 2 (April 2016): 377–402.

Radano, Ronald. "Hot Fantasies: American Modernism and the Idea of Black Rhythm." In *Music and the Racial Imagination*, edited by Ronald Radano and Philip V. Bohlman. Chicago: University of Chicago Press, 2000.

Radcliffe, Kendahl, Jennifer Scott, and Anja Werner, eds. *Anywhere but Here: Black Intellectuals in the Atlantic World and Beyond*. Jackson: University of Mississippi Press, 2015.

Rempe, Martin. "Cultural Brokers in Uniform: The Global Rise of Military Musicians and Their Music." *Itinerario* 41, no. 2 (2017): 327–52.

Reynolds, Christopher. "Porgy and Bess: An American Wozzeck." *Journal of the Society for American Music* 1, no. 1 (February 2007).

Richardson, Joe M. *A History of Fisk University, 1865–1946*. Tuscaloosa: University of Alabama Press, 1980.

Roman, Meredith. *Opposing Jim Crow: African Americans and the Soviet Indictment of Racism, 1928–1937*. Lincoln: University of Nebraska, 2012.

Roos, Julia. "Nationalism, Racism and Propaganda in Early Weimar Germany: Contradictions in the Campaign against the 'Black Horror on the Rhine.'" *German History* 30, no. 1 (March 2012): 45–74.

——. "Women's Rights, National Anxiety, and the 'Moral' Agenda in the Early Weimar Republic." *Central European History* 42, no. 3 (September 2009): 473–508.

Ross, Alex. *The Rest Is Noise: Listening to the Twentieth Century*. New York: Picador, 2007.

——. *Wagnerism: Art and Politics in the Shadow of Music*. New York: Farrar, Strauss, and Giroux, 2020.

Rothberg, Michael, and Yasemin Yildiz. "Memory Citizenship: Migrant Archives of Holocaust Remembrance in Contemporary Germany." *Parallax* 17, no. 4 (2011): 32–48.

Rowe, Mark. *Heinrich Wilhelm Ernst: Virtuoso Violinist*. Burlington: Ashgate, 2008.

Ryding, Erik, and Rebecca Pechefsky. *Bruno Walter: A World Elsewhere*. New Haven: Yale University Press, 2001.

Rye, Howard. "Southern Syncopated Orchestra: The Roster." *Black Music Research Journal* 29, no. 2 (2009): 28.

Sauer, Walter. *Von Soliman zu Omofuma: Afrikanische Diaspora in Österreich 17. bis 20. Jahrhundert*. Innsbruck: Studienverlag, 2006.

Scheck, Raffael. *Hitler's African Victims: The German Army Massacres of Black French Soldiers in 1940*. Cambridge: Cambridge University Press, 2006.

Schenbeck, Lawrence. *Racial Uplift and American Music, 1878–1943*. Jackson: University of Mississippi Press, 2012.

Schmidt, Dörte. "The Most American City in Europe: America and Images of America in Berlin Between the Wars." In *Crosscurrents: American and European Music in Interaction, 1900-2000*, edited by Felix Meyer, Carol J. Oja, Wolfgang Rathert, and Anne C. Shreffler, 72–88. Woodbridge: Boydell Press, 2014.

Schroer, Timothy. *Recasting Race after World War II: Germans and African Americans in American-Occupied Germany*. Boulder: University of Colorado Press, 2007.

Shack, William. *Harlem in Montmartre: A Paris Jazz Story Between the Great Wars*. Berkeley: University of California Press, 2001.

Shadle, Douglas. *Orchestrating the Nation: The Nineteenth-Century American Symphonic Enterprise*. New York: Oxford University Press, 2016.

Sharpley-Whiting, T. Denean. *Black Venus: Sexualized Savages, Primal Fears, and Primitive Narratives in French*. Durham, NC: Duke University Press, 1999.

Sheean, Vincent. *Between the Thunder and the Sun*. New York: Random House, 1943.

Shirley, George. "Il Rodolfo Nero, or The Masque of Blackness." In *Blackness in Opera*, edited by Naomi André, Karen Bryan, and Eric Saylor, 260–74. Champaign: University of Illinois Press, 2012.

Sieg, Katrin. *Ethnic Drag: Performing Race, Nation, and Sexuality in West Germany*. Ann Arbor: University of Michigan Press, 2002.

Silverberg, Laura. "(Re)Defining the Musical Heritage: Confrontations with Tradition in East German New Music." In *Contested Legacies: Constructions of Cultural Heritage in the GDR*, edited by Matthew Philpotts and Sabine Rolle, 124–40. Rochester, NY: Camden House, 2009.

Skelton, Geoffrey. *Wagner at Bayreuth: Experiment and Tradition*. London: White Lion, 1976.

——. *Wieland Wagner: The Positive Sceptic*. New York: St. Martin's Press, 1971.

Slobodian, Quinn. *Comrades of Color: East Germany in the Cold War World*. New York: Berghahn, 2015.

Small, Christopher. *Musicking: The Meanings of Performing and Listening*. Hanover, NH: University of New England Press, 1998.

Smith, Gerald L., Karen Cotton McDaniel, and John A. Hardin, eds. *The Kentucky African American Encyclopedia*. Lexington: University of Kentucky Press, 2015.

Smith, Helmut Walser. *The Continuities of German History: Nation, Religion, and Race Across the Long Nineteenth Century*. Cambridge: Cambridge University Press, 2008.

Southern, Eileen. "In Retrospect: Black Prima Donnas of the Nineteenth Century." *The Black Perspective of Music* 7, no. 1 (1979): 95–106.

——. *The Music of Black Americans: A History*. 3rd ed. New York: W. W. Norton, 1997.

Spencer, Jon Michael. *The New Negroes and Their Music: The Success of the Harlem Renaissance.* Knoxville: University of Tennessee Press, 1997.

Spohr, Arne. "Mohr Und Trompeter: Blackness and Social Status in Early Modern Germany." *Journal of the American Musicological Society* 72, no. 3 (2019): 613–63.

Stahl, Heiner. "Mediascape and Soundscape: Two Landscapes of Modernity in Cold War Berlin." In *Berlin: Divided City, 1945–1989,* edited by Philip Broadbent and Sabine Hake, 56–68. New York: Berghahn, 2010.

Stefaniak, Alexander. "Clara Schumann and the Imagined Revelation of Musical Works." *Music and Letters* 99, no. 2 (2018): 205.

——. *Schumann's Virtuosity: Criticism, Composition, and Performance in Nineteenth-Century Germany.* Bloomington: Indiana University Press, 2016.

Steinberg, Michael. *The Meaning of the Salzburg Festival: Austria as Theater and Ideology, 1890–1938.* Ithaca, NY: Cornell University Press, 1990.

Stewart, Jeffrey. *The New Negro: The Life of Alain Locke.* Oxford: Oxford University Press, 2018.

Stewart, Ruth Ann. *Portia: The Life of Portia Washington Pittman, the Daughter of Booker T. Washington.* Garden City: Doubleday, 1977.

Stöber, Rudolf. *Deutsche Pressegeschichte: Von den Anfängen bis zur Gegenwart.* 2nd ed. Constance: UVK, 2005.

Stoever, Jennifer Lynn. *The Sonic Color Line: Race and the Cultural Politics of Listening.* New York: New York University Press, 2016.

Stoler, Ann Laura. *Race and the Education of Desire: Foucault's History of Sexuality and the Colonial Order of Things.* Durham, NC: Duke University Press, 1995.

Story, Rosalyn. *And So I Sing: African-American Divas of Opera and Concert.* New York: Warner Books, 1990.

Stovall, Tyler. *Paris Noir: African Americans in the City of Light.* Boston: Houghton Mifflin, 1996.

Sträßner, Matthias. *Der Dirigent Leo Borchard: eine unvollendete Karriere.* Berlin: Transit, 1999.

Sysling, Fenneke. *Racial Science and Human Diversity in Colonial Indonesia.* Singapore: National University of Singapore Press, 2016.

Tallie, T. J. "Sartorial Settlement: The Mission Field and Transformation in Colonial Natal, 1850–1897." *Journal of World History* 27, no. 3 (2016): 389–410.

——. *Oxford History of Western Music.* Oxford: Oxford University Press, 2005.

Taylor, John Harper. "Ambassadors of the Arts: An Analysis of the Eisenhower Administration's Incorporation of *Porgy and Bess* into Its Cold War Foreign Policy." PhD diss., Ohio State University, 1994.

Terrell, Mary Church. *A Colored Woman in a White World.* New York: Humanity Books, 2005.

Terry, William. "The Consummate Collaborator: Conversation with William Duncan Allen." *Black Perspective in Music* 15, no. 2 (1987): 182–218.

Thacker, Toby. *Music after Hitler, 1945–55.* Burlington: Ashgate, 2007.

——. "'Renovating' Bach and Handel: New Musical Biographies in the German Democratic Republic." In *Musical Biography: Towards New Paradigms,* edited by Jolanta T. Pekacz, 17–41. Burlington, VT: Ashgate, 2006.

Thaler, Peter. *The Ambivalence of Identity: The Austrian Experience of Nation-Building in a Modern Society.* West Lafayette: Purdue University Press, 2001.

The Marvelous Musical Prodigy, Blind Tom. New York: French and Wheat, 1868.

Thurman, Kira. "'Africa in European Evening Attire': Defining African American Spirituals and Western Art Music in Central Europe, 1870s–1930s." In *Rethinking Black German Studies: Approaches, Interventions, and Histories,* edited by Tiffany N. Florvil and Vanessa Plumly, 199–234. New York: Peter Lang, 2018.

———. "Singing the Civilizing Mission." *Journal of World History* 27, no. 3 (2016): 443–71.

Timms, Edward, and Karl Kraus. *Apocalyptic Satirist: Culture and Catastrophe in Habsburg Vienna.* New Haven: Yale University Press, 1986.

Tompkins, David. "Sound and Socialist Identity: Negotiating the Musical Soundscape in the Stalinist GDR." In *Germany in the Loud Twentieth Century: An Introduction,* edited by Florence Feiereisen and Alexandra Merley, 111–24. New York: Oxford University Press, 2012.

Trotter, James Monroe. *Music and Some Highly Musical People.* Boston: Lee and Shepherd, 1878.

Trümpi, Fritz. *The Political Orchestra: The Vienna and Berlin Philharmonics During the Third Reich.* Translated by Kenneth Kronenberg. Chicago: University of Chicago Press, 2016.

Tunbridge, Laura. *Singing in the Age of Anxiety: Lieder Performances in New York and London between the World Wars.* Chicago: University of Chicago Press, 2018.

Uhl, Heidemarie. "Of Heroes and Victims: World War II in Austrian Memory." *Austrian History Yearbook* 42 (April 2011): 185–200.

Unterweger, Claudia. *Talking Back: Strategien Schwarzer österreichischer Geschichtsschreibung.* Vienna: Zaglossus, 2016.

Vehanen, Kosti. *Marian Anderson: A Portrait.* New York: Whittlesey House, 1941.

Verrett, Shirley, and Christopher Brooks. *I Never Walked Alone: The Autobiography of an American Singer.* Hoboken: John Wiley & Sons, 2003.

Wagner, Wieland. *The Ring at Bayreuth: Some Thoughts on Operatic Production.* London: Gollancz, 1966.

Wahl, Niko, Tal Adler, and Philipp Rohrbach. *Schwarz Österreich: Die Kinder afroamerikanischer Besatzungssoldaten.* Vienna: Löcker Verlag, 2016.

Walker, Corey D.B. "'Of the Coming of John [and Jane]': African American Intellectuals in Europe, 1888–1938." *Amerikastudien / American Studies* 47, no. 1 (2002): 7–22.

Walter, Bruno. *Theme and Variations: An Autobiography.* Translated by James A. Galson. New York: Knopf, 1946.

Wang, Grace. *Soundtracks of Asian America: Navigating Race Through Musical Performance.* Durham, NC: Duke University Press, 2015.

Ward, Andrew. *Dark Midnight When I Rise: The Story of the Jubilee Singers Who Introduced the World to the Music of Black America.* New York: Farrar, Straus, and Giroux, 2000.

Weber, William. *The Great Transformation of Musical Taste: Concert Programming from Haydn to Brahms.* Cambridge: Cambridge University Press, 2008.

Werner, Anja. *The Transatlantic World of Higher Education: Americans at German Universities, 1776–1914.* New York: Berghahn, 2013.

Wigger, Iris. *The "Black Horror on the Rhine": Intersections of Race, Nation, Gender, and Class in 1920s Germany.* London: Palgrave Macmillan, 2017.

Wildenthal, Lora. *German Women for Empire, 1884–1945*. Durham, NC: Duke University Press, 2001.

Wilson, Alexandra. *The Puccini Problem: Opera, Nationalism, and Modernity*. Cambridge: Cambridge University Press, 2007.

Wipplinger, Jonathan. "Performing Race in Ernst Krenek's *Jonny Spielt Auf*." In *Blackness in Opera*, edited by Naomi André, Karen Bryan, and Eric Saylor, 236–59. Champaign: University of Illinois Press, 2012.

——. *The Jazz Republic: Music, Race, and American Culture in Weimar Germany*. Ann Arbor: University of Michigan Press, 2017.

——. "The Racial Ruse: On Blackness and Blackface Comedy in Fin-de-Siècle Germany." *German Quarterly* 84, no. 3 (2011): 471.

Wright, Josephine. "Black Women and Classical Music." *Women's Studies Quarterly* 12, no. 3 (1984): 18–21.

——. " 'Das Negertrio' Jiménez in Europe." *Black Perspective in Music* 9, no. 2 (Autumn 1981).

——. "George Polgreen Bridgetower: An African Prodigy in England, 1789–99." *Musical Quarterly* 66, no. 1 (January 1980): 65–82.

Wright, Michelle. *Becoming Black: Creating Identity in the African Diaspora*. Durham, NC: Duke University Press, 2008.

Yang, Minna. "East Meets West in the Concert Hall: Asians and Classical Music in the Century of Imperialism, Post-Colonialism, and Multiculturalism." *Asian Music* 38, no. 1 (2007): 1–30.

Yoshihara, Mari. *Musicians from a Different Shore: Asians and Asian Americans in Classical Music*. Philadelphia: Temple University Press, 2007.

——. "The Flight of the Japanese Butterfly: Orientalism, Nationalism, and Performances of Japanese Womanhood." *American Quarterly* 56, no. 4 (2004): 975–1001

Zimmerman, Andrew. *Alabama in Africa: Booker T. Washington, the German Empire, and the Globalization of the New South*. Princeton, NJ: Princeton University Press, 2010.

——. *Anthropology and Anti-Humanism in Imperial Germany*. Chicago: University of Chicago Press, 2001.

INDEX

Page numbers in *italics* refer to figures.

CPSIA information can be obtained
at www.ICGtesting.com
Printed in the USA
LVHW100235200922
728806LV00020B/748/J

9 781501 759840